The Employment Interview

The Employment Interview:
Theory, Research, and Practice

ROBERT W. EDER
Cornell University

GERALD R. FERRIS
University of Illinois at Urbana—Champaign

editors

SAGE PUBLICATIONS
The Publishers of Professional Social Science
Newbury Park   London   New Delhi

To Jan, Collin, and Derek (RWE)
and Gail, Emily, and Elizabeth (GRF).

For information address:

SAGE Publications, Inc.
2111 West Hillcrest Drive
Newbury Park, California

SAGE Publications Ltd.
28 Banner Street
London EC1Y 8QE
England

SAGE Publications India Pvt. Ltd.
M-32 Market
Greater Kailash I
New Delhi 110 048 India

Printed in the United States of America

Library of Congress Cataloging-in-Publication Data

Main entry under title:

The employment interview : theory, research, and practice / edited by
  Robert W. Eder, Gerald R. Ferris.
      p.   cm.
    Bibliography: p.
    ISBN 0-8039-3270-7. — ISBN 0-8038-3271-5 (pbk.)
    1. Employment interviewing.   I. Eder, Robert W.   II. Ferris,
  Gerald R.
  HF5549.5.I6E48   1988
  658.3'1124—dc19   88-36718
                                                               CIP

FIRST PRINTING 1989

Contents

Preface

Overview

One of the ironies in employment practice is the emphasis that is placed on the relatively unstructured, face-to-face interview to arrive at selection decisions within organizations, despite the interview's questionable validity in predicting job success when compared to other selection techniques (i.e., biographical information, work samples, pencil & paper tests). Recent literature reviews have suggested that low interview validity is likely the result of both passive and active judgment errors made by interviewers as they gather, retrieve, and process applicant information. Questions persist about the degree to which the interview makes an incremental contribution to better selection decisions.

Research has advanced our knowledge of the employment interview in a number of key areas, most notably in understanding interviewer cognitive processes. New research efforts have begun to examine interview judgment from alternative theoretical perspectives by focusing on preinterview impression effects, structured question formats, interviewer-applicant process dynamics, applicant impression management strategies, situation variables, and their combined effects on the interviewer's information processing system. Still, much of the research on the interview is fragmented and disjointed, and no integrative theories have been offered to capture interview judgment in its totality. In reality, the gap between interview research and the practice of interviewing remains considerable.

The primary purposes of this edited volume are (1) to create a forum for the integration and cross-fertilization of existing research efforts that reflect the state of the art in the employment interview, (2) to stimulate new streams of employment interview research, and (3) to consider the implications this research has for enhancing interviewer performance. As the book's title suggests, there is a need for assessment and promotion of theory, research, and practice of perhaps the most frequently used organizational decision making tool—the interview. The last book published with a similar ambition was authored by Webster (1982) who reconstituted what was known in the empirical literature about employment interviewer judgment within a cognitive information processing theory. This book seeks to build upon and extend Webster's vision of stimulating new research by creating

11

a forum for the ideas of thirty authors, whose collective body of research reflects multiple theoretical perspectives.

As editors our charge was to provide the reader with an integrated, thorough, and cogent examination of these distinct research streams in a manner conducive to advancing both research and practice. First, an integrative framework is offered at the end of Chapter 1 to group research efforts that address similar key variables, and to guide the reader through the diversity of research efforts that exist today. Second, introductory comments before each section describe how each group of chapters relates to one another and to the integrated framework as a whole. Third, contributing authors were encouraged to extrapolate into the future their particular line of research, raising subsequent issues in need of further investigation. Fourth, each chapter was reviewed and revised where possible to improve readability. And finally, the book concludes with a commentary/discussion section that summarizes this volume's implications for theory building, research methods, and effective practice.

The book is particularly appropriate (1) for researchers and graduate students, as a resource for stimulating new research streams on employee selection in general, and the employment interview in particular, (2) for instructors, as a textbook supplement for Industrial/Organizational Psychology and Human Resource Management seminars on employment practices, and (3) for advanced practitioners, as a reference source for auditing and updating employment interview procedures and policies. Edited research volumes, with their emphasis on advanced work, frequently create initial difficulty for someone unfamiliar with the topic. Therefore, two chapters were added to the beginning of this edited volume. Chapter 1 familiarizes the reader with the history of employment interview research, placing these diverse research efforts in both historical and integrative perspective. Chapter 2 reviews research design principles with regard to common threats to the internal and external validity of employment interview research.

Origins and Acknowledgements

We would like to take a moment to share with you the origins and history behind this effort; we think it is a story worth telling. In the spring of 1986, John Bernardin, program chair for the Personnel/Human Resources Division, asked Bob Eder to be the discussant for a paper session on the employment interview at the annual Academy of Management meetings in Chicago. Not only was the session lively, but there was a desire to organize a symposium for the next meeting to further draw the member's attention to the ongoing, innovative work on the interview. A competitively reviewed symposium for the 1987 Academy of Management meetings in New Orleans was presented to a standing room only crowd. From that point you can guess what happened next. We expanded the concept for an edited volume and proceeded to get manuscript commitments from leading scholars in the field, were invited back in 1988 to present another symposium at the Academy of Management meetings in Anaheim, and finished editing the book for a 1989 release. It happened so fast, and from such modest beginnings.

A good idea still needs nurturing to grow to full potential. This book would not have been possible without the contributions and efforts made by a number of people. First, we would like to acknowledge the high quality contributions of our contributing authors, who responded in a timely fashion and demonstrated a willingness to work with us in making their manuscripts even better. It was truly a pleasure to work with them. A personal note of gratitude goes to Ann West, our editor at SAGE, for believing in this project, and for providing the support necessary to help us deliver a high quality product. The logistics of monitoring the progress of twenty-two manuscripts and thirty authors, keeping the correspondence flowing smoothly, and making what seemed to be an endless number of short deadlines would not have been possible without the help of Veronica Kollerbohm and staff at Arizona State University, West Campus during the 1987-1988 academic year, and Penny Price and staff at the School of Hotel Administration, Cornell University. Finally, and most importantly, we would like to thank our families who indulged us in this endeavor by putting up with our long hours at the office.

It was our original plan to end the preface here. However, there is one more special acknowledgement we would like to make. This book, in part, was clearly inspired by Webster's 1982 book, *The Employment Interview: A Social Judgment Process*, and the line of research he championed at McGill University. Just a few months before publication of this book we learned that Edward C. Webster had passed away on February 15, 1989. It is a profound disappointment that he did not live to see this book, though he certainly knew of its development over these past two years. Back in the fall of 1987 we had written to Professor Webster to inquire about his interest and availability as a potential contributing author to this edited volume. His brief letter, dated September 7, 1987, was one of the few negative responses we received. In his letter, he explained that he gave his complete personal library to the University of Waterloo shortly after 1982 to assist in the development of an industrial/organizational psychology program, and that it would be physically difficult for him to get back and forth to the libraries to do the quality of manuscript he would like. On behalf of the contributing authors, we leave you with his words; his passing of the baton and our collective charge. He wrote "Many thanks for the invitation to join you (as a contributing author). . . . For about two minutes after the invitation was received yesterday, I was in seventh heaven; then I came down to earth. . . . Good luck with this work, I do hope it leads to exciting research."

ROBERT W. EDER
Ithaca

GERALD R. FERRIS
Champaign

PART I

Introduction and
Research Design Precepts

The primary purpose of this edited volume is to create a forum for presenting and contrasting the diverse research streams that reflect the state of the art in the employment interview. An appropriate starting point would be to place today's diverse research efforts within a historical perspective, and to consider the inherent difficulties in conducting research on the employment interview. Even for the experienced researcher, a review of past developments and current research design concerns may prove beneficial.

More than just a review of the literature, Eder, Kacmar, and Ferris chart the historical developments and trends that have have been influential in guiding employment interview research during this century. As a retrospective, this historical review offers insight into the evolution of today's research questions. At the end of the chapter, an integrative framework is proposed that both organizes the chapters within the edited volume, and permits the reader to contrast existing work that addresses the same factor in interview judgment.

The chapter by Kacmar, Ratcliff, and Ferris reviews the common threats to the internal and external validity of research designs on the employment interview. Particular attention is paid to enhancing internal control by pretesting stimulus materials and checking for experiment demand characteristics. Similarly, the generalizability of a study's findings can be enhanced through experiment replication, longitudinal analysis, use of subjects who are familiar with the interview task, and choosing settings that reflect more the critical contextual dimensions that may impact actual interviewer-applicant decisions. These research design precepts will be the basis, in part, for the concluding commentary chapter which discusses the methodological points raised by chapters in this volume (see Buckley & Weitzel).

1

Employment Interview Research: History and Synthesis

Robert W. Eder
Cornell University

K. Michele Kacmar
Texas A & M University

Gerald R. Ferris
University of Illinois at Urbana-Champaign

Introduction

This chapter sets the stage for the remainder of the book by presenting a brief historical review of the literature on the employment interview since 1915, culminating in the presentation of a framework for integrating current research efforts. The historical review highlights key events, findings, and shifts in research trends up through the 1980s with speculation about the future challenges and developments which await tomorrow's employment interview researcher. The historical perspective taken is distinctly North American, emphasizing key developments and seminal research produced this century in Canada and the United States.

The end of this chapter introduces the chapters that comprise this edited volume by placing each chapter's unique perspective within an integrated framework. This framework attempts to synthesize the diverse theoretical perspectives and complex causal relationships that may exist between exogenous factors such as preinterview impressions, applicant strategies, interview content preplanning and interview content, and endogenous factors such as interpersonal dynamics and information processing as they combine to influence interviewer-applicant judgments and interview decision validities.

Due in part to the varied uses of the employment interview within the organization's selection process, and the multidimensional nature of interviewer and applicant decisions, each of the contributors in this book may imply a slightly different meaning of what constitutes an employment interview. As a frame of reference, the following definition of the employment interview is offered:

> the employment interview is defined as a face-to-face exchange of job-relevant information between organizational representatives and a job applicant with the overall organizational goal of attracting, selecting, and retaining a highly competent workforce.

Within the selection process, the employment interview may be used early as a recruitment or initial screening device to encourage individuals to become formal job applicants, provide a realistic job preview, and determine whether the applicant is minimally qualified. Or, the interview may take place during the later stages of the selection process where more lengthy, in-depth discussions with co-workers and supervisors are conducted, often to determine who among the finalists for the job will be chosen.

Like other selection techniques (e.g., analysis of biographical data, pencil and paper tests, work samples), the employment interview provides the organization with the opportunity to infer whether the applicant possesses the critical knowledge, skills, abilities, and interests to be successful in the targeted position. Unlike other selection techniques, standardization in the analysis of applicant qualifications is made more difficult by the informal, extemporaneous style of most interviewers, and by the interviewer's limited ability to extract veracity from applicant self-reports of alleged competence. Clearly, the inherent information processing limitations and non-job relevant biases of the interviewer disadvantage the interview in comparison with more standardized selection decision tools. Further jeopardizing interviewer-applicant exchanges of accurate information is the dual, but conflicting concerns each has over the mutual attraction and selection of one another. Both want complete and candid information, but often each is reluctant to risk candor that would diminish further interest by the other party.

How well the employment interview succeeds as a selection technique in predicting job performance has been the subject of considerable debate—a debate that runs throughout the chapters in this book. What is not debated is the continuing widespread use and reliance on the employment interview to make hiring decisions, more so than any other selection technique (see also The Bureau of National Affairs, 1983). Paradoxically, few individuals are hired without an interview despite its suspect validity. For the past half century, the employment interview has been a fundamental part of the selection process, a virtual constant in any organization's hiring formula (see also Spriegel & James, 1958). Perhaps because of this fundamental irony, few topics in the organizational sciences have received as much researcher attention as has the employment interview.

Employment Interview Research: History

In the past forty years, there have been nine published reviews of the literature (Arvey & Campion, 1982; Eder & Buckley, 1988; Hakel, 1982; Mayfield, 1964; Schmitt, 1976; Ulrich & Trumbo, 1965; Wagner, 1949; Webster, 1982, Wright, 1969). The intent here is not to comprehensively review every study on the interview, but rather to representatively sample the literature to identify significant trends that have emerged and that continue today to shape research efforts. After all, a scholarly discipline builds upon, extends, refutes, and refines the common body of knowledge created by its predecessors.

This historical review of employment interview research is organized roughly by decades. Significant developments in the evolution of employment interview research, as in the field of personnel psychology in general, were influenced by major historical events in the United States (e.g., World Wars I and II), and theoretical and methodological developments within the behavioral science research community (e.g., advent of validity generalization and meta-analytic techniques in the 1980s). Each of these developments are pictorially represented in Figure 1.1.

As can be seen in Figure 1.1, the time line begins at 1915 and continues through the year 1995. The items listed in the column next to the time line indicate major research trends concerning the employment interview during that period. The next column, entitled "Historical/Professional Developments," lists the major events that have influenced the research endeavors of organizational scientists during each time period.

Early Work: 1915-1939

During this period, academic journals focusing on employment interview research were just beginning to be established (e.g., *Journal of Applied Psychology*, 1917; *Personnel*, 1919; *Personnel Journal*, 1922). Division 14 of the American Psychological Association, which monitors the research of industrial and organizational psychologists, was not founded until 1937. Consequently, most of the early literature on the employment interview simply offered laundry lists of do's and don'ts (Wagner, 1949). There were a few notable exceptions.

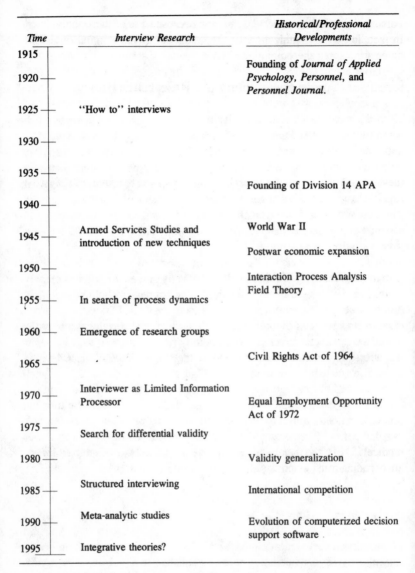

Time	Interview Research	Historical/Professional Developments
1915		
1920		Founding of *Journal of Applied Psychology*, *Personnel*, and *Personnel Journal*.
1925	"How to" interviews	
1930		
1935		
		Founding of Division 14 APA
1940		
1945	Armed Services Studies and introduction of new techniques	World War II
		Postwar economic expansion
1950		Interaction Process Analysis Field Theory
1955	In search of process dynamics	
1960	Emergence of research groups	
		Civil Rights Act of 1964
1965		
1970	Interviewer as Limited Information Processor	Equal Employment Opportunity Act of 1972
1975	Search for differential validity	
1980		Validity generalization
1985	Structured interviewing	International competition
1990	Meta-analytic studies	Evolution of computerized decision support software
1995	Integrative theories?	

Figure 1.1. A Historical Perspective of Interview Research

Scott (1915) had six personnel managers rank 36 prospective employees for a sales job after an interview. There was little agreement among the personnel managers concerning the predicted success of these individuals. In fact, in approximately 77% of the cases, the managers could not even agree if the applicant should be ranked in the top or bottom half of the group.

Follow-up studies (Scott, 1916; Scott, Bingham, & Whipple, 1916) supported Scott's initial finding that the interviewer's ability to identify successful applicants was problematic. Scott (1916) asked 13 executives to rate 12 men on their ability to sell. The average correlation of the executives was little better than chance. Scott et al. (1916) asked 20 sales managers and 3 personnel researchers to rank 24 applicants. The applicants were to prepare a 5 minute sales speech, which the interviewer could listen to if they felt the speech was the best way to determine the applicant's ability to sell. Consequently, some applicants were not asked to perform the speech. The applicant who received the largest variation in rankings was ranked second by one rater and twenty-fourth by another. The applicant with the least variation in rankings was ranked first by one rater and twelfth by another.

In a study that followed the same basic pattern as the Scott series, Hollingworth (1922) asked 12 sales managers experienced in personnel selection to interview 57 applicants following any procedure they chose. After their interviews, each manager was asked to rank the applicants. On the whole the results of the rankings showed great variability, although there was some agreement as to the best and the worst candidates. According to Wagner (1949), this study has been cited often and apparently did a great deal to shake the confidence in the interview process.

Moss (1931) asked interviewers to rate the scholastic ability of medical school applicants they had interviewed. Moss found that interview procedures could have detected 33% of the students who were admitted to medical school but who did not succeed. These results would have been encouraging if the interview procedure would not also have eliminated 23% of students earning an average of 85 or higher out of 100.

One of the few longitudinal studies performed on the interview during this period was reported by Kenagy and Yoakum (1925). These authors had one executive rate 34 newly hired salesmen from information gathered in a half hour interview. Two other executives were asked to rate the 34 salesmen based on their daily one-hour contacts during the subsequent two-week training program. After the salesmen had been out in the field for two months, sales performance was measured and then correlated with the ratings by each of the three executives. The correlations were .27 for the interviewing executive and .21 and .16 for the two interacting executives. These modest, simple correlations around .20 are not far removed from the validity coefficient estimations derived from recent meta-analytic efforts (Hunter & Hunter, 1984; McDaniel et al., 1987; Wiesner & Cronshaw, 1988).

The War Years: 1940-1949

Much of the research reported during the 1940s continued to test the reliability and validity of the interview using large military samples. It is interesting to note that the first large scale use of convenient samples in selection research was not with college sophomores but with enlistees during World War II. One such study tested how successful the interview could be at predicting success at flying (Dunlap & Wantman, 1947). The authors asked 3 interviewers, acting as a board, to study the Personal History Inventory (PHI) for 3 minutes prior to the applicant entering the room for an interview. The PHI consisted of work, health, and personal history information provided by the applicant. At the conclusion of the 25 minute interview, each interviewer rated the applicant on 9 different scales. The results showed that interrater agreement was high (.53 to .70) across all scales. However, when these predictions were compared with the results from flight school, overall prediction rates were little better than chance. Similar findings were reported two years later in a separate study by Newman, Bobbitt, and Cameron (1946).

In several studies the interview's incremental validity was questioned. Conrad and Satter (1946) conducted a study on the usefulness of the interview for the selection of 3,500 naval candidates into the Electricians' Mates School. Results of the study indicated that test scores alone predicted more accurately than tests scores combined with interview information. In another study, over 37,800 cases of acceptance into technical schools were examined for the Navy by Bloom and Brundage, as reported by Struit (1947). The authors concluded that there was a relatively insignificant gain in the ability to predict success when the interviewer's information was added to test scores.

On a more positive note, Putney's (1947) study suggested that simple decision utility of the employment interview may be more impressive than predictive validity. In this study, men who were assigned to technical schools at random were compared to individuals who were assigned based on a classification interview. Results indicated that only 29% of the randomly selected applicants completed the program successfully while 84% of the applicants selected through the interview were successful.

A second theme in this decade was the introduction of new techniques to be used in the interview. One novel approach was presented by Travers

(1941) who suggested that applicants should be rated as they carry out a practical test (i.e., the interview as a work sample). A carpenter would be asked to build a small object so that work habits and techniques could be viewed and the finished object inspected for quality. Another innovative example was suggested by Brody (1947). This author suggested that a group of 6 to 12 candidates participate in a discussion relevant to the position to be filled. Each candidate was also asked to prepare a 3 to 5 minute talk on an assigned topic. While the candidates presented their speeches and participated in the discussion, the interviewers observed the candidates' behavior and recorded their observations (i.e., mini-assessment center experience).

In Search of Process Dynamics: 1950-1969

In the period from 1950 to 1969, the United States witnessed rapid industrial growth, prosperity, and economic dominance on a global scale. Given the worldwide competitive advantage US firms enjoyed, workforce selection and rapid promotion was predicated more on initiative, nepotism, and "being in the right place at the right time" than on the credentials or abilities one presented at the employment office. Even though the employment interview had shown itself to be of somewhat low predictive value, there seemed little urgency either in replacing the interview or in questioning its continued use. Within the academic community, seminal work in interaction process analysis (Bales, 1950), field theory (Lewin, 1951), and social behavior (Homans, 1961) redirected researchers toward close observation of the interpersonal communications and process dynamics of the employment interview.

During the 1950s, field research on the interview was conducted by clinical and counseling psychologists, whose active presence in personnel departments reached its zenith during this period. Daniels and Otis (1950) were among the first to develop an unobtrusive methodology for observing and analyzing various aspects of the employment interview, the use of audio taping. With audio taping, interactions in an employment counseling interview were dividied into units that represented response categories (e.g., total number of exchanges, time the interviewer spoke, time the applicant spoke, and number of questions asked by the applicant) made by applicants and interviewers (Dipboye, 1954; Robinson, 1955). The results of these studies indicated that some counselors varied their style depending on the topic being discussed.

Another general partitioning procedure was introduced by Chappel, but reported by Matarazzo, Suslow, and Matarazzo (1956). According to

Matarazzo et al., Chappel devised a machine he called the Interaction Chronograph. The machine had keys that represented the interview participants. As the participants spoke, an observer would depress the key assigned to the participant and a line would be drawn on a constantly moving tape. When the participant stopped speaking the key was released and the line stopped. By studying the line lengths, it was possible to assign values to ten variables such as who talked most, least, and the tempo of the conversation.

By the 1960s there seemed to emerge "camps" or groups of researchers engaged in programmatic activity on the interview, typically associated with a particular geographic area or institution. One such series of studies was produced by Campbell and his colleagues (Brailey, Liske, Otis, & Prien) at Case Western Reserve University. The main focus of their research was to determine the predictive validity of interviews conducted by industrial psychologists rather than line managers. In a review of these studies, Otis, Campbell, and Prien (1962) suggested that even though the obtained validity coefficients had been modest, all were positive. However, the interview alone produced valid predictions only for dimensions that pertained to interpersonal relations.

Other groups included Maier (1966) and Janzen (Maier & Janzen, 1967), who focused on honesty and empathy in one-to-one interactions, and Carlson (1967a, 1967b, 1968) and Mayfield (Mayfield, Brown, & Hamstra, 1980) who focused on how specific types of key information alter the interviewer decision making process.

Perhaps no single group of researchers was more influential during this period than Webster and his graduate students (Anderson, Crowell, Rowe, Springbett, & Sydiaha) at McGill University who attempted to redesign the interview by addressing the interviewer's decision-making process (cf., Webster, 1964). Wright (1969) in his later literature review noted, "It would be difficult to overestimate the importance of the work done by Webster and his colleagues"(p. 394). Webster's approach to the interview redirected subsequent research for the next two decades, and was responsible for the methodological shift in emphasis from qualitative to quantitative analysis.

Among the more frequently cited conclusions from these studies was that interviewers developed a stereotype of an "ideal candidate" and then sought to match applicants against that stereotype, and that decisions were often made within the first two or three minutes of the interview. This latter assertion that interviewers routinely engage in "snap decisions" (Springbett, 1958) persists as part of our collective management lore, though Springbett's finding has never been replicated (Buckley & Eder, 1988; Buckley & Eder, in press).

In their review of the literature since 1949, Ulrich and Trumbo (1965) argued that interviewers all too frequently are asked to do the impossible because of limitations on available time and information. Their recommendation was to limit the interviewer's task to a single trait or suitability rating for which acceptable validities could be achieved. Clearly, the prospects at the beginning of the 1950s for designing a more comprehensive, valid interview process had been dimmed by the reality of a complex task and human limitations.

Interviewer as Limited Information Processor: 1970-1982

By the 1970s, it was rapidly becoming apparent that interviewer behavior was susceptible to a number of influences. Work continued to be published on the effects of verbal and visual cues such as eye contact, smiling, posture, interpersonal distance, and body orientation (Washburn & Hakel, 1973; Imada & Hakel, 1977). However, the magnitude of these effects began to be challenged as being more experimenter induced than real. For example, the finding that interviewers search for the "ideal candidate" (Hakel, Holleman, & Dunnette, 1970) was later challenged by London and Hakel (1974) who found that the stereotypes used by the interviewer to judge an applicant diminished as the evaluation of the applicant continued. While some researchers found a significant influence in the order in which applicants were presented (i.e., contrasts effects) (see also Wexley, Yukl, Kovacs, & Sanders, 1972), other researchers found insignificant or trivial effects when professional interviewers were used as subjects (Hakel, Dobmeyer, & Dunnette, 1970; Landy & Bates, 1973).

During this period, industrial/organizational psychologists began to incorporate into their research precepts from social/cognitive psychology that human rationality is "bounded" (Simon, 1975); people's cognitive capabilities are limited (Tversky & Kahneman, 1974); and that actuarial methods are consistently superior to clinical judgments like the interview (Meehl, 1965). A cognitive information processing theory assumes that information is attended to, categorized, and combined according to unique cognitive "schemas" (Taylor & Crocker, 1981; Wyer & Srull, 1981). The primary goal of this research is to study cognitive processing from information acquisition and encoding to storage and memory retrieval (Ilgen & Feldman, 1983), and to delineate the variety of information processing errors that undermine interview validity. Schmitt's (1976) review was the first to catalog the information processing bias sources that limit interviewer accuracy. Subsequent scholarly reviews built upon this cognitive information processing perspective with suggestions for interview practice, interviewer training, and future research (Arvey & Campion, 1982; Hakel, 1982; Webster, 1982).

With passage of the 1972 Equal Employment Opportunity Act, vigorous enforcement of Title VII of the 1964 Civil Rights Act directed researcher attention to the interview's legal liability. Interview researchers had a new outcome variable to address beyond reliability and validity, namely, whether the employment interview gives unwarranted advantages to members of one group over another. Perhaps due to the availability of data, research on gender bias was particularly plentiful.

Simas and McCarrey (1979) asked 84 male and female personnel officers to evaluate videotaped recruitment interviews of both male and female applicants. The personnel officers were classified by their level of authority. Results indicated that high ranking personnel officers, regardless of their sex, rated male applicants more favorably and indicated a higher likelihood of offering the male applicants a position. However, Rosen and Merich (1979) found no difference in the evaluations of male or female resumes by administrators who worked for companies with strong fair employment policies. Yet, these same administrators recommended that female applicants be given a lower starting salary than their male counterparts.

Interest in gender bias extended to research on perceived attractiveness. Heilman and Saruwatari (1979) asked male and female college students to rate applicants, both male and female, who had been judged earlier to be attractive or unattractive. The type of position the applicant was applying for was either managerial or clerical. Although results indicated that attractiveness always helped the male candidate, it helped the female applicants only when the position was a clerical one. When a women was considered for a managerial position, attractiveness worked against her. Using all male interviewers as evaluators of job resumes, Dipboye, Fromkin, and Wiback (1975) found that unattractive candidates were discriminated against.

With the passage of the Vocational Rehabilitation Act of 1973, researchers also addressed whether handicapped individuals were unfairly discriminated against in the employment interview. Kreftling and Brief (1977) found that more favorable evaluations were given to handicapped individuals than actually was warranted. However, this favorable finding was not consistent across all types of handicaps. For example, Nagi, McBroom, and Colletts (1972) reported that applicants with a history of mental illness were perceived more negatively than those without such a history.

After reviewing research on unfair discrimination in the employment interview, Arvey (1979) was able to conclude that available evidence left it unclear whether interviewers discriminated on the basis of race, age, or handicap. It was clear that females may be at risk in the employment interview, receiving lower evaluations than male applicants. However, Arvey was able to demonstrate that there was virtually no evidence, and little likelihood of ever finding such evidence, concerning the differential validity of the interview across these selected demographic groups. Although Arvey (1979) envisioned that litigation regarding unfair discrimination in the employment interview would escalate rapidly, at least in the 1980s such a prediction has not come true, attesting perhaps to the widespread trust people have in the interview.

Structuring the Interview: 1983-1989

Individuals who attempt to place the present in historical perspective are often prisoners of their own nearsightedness. Nevertheless, there are likely to be developments during the 1980s that will have a substantial influence on future interview research. The 1980s are likely to be remembered as the decade in which U.S. firms faced the reality of a world economy more likely to dominate the United States than to be dominated. Retrenchment, recession, devaluation of the dollar against key economic competitors, wage and benefit concessions, fear of corporate takeover, and the need for technological retooling have placed a premium on reducing labor costs and increasing worker productivity.

One result of the changing economic reality was renewed interest in selection validity (Hunter & Hunter, 1984; Reilly & Chao, 1982). This interest was fostered by the work of Hunter and Schmidt on meta-analytic literature review techniques (Hunter, Schmidt, & Jackson), and subsequent arguments for the validity generalization of cognitive and aptitude tests across diverse settings (Schmidt, Hunter, McKenzie, & Muldrow, 1979). By the end of the decade, at least two large meta-analytic studies had been completed on the interview (McDaniel et al., 1987; Wiesner & Cronshaw, 1988).

A second related development inthe 1980s was the growing evidence that structured interviewing techniques like situational interviewing (Latham & Saari, 1984; Latham, Saari, Pursell, & Campion, 1980) and behavior description interviewing (Janz, 1982; Janz, Hellervik, & Gilmore, 1986) yielded consistently superior predictive validities. Perhaps the century long quest for a more reliable standardized interview form was reaching fruition. Still, questions remained about the incremental validity of these more structured techniques, their practical use, and exactly how they modify the interviewer's decision process in apparently positive ways (see also Campion, Pursell, & Brown, 1988; Eder & Buckley, 1988).

And finally, like the decades before it, the 1980s may also be known for the genesis of new research streams and insights into the complex, multidimensional, cognitive task that faces both interviewer and applicant. Baron (1986) has proposed an impression management framework to explain applicant tactics that occasionally backfire, or at the very least interfere with the interviewer's ability to process, store, and retrieve job relevant information. Dipboye (1982) has questioned the incremental validity of the interview in a typical selection situation that includes prior review of applicant paper credentials. Cognitive schemas developed by the interviewer after a brief review of the candidate's resume and application materials likely guide the interview process and predetermine its outcome. In support of Dipboye's perspective, Zedeck, Tziner, and Middlestadt (1983) found that in spite of training to the contrary, interviewers may use only a limited number of the rating criteria in reaching their decision.

On the theoretical front, Dreher and Sackett (1983, pp. 323-332) have suggested treating the interviewer as an active, rather than a passive, information seeker, and focusing attention on the causal linkages in the interviewer's effort to seek, receive, and process information. Later in the decade, Eder and Buckley (1988) proposed an interactionist perspective to extend existing research to more adequately address the effects of interview context on interviewer information search strategies. This interactionist perspective places an equal emphasis on dimensions of the person and the situation as they interact within the cognitive awareness of the interviewer. However, as noted by the authors, this perspective will require more robust data analytic techniques in multivariate time series analysis to measure linear interdependence over time (Geweke, 1982; Tiao & Box, 1981).

Looking Toward the Future

Approaching the end of the twentieth century, will researchers be any closer to realizing the ambition of designing an "interview" that has both ample validity and sufficient utility to recommend to practicing managers with few reservations? Forged consensus within any scholarly profession, like crystal ball gazing, requires the unlikely task of winning over in-house skeptics. Still, there appear to be developments that are inevitable.

One such development is the further application of computer technology within a decision support system context to enhance the interviewer's information processing capability (Parsons, 1988). Perhaps new software packages are not far off that will call up the latest job description, draft job-relevant rating criteria, recommend questions, and glean relevant information from a candidate's completed application form five minutes prior to the scheduled interview. Postinterview ratings will then be entered immediately to enhance recall, analyze reliability across multiple interviewers, highlight rating inconsistencies for subsequent discussion, and calculate likely incumbent productivity. The development of parallel software for the applicant's job search efforts probably would not be far behind.

Furthermore, researchers will likely continue to focus on both interview process and outcome measures. New theoretical frameworks will examine how exogenous factors (e.g., interviewer-applicant characteristics, interview structure, interview context) alter the endogenous patterns of interviewer information processing that, in turn, may enhance interview reliability, validity, utility, and fairness.

An Integrative Framework: Synthesis

This edited volume is comprised of chapters grouped into separate sections in accordance with the integrative framework depicted in Figure 1.2. An integrative framework is seen as a first step toward ultimately building more integrative and unifying theories of employment interview judgment. The author's name and the chapter number for seventeen of the remaining twenty-one chapters in this book are noted under each component of the model.

According to Figure 1.2, interview outcomes of primary interest, namely validity and fairness, are the direct product of the interviewer's information processing system. A key component of this cognitive operation is the impression formation step used in arriving at an evaluation of the applicant's job suitability. Influencing this decision making activity are endogenous components of preinterview impressions effects and process dynamics, and exogenous components of interviewer-applicant characteristics, interview context, interview purpose, and preplanning activities. Preplanning activities include job analysis and determination of questioning strategy (e.g., using situational questions). Applicant strategies operate on the interviewer's judgment as a key component of the interview's process dynamics.

As with any effort to synthesize diverse research streams into a single framework, parsimony has simplified but not completely captured the full complexity of variable relationships. Nevertheless, the framework's intent is to guide the reader through the remainder of the book and to place each chapter within a single perspective. One of the additional benefits of an integrative framework is the potential insight one may obtain by comparing and contrasting separate works that ostensibly address the same generic factor. Furthermore, the framework may encourage future researchers to

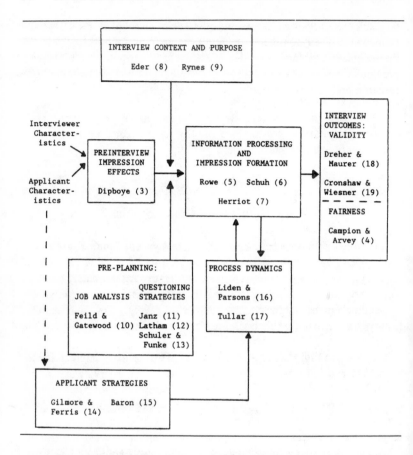

Figure 1.2. A Framework for Integrating Current Research Streams on the Employment Interview

conceptualize the interview in its totality, avoiding research designs with myopic vision and limited generalizability.

Not included in this integrative framework are four chapters. The Kacmar, Ratcliff, and Ferris chapter, which immediately follows this introduction, reviews the internal and external validity threats to the design of employment interview research. The authors' intent in this chapter is to encourage the reader to be an informed consumer of research within this field. The last three chapters in this book are commentaries by Milton Hakel, M. Ronald Buckley and William Weitzel, and James Goodale on employment interview theory, research, and practice, respectively. Each commentary author(s) reviewed all seventeen chapters included in the integrative framework. Their commentaries highlight the contributions made across the seventeen chapters, take note of conflicting viewpoints, add ideas not previously raised, and suggest future directions for employment interview research and effective practice.

2

Employment Interview Research: Internal and External Validity

K. Michele Kacmar
Texas A & M University

Shannon L. Ratcliff
Texas A & M University

Gerald R. Ferris
University of Illinois at Urbana-Champaign

Experimental research typically involves the formulation of a hypothesis such as: if a then b. The formulation of such a hypothesis is followed by the use of some method to manipulate or measure "a" in order to produce some variation in "b." If this predicted variation occurs, it provides support for the hypothesis, "if a then b."

According to Cook and Campbell (1976), a good experiment possesses the following qualities: (1) it makes temporal antecedents clear; (2) it is sensitive and powerful enough to demonstrate that a potential cause and effect could have covaried; (3) it rules out all third variables which might alternatively explain the relationship between the cause and effect; (4) it eliminates alternative hypotheses about the constructs involved in the relationship; and (5) it has results that are generalizable. Each of these qualities relates to an issue of validity including statistical conclusion, internal, construct, and external validity. While each of these validity concepts is important, the present paper is concerned with the issues of internal and external validity. More specifically, it focuses on the assumptions of internal and external validity with respect to experimental research on the employment interview that utilize a posttest-only design or designs that use pretests of an unobtrusive nature.

Experimental research, as opposed to non-experimental research, possesses a unique characteristic which contributes to its potential degree of internal validity, that is, the characteristic of control. Control is achieved in experimental research predominantly in two ways: randomization, and active manipulation or control of independent variables (Kerlinger, 1986). Experimental research controls at least one independent variable while observing the resultant dependent variable. Non-experimental research lacks this relative control of independent variables. Secondly, control can be achieved in "true" experiments through the use of randomization. Subjects can be assigned randomly to groups and groups can be assigned randomly to treatments. As a result of randomization, groups are similarly constituted (i.e., no selection problems), experience the same testing conditions and research instruments (i.e., no testing problems), and share the same global pattern of history (i.e., no history problems) (Cook & Campbell, 1976).

The degree of control offered by experimental studies may lead researchers to assume internal validity; however, internal validity is not a given in experimental research. Threats to internal validity exist and must be addressed through research design and procedures. In addressing these threats, the important but typically neglected use of pretesting of stimulus materials is examined as a means of increasing the internal validity of experimental studies of the employment interview.

The Assumption of Internal Validity in Experimental Research

An experiment represents an attempt to conceptualize the structure of relationships among variables of interest in a particular study based upon theory. Experiments are conducted so that causal inferences can be made regarding these relationships (Cascio, 1987). When conducting an experiment, the researcher attempts to test causal hypotheses by manipulating independent variables and subsequently measuring dependent variables while controlling for extraneous factors. If the experiment is conducted properly, the researcher can then conclude that any changes in the dependent variable were caused by varying the levels of the independent variable (i.e., treatment caused results). This condition can be referred to as internal validity.

Threats to Internal Validity

Threats to internal validity have been identified by Campbell and Stanley (1967) and Cook and Campbell (1976). These threats to internal validity were summarized by Fisher (1984) to include the following: (1) selection, (2) testing, (3) history, (4) maturation, (5) mortality, (6) instrument decay, (7) demand characteristics, and (8) experimenter effects.

While acknowledgement of all threats to internal validity is important, certain threats are more salient for posttest-only research designs, or designs that utilize pretests of an unobtrusive nature: selection, instrument decay, demand characteristics, and experimenter effects. Other threats present less of a problem. Specifically, history (i.e., something that happens between the pretest and posttest which is not a part of the experiment), maturation (i.e., gradual growth or decline in an individual between pretest and posttest), mortality (i.e., individuals dropping out of the experiment and thereby contributing to the pretest mean but not the posttest mean), and testing (i.e., the effects of taking a pretest on the scores of the posttest) issues are unlikely to represent salient threats to internal validity.

Selection bias refers to a lack of equivalence between subjects in the control group and subjects in the treatment group (Fisher, 1984). Random assignment of large numbers of subjects to control and treatment groups should reduce the threat of selection bias. In other instances, a pretest and/or posttest is used to assess subject equivalence prior to and after manipulation of a treatment.

However, selection bias can also occur in the use of confederates in an experiment. Equivalence must be assessed in terms of confederates or stimulus materials representing confederates in an experiment. If no assessment of equivalence is made prior to an experiment, it is not possible for the results of the study to be interpreted meaningfully or attributed to the hypothesized variance in levels of an independent variable. A study by Baron (1983) provides an example of possible confederate selection bias. One of the independent variables in his study, concerning the influence of perfume on the decision making process of the interviewer, was confederate sex. However, Baron did not determine prior to the study that the only difference between the two confederates was sex. Since equivalence was not determined, differences in the selection rates of the two confederates could not be directly attributed to sex differences. In fact, what appear to be legitimate sex differences might actually be due to differences in physical attractiveness, communication ability, or poise.

Instrument decay occurs when measurement instruments used in a study become unreliable over time (Fisher, 1984). As human observers or interviewers become more familiar with the instrument and procedures over time, stimulus interpretation changes. With experience, interviewers may become more internally consistent in their use of the instrument (e.g., scored interviewer report forms), but how they use the instrument may be quite different from initial application. Instrument decay can be minimized by training observers, periodically computing their reliability, and providing feedback and additional training as needed.

Demand characteristics provide clues to the participant about desired or expected responses (Fisher, 1984). If participants care about the outcome of a study, their perceptions of what is expected and what the experimenter hopes to find can bias their behavior (Orne, 1969). Although participants may occasionally try to live up to researcher expectations, it may not be wise to assume that a laboratory study necessarily produces artificial demand characteristics. Berkowitz and Donnerstein (1982) suggested that Orne may have based his assumption of demand effects on a "chain of speculation that does not withstand close examination" (p. 250). Whatever degree of effect demand characteristics may have on an experiment, it is not wise for an experiment to ignore their influence.

Experimenter effects represent a special subset of problems related to demand characteristics (Fisher, 1984) of which there are essentially two types. One type of experimenter effect involves experimenter expectancies which actually change subject behavior. In this instance, an experimenter's expectancies indirectly reinforce hypothesis-confirming behavior from subjects (Rosenthal, 1969).

Besides expectancies, fixed characteristics of experimenters can also alter subject behavior. Experimenter sex, age, and race have been shown to affect particpant responses in an experiment (Rosenthal, 1969). However, at this time, research has not revealed whether these influences are due simply to the presence of experimenters varying along these attributes, or whether experimenters who vary along these attributes behave differently toward participants, thereby obtaining different responses (Rosenthal, 1969).

A second type of experimenter effect occurs when participant behavior is not actually changed, but the experimenter's observation, recording, or interpretation of that behavior is contaminated by a lack of experimenter objectivity. Expectations or desires may cloud objectivity.

The Need to Pretest Stimulus Materials

Many of the threats to internal validity have occurred in employment interview research. As previously mentioned, one way to combat certain threats to internal validity is by carefully designing the research. One important but often overlooked step in designing interview research is pretesting the stimulus materials to be used in the study. Careful and extensive pretesting can help increase internal validity by controlling selection bias for confederates, exposing instrument decay, and recognizing and controlling the potential for experimenter bias to occur. Examples of interview research that have failed to pretest stimulus materials illustrate the problem.

Wexley and Nemeroff (1974) examined the influence of applicant race and biographical similarity in an employment interview. Decisions were made after subjects reviewed a job description, resume, and photograph. To ensure that the statements used in the study did indeed manipulate the two conditions being examined, the authors pretested the statements. However, once they were certain the conditions were appropriately manipulated, they attached photographs which had not been pretested. Further, the job description used to determine the job for which the individual would be hired was not pretested for racial stereotypes. Therefore, their results, which indicated that perceived similarity in backgrounds determined employment decisions, remain open to alternative explanations such as applicant suitability for the position, or attractiveness of the applicant. The absence of stimulus pretesting can also create a problem for research that uses videotaped interviews. Osburn, Timmerick, and Bigby (1981) had experienced interviewers watch two applicants in videotaped interviews, who varied in their qualifications for the job. The authors described in great detail the procedures followed to develop the materials used in the study. To create the scripts used in the videotaped interviews, behavioral items were created and pretested to insure that the two applicants were perceived as having different qualifications. After the scripts were written, professional actresses were used as the applicants and the interviewer to insure a realistic employment interview. However, no tests were made to verify that the two actresses who played the parts of the applicants were seen as comparable on various dimensions other than qualifications, such as communication ability, appearance, or attractiveness.

In a study that examined the impact of racial attitudes of interviewers, applicant race, and applicant quality on applicant ratings, Mullins (1982) pretested the appropriateness of using a student sample in terms of generalizability. However, the videotapes were inadequately pretested. Even though Mullins went to great lengths to standardize the applicants in terms of physical appearance, no attempt was made to determine whether the subjects agreed with the author in terms of similarity of the applicants' appearance and abilities.

Pretesting stimulus materials with a subset of the population can increase the internal reliability of employment interview research by controlling possible selection biases of both subjects and confederates, as well as providing valid measurement instruments. However, pretesting stimulus materials cannot guarantee internal validity. Other problems can occur when studying employment interviews which limit the internal validity of a study. One of the possible problems mentioned previously is experimenter effects.

Checking for Demand Characteristics

Three suggestions for dealing with demand characteristics were presented by Orne (1969). The first, postexperimental inquiry, simply involves holding debriefing sessions with participants. Responses from the debriefing sessions can then be used to indicate the degree to which demand characteristics have influenced the results. Orne expressed amazement over the fact that few experimenters take the opportunity to elicit participant impressions once the experiment is over.

A second suggestion for controlling demand characteristics was to use a "non-experiment." In this situation, the researcher assembles several "non-subject" groups, shows them the equipment to be used in the experiment, describes the method to be used, and asks them to complete the instruments as though they were actually participating. Comparisons between the data collected during the enacted "non-experiment" can then be compared to data collected during the actual experiment. These comparisons should be examined to determine whether the actual procedure influenced responses.

Finally, Orne (1969) suggested that simulations also can be useful in controlling demand effects. In a simulation, participants are asked to pretend that they have been affected by an experimental treatment which they did not actually receive or to which they are immune. In order for this technique to work, the experimenter who runs the session must be blind to the task, and the participants must believe that the experimenter is blind to the task. Participants are then asked to guess how actual subjects in this situation might react. Simulations can help experimenters create realistic cover stories and anticipate possible reactions to the study.

Several examples of attempts to control for demand characteristics can be found in interview research. Hitt and Barr (1989) videotaped sixteen confederates enacting a scripted description of their backgrounds. These videotapes were pretested with respect to physical appearance and communication clarity. Results from this pretest indicated that three of the sixteen confederates were more than one standard deviation away from the mean and therefore had to be replaced. After new videotapes with the three new confederates were constructed, another pretest was performed. Results indicated that none of the confederates were rated more than one standard deviation from the mean. Further tests were conducted to determine whether ratings for the experimental groups (i.e., black versus white; males versus females; old versus young) differed. Results indicated that there were no statistically significant differences among these groups. Rand and Wexley (1975) also pretested the similarity of their confederates when examining the "similar to me" effect. Among other pretests, these authors tested the similarity of the physical attractiveness of the confederates (one white and one black) by having participants rate pictures of the confederates on a seven-point scale. Pretests like the one described above are essential when one is attempting to determine the internal validity of a study.

The Assumption of External Validity

With internal validity, researchers can be assured that observed changes in the dependent variables are caused only by the intended manipulations of the independent variables. An equally important requirement for experimental research is that results be externally valid, or generalizable across times, settings, and persons. This section examines the importance of external validity in experimental research on the employment interview.

The Importance of Time on External Validity

The element of time in relation to external validity concerns the interaction of history and treatment. The need for experimental results to be externally valid across time can be addressed through replications or multiple time-series experiments which assess the stable saliency of experimental results. Replication has been defined as an examination or reexamination of someone's own findings or those of other researchers in an attempt to reproduce results (Forcese & Richer, 1973).

According to Lykken (1984), there are three methods of experimental replication: literal, operational, and constructive. Literal replication involves an exact duplication of a prior experiment including methods of sampling, measurement, and analysis. Operational replication involves duplication of a prior experiment, but only in terms of sampling and experimental procedures used. Alternatively, constructive replication involves the deliberate avoidance of conditions and procedures used by a prior researcher. Under this method of replication, a secondary researcher—through his or her own methods of sampling, measurement, and analyses—attempts to replicate the findings of a previous researcher.

While experimental replications are important (Lykken, 1984), the fact seems to be that replications are not rewarded (Denzin, 1970; Kerr, Tolliver, & Petree, 1977), which may explain why few replications are ever even submitted to journals (Campbell, 1982). It is interesting to note the wider acceptance of replication studies in the hard sciences than in the behavioral sciences.

The Importance of Setting on External Validity

External validity in relation to experimental settings concerns the plausible interaction between setting and treatment. A primary issue is the degree of accuracy with which a discovery made in one setting applies to a second setting. One area in which this interaction between setting and treatment has been scrutinized is that of laboratory and field research. The issue of external validity or generalizability in laboratory and field research has been the subject of much debate (Campbell, 1986; Dipboye & Flanagan, 1979; Berkowitz & Donnerstein, 1982).

Common criticisms of laboratory research are that laboratory settings are susceptible to experimental artifacts (Rosenthal, 1969; Silverman, 1977), ethical problems (Kelman, 1967), and artificiality (Berkowitz & Donnerstein, 1982; Dipboye & Flanagan, 1979; Fisher, 1984). Because of these issues, critics of laboratory research contend that results obtained in laboratory experiments do not generalize to real organizations.

In contrast, Weick (1964) has argued that it is not necessary for laboratory environments to duplicate real world settings in order to be valid, only that they reproduce or simulate a few of the more salient characteristics of real organizations. Similarly, Mook (1983) stated that the concern over external validity varies from experiment to experiment in terms of what the researcher wishes to generalize. The research setting, laboratory or field, should be selected according to the needs of the experiment.

For example, research on the effects of interview context on interviewer judgments should be conducted within a rich array of organizational settings. The relative sterility of a lab setting minimizes the transferability of research on interview context whose results are highly modified under different situational conditions. Further, research that is designed to emulate a real employment environment requires increased efforts to verify external validity (e.g., McIntyre, Moberg & Posner, 1980). In comparison, employment interview research that is testing the cognitive construction capabilities of interviewers when confronted with congruent or incongruent applicant information may yield laboratory results which are highly predictive of actual interviewer judgment processes. This can be seen in the research conducted by Mullins (1982), in which students were asked to view and rate videotapes of black and white applicants (i.e., incongruent applicant information).

Overall, generalizability of laboratory studies on interview decision making that are conducted within a "research only" purpose—where subjects are not held accountable for their evaluations—should be questioned.

Employment interview research, which is conducted outside the reality of organizational life, may offer only limited insight into how interviews are actually performed.

The Importance of Subjects on External Validity

Selecting subjects from an appropriate population is one of the most fundamental steps in any research project. It seems that more often than not, undergraduate students are selected. Approximately 75% of the laboratory research published in both social and industrial/organizational psychology has involved undergraduates (Dipboye & Flanagan, 1979; Gordon, Schmitt, & Schneider 1984).

The role of students as subjects in experimental research has recently been debated by Gordon, Slade, and Schmitt (1986, 1987) and Greenberg (1987). Gordon et al. contended that students are inappropriate subjects in organizational research when they do not represent a subset of the population to which the researcher is attempting to generalize findings. One area that Gordon et al. identified as problematic due to differential findings between student and non-student subjects is the research on employment interviewing. As interviewers in a hypothetical setting, students have been found to be more lenient than experienced interviewers in their evaluations (Barr & Hitt, 1986; Bernstein, Hakel, & Harlan, 1975; Dipboye, Fromkin, & Wiback, 1975).

Greenberg (1987) countered that students may provide insight into *processes* which generically operate across organizations. Following Greenberg's logic, students could be utilized in studies that are concerned with process issues (e.g., observing and rating behavior), but not in research concerned with content issues (e.g., making selection decisions). Eder and Buckley (1988) contended that students will yield as much information as would their "real world" counterparts in a skillfully designed study. For example, examining interview behavior of students who are selecting resident advisors would be similar to examining interview behavior of managers selecting employees for an organization. The debate concerning the use of the college sophomore is sure to continue. Important external validity issues on both sides have been raised and must be considered.

External Validity: Not Always Essential

No single study can assure external validity, nor is it necessary to replicate across all applicable settings. The setting often has been blamed for limiting the generalizability of a study. When the purpose of the study is to predict real-life behavior, external validity is important. However, if this is not a goal of the study, then external validity can be considered unimportant (Mook, 1983). Essentially, if the goal of the study is to determine if something *can* happen rather than if it typically *does* happen, a well designed laboratory study is sufficient. Internal validity is always essential to demonstrate with confidence that "If a then b." Whether the statement requires generalizability depends on the purposes of the research.

The importance of external validity in interview research varies from study to study. Not all threats to external validity, as delineated by Campbell and Stanley (1967), will prove germane across all studies. For example, research on discrimination in the interview may simply be trying to show that unfair discrimination can occur. This type of study should not be concerned with external validity. Much can be learned from well designed laboratory experiments on the interview, and studies of this nature should not be dismissed out of hand simply because they do not generalize to the real world. However, if the purpose of the experiment is to predict conditions under which discrimination in the interview will exist in actual organizations, external validity is of the utmost importance.

Conclusions

Experimental research, with all of its faults, still has one distinct advantage—control. The ability to control various aspects of the experiment may increase the chances of an internally valid study, but does not guarantee one. The present chapter has outlined some of the possible problems associated with experimental research on the employment interview which may decrease internal validity.

Included in this review was the problem of lack of sufficient pretesting of stimulus materials, the influence of experimenter effects, and demand characteristics. Behavioral scientists conducting experimental research on the employment interview should more carefully control for the problems that decrease the internal validity of their research.

The judgment of sufficient internal and external validity in a given study is an inductive process. One can never be certain that each has been fully addressed in a particular study. Nevertheless, observing sound experimental design principles should decrease both internal and external threats to the validity of the study's findings. Well executed, independent replications of research are often the strongest final indication that one's empirical results have captured the phenomenon as originally intended by the researcher.

PART II

Preinterview Impression Effects

Before the interviewer greets the applicant and begins the discussion, judgments are likely already being formed. Interviewer-applicant characteristics and interviewer impressions of the applicant's qualifications, based solely on a review of paper credentials, may be among the more dominant factors in biasing both the conduct and eventual outcome of the interview.

Dipboye asserts in his chapter that interviewer judgments may not add substantially to predicting job success after test scores, completed application forms, applicant resumes, and letters of reference are taken into account. Reviewers such as Ulrich and Trumbo (1965) and Mayfield (1964) noted this over two decades ago, but incremental validity remains a neglected and unresolved issue in interview research. In addition to calling for research on this important topic, Dipboye explores possible threats to incremental validity within the framework of a process model of the interview (Dipboye, 1982; Dipboye & Macan, 1988).

Campion and Arvey address the role interviewer-applicant characteristics may have in biasing interviewer judgment against protected classes (e.g., women, minorities, aged, handicapped). Legal case history and psychological research on unfair discrimination in the employment interview is reviewed. An updated examination of legal cases (1979-1988) suggests four problem areas for the interview: preinterview deterrence, selection and training of interviewers, taboo interviewer behavior, and subjectivity in evaluation. The authors recommend that more attention be devoted to job analysis, interviewer training, review of interviewer decisions, and record keeping. Based on an examination of the literature on sex, race, and age discrimination (1982-1988), no firm conclusions can be made regarding interviewer bias. Research results appear to be dependent on a variety of contextual and methodological factors, requiring additional research on the role these factors play in producing unfair bias.

3

Threats to the Incremental Validity of Interviewer Judgments

Robert L. Dipboye
Rice University

A basic assumption behind eight decades of research on the employment interview (Arvey & Campion, 1982; Hakel, 1982; Webster, 1982) is that subjective procedures should be held to the same psychometric standards as paper-and-pencil tests of intelligence, personality questionnaires, work samples, biodata instruments, assessment centers, and other more objective procedures. In other words, if selection decisions are based on an individual's judgments then these judgments should be reliable and valid. The Equal Employment Opportunity Commission (Uniform Guidelines on Employee Selection Procedures, 1978) and the Society of Industrial and Organizational Psychology (1987) have reinforced this theme in their guidelines for employee selection. Despite the accumulation of a large amount of evidence on the validity and reliability of the interview, a continuing source of ambiguity in the interpretation of this research is the overlap that exists between the content of the interview and other methods. Indeed, some of the more highly structured procedures appear indistinguishable from work samples, biographical inventories, achievement exams, or personality measures.

Over twenty years ago, both Mayfield (1964) and Ulrich and Trumbo (1965) noted this overlap in content, and questioned whether the interview itself contributes to prediction beyond what could be contributed by more objective and economical measures. Unfortunately, the issue of incremental validity seems to have been largely ignored in subsequent research and reviews. The present chapter resurrects this issue, using a process model to explain why an interview might fail to show incremental validity.

The Issue of Incremental Validity

The traditional basis for evaluating selection techniques is predictive validity, usually expressed as improvement over random selection of applicants.

Recent meta-analyses leave little doubt that interviewer judgments are better than random selection (McDaniel et al., 1987). After correcting for sources of error (e.g., restriction, range, and low reliability), trait-oriented and unstructured interviews were found to possess validities in the mid-teens to low twenties. Job-related structured interviews possessed validities in the low thirties. Even more encouraging was evidence that some types of structured job-related interviews achieved corrected validities previously found only for cognitive ability measures (i.e., the 50s).

The quantitative reviews of the validity data provide convincing support for the conclusion that interviews can improve on chance prediction. As noted by Sechrest (1963), however, a more appropriate criterion of success is incremental validity or improvement "in predictive efficiency over the information otherwise easily and cheaply available" (p. 369). Similarly, Cronbach and Gleser (1965: 36), and more recently Thumin and Barclay (1980), have argued that the validity of procedures must be evaluated on the basis of improvement over prior procedures rather than random selection. How then does the typical employment interview perform against this more stringent criterion? Unfortunately, past research findings do not provide a particularly sound basis for sweeping statements.

The problem lies mainly in the sequence of events occurring in the typical interview. Usually there is an opportunity to form initial impressions of the applicant prior to the face-to-face encounter on the basis of initial contact and appearance as well as paper credentials such as test scores, the application, and references. The interview follows, after which interviewers render their final ratings and decisions. Postinterview impressions may be shown to predict subsequent job success of applicants, but as Ulrich and Trumbo (1965) noted,

> In most studies data from the interview are inextricably confounded with biographical or other nonpsychometric data, or both, in the interviewer's predictions. Furthermore, in some cases in which no ancillary data are specified in the report, one could not be certain that such data were not available to the interviewer. (p. 113)

The usual statistical procedure for examining incremental validity is a hierarchical regression in which the criterion (e.g., applicant success on the job) is first regressed on evaluations of whatever information is available on the applicant before the interview and then regressed on both preinterview and postinterview impressions during the second step of the analysis. The extent to which R^2 increases as a consequence of adding postinterview impressions is a measure of the incremental validity of the interview.

Sechrest (1963) also has recommended correcting for unreliability in the predictors before entering them in the regressions to make sure that increments in R^2 reflect more than improved reliability associated with an increased number of predictors.

To fully examine the extent to which the interview uniquely contributes to the prediction of the criterion, Ulrich and Trumbo suggested a three group research design to provide a clear assessment of the interview's validity. Specifically, one group of interviewers would evaluate applicants before and after the interview based on whatever information were available. The prediction obtained from preinterview assessments would then be compared to the prediction obtained from postinterview assessments. They also suggested a control group in which the order of interview and ancillary data would be reversed and still another control in which predictions would be based solely on ancillary data.

The validation study suggested by Ulrich and Trumbo (1965) has yet to appear in the published literature, and consequently the issues they raised remain largely unaddressed. The few attempts to separate the contribution of preinterview impressions from postinterview impressions that have appeared in the literature are not encouraging. Among the most discouraging of these studies was the landmark validation of the Veteran Administration's assessment of potential trainee in clinical psychology (Kelly & Fiske, 1951). The highest validities obtained came from evaluations of the student's paper credentials, objective test scores, an autobiographical essay, and scores on projective tests (mean $r = 34$ with r's ranging from .19 to .48). The addition of a two-hour intensive interview to the above information not only failed to improve prediction but was associated with a smaller mean validity coefficient (mean $r = .27$ with r's ranging from .22 to .33)! In a more recent study, Gorman, Clover, and Doherty (1978) had each of eight graduate students predict the performance of undergraduates on tests of their knowledge of psychology. A comparison was made between the predictive validities obtained from judgments of only paper information in the form of a profile of six cues (i.e., student sex, high school rank, four ACT scores) and the validities obtained from judgments of both paper information and a brief interview. Minimal evidence was found for incremental validity, with five of the eight interviewers achieving higher validities with only the paper profiles than with the combination of paper and interviews. Waldron (1974) presented some evidence for the incremental validity of an interview used in the selection of naval recruits, but unfortunately confounded interview evaluations and objective paper credentials.

The obvious way to guarantee that postinterview impressions contribute to prediction is to withhold the ancillary data on applicants. Even in such a situation, Ulrich and Trumbo (1965) noted that one could still question whether the same or higher "predictive efficiency could not have been achieved from other, probably less expensive sources." Tubiana and Ben-Shakhar (1982), for example, found that interviewer assessments of motivation to serve in combat added an additional 4% of variance to the prediction of success in military training beyond the contribution of three objectively scored predictors (i.e., knowledge of Hebrew, level of education, and ability test scores). A questionnaire measure of motivation to serve in combat contributed slightly more to the prediction of the criterion, however. The interview was subsequently replaced by the questionnaire without any loss to predictive validity (possibly a gain in validity of a combined predictor) and with a great profit in terms of time, manpower, and money. Similar results were reported by Campion, Pursell, and Brown (1988). They designed a highly structured interview that proved quite successful in predicting the success of entry-level paper mill employees, but failed to contribute to the prediction of the criterion above the level of prediction achieved with test scores alone. Ability tests offered an alternative to the interview that was just as predictive and probably less costly.

The findings of Tubiana and Ben-Shakhar (1982) and Campion et al. (1988) suggest that the most efficient solution to the problem of incremental validity is to do away with the interview altogether and substitute paper-and-pencil measures. This is not a realistic solution in many organizations. For instance, Campion et al. reported that the interview they designed was more acceptable to management and consequently was retained as the major basis for selection decisions. For a variety of reasons, many organizations will continue using interviews even when the same results can be achieved with cheaper methods. Moreover, the typical interview will probably continue to be wide-ranging, unstructured, and intertwined with other applicant information.

Given this less than ideal state of affairs, research is needed on the factors influencing the extent to which the validity of postinterview impressions can rise above the baseline levels of prediction achieved with impressions of applicants' paper credentials alone. To improve incremental validity, a better understanding is needed of the impact of pretervew impressions on postinterview impressions and the factors mediating this influence. A process model of the interview (Dipboye, 1982; Dipboye & Macan, 1988) is presented which perhaps can provide insight into these mediating factors.

Evidence for a Preinterview Impression Effect

The process model offered by Dipboye (1982) describes the interview in terms of three phases. In the preinterview phase, the interviewer has an opportunity to form impressions of the applicant based on paper credentials such as test scores and the application. The interview phase consists of the face-to-face conversation between the interviewer and applicant. Finally, in the postinterview phase, the interviewer forms impressions of the applicant's qualifications and renders decisions such as to hire, not hire, or to seek more information. Although this sequence of events does not describe all interviews, it does seem descriptive of the typical or modal interview. The main concern of the present chapter is the extent to which the second phase of the above process can contribute to the prediction of applicant success, above and beyond the prediction achieved with just the first phase.

The interview seems most likely to contribute to the prediction of a criterion to the extent that the information gathered during this phase is kept independent of information gathered in the first phase and considered on its own merit. Contrary to this ideal, however, research on social perception (Schneider, Hastorf, & Ellsworth, 1979) has shown that final judgments can be unduly influenced by initial impressions. There is no reason to believe that interviewers are immune from primacy effects. This leads to the basic proposition of the process model (Dipboye, 1982); that is, postinterview impressions of an applicant's qualifications are positively related to preinterview impressions.

Studies Examining the Correlation of Preinterview and Postinterview Impressions

In support of the process model, at least five studies have shown substantial relationships between postinterview impressions of an applicant's qualifications and preinterview impressions of paper credentials such as the application, test scores, and references. The earliest evidence of a preinterview impression effect was reported by Springbett (1958). Interviewers from several industrial settings evaluated the suitability of applicants three times: once on the basis of the application form, another time on appearance alone, and a third time based on all information. The order of presentation of appearance and the application was varied, but the total impression was always last and followed the face-to-face interview. Overall, 81 percent of the final decisions agreed with impressions formed from the application, and 62 percent agreed with impressions formed from appearance. When the application came first, 87 percent of final decisions agreed with impressions based on the application. A second study conducted with eighteen Canadian army personnel officers and three applicants yielded essentially the same results. Combining the results of the two studies, 90 percent of applicants accepted on the basis of both application and appearance were accepted after the interview. Only ten percent of applicants who were rejected on the basis of both application and appearance were later accepted after the interview.

Four subsequent studies have reported additional support for the above proposition, although the size of the relationships found generally has been smaller than those reported by Springbett. Phillips and Dipboye (1989) had 34 interviewers evaluate the qualifications of candidates for stockbroker positions before the interview, on the basis of their applications and a test score, and then after the interview. Preinterview evaluations on a multiple-item measure of qualifications were positively related to postinterview impressions on the same measure, with an obtained correlation of .63 ($p \leq$ .001). To further explore this relationship, an examination was made of an item in this composite pertaining to actual willingness to hire. Of those interviewers stating that they would recommend or would strongly recommend hiring the applicant before the interview, 80 percent said they would take one of these options after the interview. Of those stating they would not recommend or would strongly not recommend hiring before the interview, 54 percent said they would take one of these options afterward. Interviewers also evaluated the applicant as having done a better job answering questions during the interview, the more positively they evaluated the paper credentials before the interview ($r = .44$, $p \leq .01$).

Macan and Dipboye (1988) asked 120 recruiters at a university placement center to evaluate the qualifications of college students before and after interviews on their overall qualifications. Despite the fact that very little information was provided to recruiters (i.e, types of courses taken, major, work experience, but no transcript of grades), preinterview impressions of applicants were positively related to postinterview impressions ($r = .54$, $p \leq .01$). Similar to the findings of Phillips and Dipboye (1989), interviewers evaluated the applicant as having done a better job in answering questions during the interview the more favorable their impressions of the applicant before the interview ($r = .37$, $p \leq .01$).

Russell, Persing, and Dunn (1986) examined a situation in which 117 students interviewed for admission to a university's elementary education teacher preparation program. Candidates were first evaluated on the basis of their paper credentials, which included tests scores in reading, spelling, language, mathematics, and writing, work history, an autobiography, letters of reference, and a transcript of college grades. At the next step two members of an admissions committee conducted a 20 to 25 minute interview and evaluated the applicant using 10 criteria. The overall evaluation of the applicant's paper credentials in the preinterview phase was positively related to their evaluations of the interview ($r = .49$, $p \leq .001$).

In the research reviewed so far, ratings were aggregated across interviewers in computing the correlations. In contrast to these studies, Dougherty, Ebert, and Callender (1986) examined the preinterview effect at the level of the individual interviewer. Three untrained interviewers rated applicant test scores and the application before the interview. These preinterview ratings of applicant test scores were closely related to postinterview evaluations of applicant qualifications for each of the interviewers (r = .80, .80, and .91). Similarly, the correlations of preinterview ratings of applications and postinterview evaluations of the applicants' qualifications were also substantial (r = .61, .49, .50). Training in interviewing techniques was found to reduce the effect, but the correlations remained substantial (r = .36, .57, and .63 for test scores and r = .29, .11, and .41 for the application).

Consistent with the evidence that postinterview impressions tend to conform to preinterview impressions, there is some evidence that postinterview evaluations of paper credentials and the interview performance of the applicant are highly correlated. In a recent example, Powell (1986) examined the intercorrelations of the ratings of 53 college recruiters of 145 applicants on eleven characteristics. A correlation of .63 was observed between evaluation of the applicant on a personal factor, consisting of information gleaned exclusively from the interview such as personal appearance and communication ability, and evaluations on a credentials factor, consisting of extracurricular activities and work experience.

Studies Examining the Correlation Between Objective Credentials and Ratings of Interview Factors

The correlation observed from the above studies could simply reflect the fact that preinterview impressions and postinterview impressions are tapping similar psychological constructs. For instance, persons with high test scores, good grades, relevant work experience, and extracurricular activities may receive higher postinterview evaluations of their interview performance because they actually make better impressions in the interview. The few studies that have reported the correlations between *objective* credentials and ratings of interview performance provide little support for this contention. Factor analyses have revealed that these two types of information usually load on separate factors (James, Campbell, & Lovegrove, 1984; Kinicki & Lockwood, 1985; Shahani & Dipboye, 1988).

Even more important, the correlation between objectively scored paper credentials and ratings of the interview is usually quite low. Sparks and Manese (1970) found that the mean correlation of interview ratings and a test score was .27 when interviewers were aware of the applicants' test scores and only .10 when interviewers were unaware of the test scores. Kinicki and Lockwood (1985) found that recruiters' ratings of applicant interviewing skills had a correlation of .27 with objectively scored relevance of work experience and a correlation of .20 with objectively scored scholastic record. Ratings of interview impression had a correlation of .26 with scholastic record and .28 with relevance of work experience. Shahani and Dipboye (1988) reported similar results in a study in which over 2000 applicants to a small private university were rated on 12 dimensions on the basis of 30 minute interviews. Consistent with the findings of the other studies reviewed here, the correlations of ratings on these dimensions and objective scores derived from the paper credentials (i.e., college board exams, evaluations of essay, rank in class) were very small (mostly in the 0 to .10 range). In addition to these findings, McDaniel et al. (1985) examined data from ten studies and found a median correlation in the .20's between objective test scores and interviewer ratings.

Conclusions

Hakel (1982, p. 136) concluded in a review of the interview research, "It is abundantly clear that whatever information occurs first has a disproportionate influence on the final outcome of interviews." The first information on an applicant is usually in the form of paper credentials, and the present review suggests that these credentials indeed have a disproportionate influence on impressions formed from the interview itself. Before proceeding to a discussion of possible mediators of this effect, however, two observations should be made. First, the effects of paper credentials on later impressions found in the above research probably reflect more than order of presentation. Test scores, the application, references, and other paper credentials can be a rich source of verifiable and valid impressions which can overwhelm ambiguous interview information. Second, a preinterview impression effect does not necessarily imply a "snap judgment" in which interviewers reach a final decision before or very early in the interview. Springbett found in a pilot study with eight Canadian Air Force interviewers and twenty interviews that final judgments were reached within an average of four minutes (discussed in Hakel, 1982; Buckley & Eder, 1988). Although this finding has been cited often, the original research was limited by methodological problems and subsequent attempts to replicate have failed (Hakel, 1982; Buckley & Eder, 1988). Determining exactly when decisions are reached is not as important to the present discussion, however, as the fact that postinterview impressions tend to conform to preinterview impressions (Dipboye, 1982, p. 580).

Cognitive and Behavioral Mediators of Preinterview Impression Effects

Although the obvious way to avoid preinterview impression effects is to have different persons evaluate the credentials and the interview of an applicant, the main concern of the present chapter is with the more typical situation where the same person performs both tasks. The research findings reviewed so far cast doubt on the ability of postinterview impressions in this situation to increase prediction above the levels achieved with just preinterview impressions. The nonindependence of impressions formed in the preinterview, interview, and postinterview phases appears to be a factor contributing to the problem. Moreover, the low correlations of objective credentials and interview ratings suggests that a goodly portion of the variance in the correlation of preinterview and postinterview impressions can be attributed to bias. Why might preinterview impressions bias later impressions and consequently detract from the incremental validity of the interview? An answer to this question requires an examination of the behavioral and cognitive processes mediating the preinterview impression effect.

Cognitive Categorization in the Preinterview Phase

As stated previously, the typical selection interview begins with interviewers forming impressions of the applicant before the interview from paper credentials. The face-to-face interview then follows, culminating in the formation of overall impressions of the applicant's qualifications after the interview. These impressions then form at least a partial basis for the decisions the interviewer is empowered to make regarding the status of the applicant. At the first step of this sequence, the act of previewing an applicant's credentials can set in motion a process by which applicants are placed in categories such as the "ideal or highly qualified applicant," the "typical" applicant, or the "unqualified applicant." The interviewer's conception of the prototypical member of the category can then guide and influence the subsequent gathering and processing of information on the applicant. The immediate outcome of this cognitive categorization is that interviewers form expectancies for how applicants will present themselves in the interview.

Indeed, Fiske and Taylor (1984) noted that distinctions can be made among terms such as category, stereotype, prototype, and schema but "the common point in the term schema and related terms is this: general expectations guide processing of specific data" (p. 148). Supportive of this view,

Macan and Dipboye (1987) found that subjects given preinterview information that a candidate possessed high qualifications had higher expectations that the applicant would give good answers to the questions of the
interviewer, display the traits of the ideal job candidate in the interview,
and make specific statements that were consistent with the schema of the
ideal candidate. Undoubtedly, there are wide differences among interviewers
in the schemas that influence their preinterview impressions. An interesting
area for future research will be to examine these differences and their impact on subsequent gathering and processing of information. For example,
one could predict that the interview is less likely to contribute to the prediction of applicant success for those interviewers whose schema leads them
to emphasize attributes contained in the paper credentials.

Behavioral Confirmation of Expectations

The expectations that interviewers form in the preinterview phase can
be self-fulfilling in the sense that they cause the applicant to respond in
ways that confirm these expectations. In other words, interviewers who are
favorably impressed with an applicant's credentials cause the applicant to
appear highly qualified in the interview, whereas those with unfavorable
impressions cause the applicant to appear unqualified. Thus, interviewers
discover in the interview no more than was expected, and the interview
fails to contribute unique information to the prediction of the criterion.

The crucial mediating factor is the interviewer's conduct of the interview.
A considerable amount of laboratory research has demonstrated that interviewers who have favorable attitudes toward an applicant tend to show more
signs of approval and fewer signs of disapproval in their verbal and nonverbal behavior (Dipboye, 1982; Dipboye & Macan, 1988). Farina and Felner
(1973) provided an interesting demonstration of this by having a confederate
interview for jobs in 32 different firms. In 16 of the firms, the confederate
stated in the application that he had been traveling the last nine months,
whereas in the other 16 firms he stated that he had been in a mental hospital
during the same period. Recordings of the interviews revealed that interviewers were uniformly less friendly in their conduct of the interview when
the applicant was believed to have been in a hospital. Also, when the applicant asked what his chance of finding employment was, interviewers
expressed lower expectations for the applicant when he claimed to have
suffered from mental problems.

There are at least two ways in which a behavioral confirmation might
follow from biased conduct of the interview. One possibility is that the interviewer's behavior influences the motivation of the applicant to make a

favorable self-presentation. Applicants who perceive favorable attitudes can be encouraged to try even harder in attempting to present their qualifications. Applicants who perceive negative attitudes, on the other hand, might cease trying to create a good impression, or their anxieties might detract from these attempts. An interviewer's actions also can lead to a behavioral confirmation by restricting the range of the applicant's responses. For example, if applicants are asked only about the poor aspects of their credentials, evidence supportive of their qualifications may remain uncovered.

On the other hand, spending most of the interview recruiting or engaging in small talk is unlikely to allow discovery of much negative data. The findings of at least two laboratory studies demonstrate that initial impressions of credentials can bias spontaneously generated questions (Macan & Dipboye, 1988; Binning, Goldstein, Garcia, Harding & Scattaregia, 1988). Although questions do not inevitably trap applicants into confirming an interviewer's hypotheses (Macan & Dipboye, 1988; Sackett, 1982; McDonald & Hakel, 1985), it still seems possible that initial impressions can lead to lines of inquiry that neglect some important topics and overemphasize others. Some indication of this comes from a study by Tengler and Jablin (1983) in which college recruiters were found to use many closed questions and relatively few open-ended questions at the beginning of the interview. Just the opposite was found toward the end of the interview. The authors speculated that "interviewers were basing their employment decisions about applicants on very limited amounts of information" and "were not allowing applicants to 'display' themselves early in the interviews" (p. 262), possibly reflecting an attempt on the part of the interviewers to test their stereotypes regarding the ideal applicant.

Cognitive Mediators

Another way in which preinterview impressions can limit the incremental validity is by biasing the interviewer's processing of information. This has been shown in laboratory research in which the level of preinterview impressions has been manipulated and the effects on postinterview impressions examined. Such research cannot be used to estimate the frequency or strength with which preinterview effects actually occur in the real world, but lab studies can contribute to an understanding of the cognitive processes accounting for these effects when they *do* occur. The research shows that final evaluations of applicants generally conform to evaluations of applicants' paper credentials before the interview, even when the interview refutes these impressions (Belec & Rowe, 1983; Dipboye, Stramler, & Fontenelle, 1984; Latham, Wexley, & Pursell, 1975; Macan & Dipboye, 1987; Rasmussen, 1984; Tucker & Rowe, 1979).

Postinterview impressions may conform to preinterview impressions because interviewers fail to recall information that is inconsistent with their expectations and recall primarily the information that is consistent with these expectations. Dipboye et al. (1984) found biased recall among subjects who were given favorable or unfavorable applications, viewed videotaped interviews with the applicants, and then stated the things they learned about the applicants. Subjects recalled more negative information from an interview when there was an unfavorable application. In some cases the differences were quite striking. One interviewee, for example, was seen as alert, enthusiastic, expressing himself well, and well groomed when he conveyed a high level of qualifications in the application. The same interviewee was perceived as nervous, quick to object to the interviewer's assumptions, and lacking self-confidence when he conveyed a low level of qualifications in the application.

Despite these findings, memory and impression appear unrelated in the few social psychological experiments that have examined both within the same design (see also Carlston, 1980). The findings of a more recent experiment (Macan & Dipboye, 1987) suggest that a biased *interpretation* of what is recalled is a more important mediator than is selective recall. In this study, interviewers allowed to take notes were compared to interviewers who were not allowed to take notes. Greater accuracy of recall of information from the interview was found for those taking notes. Nevertheless, impressions of the applicant's performance in the interview were just as biased by application qualifications with note-taking as without. Similar to the malleability of trait inferences that has been found in basic social cognition research (Srull & Wyer, 1979), interviewers in this study seemed to interpret most of what they recalled on the applicant as consistent with their preinterview impressions. This study brings attention to the fact that one can almost always infer from any single statement or behavior of an applicant more than one trait-schema. Consider, for example, an applicant for a sales job who expresses a dislike for large gatherings and love of solitude. Normally one might consider this a sign of introversion, lack of sociability, and other traits incongruent with the prototypic salesperson. In the context of favorable prior impressions, however, the same statement could be construed as rugged independence, individualism, and other prototypic sales traits.

Biased interpretation of information also can occur in the form of the causal attributions interviewers make for applicant behavior in the interview. Tucker and Rowe (1979) found that students with favorable preinterview impressions were more likely to attribute past successes of an applicant to internal causes (e.g., the applicant's effort, ability) than were students with unfavorable preinterview impressions. Students with favorable preinterview impressions were less likely to attribute past failures of an applicant to internal causes than were students with unfavorable preinterview impressions. Rowe and her associates have examined attributions for successes and failures in the interviewee's past work history. Interviewers make causal attributions for not only the content of the applicant's statements but also the style with which they present their qualifications. For example, a nervous, incoherent self-presentation could be attributed to a lack of qualifications on the part of the applicant or to the way the interviewer conducted the session. Likewise, a polished self-presentation could be attributed to the high qualifications of the applicant or could be seen as a well-rehearsed act. Phillips and Dipboye (1989) asked managers screening applicants for stockbroker positions to indicate how well each applicant had performed in the interview itself and whether this performance was the result of their possession (or lack) of the attributes required for the job or merely a "fluke." Consistent with the research of Rowe and her associates, as managers' preinterview impressions became more favorable, they were more likely to attribute a good performance in the interview to the applicant's possession of the requisite traits and a poor performance to a "fluke."

How Can Confirmatory Biases Limit Incremental Validity?

Whether subjects show biases in the recall or interpretation of the applicant's behavior, the effects of prior impressions on processing information in the interview can bring behavioral confirmation full circle. Interviewers' preinterview impressions lead them to conduct the interview in ways that fulfill their impressions. In turn, their processing of the information increases their confidence in the correctness of their impressions. Preinterview impressions can set in motion confirmatory biases, but these biases do not necessarily yield "bad" decisions. Granted, preinterview impressions based on nothing but appearance and an initial encounter seem unlikely bases for valid prediction (Borman, 1982), but impressions based on information such as biodata and test scores can be highly predictive. To repeat the essential thesis of this paper, the primary threat of preinterview impressions is not to the basic validity of interviewer assessments considered alone, but to the incremental validity of these assessments.

Confirmatory biases can prevent postinterview impressions from contributing to the prediction of the criterion in at least two ways. These biases could prevent the interviewer from generating and retaining new information. Once their initial impressions are fulfilled, interviewers seem less likely to seek additional, unique information which might improve on the prediction obtained from preinterview impressions alone. Moreover, multicollinearity may be introduced in the form of high correlations between impressions of the credentials, and impressions based on the interview. The resulting redundancy in information can place a ceiling on the extent to which postinterview impressions improve prediction.

In addition to, or instead of, the above scenario, another way in which confirmatory biases can reduce incremental validity of postinterview assessments is through attenuating the reliability of these assessments. Interviewers exposed to the same basic information on an applicant can differ markedly in their evaluations (Valenzi & Andrews, 1973; Hakel, 1971). In many cases this lack of agreement reflects differences in the knowledge structures that interviewers bring to the interview situation (i.e., differences in prototypes, schemata, implicit theories). For example, one interviewer may see high ability test scores as characteristic of a highly qualified candidate, whereas another may emphasize work experience and see high test scores as characteristics of low social skills. Idiosyncratic views of the applicant in the preinterview phase can lead to variations in the conduct of the interview and the processing of information from the interview that adversely affect the reliability of postinterview assessments (Dipboye, Fontenelle, & Garner, 1984). Reduced reliability of postinterview assessments can, in turn, severely reduce or eliminate their contributions to prediction.

Boundary Variables

Although past research seems to have yielded more support for the process model described here than for alternative models, interviews do not always result in self-fulfilling prophecies. It is important then for future research to provide competitive tests of at least three alternative models. One possibility is that interviewers remain relatively unbiased by preinterview impressions and apply diagnostic strategies to the gathering and processing of information. Another is that they adopt disconfirmatory strategies. Thus, highly favorable impressions might lead an interviewer to stress the weaknesses on an applicant, while deemphasizing the positive information (see also McDonald & Hakel, 1985). Still another possibility is a "mixed model" in which interviewers show different combinations of these processes. An interviewer might, for example, show confirmatory biases in their processing of information while remaining diagnostic in conducting the interview.

Research is needed to determine the conditions under which each of these alternatives is most likely to occur. In previous presentations of the process model (Dipboye, 1982; Dipboye & Macan, 1988), confirmatory biases were hypothesized to occur when (1) interviewers are highly confident of their preinterview impressions of the applicant and applicants are unsure of how they will do in the interview, (2) when interviewers are committed to their preinterview impressions as a result of making these impressions explicit and public, (3) when interviews are unstructured in the sense that requirements of the job and procedures for interviewing and evaluating applicants are unstated or vaguely stated, and (4) when interviewers are untrained in effective interviewing techniques and unaware of the possible biasing effects of their preinterview impressions. In addition to specifying the conditions under which the model is most likely to hold true, these variables also suggest possible ways to improve incremental validity. For example, cultivation of a hypothesis-testing orientation through interviewing procedures and training seems to be a particularly promising strategy for enhancing the incremental validity of the interview (see also Janz, 1982).

Research will undoubtedly lead to revisions in the process model, but even if some of the predictions fail to receive substantial support, they may point the way to important research questions. Indeed, the main virtue of this and similar conceptual schemes which have been presented in recent years (Dreher & Sackett, 1983; Schmitt, 1976) is that they present a more realistic road map for future research on the interview than the rather narrow models dominating past studies. Too much of the past research has focused on *just* the reliability and validity of judgements, or *just* cognitive or social processes. To guide future work, more integrated and holistic models are needed to capture the interrelationships among cognitive and behavioral events in the interview and judgments that are made before and after the interview (see also Eder & Buckley, 1988).

The clear implication for future research of a process approach, such as the one presented here is that interviewers and applicants need to be tracked as they move through the various phases of the selection process. A comprehensive examination of all phases of the interview has yet to be conducted. Such a study would start with measures of the impressions formed in the preinterview phase, followed by monitoring the actual behavior of applicant and interviewer in the interview phase. Later, an assessment would be made of the information recalled by the interviewer from the interview, and of the final impressions and decisions formed on the basis of this information. Following up from this analysis of behavioral and cognitive processes, one could examine the degree of predictive validity achieved by interviewers in their postinterview evaluations. An integrated, multiphasic approach such as this could allow one to profile the characteristics of interviews that succeed and those that fail to contribute in an incremental manner to the predictions of applicant success. The process model has been presented in the hope that it will provide a better guide for this type of research than the fragmented and narrow conceptualizations dominating past work on the interview.

A Postscript on the Multiple Functions of the Interview

The focus of this chapter has been the use of the interview in selection. To repeat an earlier assertion, interviews used for the purpose of selection should be held to the same standards applied to more objective procedures, including the stringent standard of incremental validity. In closing, the author would add to this affirmation a note of realism. At the same time that attempts are made to improve efficiency of selection, one must not forget that unstructured interviews can fulfill a variety of other functions. They serve as vehicles for recruiting, counseling, informing, and maintaining good public relations. They can even be a means of allowing organizational members to participate in the selection process, of affirming the values of the organization, and maintaining the organizational culture. Klitgaard (1985) brought attention to this last function of the interview when he noted that

> The declaration of what is being sought—vague and idealistic as that may be—and the involvement of culture's best representatives . . . help to create and reinforce an institution's mission. This is so even if someone comes along and shows that what is sought cannot be reliably measured or effectively predicted. (p. 191)

The value of interviews in achieving these other goals provides a possible explanation for why interviews continue to be used, and perhaps *should* be used, even when they fail as efficient tools of selection. The primary challenge of future research on the interview is to determine how organizations can strike a balance among these often conflicting objectives.

4

Unfair Discrimination in the Employment Interview

James E. Campion
University of Houston

Richard D. Arvey
Industrial Relations Center
University of Minnesota

Almost ten years ago, Arvey (1979) reviewed the literature regarding unfair discrimination in the employment interview. At that time, as is true today, the interview was the most widely used method of evaluating job candidates despite a long history of research findings suggesting it is among the least reliable and valid predictors of job behavior (Arvey & Campion, 1982). Arvey (1979) had suggested that interviewers may be biased against women and other protected classes, and, hence, highly vulnerable to legal attack.

Although there had been few discrimination cases involving the interview, two key problem areas were identified by Arvey (1979). The first was an interviewer questioning strategy that conveys an impression of discriminatory intent. The second was the interviewer's use of questions that had a differential impact or adverse effect on protected class members but had no relationship to job requirements. Arvey concluded his article by appealing for more research on the role of unfair discrimination in the employment interview. It was his hope that research findings rather than data-free court decisions would guide future employment practice in this area. This chapter updates the 1979 review by summarizing both recent court cases and psychological research, and by recommending guidelines for future practice and research.

AUTHORS' NOTE: We gratefully acknowledge the help of Gail Sissons, Law Librarian, University of Houston.

Legal Aspects of Interviewing

To prepare for this review, Federal and State court decisions were examined that included the employment interview as a fair employment practice issue. The main source of reference material was the Commerce Clearing House series, *Employment Practices Decisions (EPD)* (1979-1988). This hand search was supplemented by two computer-aided search programs, *Lexis* (1987) and *WestLaw* (1987). The reader may be interested to know that the interview was an issue in fewer than 1% (72) of the more than 8,000 cases reported between 1979-1987. The interview was most often referred to in sex (47%) and race (31%) discrimination suits followed by age (12%).

Space limitations prevent a detailed review of each case. Instead, a summary is presented that describes four areas that appear problematic for the interview. These problems areas are (a) preinterview deterrence, (b) selection and training of interviewers, (c) taboo interviewer behavior, and (d) subjectivity in evaluation. Important issues are first illustrated with court cases, and followed by recommendations for practice.

Preinterview Deterrence

There are several legal risks in the recruitment and prescreening of applicants. These hazards include not advertising for openings, using word-of-mouth advertising, giving preference to relatives and friends, callback procedures, discouraging applicants, and the use of unnecessary job experience requirements. Interviewers often participate in these efforts and, therefore, should give careful thought to the impact of their actions on protected class members.

In *Kraszewski v. State Farm* (1985), a class action suit was filed on behalf of deterred female applicants for the job of insurance agent. When the suit was filed in 1981, 99.6% of the organization's agents were male. The firm did not advertise or post openings. Instead, it relied on word-of-mouth recruiting by its male work force, which was augmented by a policy of nepotism favoring male relatives. Testimony supported the claim that female applicants were actively discouraged, lied to, and misinformed about the nature and availability of agent positions. Until 1979, company brochures portrayed only male insurance agents. The organization was found guilty of discouraging female applicants.

Selection and Training of Interviewers

In several cases, the court criticized the race and/or sex makeup of the interviewing team, and its training and experience in the hiring process.

For example, in *Gilbert v. City of Little Rock* (1986), the city was criticized for denying black police officers promotional opportunities based on oral exams given and evaluated by an all white supervisory group. In *EEOC v. American National Bank* (1979), the court criticized the bank's systematic rejection of black applicants because all officials involved in the decision-making process were white, none had received formal interview training, and only a few had previous hiring experience.

Court criticisms of inadequate interviewer training were also evident in *Green v. USX Corporation* (1988) and in *Bailey v. Southeastern Apprenticeship Committee* (1983). In the former case, the court criticized the defendant in a race discrimination suit for not providing formal instructions to interviewers, and for the apparent lack of education or experience requirements in selecting interviewers. The 1983 case questioned both the appropriateness of an interviewing format that had not been reviewed since 1972, and the adequacy of interviewer training. The court ruled that given outdated interview questions and ambiguous instructions, the interviewing procedure was defective and likely to result in disparate appraisals.

Taboo Interviewer Behaviors

The courts have also raised doubts about the appropriateness of certain interviewer behaviors, especially when interviewer questioning varies across groups of applicants. Of particular concern has been interviewer questions on applicant arrest and conviction records, physical and mental handicaps, and marital and parental status. In *Reynolds v. Sheet Metal Workers* (1980), inquiries about arrest records on the application form and during the interview produced disparate impact for black applicants to an apprenticeship program. The court concluded that arrest records played a role as a chilling factor as well as an element affecting interviewer judgment of applicant job suitability, rejecting the employer's claim that arrest records were not used in arriving at the evaluation.

An example involving mental handicap is *Doe v. Syracuse School District* (1981). The school board violated the law when interviewers asked applicants whether they were mentally ill or had been treated for a mental illness. The plaintiff, who admitted he had suffered a nervous breakdown during his military service, was examined by the school district's physician and declared physically and mentally qualified for the teaching position. Still, he was not hired. The court concluded that the inquiries regarding his handicap were unrelated to the applicant's ability to do the job.

In *King v. TWA* (1984), questions were asked regarding marital and parental status. A black women applied for a position as a kitchen helper. The interview consisted of questions about her recent pregnancy, her marital status, and the nature of her relationship with another TWA employee, who had filed an earlier EEOC complaint. She was also asked about the number of children she had and whether they were illegitimate, about her childcare arrangements, and about her future childbearing plans. The company gave other reasons for rejecting her, but the court concluded that they were pretextual for two reasons. One, the offensive questions were not asked of anyone else. And two, a previous TWA personnel officer testified that the interviewer had a history of discriminating against female applicants with children because he felt childcare problems created an unacceptably high risk of absenteeism.

Other examples of inconsistent application of standards include *Smith v. American Service Company* (1984) and *Thorne v. City of El Segundo* (1983). Both cases involved inconsistent use of polygraph interview findings. In addition, there has been at least one case of adverse impact in the use of polygraph examinations. In *Moon v. Cook County Corrections Board* (1988) records showed that while 72.5% of black applicants for corrections officer failed the polygraph, only 21.5% of white applicants did. However, problems with the polygraph interview may soon disappear due to legislative fiat. Congress has prohibited its use except for a very narrow range of jobs and circumstances (Camara, 1988).

Finally, one case involved sexual harassment in the interview. In *Phillips v. Plaquemines Parish School Board* (1985), the plaintiff filed suit to be reinstated in his job as principal, which he lost because of a charge of sexual harassment. During an interview with a 21-year-old female applicant he expressed a desire to have a sexual relationship with her and later, during a school tour, he placed his hand on her neck and attempted to lead her forcefully down a hallway toward some empty classrooms. A former teacher at the school also testified about unwelcome sexual advances she had received two years earlier from the plaintiff. The court supported the Board's decision for dismissal.

Other issues raised about interviewer behavior concerned note taking during the interview, length of the interview, interviewer feedback to the applicant, and record keeping. In *EEOC v. Tecumseh Products* (1983), interviewers, when making exceptions to hiring rules, explicitly noted in writing that some applicants were young. In *EEOC v. Spokane Concrete* (1982), the court criticized a five minute interview as perfunctory and designed to discourage the applicant. In *Pushkin v. University of Colorado* (1981), a handicapped applicant for a psychiatric residency was given feedback from the interviewing team that the reason for his rejection was his handicap. The University argued that he was not qualified apart from his handicap. However, the court ruled that they altered their reasons after-the-fact and found for the plaintiff. Finally, lost records of interview notes were noted in two recent decisions that resulted in victories for the plaintiffs (*Green v. USX Corp.*, 1988 and *Colon v. Sorensen*, 1987).

In summary, the courts have identified several interviewer behaviors that can support charges of illegal discrimination. The issues raised in questioning technique, feedback to the candidate, record keeping, and so forth should be considered when training interviewers and developing interview procedures.

Subjectivity in Evaluation

The problem of subjectivity is often raised whenever the interview is criticized. It is argued that, when interviewers are not given clear guidelines for evaluating a candidate, subjectivity guides the process and provides a ready mechanism for illegal discrimination.

For example, in the previously noted case of *Reynolds v. Sheet Metal Workers* (1980), the interview was the most important part of the process and it was subjective. Categories such as attitude, interest in trade, and work experience were evaluated without the benefit of guidelines to distinguish between good and bad attitudes, high and low interest in the trade, and so on. Furthermore, the court pointed out that interviewers' judgments were not subject to review, and there was no attempt to validate the interviewer's judgment.

In *Harless v. Duck* (1980), police department representatives admitted that the grading of interviews was subject to a host of errors due to unstandardized conditions, rater bias, and the lack of objective criteria. The court concluded that the interview was not job related, and thus rife with potential for discrimination. A more recent example is *EEOC v. Rath Packing* (1986). Here the employer was unable to show that the interview-based selection procedure, which resulted in a 95% male work force, was job related. In testimony the interviewer could not identify the qualifications and criteria that were being used. The court concluded that sex was the sole identifiable element explaining their hiring pattern. Finally, in a reverse discrimination case (*Lucas v. Dole*, 1987), a subjective interview was noted by the court as one factor in ruling for the plaintiff.

Conclusions Regarding Interviewing Practice

This review suggests several actions that can be taken to enhance the legal defensibility of the employment interview. Although implementing all these steps is unnecessary or impractical for many jobs, employers in high risk situations (i.e., interviews having disparate impact on protected classes) would benefit from adopting some of these practices. Finally, several of these suggestions also have been found useful in defending performance appraisal systems (Barrett & Kernan, 1987; Cascio & Bernardin, 1981; Feild & Holley, 1982), so efforts in one area may help in the other.

Develop job descriptions. In evaluating interview cases, the courts focus on job relatedness and uniformity of application in making their rulings. Often the courts have criticized the lack of job descriptions to guide the interviewer. The availability and use of job descriptions for developing interview objectives, questioning strategy, and evaluation standards should encourage job relatedness and uniformity to counter charges of subjectivity.

Selection and training of interviewers. Several courts discussed the race and sex makeup of the interviewing team, their training, and their background. An all-white male interviewing team with little experience was seen as detracting from the interview's objectivity and job relatedness. Carefully selected and trained interviewers should minimize exposure to lawsuits.

Questioning techniques. This area, although partially addressed in the first two recommendations, warrants special attention. Questioning technique is carefully examined in courts to support arguments of illegal discrimination. Questions should be job relevant, and asked of all applicants. Questions or interviewing strategies that produce disparate impact should be closely examined and revised toward greater job relevancy.

Introduce review. Usually the interviewer, alone, decides on objectives, question strategy, and evaluation standards. Anything that can be done to introduce additional review of these elements would counter subjectivity arguments. For example, the use of multiple interviewers or panel interviews might help. Also, the introduction of management committees to review interviewer findings and recommendations might also counter subjectivity arguments.

Keep records. A serious problem for some organizations in defending their practices was a lack of record information which would have allowed them to document the job relatedness of their selection procedures. Often organizations had to rely on the memory of those involved to reconstruct events. Undocumented, after-the-fact reconstructions are not given much credence by the court. A system for recording and storing this information for several years would be useful in defending against lawsuits.

Monitoring for disparate impact. Monitoring interviewer decision results for disparate impact would appear to be a prudent and preventative step. Based on the present review, approximately 50% of the cases were ruled in favor of the defendant. The most successful defense was showing that the interview did not have a disparate impact on a protected class. When an organization acknowledges that it noticed the disparate impact result and took specific action to assure fairness, the employer's defense is bolstered.

It should be noted that there has been controversy regarding the appropriateness of the plaintiff using disparate impact evidence in cases involving subjective decision-making practices (e.g., *Harris v. Ford*, 1981; *Griffin v. Carlin*, 1985). However, a recent Supreme Court ruling (*Watson v. Fort Worth Bank and Trust*, 1988) unanimously held that disparate impact analysis is appropriate when evaluating subjective employment criteria. In this case, an employer's practice of promoting bank employees based on the subjective evaluations of an all white supervisory corps resulted in adverse impact against blacks. On the more important issue of whether use of such subjective criteria is subject to the test of *Griggs v. Duke Power* (1971), the court was divided. A plurality of the judges (O'Connor, Rehnquist, White, and Scalia) indicated that the burden would be less for the employer when using subjective practices. However, three of their colleagues (Blackmun, Marshall, and Brennan) were adamantly opposed to more lenient evidentiary standards and wrote an opposing opinion. If the pluraity view prevails, it would be easier for employers to defend subjective employment practices and we might expect less effort devoted to validating interview practices. Final resolution of these issues will have to await additional Court action.

Research on Unfair Discrimination

Previous reviews by Arvey (1979) and Arvey and Campion (1982) summarized literature pertaining to sex, race, age, and handicap bias in the employment interview. In the present chapter, trends and issues associated with this research stream are noted, and relevant research is summarized in order to illustrate salient points.

First, more recent research on bias against protected classes qualifies the earlier presumption of pervasive interviewer bias. It appears that as more information becomes available to the interviewer, reliance on minority stereotypes diminishes. For example, Tosi and Einbender (1985) reviewed 21 studies investigating gender bias, showing that judges faced with limited information about candidate competence or job requirements tended to make biased or stereotyped judgments; but also that those with more information did not. Powell (1987) drew a similar conclusion in his recent review of gender effects on recruiter's responses. The work of Heilman (1984) and Heilman, Martell, and Simon (1988) serves as a good illustration. Both studies showed that positive job-related information enhances ratings assigned to female job candidates and removes their disadvantage when compared to males. Conversely, when job-related information was limited or not available, females were rated less favorably than males. Previous research that presented very limited information might have had the effect of artificially "enhancing" bias effects based on simple demographic or visual cues.

Second, recent research reflects a growing awareness that contextual and other personal variables need to be considered in combination with minority characteristics in investigating interviewer bias. An example of this thinking is reflected in a study by Heilman (1980) where she suggested "that situational factors can preclude, or at least reduce, the likelihood of discriminatory personnel decisions although they leave the decision-maker's stereotypic belief system intact" (p. 387). As support for this proposition, Heilman (1980) reported the results of a study in which interviewers evaluated a female candidate's application form along with interviewing seven additional candidates. The percent of women in the applicant pool was manipulated so that the pool included either 12.5, 25, 37.5, 50, or 100% females. Results suggested that when women represented 25% or less of the total pool, the female applicant was evaluated more unfavorably than if the pool reflected a larger percentage of female applicants. Similar results were recently reported for older applicants (Cleveland, Festa, & Montgomery, 1988).

The type of job for which applicants are being considered is another contextual variable which appears to mediate sex bias effects. The findings that females are given higher evaluations than similarly qualified males for jobs which are stereotypically female has been frequently replicated. Arvey, Miller, Gould, and Burch (1987) conducted a study involving 558 applicants in one year and 774 the next, where both sex and age were correlated with interview judgments. The results showed that females were given significantly higher evaluations than males; older applicants were also evaluated more favorably. The job was a retail clerk position in specialty-food stores across the U.S. The authors concluded that these findings corresponded to their prediction of higher evaluations for females given the sex-stereotyped nature of the job. A similar study by Parsons and Liden (1984) also found that females were given higher evaluations for low-level jobs in an amusement park.

Gordon (1984) studied the effect of accountability on interview judgments in conjunction with age. Videotaped interviews portraying 25, 40, and 55 year old applicants were rated by 120 undergraduates. Subjects gave more positive evaluations to the 25 year olds, and this was enhanced when subjects were made to feel accountable for their evaluations.

In sum, contextual and situational variables are important factors serving to limit the extent to which one can safely make broad generalizations regarding the type and extent of interview bias.

Third, research methodologies appear to make a difference when investigating interview bias. Most of the early research in this area relied heavily on stimulus materials based on resumes and "hypothetical" applicants. However, recent research has begun to use methods which more fully approximate "real" interview situations (e.g., using videotape materials), or are conducted in actual field settings. For example, Mullins (1982) used video-taped stimulus materials to examine interviewer ratings of high and low quality candidates role-played by black and white males. The study used 176 white business administration students who viewed the videotaped interviews. Results suggested that the most important variable influencing the interview ratings was applicant quality, but that the black applicant was significantly favored over the white applicant. However, in a field study examining actual interviewer ratings of candidates for positions in an amusement park, Parsons and Liden (1984) found lower ratings for black applicants as compared with white applicants on several rating dimensions. One must be careful, however, in evaluating this study because the black and white candidates evaluated under these actual job interview conditions may not have had the same qualifications. That is, the job candidate qualifications are not controlled or held constant as they are in the resume or videotape methodologies (see Kacmar, Ratcliff, and Ferris, this volume).

When more contextually rich and sophisticated research methods are used, puzzling differences occur across studies. For example, in two studies (Young & Allison, 1982; Young & Voss, 1986), candidate age was manipulated by using otherwise equivalent resumes. These results suggested that younger teacher candidates (age 29) were rated higher than older candidates (age 49). However, Young and Ponder (1985) found no age bias when candidates were presented on videotape or when interviews were role played. In attempt to integrate these findings and better understand possible methodological artifacts, Ponder (1987) manipulated the mode of candidate information into four levels: resume only, resume plus candidate photograph, resume plus interview script, or resume plus videotaped interview. Results indicated no significant differences for age nor any significant interaction between age and mode of information transmittal. When more "realistic" interview studies are conducted using field and videotape methods, the findings on bias are still mixed and inconsistent.

Fourth, research has begun to examine the information processing variables that may explain how and why bias and discrimination occurs in the employment interview. For example, Graves and Powell (1988) examined the role of perceived similarity, interpersonal attraction, and subjective and objective qualifications on recruiters' evaluations in a field setting. Sex of applicant did not affect recruiters' evaluations; instead, subjective qualifications were most important and mediated the effects of the other variables. Giles and Feild (1982) examined the accuracy of interviewers' perceptions of the importance of intrinsic and extrinsic job factors to male and female applicants. While these authors showed that male recruiters were more accurate for males than for females, and that the recruiters overvalued the importance of the intrinsic factors for both males and females, no link back to the interviewer final judgments was made. Seigfried and Pohlman (1981) examined the effect of task and order in the rating of female and male applicants using undergraduates as subjects. Postponement of the hiring decision had no effect on ratings or on the hiring decision, but the order in which the applicants were seen did interact with sex. Interviewers were more lenient in evaluating a male who was seen after a female than in evaluating a female who followed a male. Finally, McDonald and Hakel (1985) and Binning, Goldstein, Garcia, and Scattaregia (1988) examined the effects of preinterview impressions on questioning strategies on same- and opposite-sex employment interviews.

Conclusions Regarding Research Evidence on Bias

Based on the research of the past decade, there appears to be a need to be tentative with regard to firm conclusions about bias in the employment interview. Gender bias is substantially affected by contextual and situational variables, making it difficult to conclude that automatic bias exists against females in the interview. Instead, bias, when it does occur, appears to be a function of the type of job, amount of job information available to the interviewer, and as noted in earlier reviews, the qualifications of the applicants.

Similarly, there is insufficient evidence to draw firm conclusions regarding racial bias in interviewer judgment. It appears that when studies are conducted using resume materials, blacks receive more favorable evaluations. In the one study that used a field setting, the evidence suggested that blacks received lower evaluations. Obviously, research results involving resumes and undergraduate students are suspect because of possible subject sensitivity to equal employment opportunity issues. The research on age bias is quite mixed. Again, these findings seem influenced by contextual variables and research methodologies. Finally, recent research has not dealt with interview bias against handicapped applicants, so readers are referred to earlier reviews (Arvey, 1979; Arvey & Campion, 1982).

Future Research on Unfair Discrimination in the Interview

There remain a number of methodological issues that need expansion and clarification if substantial progress is to be made on this more recent body of mixed and conflicting findings. First, more research is needed to specify the differences in outcomes in interview bias using different methodologies. The work by Ponder (1987), in which a variety of methodological procedures were used to explore age bias is a good example. A more complete understanding is needed concerning how much of detectable bias is due to particular methodologies.

Second, greater efforts in employing "real life" interview situations are needed in future research designs. Perhaps researchers should consider observing actual interviews as they unfold, or videotaping interviews to analyze later. Actual interviewers should be used as subjects in contexts associated with real job openings in order to understand more fully actual interview judgment outcomes. It will be necessary in these field studies to control for differences in actual candidate qualifications.

Third, more effort should be made in understanding some of the micro-level behavioral processes that might be involved in interview situations, and their covariations with bias. For example, perhaps subtle behavioral differences emerge when males interview females, females interview females and so forth, which could account for differential evaluations. Researchers fail to systematically collect and analyze such data in interview contexts, yet there exist plenty of examples of studying streams of behavior in other kinds of settings (Weick, 1968). During interview training workshops, the second author observed that female interviewers and applicants seemed to lower their voice volume and sit closer when they seem to "hit it off" in the interview. Would this observation be verified if investigated more scientifically? Would such behavioral differences lead to differences in evaluation?

Fourth, what are the implications of differential evaluations in terms of predictive bias? While the issue has been raised previously (Arvey, 1979), there have been two investigations of whether differential evaluations produce different regression lines when predicting job performance. In the first study, Arvey, Miller, Gould, and Burch (1987) found that even though females received higher evaluations, the regression lines for males and females were similar. Similar findings were reported by Campion, Purcell, and Brown (1988), who examined the fairness of a highly structured interview with respect to both race and sex.

Fifth, more research is necessary to investigate the interview evaluations and outcomes associated with other characteristics not formally protected via current laws. For example, what kinds of interview outcomes are associated with applicants who are homosexuals? With candidates who have AIDS? There is a dearth of research associated with religious preferences in the interview as well as with national origin. What forms of sexual harassment occur in the employment interview?

Sixth, can interviewer training reduce bias? Virtually nothing is known regarding whether interviewer bias can be reduced or eliminated via training procedures. Part of the problem is identifying and quantifying bias in order to make it and the processes salient for trainees. Once this is accomplished, it may be useful to apply the training techniques developed to reduce rating errors in this area. Recent work by Hedge and Kavanagh (1988) has suggested that workshops focusing on observation skills and decision training are most useful in enhancing rater accuracy. These methods also may be useful in reducing interviewer bias in regard to sex, race, age, and handicap.

Finally, research should investigate whether "format" features of the interview affect interview bias. For example, does the use of board interviews, which include a proportionate mix by sex, race, and so forth, reduce differential evaluations? Also, does any reduction in differential evaluations impact the relative validity of the interview, or result in differential regression lines? Does the use of structured interviews diminish differential evaluations? To date, little research exists that investigates these format features, yet they figure prominently in many legal cases.

Conclusion

Judgment, fairness, and legal liability play an important role in employment practice, even though the present review showed that fewer than 1% of discrimination cases involve the employment interview. Errors by interviewers can leave the company open to costly and time consuming charges of unfair discrimination. Thus, employers and interviewers must be sensitive to the subtleties of discrimination against females, minorities, the aged, the handicapped, and other protected classes. More research is needed to develop interviewing practices that improve job relatedness and reduce subjectivity. Most importantly a better understanding is needed concerning the process and contextual factors that produce unfair bias, and how interviews can be designed to diminish bias. Research in these areas and related interventions should not only increase interview fairness and defensibility, but should also benefit employee productivity and morale.

PART III

The Interviewer's Decision-Making Process: Shortcuts and Short Circuits

There are always two applicants in each interview, the "real" and the "make believe." The interviewer's task is to determine which is which. Accurate judgment of an applicant's job-relevant qualifications is dependent on the interviewer's ability to gather, store, organize, combine, and evaluate the information both provided and inferred by the applicant's behavior. The demands of this cognitive task are made more difficult by the "shortcuts" and "short circuits" that characterize virtually all human information processing. The following three chapters represent ongoing research efforts to conceptualize, measure, and understand how interview decisions are confounded by human cognitive limitations.

Rowe examines and refines the finding from the McGill University studies which reported that greater weight is attached to unfavorable information by decision makers. The differential effects of unfavorable information on employment decisions is reviewed and some of the explanations for the cause of the effect are discussed. Two studies which attempted, but failed, to alter the negativity bias are described. An alternative explanation of the unfavorable information effect derived from work on confirmatory bias in hypothesis testing is also offered.

Schuh's chapter builds upon Webster's (1982) assertion that interviewers employ multiple decision models to acquire information from applicants and to make selection decisions. Both distinct decision styles and cognitive structures that interviewers may use are described, as well as their implications for future research to improve decision accuracy.

Herriot reviews one of several social psychological theories that is applicable to the employment interview—namely, attribution theory. The theory is reviewed in terms of its historical development, with particular attention paid to biases in attributions, attributions to dispositional and situational factors, and self-attributions. A macro-analysis of the interview in terms of attribution theory is presented, together with a review of the relevant literature.

5

Unfavorable Information and Interview Decisions

Patricia M. Rowe

University of Waterloo

The publication of Webster's 1964 book on the employment interview produced a major shift in research away from studies of the reliability and validity of the interview to studies examining the factors influencing the decisions made by interviewers. In the years since then hundreds of studies have been published which have examined a variety of such factors, including contrast effects, stereotypes of good applicants, unfavorable information, minority bias, nonverbal behavior and a host of other major and minor factors. Much of this literature has been reviewed by Schmitt (1976), Arvey and Campion (1982), and Webster (1982). As more knowledge of the roles these factors play and of their complex interactions has been gained, a better understanding of the selection interview process has developed.

One of the earliest findings from the McGill studies, and one that continues to stimulate research, is the greater impact unfavorable information has on selection decisions, as compared to favorable information. In 1958, Springbett noted that a small amount of unfavorable information resulted in a reject decision. In fact, he found that a single early unfavorable rating resulted in a reject decision in 84.5% of his cases; the interviewer seemed more interested in negative than in positive information. Subsequent research has confirmed and elaborated upon the earlier findings.

Further Studies of the Unfavorable Information Effect

Research since Springbett's (1958) finding has addressed some of the parameters of the unfavorable information effect. Several studies have ex-

AUTHOR'S NOTE: This work was supported in part by a grant from the Social Sciences and Humanities Research Council of Canada. The author would like to thank Michael O'Driscoll, Phil Bryden, and Willi Wiesner for their helpful comments on an earlier draft of this paper.

77

amined the relative weight of favorable and unfavorable information. Bolster and Springbett (1961) found that, on average, 8.8 items of favorable information were required to change an initially unfavorable impression, but only 3.8 items of unfavorable information were required to alter an initially favorable impression. Rowe (1963) reported that the correlation between number of applicants accepted and ratings of unfavorable characteristics was .61, while the correlation with favorable characteristics was .31. Carlson and Mayfield (1967) reported that unfavorable information was weighted approximately twice as heavily as favorable information. However, on the basis of a carefully designed study, Hollman (1972) argued that interviewers place too little weight on favorable information rather than too much weight on unfavorable information. Whatever the appropriate weighting system may be, it is clear that unfavorable information outweighs favorable information.

Many studies have been concerned with the temporal placement of favorable and unfavorable information. In general, primacy effects, or the greater impact of initial information, are encountered only when a final judgment is required (e.g., Bolster & Springbett, 1961; Peters & Terborg, 1975), and recency effects, or the greater influence of later information, are encountered when repeated judgments are required (Belec & Rowe, 1983; Farr & York, 1975). One study (Tucker & Rowe, 1979) demonstrated the differential effects of favorable or unfavorable information that occurs at the beginning of an interview: following unfavorable information, applicants were given less credit for successes (i.e., fewer internal attributions) and more blame for failures (i.e., more internal attributions), but following favorable information, more internal attributions were made for successes and fewer internal attributions for failures.

The unfavorable information effect is not restricted to the employment interview. Levin and Schmidt (1970), among others, have noted the pervasive influence of unfavorable information in impressions of people. Nor is the unfavorable information effect limited to situations in which both favorable and unfavorable information are present. Miller (1968) presented subjects with equally polarized sets of favorable or unfavorable adjectives. When these sets of adjectives were presented to subjects as hypothetical people, unfavorable descriptions were rated significantly further from the indifference point than were those containing only favorable adjectives. Hamilton and Zanna (1972) also used only favorable or unfavorable adjectives paired with neutral adjectives and found likableness ratings to be more influenced by the unfavorable adjectives than the favorable ones.

It is important to note some qualifications to this unfavorable information effect. Hakel, Dobmeyer, and Dunnette (1970) found that the impact of unfavorable information was a function of the judged importance of the information: the more important the information, the greater the effect of unfavorable evidence. Constantin (1976) found unfavorable information judged relevant to the job produced lower ratings than irrelevant unfavorable information, but the relevancy of favorable information had no such effect. There are also large individual differences in response to unfavorable information, as first suggested by Rowe (1963), who reported striking differences among interviewers in the number of applicants accepted. Later work demonstrated that some people seem more susceptible than others to unfavorable information, insofar as the number of individuals who place greater reliance on unfavorable information increases as the proportion of unfavorable information about an applicant increases (Miller & Rowe, 1967). Mayfield and Carlson (1966) found high interrater and intrarater variability in ratings of items of information (i.e., some items are rated quite favorably by some raters and quite unfavorably by other raters). London and Poplawski (1976) found that females rated others more favorably than did males, while Belec and Rowe (1983) found that women made more internal attributions than did males about past successes and failures. Bernstein, Hakel, and Harlan (1975) found employment interviewers to be less lenient than students in their judgments, and there is some evidence (Rowe, 1963) that interviewers with extensive experience are less lenient than those with limited experience.

Explanations of the Unfavorable Information Effect

Why is unfavorable information more important than favorable information in selection decisions? Consider the reinforcement argument first offered by Springbett (1958), and refined more recently by Rowe (1984). Springbett suggested that the unfavorable information effect was created and sustained by the system of rewards and punishments typically provided to employment interviewers. As shown in Figure 5.1, decision makers are simply doing the jobs expected of them when the good applicant is accepted and the poor one is rejected. Positive feedback or praise for such decisions is rare. But of the two kinds of error, only that of accepting the candidate who lacks the necessary abilities and skills for the job has any serious consequences for the decision maker. Negative feedback about these employees is almost certain. In contrast, the other error, rejecting good candidates, is likely to go undetected and therefore unpunished. In other words, the costs of false positives are greater than the costs of false negatives (see Eder, this volume). As Springbett argued, it is not surprising that the interviewer develops an attitude of caution and a high degree of sensitivity to negative evidence in an attempt to avoid hiring poor candidates.

Other writers have dealt more explicitly with the costs associated with the two types of error. For example, Kanouse and Hanson (1972) suggested that the negativity bias in attributions of value came about because people are cost-oriented (i.e., regard costs as more important than rewards), and are more motivated to avoid potential costs than to look for potential rewards. A number of more recent studies (e.g., Tversky & Kahneman, 1981) have shown that people make different choices depending on whether they see the problem as offering an opportunity for a gain or for a loss. The evidence indicates that individuals are more averse to putting a gain in jeopardy than they are toward risking a loss.

In the selection context, this cost-benefit approach suggests that decision makers would be more averse to accepting a poor applicant than to rejecting a good one; as a result they would adopt a more conservative (less risky) attitude toward acceptance. Costs are likely to be more salient in situations where the decision will have a direct impact on the decision maker (Rowe, 1984; Eder & Buckley, 1988). For example, when future contacts with the accepted candidate will be long and close, such as with a member of one's own staff, a cost orientation is very likely. Similarly, the more accountable for the decision an interviewer is, and the more salient constraints on the interviewer are, the greater is the likelihood of a cost orientation. Some support for this notion comes from a study by Rosen and Mericle (1979) who found that a strong statement of fair employment policies tended to be associated with fewer acceptances of both males and females than did a weak statement.

An alternative way of conceptualizing selection decisions is in terms of signal detection theory (Swets, Tanner, & Birdsall, 1961). Translating the matrix in Figure 5.1 into signal detection terms means that acceptances of good applicants would be labelled as hits, rejections of good applicants as misses, acceptances of bad applicants as false alarms, and rejections of bad applicants as correct responses. Signal detection theory would say that the selection decision maker is applying a conservative criterion in order to minimize false alarms. By casting the problem in signal detection terms the possibility is raised of a different and perhaps more useful approach to selection, such as measuring the confidence level for each decision in order to evaluate better the "sensitivity" of the decision maker. Signal detection theory would also predict that changing the criterion for hits would result in changes in the matrix of responses.

Both the reinforcement argument and signal detection theory imply that reliance on unfavorable information should be altered if the relevant fac-

| Type of Applicant | Type of Decision | |
	Accept	Reject
Good	Valid Acceptance (doing one's job)	False Rejection (a mistake, but not noticed)
Bad	False Acceptance (a serious mistake, much criticism)	Valid Rejection (doing one's job)

Figure 5.1. Selection Decisions and Their Consequences

tors are changed; that is, by changing the reward structure or the criterion for hits and misses. It has been suggested elsewhere (Rowe, 1984) that the hockey or baseball scout provides a good example of a selection decision maker with a different reward structure. In professional sports, the scout's decisions are more costly if his or her rejects happen to include a player chosen by another team who becomes the rookie of the year. By contrast, selecting a player who attends the first tryouts but is subsequently cut from the team produces little in the way of punishment. In this situation, one would expect that favorable information would have greater salience than unfavorable information.

Two Studies Manipulating Costs

Two recent studies at Waterloo have attempted to change the criterion for acceptance and to make false rejections more costly, thus reducing the impact of unfavorable information and increasing the acceptability of applicants. The first study, a master's thesis by Vogler (1984), examined the effects of two situational factors, availability of skilled workers and training costs, on 267 student assessments of three job candidates. Skilled workers were either rare or readily available, training costs were either cheap or expensive. Moreover, half of the subjects were provided with a memo, purportedly from the vice-president of the organization, reminding them of their specific availability/training condition and its consequences for the organization. It was predicted that more favorable ratings would be given in those situations where skilled workers were in short supply and/or training costs were low, and that the memo would increase these effects. The candidates represented three levels of favorability: very favorable (VF), moderately favorable (MF), and marginal (M).

Two measures were analyzed for each description, a composite score of suitability and an accept/reject decision. The suitability means for the three candidates as a function of the two situational variables are shown in Table 5.1. Analysis of variance revealed no significant differences as a function of labor availability, training costs, or memo conditions, nor were there any significant interactions among these variables. The analysis of the accept/reject data supported the suitability findings in that no significant differences were found for any of the applicants as a function of training costs or memo condition, or for the moderately favorable or marginal applicants as a function of labor market. Table 5.1 also contains the results of the manipulation check. Subjects were asked whether it was worse to accept an unsuccessful candidate or to reject a successful one; responses were given on a 6-point scale with lower scores indicating false acceptances as more serious errors. Analysis of variance revealed significant effects for labor availability, training costs, and the interaction between them, but not for memo condition. In all cases the subjects responded in accordance with the intended manipulations. Most notably, subjects in the rare skill/ cheap training condition considered rejecting a potentially successful applicant to be more of a mistake than accepting an applicant who proves to be a poor worker.

The results of the manipulation check indicated that these subjects distinguished between error costs in the four experimental conditions. However, the experimental manipulations were not sufficient to modify selection strategies or to reduce the negativity bias of the subjects, although subjects did acknowledge the relationship between situational manipulations and the relative costs of different kinds of error.

A second study by Mifsud (1988), represented a further attempt to reduce the impact of unfavorable information. Three conditions were employed: a situational manipulation (rare skills/cheap training), an accountability condition in which the progress in other organizations of applicants not hired would be monitored, and a control condition. The five hypothetical candidates included two extreme candidates, one very favorable and one very unfavorable, and three marginal candidates. The marginal candidates had been shown in previous work to be very sensitive to small shifts in assessment. A total of 60 students rated the suitability of the candidates, rank ordered the five candidates, and made an accept/reject decision for each one. No differences among the three conditions were found for suitability ratings, rankings, or accept/reject decisions.

In this study, a more detailed manipulation check was carried out. Subjects were first asked three general questions about how much criticism a personnel officer could expect for hiring an incompetent worker, for not

TABLE 5.1. Mean Suitability and Manipulation Check Measures[a]
as a Function of Labor Market Conditions and
Cost of Training

Labor Market Availability	Training Costs			
	Cheap		Expensive	
Rare	VF	24.84	VF	26.36
	MF	23.18	MF	21.78
	M	21.04	M	20.85
	MC	4.16	MC	3.12
Common	VF	24.51	VF	25.58
	MF	22.74	MF	23.87
	M	22.22	M	20.79
	MC	3.24	MC	3.11

SOURCE: Adapted from Vogler, 1984

NOTE: VF = Very favorable, MF = Moderately favorable, M = Marginal applicants, MC = Manipulation check measures.

[a]Suitability ratings are a composite score, manipulation checks are based on a 6-point rating scale with low scores indicating false acceptances as more serious than false rejections. No significant effects for suitability ratings were found as a function of training costs or labor market availability; however, the manipulation check measures were affected by training costs, availability, and the interaction of the two variables.

hiring a potentially successful worker, and whether it was worse to accept a poor worker or reject a good one. Then they were asked to answer the same three questions with respect to the decision task that they had just completed. The analysis of the manipulation checks revealed no significant effects as a function of experimental condition for the general questions, nor for the question of criticism for false acceptance in the decision task. However, significant effects were found concerning criticism for false rejections; and the differences approached significance for the relative importance of the two types of errors. For both of the latter items, subjects in the ''monitor'' condition rated false rejections as more serious than false acceptances.

These results indicate that the subjects in the three conditions did not differ in their general orientation to the costs of different kinds of errors, but did appreciate that in the special conditions of the experiment, different costs were associated with different kinds of errors. Therefore, just as in the Vogler (1984) study, subjects recognized the costs of errors, but did not alter their assessment or selection behavior.

The failure to find any evidence in these two studies of the effect of changing the system of rewards and punishment for interviewers puts explanations for the unfavorable information effect derived from reinforcement and signal detection theories into considerable question. While the particular system of rewards experienced by employment interviewers may be as Springbett (1958) described, it is not necessarily true that the system is responsible for producing the interviewer's reliance on unfavorable information. Perhaps some other mechanism is responsible for the unfavorable information effect. Alternatively, it may be that the selection decision task is so strongly associated with the motivation to avoid false acceptance errors that subjects could not adopt a new strategy in accordance with the demands of the experimental conditions. Further research on this issue is very much needed. Eder and Buckley (1988) have suggested using professional interviewers as subjects, manipulating costs in a more salient way, and examining interviewers' confidence levels as a function of different situational factors (e.g., labor availability, accountability, and so on).

To this point the literature discussed has dealt with the way unfavorable information is attended to and utilized when it is available. For the most part these studies have treated the interviewer as a passive recipient of information, not as the active seeker of information emphasized by Dipboye (1982) and Dreher and Sackett (1983). Earlier, however, Springbett (1958) speculated beyond the question of the weight placed on unfavorable information to suggest that the interview was a *search* for negative information, that interviewers actively try to discover any unfavorable information about each applicant. Until recently, investigators largely ignored this negative information seeking aspect of the interview. Before turning to those studies, however, it is necessary to consider the literature in the hypothesis testing area.

Hypothesis Testing Research

A number of studies in the hypothesis testing area have suggested that people are prone to a "confirmation bias," and that this interferes with effective decision making. Klayman and Ha (1987) term this bias a *positive test strategy* or the tendency to test cases that are expected or known to have the property of interest, rather than to test cases that are expected or known to lack that property. Several studies in the impression formation area provide concrete examples of the positive test strategy. For instance, Snyder and Swann (1978) and Snyder (1981) have demonstrated that people use an information gathering strategy that is likely to confirm the hypothesis they hold about the personality of others. In their studies, some subjects were asked to judge whether or not an individual was an extrovert, while other subjects were asked to judge whether the individual was an introvert. The subjects were required to select interview questions from a list that has been categorized as typically asked either of extroverts or of introverts. The result indicated that people prefer to ask questions that confirm their initial hypothesis (e.g., those testing the hypothesis of extrovert selected questions likely to confirm extroversion).

Two studies, by Sackett (1982) and McDonald and Hakel (1985), attempted to apply this work in the selection area. Sackett explored the effect of preinterview impressions on the questioning strategies of interviewers. He found little evidence to indicate that interviewers seek confirmation of their initial hypotheses. In particular, confirmatory hypothesis testing was not found with experienced interviewers as subjects, nor with student subjects in an explicit interview context. However, Sackett did find that interviewers consistently preferred questions seeking positive information to questions seeking negative information regardless of the initial impression of the applicant.

McDonald and Hakel (1985) also failed to find any evidence of confirmatory information seeking in a more thorough examination of Snyder and Swann's (1978) theory. Worth noting, however, is that both the Sackett (1982) and McDonald and Hakel (1985) studies used a fixed list of questions from which subjects chose the 15 questions they wanted to ask the applicant. Such a procedure is quite different from the typical unstructured interview where interviewers generate their own questions.

A recent study by Binning, Goldstein, Garcia, Harding, and Scattaregia (1988) used this more appropriate methodology of free questioning. Subjects reviewed a job description, resumes, and application blanks, and then were asked to generate a list of questions for the applicant. In addition they completed the question selection task used by Sackett (1982). Their findings indicated differential question strategies as a function of applicant suitability; more questions designed to elicit negative information were asked of low-suitability candidates than a high-suitability candidates. However, regardless of the applicant's suitability level, subjects consistently generated more positive questions than negative questions (see Bining et al., 1988: Table 1, p. 33). Analysis of Sackett's questions replicated his failure to find any effect of initial impressions.

Taken together, then, these studies of information seeking behavior in the interview (1) demonstrate the applicability of the hypothesis testing literature to the selection interview, (2) indicate that methodological differences may obscure effects of initial impressions, and (3) fail to support

Springbett's claim that the interview is a search for negative information, and instead provide evidence that interviewers prefer to ask positive questions.

The Positive Test Strategy and Selection Decisions

The studies just reviewed lend some credibility to the notion that interviewers, like all people in impression formation situations, tend to adopt a positive test strategy. But what does a positive test strategy mean in the employment interview? In any selection situation interviewers may test whether an applicant is a member of the target group of actual good applicants (i.e., a positive hypothesis test) or whether the applicant is outside the target group and so a potentially incompetent worker (i.e., a negative hypothesis test). In the first case, favorable information supports the hypothesis but is not conclusive as to whether the applicant is actually a good applicant, while unfavorable information, which indicates that the applicant does not meet minimum standards for the job, proves the hypothesis false; that is, the applicant is a poor applicant and should be rejected. If the unfavorable information is less critical, it will at the very least put the hypothesis in some doubt. With a negative hypothesis test, the applicant is hypothesized as not fitting the target group; unfavorable information would support the hypothesis and the applicant would likely be rejected. If contradictory (i.e., favorable) information is obtained in the negative hypothesis test, then there is some indication that the hypothesis is wrong. Thus, with a negative test strategy, one positive item is unlikely to lead to acceptance, but with a positive test strategy, one negative item may lead to rejection, or at least a tendency towards rejection.

Under these circumstances a positive test strategy is more likely to permit the detection of a potentially incompetent worker. Also, unfavorable information will have more impact because it provides strong evidence regarding the appropriate classification. As Klayman and Ha (1987) suggested, when people have to live with their mistakes, they are more likely to focus on false positives than on false negatives, thus showing a greater concern for sufficiency than necessity. "That is, the tester may simply be more concerned that all chosen cases are true than that all true cases are chosen" (Klayman & Ha, 1987, p.216).

It is clear from this analysis that a positive test strategy is best for selection decision makers; it is more likely to permit the detection of potential false acceptances. Furthermore, considering the interview in terms of hypothesis testing also helps to better understand the importance of unfavorable information. Rather than the interview being a search for negative information as Springbett (1958) thought, it is a search for confirmation of a positive hypothesis. But when the interviewer encounters negative information it is much more important than positive information because it disconfirms the hypothesis that may change the final decision. As Hamilton and Zanna (1972) suggested, unfavorable evidence has greater information value in this situation than favorable evidence.

Perhaps the relevance of the positive test strategy becomes most apparent when one considers the interviewer's use of what was called in the McGill studies (Webster, 1964), a "stereotype" of the ideal worker for a particular job. This term is probably misleading insofar as it implies that additional characteristics not noted in the original assessment are attributed to the person as a function of assignment to a category. A better term is "prototype" as used in the cognitive literature by Rosch (1975). Regardless of the term used, the evidence (e.g., Sydiaha, 1959; Rowe, 1963; Hakel, Hollman, & Dunnette, 1970; Rothstein & Jackson, 1980) has indicated that each applicant is compared to the ideal, and accepted or rejected depending on the degree of similarity of the applicant to the prototype. Note, however, that such a matching process runs counter to the notion of the interview as a search for negative information. Conceptualizing the interview as a search for evidence which will support the hypothesis that the applicant is a potentially good worker, however, is in keeping with the notion of an ideal applicant prototype.

In general, a positive test strategy will also lead interviewers to ask more positive questions of an applicant, as Sackett (1982) and Binning, Goldstein, Garcia, Harding, and Scattaregia (1988) found. It is also not surprising that reject decisions are more resistant to change (Springbett, 1958), and that more favorable information is required to change an initially negative decision than unfavorable information to change a positive decision (Bolster & Springbett, 1961). Furthermore, it might be expected that reject decisions would be made faster than accept decision, as was found in a field study by Tucker (1976), using a within-subjects design. Probably because of the large individual differences neither Tucker, nor a later study by Huber, Neale and Northcraft (1987) was able to detect these time differences in between-subject designs.

The positive test strategy may also be moderated by various factors. Thus, Binning et al. (1988) found that initial impressions affected the frequency of negative questions asked. It would also be expected that questioning strategies would be affected by the answers given by the applicant during the course of the interview. Binning et al. found male and female interviewers to alter their strategies as a function of whether they were preparing to interview an applicant of the same or opposite sex. Similarly, some of the individual differences in response to unfavorable information noted earlier, including the greater leniency of females (London & Poplawski, 1976), inexperienced interviewers (Rowe, 1963), and student subjects (Bernstein, Hakel, & Harlan, 1975) may be related to questioning strategies.

A number of situational factors known to influence selection decisions might also be related to differences in positive hypothesis testing (see Eder, this volume). Factors such as hiring quotas (Carlson, 1967a), accountability (Rozelle & Baxter, 1981), need to justify decisions (Hagafors & Brehmer, 1983), and fair employment practices (Rosen & Mericle, 1979) may all be seen as pressures on the decision maker which increase the likelihood of positive hypothesis testing. The role played by the interview in the selection process is also important: Interviews of a short list of candidates, all of whom are potentially excellent employees, are likely to follow a positive hypothesis testing strategy. Similarly, recruitment interviews where the objective is to attract personnel should also adopt this strategy, and should also utilize few negative questions. However, where the goal is to reduce a very large number of applicants, as in screening interviews, the positive testing strategy may not be followed. Some support for these different predictions comes from a study by Huber et al. (1987) who examined the effects of framing (i.e., the manner of presenting choice alternatives) on selection decisions. Subjects were instructed either to identify those applicants they would *not* interview (i.e., a rejecting frame) or to identify those that they would interview (i.e., an accepting frame). Subjects using an "accepting" strategy accepted fewer applicants but judged those accepted to have a higher probability of success than did subjects with a "rejecting" strategy.

A number of situational factors known to influence selection decisions might also be related to differences in positive hypothesis testing; see paper by Eder in this volume. Factors such as hiring quotas (Carlson, 1967a), accountability (Rozelle & Baxter, 1981), need to justify decisions (Hagafors & Brehmer, 1983), and fair employment practices (Rosen & Mericle, 1979) may all be seen as pressures on the decision maker which increase the likelihood of positive hypothesis testing. The role played by the interview in the selection process is also important: interviews of a short list of candidates, all of whom are potentially excellent employees, are likely to follow a positive hypothesis testing strategy. Similarly, recruitment interviews where the objective is to attract personnel should also adopt this strategy, and should also utilize few negative questions. However, where the goal is to reduce a very large number of applicants, as in screening interviews, the positive testing strategy may not be followed. Some support for these different predictions comes from a study by Huber, Neale and Northcraft

(1987) who examined the effects of framing (i.e., the manner of presenting choice alternatives) on selection decisions. Subjects were instructed either to identify those applicants they would *not* interview (i.e., a rejecting frame) or to identify those that they would interview (i.e., an accepting frame). Subjects using an "accepting" strategy accepted fewer applicants but judged those accepted to have a higher probability of success than did subjects with a "rejecting" strategy.

The analysis presented here confirms the early research indicating the importance of unfavorable information in the interview, but does not support Springbett's (1958) proposal that the interview is a search for negative information. Rather, the interviewer is seen as possessing a prototype of the ideal candidate and hypothesizing that the applicant fits the prototype. Each piece of favorable information tends to confirm the hypothesis while each piece of unfavorable information tends to disconfirm the hypothesis. The interviewer's cost orientation makes disconfirmation more important that confirmation, and thus unfavorable information is more important to the interviewer than favorable information. Further research is necessary to evaluate the role of positive hypothesis testing in the selection interview.

6

Interviewer Decision Styles

Allen J. Schuh
California State University, Hayward

Webster (1982) concluded from his review of the literature on interviewer decision making that interviewers employ several distinct decision styles. Among these decision styles are the "conflict model" (Janis & Mann, 1977), the "cognitive information processing models" (Bayesian, correlational, or variance analysis) (see also Slovic & Lichtenstein, 1971), and the "feeling or affect model" (Zajonc, 1980). Webster (1982) pointed out that the prevalence of distinct decision styles had not been recognized and accounts for many conflicting findings across studies.

The purpose of this chapter is to extend Webster's (1982) earlier work on decision styles. Decision styles may be manifested in all of the tasks to which an interviewer must attend. Attention affects concentration and listening accuracy. Accuracy of description affects the quality of prediction. Greater predictive validity should result from a more complete mapping of the interviewer's decision style.

Decision Style Description

How does decision style affect perception, accuracy of observation, and interjudge reliability? Suppose a person is standing on the rim of the Grand Canyon of the Colorado River. If that person experiences a sense of awe, grandeur, and breath-taking beauty, the person's feelings predominate. If the person sees the Canyon as a photograph might represent it, the person's visual sensation predominates. If the person tries to understand the Canyon in terms of geological principles and theory, then the person's cognitive and abstract reasoning predominates. If the person sees the Canyon as a mystery of nature possessing deep significance whose meaning is partially revealed or felt as mystical experience, then the person's intuitive perception prevails (Hall & Lindzey, 1978; Jung, 1971).

Now assume that a complete and accurate description of the Canyon is desired. Asking 100 people, knowing nothing about their decision style, would yield little interrater agreement. A more preferred strategy might be to determine first what decision style they are utilizing to combine observations by subgroup decision style for a more complete and accurate description. Naturally, this implies that description accuracy and completeness, not overall interrater agreement, becomes the judge's goal. Pursuit of higher judgment reliabilities provides no assurance that greater "accuracy" is being obtained.

Incorporating multiple interviewer decision styles should yield more complete and accurate information, and subsequently lead to better decisions. Picture an interviewer sequentially gathering information (at a unit cost), and updating prior beliefs in a Bayesian manner. Eventually the interviewer must stop collecting information and make a decision. The interviewer also has uncertainty regarding the actions of competitors who are bidding for the same talent in the same recruiting environment. It is a classic game theoretic setting with a cone shaped continuation region. The effect of more precise information is to shrink the cone and lead to an earlier expected decision time. Any aids the decision maker could employ that would yield more complete and accurate information should give the interviewer a competitive advantage in the recruiting arena. Whatever the interviewer's decision style, information is needed that the other styles may provide.

A decision style influences the gathering, storing, combining, and evaluation of information. A decision style is the architecture of a person's previously developed concepts which are linked logically into what is referred to as a "logical-mathematical" cognitive structure. Synonyms for these structures in the literature include: mental models, knowledge structures, cognitive maps, scripts, frames, and schemata (Henderson & Nutt, 1980; Kilmann & Mitroff, 1976; Ramaprasad & Mitroff, 1984). These cognitive structures may reflect simple cause-effect models or very complex personal theories. An interviewer's cognitive structure will determine what factors and relationships will be observed (Piaget, 1974; Posner & McLeod, 1982; Ramaprasad, 1987).

Future research efforts may enhance one interviewer's competitive advantage over another. A related concern is how one draws upon and combines information taken from different cognitive structures without information loss or subjugation arising from opposing structures. A start to the problem would be in screening participants in an interview experiment for variance in decision styles and cognitive structures they are likely to use. One would need to categorize accurately the exact number of different decision styles being used for a given judgment task. Jung's (1971) work suggested there were four basic styles while Webster (1982) suggested three. Is Jung's (1971) feeling function the same as Webster's (1982) affect model? Is Jung's (1971) sensation function the same as Webster's (1982) cognitive information processing model?

It is also quite likely that the interviewer's decision style may change as a function of the interview context. What decision style tends to be preferred when the interviewer is in a position of high accountability or risk? Webster (1982) pointed out that the presence or absence of interviewer stress was the most important variable that differentiates interviewers. Nonrational feelings intrude and distort evaluations when something personal is at stake.

Cognitive Structures and Process Elements

Research on verbal listening skill suggests that a person's ability to listen effectively is based on attention or concentration, and the information processing system of productive thought from long term storage which permits the message to be integrated at the time of listening and extended beyond the time of listening (Lundsteen, 1979; Schuh, 1978; 1980). Attention is the state of concentration or capacity to be receptive to the verbal message. Few people can concentrate on a stimulus for more than 20 seconds without shifting focus. The shift can be to another element within the parameters of the message content, to an associated thought that the message brings to mind, or to something entirely unrelated. There are wide individual differences on these issues (Boileau, 1983; de Beaugrande, 1982; Watson & Barker, 1984).

The human information processing system has only a few basic constraints, namely, the number of chunks held in short-term memory and the time to process each chunk (Wickelgren, 1981). Better listeners have a larger short-term memory and a greater speed of retrieving word meanings (Devine, 1978; Just & Carpenter, 1977; Kean, 1982). The listener applies a set of rules to abstract the meaning of communication. A rule summarizes elements by constructing superordinate terms or concepts. After these rules have been applied, the original is transformed into a logic structure that represents the topic and major points but eliminates many of the redundancies and irrelevancies contained in the original communication. Evidence shows that the way people comprehend, summarize, and remember is consistent with a theory of structures (Kintsch, 1982).

The adequacy of the cognitive structure to organize and hold information in long-term storage separates, typically, the expert from the novice interviewer. The expert has a system of rules for storing and retrieving results of partial calculations en route to the complete solution coupled to an algorithm for reducing the complexity of the calculation. Capacities are not affected by practice; what is stored is. The literature shows that experts and novices identify different aspects of a problem as relevant. Experts develop categories that are more abstract than are novices'. Experts store information in larger chunks, and combine information in a more highly integrated and complete fashion (Honeck, Firment, & Case, 1987; Schwartz & Griffin, 1987).

Future research must be conducted to determine the extent to which an interviewer's cognitive structure can be augmented (Hogarth & Makridakis, 1981; Kleinmuntz, 1985). An augmented cognitive structure should reduce interviewer training time. Related work on artificial intelligence algorithms may prove useful in increasing cognitive structure capacity (Hunt, 1986; Kolodner, 1984). The implications for interviewer selection suggest that a personnel director should choose those who have greater knowledge of word meanings, a larger short-term memory span, greater speed of retrieval of word meanings, and better ability to concentrate, and see how they compare with those who fall on the less favorable side of these measures.

Decision Style Strategies and Criterion Environments

There are several decision strategies for choosing an applicant where the probability of the criterion environment is uncertain within a specified time horizon. As mentioned earlier, decision style is reflected not only in the acquisition and confirmation of applicant information, but also in the selection decision, which includes an estimate of the most likely criterion environment. Which of the several available strategies the interviewer chooses reflects another dimension of the interviewer's decision style. Subjective probability is at issue where the estimate of the most probable criterion setting depends upon the cognitive structure of the person making the decision. Six well documented strategies have been described (Agee, Taylor, & Torgersen, 1976; Bierman, Bonini, & Hausman, 1986; Eppen, & Gould, 1984; Markland, 1983). It will be shown how they operate as alternatives within the context of a simple selection decision.

Consider applicants (Bobby, Stacy, and Kim) for a position in personnel where the one successful applicant will eventually be assigned to a subspecialty based on future unknown organizational demands. Applicants will be considered for different criterion environments, or in this case the subspecializations of (1) selection, (2) compensation, and (3) training. Here, the interviewer does not know with certainty at the time of the hiring decision which subspecialty will require the person's full attention once in the position.

Row and column entries represent the most reliable estimate of the expected payoff on the criterion for the applicants' cumulative performance at the time horizon. Scores are in traditional T-score form with a mean of 50 and standard deviation of 10.

	Criterion Environments		
	1	2	3
Applicant			
Bobby	75	50	46
Stacy	45	82	56
Kim	40	56	90

The table shows that if the eventual criterion environment is "1" (Selection) then Bobby would have been the best choice. But, if criterion "2" (Compensation) happens then Stacy would have been the best choice. If criterion "3" (Training) happens then Kim would have been the best choice. The first decision strategy to be considered is the "principle of insufficient reason" (i.e., the Laplace), that assigns equal probability to each criterion. Here, there are three criteria, so all row-column entries would be multiplied by .33 and the products summed across the rows. The largest sum is the best alternative.

For Bobby: (.33) 75 + (.33) 50 + (.33) 46 = 57.
For Stacy: (.33) 45 + (.33) 82 + (.33) 56 = 61.
For Kim: (.33) 40 + (.33) 56 + (.33) 90 = 62.

Since 62 is the largest sum, the choice would be Kim.

The second method to be considered is to improve the estimates of relative probability of criterion categories rather than just assuming that they are all equal. There might be an a priori estimate, as in Bayesian analysis, that the first criterion is more probable than the others. Thus, a probability of .50 could be assigned to the first criterion, .25 to the second criterion, and .25 to the third criterion. The sequence of calculations would be repeated to see the effect of the refinement of the probability estimate.

Bobby: (.50) 75 + (.25) 50 + (.25) 46 = 61.5
Stacy: (.50) 45 + (.25) 82 + (.25) 56 = 57
Kim: (.50) 40 + (.25) 56 + (.25) 90 = 56.5

Since 61.5 is the largest sum, the choice would now be Bobby.

The third strategy is called the "maximin" criterion (i.e., the Wald), which assumes the worst case will happen: minimize the maximum loss. The smallest score is observed for each applicant, and the largest score is selected. In the example above, Bobby was 46, Stacy was 45, and Kim was 40. The largest minimum value was 46 (Bobby).

The "maximax" method (i.e., complete optimism) is a method that assumes the very best outcome will occur. The interviewer selects the applicant with the most optimistic outcome (or largest payoff). The largest row-column entry is 90 (Kim).

The fifth method requires the interviewer to calculate the "minimax regret" (i.e., the Savage). Regret is the difference between actual and possible payoff that could be received if the interviewer knew which criterion was going to happen. A new opportunity cost payoff matrix (regret matrix) is established. The interviewer attempts to minimize potential decision regret. The largest number in each column is subtracted from each other number in the same column. The applicant that minimizes the maximum regret is chosen. The new regret matrix would look like this.

Applicant	Criteria			
	1	2	3	Maximum Regret
Bobby	0	32	44	44
Stacy	30	0	34	34
Kim	35	26	0	35

The minimum maximum regret in the matrix is Stacy at 34.

The sixth method to be examined is the "coefficient of optimality" (i.e., the Hurwicz). The total probability (1.00) is proportioned to the largest and smallest payoffs for each applicant. The interviewer ignores other payoffs. In the example, let us assume the probabilities are proportioned .6 to the largest and .4 to the smallest value for each applicant.

$$\text{For Bobby:} \quad (.60)\ 75 + (.40)\ 46 = 63.4$$
$$\text{For Stacy:} \quad (.60)\ 82 + (.40)\ 45 = 67.2$$
$$\text{For Kim:} \quad (.60)\ 90 + (.40)\ 40 = 70$$

By this weighting Kim (70) would be selected.

Clearly, the interviewer is directed to a rational strategy depending upon decision style used. Decision style determines which rational outcome is chosen from among the legitimate methods which offer a solution.

Conclusion

Research is needed to answer questions such as, whether an interviewer working under the conflict model (Webster, 1982), tends to choose a pessimistic strategy such as the maximin or minimax regret, or whether an interviewer working under a cognitive information processing model (Webster, 1982) tends to choose one of the more optimistic strategies such as the complete optimism or coefficient of optimality. Perhaps those with decision styles predicated more on affect (Jung, 1971; Webster, 1982) use the pessimistic decision strategies.

Such hypotheses would follow from Webster's (1982) review. Webster argued that experienced interviewers under conditions of high accountability use different decision styles than those employed by student subjects in a laboratory setting. To researchers, and professionals, who choose to move into the exploration of decision styles, a wide, new, and productive world awaits.

7

Attribution Theory and Interview Decisions

Peter Herriot
University of London

Reviews of the employment interview literature (Schmitt, 1976; Arvey & Campion, 1982) have remarked upon the low level of theoretical development in the area, and have advanced descriptive frameworks of the independent and dependent variables found in the literature. Arvey and Campion (1982) are particularly critical of the absence of theoretical paradigms from social psychology, and argue that the psychometric properties of the interview have dominated research at the expense of its social features. Where research and theory from social psychology have been introduced, they have tended to be micro-analytic in scope. For example, the effects of the non-verbal communication style of the applicant upon interviewer decisions have been exhaustively explored (e.g., Imada & Hakel, 1977). However, the use of person perception theory to examine the interviewer's inferences from such behavior to judgments about applicants has been largely absent from the literature. More macro-analytic social psychological analysis of the interview as a dynamic interactive social episode is likewise notable for its absence. Perhaps this is because selection for employment is consistently construed as the assessment of the applicant by the organization, rather than as a social process (Herriot, 1988).

This chapter illustrates how one social psychological approach, that of attribution theory, may contribute to a better macro-analytic understanding of the employment interview. In the absence of a coherent body of attributional research on the interview, a brief historical account of attribution theory is presented, which owes much to Eiser (1986). Propositions and hypotheses derived from the theory are described, followed by a review of what little evidence does exist with regard to interview decisions.

Rational and Biased Attribution

The history of attribution theory and research is marked by the same developmental sequence as has characterized other areas. The original theoretical proposition is that people act in a rational way, basing their judgments upon the evidence available to them. This was amended by research findings indicating that a variety of suboptimal shortcuts were used by individuals in obtaining their causal evidence, and that perceptual biases often guide whatever evidence is obtained. This theoretical development was accompanied by methodological advances which recognized that experimental subjects acted rationally because experiments were set up in such a way as to permit them no alternative but to do so.

The theory of rational attribution was initially outlined by Heider (1958), who proposed the covariation principle; that is, a person's behavior tends to be attributed to causes which are present at the time, and absent when that behavior does not occur. Kelley (1967) carried the covariation principle further, suggesting three forms of such covariation: consensus, distinctiveness, and consistency. Consensus refers to the fact that people behave in the same way in a particular situation; distinctiveness means that the person does not behave like this in other situations; and consistency indicates that the person usually behaves like this in this situation. Kelley proposed that when there was high consensus, high distinctiveness, and high consistency, the inference about the cause of the person's behavior would be a situational one (i.e., their behavior would be attributed to the situation in which they found themselves). Suppose Fred wears a suit when he attends an interview. If other people attending interviews also wear suits, if Fred does not normally wear suits, and if he has worn suits before to interviews, then it can logically be concluded that he is wearing a suit because he is attending an interview (i.e., situational attribution).

Now consider a different pattern of covariation: low consensus, low distinctiveness, and high consistency. Suppose Fred attends an interview smoking a fat cigar. Few people attend interviews smoking, Fred tends to smoke whenever he goes, and he's taken cigars into interviews before. The attribution in this case is likely to be dispositional; Fred is smoking at the interview because he is the sort of person he is.

In the first case, there would be less confidence if consistency was low; that is, if Fred did not usually wear suits to interviews, one might not be so sure that he was wearing one because it was an interview. Similarly, in the second example, if Fred did not normally smoke at interviews, there would be less confidence in attributing his smoking to the sort of person he is. It might, for example, be a particularly stressful interview.

Kelley (1972) went on to suggest that people do not wait until they have accumulated enough evidence about covariation before they make attributions. On the contrary, they often do so on the basis of very little evidence indeed. For example, they may use the pattern of high consensus, high distinctiveness, and high consistency as a causal schema; an already existing theory about what causes are associated with what behavior. In this case, they may only need high consensus and high distinctiveness information to make a situational attribution. They need only know that most people wear suits to interviews and that Fred does not usually wear suits. Kelley assumed that people work on the basis of relatively few such schemata. For example, high consensus, high distinctiveness, and high consistency for a situational attribution; low, low, high for a dispositional attribution; and low, high, low for a circumstance attribution. An example of the latter might occur if few people smoke cigars at interviews; Fred rarely smokes; and Fred hasn't smoked in interviews before. One would then attribute Fred's smoking to a particular circumstance rather than to either the interview situation in general or to Fred's personality (e.g., if the interviewer offered Fred a cigar because he was smoking one himself).

Early experiments supported these hypotheses (e.g., McArthur, 1972). However, they presented subjects with statements indicating the nature of the covariance involved. They did not leave them to discover covariance for themselves from naturally unfolding events. Later research indicated that people may not be as good at perceiving covariation as Kelley (1972) assumed they were. That is, people do not habitually act as virtuous scientists (Crocker, 1981). People often apply causal schemata when they do not actually fit the evidence. They see relationships between events when such relationships do not in fact exist, and they fail to spot unanticipated relationships when they do exist. In summary, attributions of the causes of other people's behavior are likely to be as much a consequence of personal theories and expectations as of an impartial scrutiny of the evidence.

Research has subsequently investigated the major forms of attributional bias that result from covariation not objectively observed. For example, there is the *self-serving* bias, where desirable outcomes are attributed to oneself, and undesirable ones to one's situation. Applicants may attribute good examination results to their own ability, and bad ones to poor advice. Interviewers may congratulate themselves upon punctual completion of an interview but blame applicants for over-runs.

Another bias is to assume *false consensus*; that is, to suppose that most people share one's own expectations, beliefs, and attitudes. An interviewer might believe that everyone thinks an applicant should never ask a question until invited to do so at the end of the interview. An applicant who violates this expectation might be considered "brash." In fact, the interviewer's false consensus has resulted in a mistaken dispositional attribution.

A further bias is known as the *actor-observer divergence*, and describes the tendency of people to attribute their own actions to the situation, but the same actions when carried out by other people to those people's dispositions. Both applicants and interviewers may cough nervously and fiddle during the interview. The applicant will believe that this nervous behavior is a result of the situation, whereas the interviewer will attribute it to the applicant's anxious disposition. Interviewers will believe that their fidgets are due to the situation (e.g., "why should a line-manager like me be doing personnel work?"), whereas the applicant will attribute them to a lack of straightforwardness in the interviewer's conduct of the discussion.

Finally, there is the so-called *fundamental attribution error*, where people underestimate the situational factors and overestimate the dispositional ones in their assessment of another's behavior. For example, interviewers will tend to believe that applicants are behaving anxiously because they are anxious people rather than because they are in an interview.

Recent research suggests cognitive explanations for most of these biases, although there are obvious motivational explanations for some of them. The need to enhance or preserve self-esteem is likely to underlie the self-serving bias, while false consensus may reflect an effort to appear "normal" to oneself or others.

However, there is strong evidence for cognitive explanations in terms of perceptual salience. Actors pay attention to their environment, and observers pay attention to the actor. When actors are, for experimental purposes, made to look at themselves behaving, they make more dispositional attributions; when observers are shown the actor's point of view by video, they make more situational attributions (Storms, 1973). The same effect can be obtained by forcing observers to empathize with actors (Regan & Totten, 1975). This line of research suggests that when interviewers are asked to empathize with applicants, interviewers are more likely to attribute applicant behavior to the interview situation.

The overwhelming emphasis on situational versus dispositional attributions in attribution research has been modified to a considerable extent. First the "hydraulic" assumption that a decrease in situational attribution parallels an increase in dispositional attribution has not held up (Lepper, 1973). People do not always look for a single cause for behavior. When they believe it is important to be accurate in their attributions, they employ combinations of dispositional and situational attributions (Kassin & Hochreich, 1977). In the employment interview, this implies that if interviewers take their job seriously, they could interpret the application form as indicating achievement in light of opportunities; or, they could distinguish trait from state anxiety at the interview.

Moreover, a variety of other attributions have been evidenced. For example, Weiner (1979) listed attributions to ability, effort, task difficulty, and luck. The former two were internal (dispositional); the latter two external (situational). However, he also differentiated the four attributions in terms of their stability and their controllability. Ability and task difficulty were relatively stable, and therefore predictable; effort and luck were inherently unstable and unpredictable. On the other hand, ability and luck are essentially beyond the individual's control, while effort and task difficulty are to some extent within it (e.g., they can attempt tasks of differing degrees of difficulty).

When research designs are less manipulative, however, it becomes evident that ability, effort, task difficulty, and luck are only four among many other commonly used attributional explanations for behavior (Darley & Goethals, 1980). Mood, personality, fatigue, and interest, for example, are often mentioned, while luck is rarely adduced as an explanation.

Recent research has also modified the assumption that people habitually make attributions about behavior. The demand characteristics of laboratory experiments ensure that subjects respond with explanations for hypothetical events. In everyday life the need to explain other's behavior is less pervasive than one would expect from laboratory research. On the other hand, Weiner (1985) demonstrated that many situations occur where people offer explanations for others' behavior without being asked for them. People tend to do so when the behavior or event is unexpected, in particular where there is a failure in achievement or action. For example, an interviewer might pay particular attention to unusual performance in the achievement record or during the interview, and make attributions on the basis of this evidence alone (Constantin, 1976). Unusual behavior in the interview often involves breaking the interviewer's rules about how interviews should be conducted (Herriot, 1981; see Tullar, this volume). Hence, negative dispositional attributions may be made. Moreover, solid achievements may be ignored because they are not unusual across a large well-qualified applicant pool.

Self-Attributions

There is an equally extensive body of theory and research about attributions of the causes of one's own achievements and behavior. In this literature, interest has focussed not so much upon the general processes underlying attribution, but rather upon individual differences in the extent to which people attribute their own behavior to dispositional or situational causes.

Rotter (1966) termed this dimension of individual difference the "locus of control." He followed Heider (1958) in the false assumption that more dispositional attributions necessarily mean fewer situational attributions. Rotter devised a questionnaire to measure the extent to which individuals were internal (dispositional) or external (situational) attributers of their own behavior. Noting the existence of Marxists or radical Conservatives is not needed to remind one that people have different explanations for their own experience in society. However, it is useful to remember that to the extent that particular cultures exemplify political ideologies, internal or external locus of control is likely to be valued differently. Hence, in capitalist societies, internal locus of control is likely to be expected and valued, while in socialist ones, external or communal locus will be approved. Consequently, applicants' willingness to take personal responsibility for both failures and successes is likely to be approved in the USA and the UK. Indeed, the very use the terms "failures" and "successes" implies an internal locus.

However, likely approval for an internal locus of control is by no means the only implication of self-attributions. If one carries on through the inferential sequence, those with an internal locus of control are likely to attribute their behavior to ability and effort. Since effort is more under their control than ability, they will try hard, persist when failing, and be attracted to those activities which permit them to succeed (Weiner, et al., 1971). The individual payoff is greater self-esteem, since they will achieve successes which they can attribute to their own efforts.

The other side of the coin is the explanation for "failure" which people with an internal locus of control will infer. They will believe they have failed because of a lack of ability or effort, especially effort. Hence, they will feel ashamed of their failures, just as they feel proud of their successes. If these emotions are expressed in the interview, then they are likely to have an impact upon the interviewer's judgments. In particular, if the interviewer shares a similar internal locus, such expressions may be approved. On the other hand, the low self-confidence resulting from failure may be treated as a negative attribute.

In contrast, external locus of control results in a different attributional pattern. People with this attributional style tend to attribute their successes to their opportunities and their failures to their lack of them. While self-deprecation of success may still occasionally be considered a virtue, "excusing" one's "failures" certainly is not, even though this attribution may be perfectly justified by the facts. Hence, applicants with an external locus of control are apt to be assessed less favorably by the interviewer.

Locus of control is not the only possible dimension of individual differences in self-attribution, however. As Weiner et al. (1971) have pointed out, individuals may differ in other ways in their preferred explanations.

Some may prefer stable or controllable causal explanations. Others may go for unstable or uncontrollable ones. Those who prefer the former attributions will feel more confident in making predictions of future performance on the basis of their past record. They will believe themselves likely to perform well if they have had previous successes which they attribute to stable or controllable factors. They will predict failure for themselves if they have previously not performed well. On the other hand, those who favor unstable or uncontrollable explanations will not feel so able to predict or effect outcomes.

Covariation in the Employment Interview

Up to this point in the chapter, the employment interview has been mentioned only by way of illustration of general attributional concepts. A general, macro-analytic application of the theory is now attempted, together with some methods for testing the theoretical propositions. Since these methods are predicted to increase the accuracy of attributions and hence the validity of the interview, both organizations and researchers may support a research program to test attributional hypotheses. Two sets of theoretical propositions are advanced. The first proposes the existence of beliefs in certain patterns of covariation which are likely to lead to mistaken dispositional attributions. The second refers to the consequences of individual differences in attributional style. One should note that these attributional biases are exhibited by both the interviewer and the applicant (see Rynes, this volume).

It is proposed that there are basic assumptions about covariation normally held by both parties to the employment interview. Specifically, they falsely believe that there is *high consensus*. That is, they assume that the same expectations are held about each other's behavior in the interview, whereas, in fact, they are likely to vary. The rules of the game are neither clear nor universally held. The consequence of the false assumption of high consensus is that each party perceives the other as breaking the rules, and makes unfavorable dispositional attributions about them. Subsequently, satisfaction with the interview is low, affecting decision outcomes for both parties.

The second false assumption is that of *low distinctiveness*. That is, the parties believe that the others behave in work life as they do in the interview. The fact is that the overall predictive validity of the interview (e.g., with certain exceptions) belies this assumption. Each party has unrealistically high confidence in predicting the other's work behavior.

The third false assumption is that of *high consistency*. That is, both parties believe that the other behaves in the same way in other interview situations. The overall low reliability of separate interviewer judgments of the same applicant does not support this assumption, although low inter-rater reliability can be a consequence of different interviewer interpretations as much as of different applicant behavior. The consequence of the false assumption of high consistency is that both parties are too confident that the single interview they share is a reliable assessment.

Therefore, it is proposed that the overall covariation pattern assumed by both parties is that of high consensus, low distinctiveness, and high consistency. Assumptions of low distinctiveness and high consistency are likely to produce dispositional attributions. This is because the attributional pattern "low, low, high" is preferred for this purpose (Kelley, 1972). Hence, interviewers and applicants will be confident in making dispositional attributions about each other, since they believe that the evidence warrants these inferences. However, in fact, the covariation pattern in the employment interview is typically low consensus, high distinctiveness, and low consistency—more appropriate for making attributions to circumstance. If there is little agreement in expectations of interview behavior, little similarity between interview behavior and behavior in other situations, and little similarity in behavior across different interviews, then all that can be inferred is that behavior was a function of the specific occasion. The consequence is that both parties repeatedly and confidently make dispositional inferences from interview behavior when such inferences are unwarranted.

These effects of false assumptions are enhanced by habitual biases, which further distort accurate attributions. The tendency to make dispositional attributions where they are not appropriate is increased by actor-observer divergence. That is, each party believes that the other's actions in the interview are dispositionally caused, and that their own are situationally produced. And, the fundamental attribution error will also operate; both parties will overestimate the dispositional causes of the other's behavior.

Finally, there is pressure upon both parties to make dispositional attributions. For the interviewer, the primary purpose of the interview is assessment of the applicant; for the applicant, the character of the interviewer may provide their only clue as to the character of the organization. Both parties are therefore motivated to make dispositional attributions.

Various interventions in the interview procedure may be used to test these attributional propositions. These may take two forms. First, interventions may be aimed at actually changing the covariation principle involved so as to make dispositional inferences justified. Second, interventions may seek to persuade the parties that the existing covariation principles do not provide adequate grounds for dispositional inferences.

In terms of changing the covariation principle involved, false high consensus is considered first. The falsity of an assumption of high consensus is evidenced by Herriot and Rothwell (1983), who demonstrated that although interviewers expected the applicants to talk more about themselves, applicants expected the interviewer to talk more about the job. The degree to which the applicants talked about themselves actually predicted interviewer's judgments of suitability. Applicants were more likely to be rejected when they asked for information, opinions, or suggestions from the interviewer (Sydiaha, 1961). An appropriate experimental intervention would be to induce the parties to make explicit their expectations at the beginning of the interview, and to negotiate an agreement regarding topic coverage and other behavior.

As a consequence of such an intervention, true consensus would increase. Dispositional inferences based on the other party's unexpected behavior in breaking the rules would be justified, since such transgressions would involve reneging on negotiated contracts; false dispositional inferences based on mistaken beliefs that the other's expectations were the same as one's own would decrease. Moreover, satisfaction with the interview would increase, provided that agreements were kept. Hence, applicants would be more likely to accept a job offer, while interviewers would be more likely to give the applicant a favorable judgment. Certainly, there is evidence that applicants welcome interviewers who exhibit an interested and supportive manner, ask questions in areas where the applicant can demonstrate technical competence, and give adequate job information (Harn & Thornton, 1985; Keenan & Wedderburn, 1980; Schmitt & Coyle, 1976). For interviewers, the applicants' interview skills are important, especially their expression of ideas, their appearance, and their job knowledge (Kinicki & Lockwood, 1985). However, the fact that the parties welcome such behavior does not necessarily imply that they expect it.

As far as distinctiveness and consistency are concerned, the continued widespread use of the interview as an assessment device suggests that practitioners believe it is a valid (low distinctiveness) and reliable (high consistency) procedure. The evidence, of course, generally has indicated otherwise (Hunter & Hunter, 1984; Schmitt, Gooding, Noe & Kirsh, 1984). Interventions aimed at ensuring low distinctiveness and high consistency have already been attempted with some success. Arvey, Miller, Gould, and Burch (1987) sampled the work situation based on actual interview behavior, while Latham and Saari (1984) and Weekley and Gier (1987) sampled it theoretically by asking applicants how they would behave in certain hypothetical job-related situations. In these cases, the predictive validity of the procedure was greatly increased above that typically obtained. This was due to the low distinctiveness induced by the similarity of interview to job behavior, and to the high consistency consequent upon the standardization of the questions. The covariation principles were thus more appropriate for dispositional attributions to be made. However, the improved validity might not have been due to more accurate dispositional attributions so much as to the fact that the interviews were job samples. In other words, mediating inferences to dispositions might not have occurred.

The interventions listed thus far have been devised so as to render the covariation principles more appropriate for making dispositional inferences. However, another form of intervention is to decrease attributional biases, especially those of interviewers. Attempts to remediate general biases in the interview have not had great success. In those cases where success has been reported, lengthy training has been required to decrease one specific bias. An example is the work of Wexley, Sanders, and Yukl (1973) in reducing the contrast effect. However, there are no reports of attempts to remediate attributional biases. Training in empathizing or in literally seeing the situation from the applicant's viewpoint would be likely to reduce the fundamental attribution error of attributing too much to disposition, and too little to situation. Such training should result in fewer dispositional attributions based on interview behavior which is in fact situationally caused. Hence, one would expect a decrease in the number of dispositional attributions made by interviewers, and an increase in the accuracy of the ones that are made.

The pressure on the interviewer and the applicant to make dispositional attributions can be reduced by experimental intervention. The interviewer can be asked to rate only three or four attributes. Interviewers make use of only two or three attributes in their decision making, however many they are required to rate (Zedeck, Tziner, & Middlestadt, 1983). Thus, the interviewer can concentrate on the few important attributes. As fas as the applicants are concerned, realistic job information provided before the interview (Premack & Wanous, 1985) can reduce applicant need to infer the character of the organization from that of the interviewer. Hence, one would expect interviewer dispositional attributions to decrease in number as a consequence of a realistic job preview.

Individual Differences in the Interview

A second area of attribution theory which may be applied to the employment interview is that of individual differences in attributional style. Interviewers and applicants may habitually prefer certain attributional explanations to others. Some may prefer dispositional attributions in terms of ability, personality, or effort, others situational ones in terms of opportunity, luck, or task difficulty. Some may opt for relatively stable causes: ability, personality, task difficulty, which can permit prediction over time, while others choose unstable explanations: mood, effort, and luck, for example. Some prefer attributions to features that are under the individual's control such as effort, or task difficulty, whereas others attribute features that are uncontrollable, such as ability, personality, or opportunity.

The existence of such individual differences means that the same behavior is interpreted very differently, both by different interviewers working for the same organization, and across applicants being interviewed for the same position. Low interrater reliability in rating the same applicant on the same interview suggests that the interviewers differ in their attributional biases. Some evidence suggests that variability in attribution is evidenced even more in assessment of the application form, since interrater reliability is even lower than for the interview (Dipboye, Fontenelle, & Garner, 1984). Differences in attributional style between applicant and interviewer are apt to result in unfavorable dispositional attributions. For example, applicants' situational explanation of their career in terms of the limited opportunities open to them is apt to be regarded as an excuse by interviewers who favor controllable dispositional attributions such as effort.

One intervention would be to define the dispositional attributes to be inferred and rated by interviewers, thereby removing some ambiguity and variation. The prespecification of what behaviors in which job-related situation would be counted as evidence of each dispositional attribution of interest would also decrease the effect of individual differences. This information would double its effect if it were communicated to applicants. They would learn what attributes the organization was looking for and what sort of evidence it would consider appropriate. This would be particularly helpful in the completion of the application form, where it is often unclear what sort of achievement the organization is looking for. Moreover, the organization can clarify that its requests for information on personal background are relevant to the assessment, insofar as dispositional attributions made on the basis of achievements in the light of opportunity are likely to be more accurate than those made on the basis of achievements alone.

Moreover, the identity of the dispositional and situational attributions chosen to be assessed is of importance. They should be stable attributes, since prediction is only possible on the basis of stable variables. Since intellectual aptitude has been shown to be a powerful prediction of job performance in all occupations (Hunter & Hunter, 1984), it should be one of the attributes rated. It is also important that the interviewer be familiar with actual job demands (another relatively stable variable). There is some evidence that this latter information reduces the effect of irrelevant information on interviewers' decisions (Wiener & Schneiderman, 1974) and more accurately discriminates between qualified and unqualified applicants (Osburn, Timmreck, & Bigby, 1981). Recent work by Raza and Carpenter (1987) has demonstrated that applicants for higher level jobs are rated more highly on intelligence, attractiveness, likability, skill, and employability. However, they do not receive more recommendations for hiring, indicating that the job does indeed serve as a moderating variable. While these authors were confident based on their results that skill and intelligence attributions weigh heavily in interview decisions, Herriot and Rothwell (1983) found that the nature of attributions changed as a consequence of the employment interview. Attributions to intelligence and interests based on the application form alone, decreased in frequency after the interview, whereas attributions to applicant personality increased.

One consequence of these proposed interventions is greater judgment reliability and predictive validity, based on shared explicit job-relevant evidence and dispositional inferences. Individual differences in applicants' attributional style can also be predicted to affect outcomes. The relationship between the applicant's qualifications and a positive interviewer decision will be moderated by the extent to which applicants accept controllable dispositional explanations for their own behavior. Specifically, applicants with a preference for such explanations will credit themselves for their successes and blame themselves for their failures. Hence, their degree of self-confidence will vary considerably, whereas that of an applicant with a preference for situational explanations will vary little. Confidence is expressed and assessed through such non-verbal signals as eye-contact and facial expression. Interviewers tend to assess such signalled self-confidence in the light of the applicant's record. Tessler and Sushelsky (1978) found an interaction effect between qualifications for the job and eye contact, such that those who had good qualifications but made no eye contact were considered to lack self-confidence and be less suitable. A generally unfavorable prior impression of an applicant, such as that conveyed by a reference report, can lead interviewers to give applicants less credit for successes and more responsibility for failures (Tucker & Rowe, 1979).

The selection of attributes to be rated and the specifications of the evidence to be used to support such ratings will help to reduce the importance of applicant self-confidence signals for interviewers' decisions. Interviewers will know what they are looking for in the application form, and will be able to assess how justified the applicants' degree of self-confidence really is. They will be less likely to be deceived by skillful self-presentation.

To conclude, attribution theory has much to offer as an explanation at the macro-level, from which the relationship between interview behavior and the applicant-interviewer inferences can be drawn. At the level of specific behaviors, the particular attributes to be inferred from them, and the relationship of these attributes to others and to decisions, person perception and behavioral decision theories are likely to prove more effective. However, one of the benefits of attribution theory is that it leads to macro-level interventions which can both lend support to the theory and improve the effectiveness of interviews. Unfortunately, most dispositional attributions are difficult to measure unobtrusively within actual interview settings and their relationship with judgment reliability and validity are not easily investigated.

PART IV

Interview Context and Purposes

Recent reviews of the interview literature have concluded that low selection interview validities, relative to biodata, aptitude testing, or work samples, are likely the result of interviewer information processing errors. The cause of faulty interview judgment is assumed to rest largely within the individual interviewer. Yet the reality is that even experienced, well-trained interviewers modify their behavior under a variety of situational constraints—some of which are a function of organizational requirements (e.g., interview purpose, level of assigned decision making responsibility), and some of which are directly perceived by the interviewer (e.g., task clarity, judgment accountability, risk in making a false positive decision). Arvey and Campion (1982) noted that "An important 'hole' in the interview research area is the lack of investigations dealing with situational factors as they impact interviewers" (p. 311). The following two chapters attempt to expand theory and research from its myopic attention on the individual interviewer by considering the potential influences of interview context on both applicant and interviewer decision processes.

Eder offers an interactionist perspective to conceptualize how key dimensions of interview context may operate on the cognitive capabilities of the interviewer. A taxonomy of situational factors are delineated, related research reviewed, potential areas for research suggested, and methodological implications discussed. Four distinct dimensions of the interview context, as perceived by the interviewer, are examined: task clarity, interview purpose, decision risk, and accountability.

Rynes reverses the traditional focus in employment interview research from applicant selection to applicant attraction. A model is developed on the factors that may influence the extent to which recruitment versus selection objectives predominate in a given interview situation, and the subsequent effect this shifting perception of interview purpose may have on both interviewer behavior and recruitment success (i.e., selected applicant accepts job offer). Rynes comments on the inadequate conceptualization of applicant attraction processes, and the need for research on improving the employment interview as a recruitment device.

8

Contextual Effects on Interview Decisions

Robert W. Eder
Cornell University

Recent reviews of the employment interview literature (see also Arvey & Campion, 1982; Hakel, 1982; Reilly & Chao, 1982; Schmitt, 1976) have concluded that the likely cause of faulty interview judgment rests largely within the individual interviewer. Each of these reviews concluded that low selection interview validities relative to biodata, aptitude testing, or work samples, are likely the result of interviewer information processing errors. Originally founded on person perception theory, and more recently cognitive information processing theory, employment interview research has conceptualized interviewer judgment as a distinct cognitive event, where research is conducted to better understand the complex perceptual processes that interact to create overall assessments of applicant qualifications (see also Dipboye, 1982).

In comparison with biographical inquiries, written tests, or performance simulations, the employment interview is usually conducted under conditions which can best be called variable. The employment interview is tailored to suit individual or organizational preferences; this undermines the notion of standardized testing, a fundamental requirement in test validation, and threatens the validity generalization of the employment interview as a selection test. A common recommendation to improve interview validity has been to standardize the interview process on dimensions such as the evaluation criteria to be considered, question sequencing, and interview length (Washburn & Hakel, 1973).

More recent efforts to standardize the employment interview have focused on structured interviewing techniques (Campion, Pursell, & Brown, 1988; Janz, 1982; Janz, Hellervik, & Gilmore, 1986; Latham, Saari, Pursell, & Campion, 1980; Latham & Saari, 1984). However, interview context is more than the standardization of interview content. It also includes interviewer and organizational efforts, conscious or unconscious, that alter the context within which the interview is conducted (e.g., allotted interview length, relative importance of candidate attraction and/or selection, decision accountability). Providing an interviewer with a guide or framework to structure the interview (Arvey, Miller, Gould, & Burch, 1987; Carlson, Schwab, & Heneman, 1970; Heneman, Schwab, Huett, & Ford, 1975; Schwab & Heneman, 1969) has been but one successful intervention to modify the interview context in order to improve judgment reliability and validity.

The reality is that even experienced, well-trained interviewers operate under a variety of situational constraints; some of which are a function of organizational requirements (e.g., interview purpose, level of assigned decision making responsibility), and some of which are directly perceived by the interviewer (e.g., task clarity, judgment accountability, risk in making a false positive decision). Yet little is known about how the interview context affects interviewer judgment.

The thesis of this chapter is that employment interview judgment also occurs within a multi-dimensional context, where exogenous situational factors may alter and interact with the interviewer's cognitive capabilities to produce systematic variance. Arvey and Campion (1982) noted that "An important 'hole' in the interview research area is the lack of investigations dealing with situational factors as they impact interviewers" (p. 311). Arvey and Campion suggested that interview outcomes are the result of combinations of applicant, interviewer, and situational factors. This chapter offers a theoretical framework for focusing future research on interview context, proposes a taxonomy of situational factors, and recommends modifications in subsequent research designs.

A major impediment to research on the effects of interview context is the myopic theories that have guided researchers. Reliance on intrapsychic explanations for observed variance across interview judgments has not only served to de-emphasize the importance of situational factors, but also has resulted in restricted and/or misplaced organizational efforts to improve interviewer effectiveness. Training interviewers to reduce information processing errors assumes one can pinpoint the sources of interviewer bias, distinguish what constitutes "true" perception, and make a permanent change in subsequent interviewer judgment processes. An alternative, and more reasonable, strategy may be to engineer the interviewing context to elicit a more accurate assessment of job suitability. However, such a strategy would require an understanding of how situational factors influence interviewer judgment (see also Webster, 1982).

Extending Current Theory

Both implicit personality theory and cognitive information processing theory posit that the individual alone is the determinant of behavior, and that introspection and self-reports are the primary data collection methods for capturing, respectively, personal trait configurations and specific information processing strategies. Neither theory offers a research framework for examining either the main or interactive effects of situational factors. Eder and Buckley (1988) proposed the adoption of an interactionist perspective (Endler & Magnusson, 1976; Lewin, 1951; Murray, 1938) to provide a conceptual and theoretical framework for extending existing research on interview judgment to more adequately address the effects of situational factors. An interactionist perspective places a more equal emphasis on dimensions of the person and the situation as he or she interacts within the cognitive awareness of the interviewer. In recent years, the interactionist perspective has been offered as a theoretical framework to focus research attention on the often ignored role of situation variables in organizational behavior research (Schneider, 1983; Terborg, 1981).

An interactionist perspective conceptualizes behavior as a function of the multidirectional interaction (feedback) between the individual and the situation encountered. In interactionist research both discrete levels of situation and person factors are used, constrained by researcher control over the heterogeneity of both factors within the research design. The person is assumed not only to react to the situation but also to create or enact the situation, which, in turn, influences future behavior. Schneider (1983) has advocated a definition of interaction as "reciprocal action-transaction." This definition suggests "that the natural ebb and flow of people and settings are continually affected by each other, and that oneway causal inferences fail to adequately represent the reality of most work settings" (p. 10).

On the situation side of the reciprocal interaction, the psychological meaning of the situation for the individual is the determining factor. Interactionist theory provides a basis for parsimonious dimensionalization of the interview context. In contrast, Arvey and Campion (1982) listed situation variables such as political, legal and economic forces, the role of the interview in the selection system, selection ratio, physical setting of the interview, and interview structure (i.e, question sequencing). Atheoretical approaches to identifying situational factors that are relatively stable, and yet also naturally variant, are unlikely to yield viable taxonomies. For example, Peters, O'Connor, and Rudolf's (1980) free response questionnaire methodology for determining situational constraints on individual performance produced a taxonomy which has yielded few substantive effects in field experiments. Commenting on the weak empirical support for their taxonomy, Peters, O'Connor, and Eulberg (1985) noted that individuals viewed these constraints as salient. However, in practice, they perceived their actual work environments to be fairly devoid of these same constraints. Furthermore, the cumulative presence of these objective constraints did not appear to combine in a linear fashion. Following the logic of the interactionist perspective, if cognition and situation interact in a multi-faceted fashion, then it is the assigned psychological meaning given to the situation and not the physical, objective dimensions of the situation that likely will influence interview judgment.

On the person side of the reciprocal interaction, cognitive factors are the essential determinants of behavior. The psychological meaning of a situation can be dominated by the perceiver's cognitive characteristics when exposure and observations are limited. In other words, not all employment interviews would be equally susceptible to the effects of interview context. It is very likely that judgments made by corporate recruiters during brief, informal, and unstructured college campus interviews are predominantly a function of the recruiter's unique cognitive characteristics. However, reliance on interviewer cognitive characteristics to predict final job interview decisions by a supervisor for a specific key position within the work unit is more problematic.

Dipboye (1982) reported that certain interviewer cognitive characteristics (e.g., schemas and subjective stimulus values from the review of candidate application materials), may be so powerful that they dictate both the conduct of and the decision reached in an interview. He contended that pre-interview evaluations of applicants tend to be self-fulfilling; information is attended to, recalled, and interpreted consistent with pre-interview evaluations. However, Dipboye (1982, p. 585) cautioned that pre-interview evaluations are likely to affect interviewer judgment, "only to the extent that (a) the organizational policies, standards, and procedures for conducting the interview are unstructured." The role of interview context and, in particular, the perceived psychological meaning of the interview situation may both interact with and diminish the main effect of interviewer cognitive characteristics.

The point is, of course, that individual cognitive differences exist at the very beginning, before "objective" differences in the situation can play any part in modifying them. Thus, from the beginning, the situation must be specified in terms of the particular individual experiencing it. This inseparability of the interviewer's cognitive make-up and what is perceived, creating a "personal reality," is precisely the interactionist perspective. From the interactionist perspective the individual is an active agent, capable of directing behavior and enacting environments in a goal-oriented fashion. However, choices of action are partially limited by the variability of the situations enacted, and by each person's unique cognitive processes. Consistency in interviewer judgments across applicants can be explained either in terms of consistency in the individual's choice of enacted interview context and the predictable effects the context has on interview judgment, or in terms of the consistency of individual information processing patterns across interview situations.

The remainder of this chapter delineates a taxonomy of situational factors, reviews related literature, suggests potential areas for research, and discusses the methodological implications of employing an interactionist perspective for future research designs. Other researchers have described in considerable detail the cognitive information processing system (see also Ilgen & Feldman, 1983), and how interviewer cognitive characteristics may directly affect interviewer judgment within an interactionist framework (see also Eder & Buckley, 1987, 1988). What is less well understood is how the psychological meaning of the interview context may also influence interview judgment in a systematic, predictable manner.

Taxonomy of Situational Factors

The following taxonomy of situational factors are organized into four distinct dimensions each of which influences interview judgment: task clarity, interview purpose, decision risk, and accountability. These situational factors are offered as prospective dimensions of psychological meaning rather than objective situation parameters (see also Arvey & Campion's model, 1982). In essence, the interview context signals to the individual the interviewing purposes, risks, benefits and responsibilities in varying degrees of task clarity.

Task Clarity

Task clarity is a function of two broad issues: (a) the array and clarity of task demands placed on the interviewer and (b) the extent of interviewer preparation and training. Prior research has suggested that the level of task difficulty moderates the relationship between task performance and an individual's ability or motivation (Schneider, 1978; Terborg, 1977). The desired psychological state for the interviewer is one of high confidence in knowing what to look for in the interview and how to treat the information provided by the applicant.

Osburn, Timmrick, and Bigby (1981) found that specificity of evaluation criteria facilitates discriminability across job applicants. Behaviorally-specific criteria that capture job-relevant information not previously tapped by other sources (e.g., review of application, resume or other biographical data), and that are recorded on a scored interview report form increase incremental validity. Likewise, familiarity with target job content, skill requirements, and historical performance difficulties may also improve interview validity by focusing the interviewer's attention on more salient job information.

Interviewers who are given more complete job information make decisions with higher inter-rater reliability (Langdale & Weitz, 1973), a necessary pre-condition of interview validity. Frequently, only broad job categories or occupational groups form the basis against which interview judgment is rendered (e.g., recruitment interviews). The more complex the job the greater difficulty in adequately assessing a candidate's qualifications, and, hence, the more reliance is placed on the interviewer's cognitive skills to form a valid judgment.

One approach to improving task clarity is through interviewer training. Interviewer training clarifies pre-interview expectations and modifies the interviewer's behavior when conducting the interview. In essence, researchers (Gilmore & Ferris, 1980; Howard & Dailey, 1979) have suggested that interviewer training's primary effect is to enhance decision making through increased task clarity. However, training effects may be limited by interviewer cognitive capability when evaluation criteria are highly abstract (e.g., manager, teacher). According to Zedeck, Tziner, and Middlestadt (1983), interviewers may use only a few rating dimensions in determining their decision, even when given a more extensive list of evaluation criteria. Whether interviewers can be trained to use a more complete range of information categories, and whether such an intervention results in better decisions is a question in need of further empirical testing.

Another factor that may constrain task clarity is job complexity. For example, Tullar, Mullins, and Caldwell (1979) found that as allotted interview time increases, decision time increases, and "primacy" effects wane. Decisions were made more quickly when the interviewer was informed that the interview was to last only fifteen minutes. If the interviewers were informed that the interview was to last thirty minutes, decision times were significantly longer. However, the more interesting finding in Tullar et al. (1979) is the potential interaction between allotted interview time and job complexity. With complex jobs, longer allotted interview time may increase interview validity. With less complex jobs, a longer allotted interview time may cause the interview to drift into issues less likely to be job relevant, reducing interview validity.

Efforts to improve task clarity and focus attention on job-relevant criteria should delay the onset of a "snap decision" by the interviewer, which might otherwise be grounded on candidate appearance, stereotyping, and personal liking (see also Buckley & Eder, 1988). Tullar et al. (1979) demonstrated the potential interactive effects of allotted interview time and candidate qualifications on both decision time and evaluation level. With a longer allocated interview time interviewers who took more time to make a decision gave the low-quality candidates higher ratings and high-quality candidates lower ratings. Apparently, the enhancement of task clarity through such approaches as interviewer training is likely to curtail "snap decisions" that yield more extreme ratings. This would be particularly true of interviews conducted under less time pressure.

Investigating the upper limits of interviewer training on cognitive processes requires more systematic research on judgment patterns across a divergent set of interview situations. One might expect that a lack of task clarity in the interview situation would correlate with quicker, more extreme judgments, a reluctance to quantify candidate performance, higher short-term memory loss, and decisions that are more frequently made on the basis of nonspecific, nonjob-relevant criteria.

Interview Purpose

Employment interviews have the dual purpose of applicant attraction and selection. Each interviewer interprets the extent to which a greater or lesser importance is to be placed on each interview purpose for which information is being gathered. There are several instances in which attraction, rather than selection, becomes a prime consideration. Early interviews in the selection process may be recruitment efforts to generate a large qualified applicant pool, and final interviews may be conducted as "closers" to be sure the applicant has been sold on the advantages of joining the organization. Ignoring applicant attraction may reduce offer acceptances by applicants who may perceive the organization, through the interview experience, as being indifferent toward the applicant.

The role of evaluation purpose in information processing, while absent from employment interview research, has received increased attention in the performance appraisal literature (DeNisi, Cafferty, & Meglino, 1984). Performance ratings have been reported to be higher (i.e., more lenient) when the rating purpose was administrative rather than for counselling or feedback only purposes (McCall & DeVries, 1976; Meyer, Kay, & French, 1965). Beyond differential motivations created by rating purpose (DeCotiis & Petit, 1978), the purpose for which one is seeking information may also influence what types of information are sought and how that information is later stored (see also Eder, Fedor, Buckley, & Longenecker, 1988). Recruitment interviews may prompt interviewers to search for and organize information around the candidate's own career goals, while selection interviews may prompt interviewers to search for and organize information about the candidate's possession of traits assumed to be associated with job success (see also Hoffman, Mischel, & Mazze,1981). Williams, DeNisi, Blenco, and Cafferty (1985) found that different purposes may also trigger rater preferences for distinctiveness versus consensus information. It may well be that recruiters in their interviews search for consensus information that this candidate is or is not in the feasible set, while interviewers who are making a choice from among a handful of finalists are looking for distinctiveness information.

Carlson, Thayer, Mayfield, and Peterson's (1971) study comes closest to examining the effects of interview purpose on interview judgment. They found that in a situation where quotas were stressed, the inexperienced interviewer was more likely to accept a less qualified candidate than an experienced interviewer. Though interviewer cognitive processes were not directly examined, the study's findings suggest that experienced interviewers are more able to enact the psychological meaning of judging candidates under heightened selection utility purposes.

The majority of published interview studies can best be described as initial screening interviews, where with limited exposure, the interviewer is asked to make an overall assessment of candidate suitability. Even when the stated interview purpose is to make an accept-reject decision, frequently the decision is made in the fictitious context of a "for research only purpose." Therefore, recent research findings on the employment interview may actually be more reflective of an interview under a joint attraction-selection purpose, than purely for selection purposes.

Whether dictated by the selection situation or as a function of preferred style, interviewers differentially perceive the extent to which candidate attraction and selection is to be emphasized. Yet, no published research to date has examined whether interviewers employ distinctly different cognitive processes as a function of the perceived importance of candidate attraction and/or selection (see also Zedeck & Cascio, 1982), or what factors actually trigger shifts in perceived interview purpose both before, during, and after the interview.

Based on recent performance appraisal purpose research, it is quite likely that an interviewer's information processing system is substantially modified by interview purpose. In a screening interview where candidate attraction is important, one might expect that the interviewer will draw upon basic person perception and/or signal detection mechanisms to assess adequate qualifications for the position. Hence, interviewer judgment may be more a function of cognitive characteristics when the interview purpose focuses more on attraction than selection. However, when the interview purpose is selection, the interview context may emerge as a significant influence on interviewer judgment. For example, the interviewer, under a selection purpose, may attend more to job relevant criteria than basic interpersonal liking, as predicted by the interviewer's implicit personality theory. Overall, the role of interview purpose would seem to play a greater role in understanding interviewer decision making than has been previously addressed in the literature.

Decision Risk

Perceived decision risk (i.e., the cost of making a hiring mistake) is a cost expressed in both organizational and personal terms. In selection a false positive probability is a function of the historical record of incumbent success (i.e., hires/applicants) and the validity coefficient of the interview (i.e., strength of association between test score and subsequent job success). Jobs in which few incumbents fail present a lower false positive risk compared with jobs that have occasional poor performers. The selection ratio is a direct function of the changes in the relative demand for employees in the job category (i.e., hiring quotas) and the recruitment effort put forth to generate a large qualified applicant pool.

Webster (1982) was among the first to posit that changing labor market dynamics, both internal and external, which affect the size of the applicant pool, may also alter the interviewer's judgment. Candidates with equivalent qualifications may be differentially evaluated as a function of perceived labor market conditions (see also Carlson, 1967a). If recruitment efforts have been only moderately successful and market conditions appear tight, the candidate may receive inflated ratings as interviewer efforts shift more to attraction purposes. On the other hand, if the available pool of qualified candidates appears to be large by historical standards, candidates may receive more stringent ratings. While base rate, selection ratio, and interview validity determine the probability of a false positive, the cost of making a hiring mistake is a direct function of the economic importance of the job to the organization (e.g., clerical worker versus middle manager) and the interviewer (i.e., likely colleague versus a hire for another department).

Personal decision risk increases if the interviewer is likely to be the job candidate's supervisor or coworker. As perceived decision risk increases, interviewer judgment may be affected by candidate qualifications (see also Tullar et al., 1979). Under conditions of high decision risk lower quality applicants may receive lower than expected evaluations, while under low decision risk higher quality applicants may receive higher than expected evaluations. To date, no published research has systematically examined interviewer judgment across interviews that vary in decision utility for the organization, and that may modify interviewer motivation toward the interview task. Again, recent developments in performance appraisal research (DeCotiis & Petit, 1978; Kane & Lawler, 1979; Bernardin & Buckley, 1981) have suggested that interviewer motivation should not be overlooked in understanding interviewer judgment validity.

Accountability

Another way to increase interviewer motivation is to hold interviewers accountable for their information gathering and final judgments. As will be evident in the research to be discussed, there are subtle distinctions between "feeling responsible" and "being held accountable" in either an ambiguous or nonambiguous situation.

Feeling responsible. Feeling responsible for the interview decision is a function of several factors: personal decision risk, relative emphasis on the interview in the selection process, and single versus board interviews. The former two factors are closely related to perceived decision risk. Higher perceived decision risk increases feelings of decision responsibility. However, feelings of greater responsibility do not necessarily increase decision risk. For example, a supervisor could conduct a ten minute interview to hire a clerical worker and hire the person "on-the-spot" immediately after a cursory interview. Clearly, there is sole responsibility for the decision, but a hiring mistake may not be seen as a major cost.

Interviewer decision-making responsibility increases to the extent that the interviewer's judgment is more heavily weighted in making the final determination. One might expect that individual, rather than group interviews increase decision-making responsibility. The presence of other interviewers may dilute responsibility rather than enhance individual effort (see also Albanese & Van Fleet, 1985). For example, Weldon and Gargano (1985) found support for the concept of "social loafing" in decision-making groups; shared responsibility leads to less effortful judgment. However, they noted that when the individual's contribution to the group decision was known, not anonymous, social loafing disappeared. Yet, Moore and Lee's (1974) findings suggested there is no difference in interview judgment as a function of individual or group decision making.

The issue may be how a board operates, rather than whether the decision is an individual or group product. The individual's perceived psychological meaning of personal responsibility would largely depend on the composition and history of the group as well as the group decision-making style. Felt responsibility may be enhanced when the process of board interview decision making includes the sharing of individual written assessments, opinion generation, and requested rationale from each person before group consensus. Given the prevalence of team or board interviews, more research on the benefits and liabilities of group interviewing is needed.

Being held accountable. Being held accountable presents the interviewer with an external validity threat. The strategies individuals develop for coping with the contextual demand for accountability will depend, in part, on whether the perception of accountability is pre- or postjudgment, and the degree of ambiguity that exists in the interview context with regard to the person or persons to whom one's judgment is held accountable. The simple expectation that one may have to justify a forthcoming decision appears to reduce information primacy effects and to increase recall of significant information (Tetlock, 1983b).

Rozelle and Baxter (1981) manipulated accountability and responsibility for judges prior to their assignment to watch interview videotapes. Those in the high accountability condition were told their ratings would be discussed at a staff meeting and that applicants would have access to their reports. Other judges were assured that all ratings were confidential and would not be revealed to anyone (i.e., low accountability). Similarly, members of the high responsibility team were assured their ratings would be used to reach a decision. Those with low responsibility knew decisions had already been reached. Judges who worked under the constraint of high accountability and to a lesser extent, high responsibility, provided descriptions that more accurately reflected applicant characteristics. In a similar fashion, McAllister, Mitchell, and Beach (1979) reported that participants in a business simulation experiment employed more analytic and complex judgment strategies the more personally accountable they felt for their decisions. This was particularly true when the decision was perceived to be important and irreversible. Thus, preexposure accountability may induce interviewers to become more thorough and vigilant information processors, who are more willing to revise initial impressions in response to changing evidence (Tetlock, 1983b, p. 319).

Felt postjudgment accountability may produce more variance in interviewer decision levels, though not necessarily more accuracy, when compared to prejudgment accountability situations. When one does not know the views of the person to whom one will be held accountable, interviewers likely engage in preemptive self-criticism (Tetlock, 1985, p. 316). Counterarguments, which potential critics could raise, are formulated to avert the appearance of flawed reasoning and subsequent loss of esteem. In this context, postjudgment accountability may have no effect on enhanced information recall, but may activate more complex decision schemas for evaluating the recalled information. The rationale is more extensive, not necessarily more accurate.

When the views of those to whom the interviewer is held accountable are known, interviewers are more likely to shift their opinions toward those of others in the interview context (see also Tetlock, 1983a). Interviewer judgments will be strategically shifted to the extent that the individual engages in political behaviors, such as impression management or self-serving attributions. The label of self-serving attributions refers to the tendency of a highly accountable interviewer to take credit for hiring successes and to deflect blame for hiring failures. Staw, McKechnie, and Puffer (1983) found that corporate administrators gave more self-serving attributions in letters to stockholders as a function of their concern about the volatility in the company's stock price. Of interest was the finding that enhancement statements when the stock price rose were as prevalent as defensive statements when the stock price dropped. Again, rationale is more enmeshed, not necessarily more valid. Postjudgment accountability not only fails to enhance self-critical thinking upon entering the interview task, but also likely exacerbates the biases and information processing errors that are inherent in human decision making.

Tetlock (1985, p. 320) concluded that the findings on accountability, "support contingency models of judgment and decision-making which challenge the universality of the cognitive miser portrait of how people think." This literature would suggest that interviewers have a capacity to adopt different strategies and styles of information processing in response to changing interview circumstances.

Overall, the relative effects of interview context on interview judgment may depend on the degree of task definition, interview purpose, decision risk, and personal accountability perceived by the interviewer. To the extent that these situational factors are highly specific and salient to the individual, interview context will have a proportionally profound effect on interview judgment.

Implications for Future Research Designs

First, researchers should be encouraged to conduct employment interview research within more realistic settings that naturally vary across salient situational factors. In particular, interviewer accountability and interview purpose should be examined explicitly within the interview context. The relative sterility of a lab setting minimizes the transferability of employment interview research whose results are highly modified across different interview contexts. When researchers use subject or stimulus extremes while sampling minor situational variation, one should not be surprised that personalistic theories of interview judgment are once again confirmed.

Second, employment interview research conducted outside the reality of organizational life may offer little insight into how interviews are actually performed. Most experiments on the employment interview are conducted within a "research only" purpose, where subjects are not held accountable for their evaluations. Furthermore, the interview is almost always treated as the sole component of a hypothetical selection process. In actual selection models, interview information is combined with other predictor information before a final summative decision is rendered. However, most published research asks the interviewer to make a single rating of suitability, or to accept or reject the applicant based solely on a brief interview. The innate multidimensionality of the evaluation task is ignored. Summative ratings, comparative ranking, and/or simple decisions to accept or reject may decrease both interviewer decision time and validity, compared with nonsummative evaluations across multiple criteria. In reality, selection models often include a variety of steps in a sequential decision process, each contributing to the determination of overall qualifications. The incremental validity of the employment interview will remain an unanswered question until interview research is conducted within the organization's actual selection process.

Finally, the situational factor taxonomy offered in this paper requires construct validation. The salient dimensions of the interview context need to be empirically confirmed as distinguishable features which potentially alter interviewer judgment processes. The interactionist perspective suggests, for example, that the simple presence or absence of interviewer training, or the use of a scored interview report form, should be conceptualized within the interviewer's perception of task clarity. A further complication to this perspective is the likelihood that not all objective changes in the interview context will be equally attended to by interviewers, who may continue to enact an interview context consistent with personal preference. The four situational factors discussed are not necessarily exhaustive nor fully operationalized.

For example, the physical environment itself may be a hindrance to interviewer information processing. Siegal and Steele (1980) found that noise-distracted interviewers made more extreme judgments and changed them more frequently in repeated administrations of a questionnaire. They concluded that noise distraction interfered with information integration. Perhaps there should be a fifth dimension that includes physical environment enhancers and/or distractors. Such a dimension may include aspects of perceived time pressure to complete the interview quickly as a function of competing job demands at the time (i.e., work stress), and the extent to which the interview is conducted in a physically comfortable, private, uninterrupted setting.

Interview purpose has been stated simply as the extent to which attraction and selection purposes are accentuated. However, a number of other interview purposes may be operating (e.g., to insure that only individuals with certain value orientations are hired, to hire someone who will make me look good in comparison, to demonstrate power and influence over coworkers) with no assurance that the purpose(s) assigned by the organization is the purpose(s) perceived by the interviewer (see also McIntyre, Smith, & Hassett, 1984, p. 155). As stated earlier, interview structure is often at the discretion of the interviewer. Interviewers may define the interview context to replicate behavior patterns that are consistent with personal beliefs of past task mastery (see also Diener, Emmons, & Larsen, 1984; Wortman, 1976). The extrinsic motivation ostensibly provided from assigned decision-making accountability may be subjugated by the interviewer's personal goals (Deci & Ryan, 1984). Therefore, confirming a stable taxonomy of situation variables may be dependent on an increased understanding of the interviewer's information processing system as it operates to define the interview context.

In conclusion, there is a common metaphor that perhaps best captures the point of view of this chapter's thesis on employment interview research. Researchers may achieve more progress in closing the gap between interview research and interviewing practice by pulling back to "see the forest from the trees." Like the five blind men who each offered widely variant descriptions of an elephant based upon the particular part of the mammal each was touching, the price one pays for seeking greater detail is misrepresentation of the phenomenon within its broader context. Previous reviewers of the employment interview literature (Wright, 1969; Mayfield, Brown, & Hamstra, 1980; Arvey & Campion, 1982; Hakel, 1982), recognizing the extemporaneous nature of interviewing, have repeatedly suggested that research might benefit from considering the interview in its totality. In part, this requires a research framework that departs from a purely microanalytic approach to a paradigm that captures the interrelationships between the interviewer's cognitive characteristics and salient dimensions of the interview context.

9

The Employment Interview as a Recruitment Device

Sara L. Rynes
Cornell University

The employment interview is an interactive process through which organizations and individuals mutually assess and select one another. Despite this fact, interview research has focused mainly on its function as an organizational selection and screening device. In comparison, the interview's role in recruitment (i.e., in attracting applicants and influencing their job choices) has received far less attention.

In part, the dominance of selection over recruitment research probably reflects the generally loose labor markets of the past fifteen years. Blessed with large numbers of first-time workers and rising female labor force participation rates, employers have typically been in the enviable position of choosing among large numbers of applicants. Now, however, demographics are changing and employers are expected to confront long-term labor shortages in many sectors (Bernstein, 1987; Hanigan, 1987; Johnston, 1987).

As applicants become scarce, employers devote increased attention to applicant attraction and retention (Malm, 1954; Merrill, 1987). Accordingly, recognition of the interview's role in recruitment is likely to grow in future years. This chapter considers the implications of viewing the interview from a recruitment, rather than a selection, perspective.

Interviews and Applicant Attraction: A Model

Efforts to understand, evaluate, and improve recruitment have been hampered by inadequate conceptualization of the applicant attraction process (Guion, 1976; Rynes, Heneman, & Schwab, 1980). Fortunately, the

AUTHOR'S NOTE: This chapter benefitted substantially from the comments of Robert Eder, Judy Olian, Donald Schwab, and M. Susan Taylor. However, the author retains sole responsibility for any errors of substance or interpretation.

relationship between recruitment activities and applicant attraction has received increasing attention in recent years (e.g., Rynes, in press; Schwab, 1982; Wanous, 1980).

Figure 9.1 presents a model of the relationship between the recruitment process and applicant attraction, with emphasis on the employment interview. The model is first outlined briefly; then discussed in more detail.

Model Overview

Employment interviews are both recruitment and selection devices. However, as the model shows, several factors are believed to influence the extent to which recruitment versus selection objectives predominate in any given interview.

In general, the relative emphasis placed on recruitment versus selection is hypothesized to flow from labor market (e.g., relative supply and demand) and vacancy characteristics (e.g., job and organizational attractiveness). These variables are hypothesized to have both direct and indirect effects on the extent to which recruitment is emphasized in the employment interview. In general, recruitment emphasis is hypothesized to increase when applicants are scarce, and vacancies unattractive.

However, vacancy and market characteristics influence not only the interview, but other recruitment activities as well (e.g., number and type of recruitment sources, selection and training of organizational representatives). These, in turn, may exert an independent effect on interview objectives through their impact on applicant and interviewer characteristics. For example, to the extent that only exclusive recruiting sources are used (e.g., executive search firms or top-tier universities), recruitment would be expected to become more important in the interview, relative to screening. Similarly, to the extent that tight labor markets lead to increased recruitment training, recruiters and other organizational representatives would be expected to be more sensitive to the recruitment aspects of selection procedures.

More directly to the point of this chapter, differences in the relative importance of recruitment versus selection are hypothesized to influence the conduct, and outcomes, of the employment interview. This can occur in several ways. For example, interviewers can change either their nonverbal (e.g., body language) or verbal behaviors (e.g., time spent talking), as well as the content of what is discussed (e.g., applicant qualifications versus vacancy characteristics).

Interviewer behaviors are further hypothesized to influence applicant behaviors (e.g., Dipboye, 1982; Eder & Buckley, 1988), which in turn can

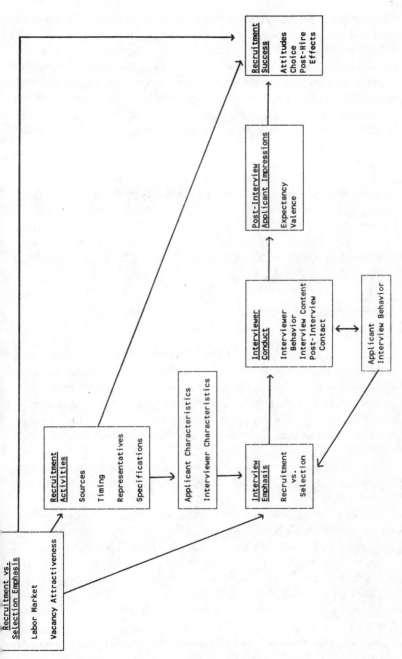

Figure 9.1. The Employment Interview as Part of the Applicant Attraction Process

129

either reinforce the interviewer's initial emphasis, or cause a readjustment toward a greater emphasis on either recruitment or selection.

Following the interview, the applicant makes a number of judgments and decisions which determine the success of the recruiting effort. Specifically, based on the interview and other recruitment experiences, applicants assess the likelihood of receiving an offer (expectancy), and the probable attractiveness of that offer (valence). These assessments, in turn, are believed to influence job choices (Schwab, Rynes, & Aldag, 1987; Vroom, 1966; Wanous, 1977).

However, as the model indicates, the extent to which recruitment activities are able to influence recruitment success (particularly job choice) is limited by other factors, most notably the attractiveness of the applicant's other alternatives. Generally speaking, an applicant's alternatives are likely to be a function of labor market conditions and the applicant's particular qualifications (Thurow, 1975). This implies that there are inherent limits to the ability to attract candidates through conventional recruitment activities, including the interview.

Determinants of the Balance
Between Recruitment and Selection

Market and vacancy characteristics. Generally speaking, the importance of the recruitment function increases as demand for labor outpaces supply. However, changes in aggregate vacancy or unemployment statistics will imperfectly reflect the importance of recruitment to any given organization. For example, well-known and highly attractive companies like IBM are likely to generate thousands of unsolicited applications even in full employment economies.

Thus, the importance of recruitment also depends on characteristics of the particular vacancy. In general, attraction seems to be most difficult when there is a poor organizational image, low pay, or few opportunities for advancement. Not surprisingly, then, industries such as retailing and food service are currently placing considerable emphasis on innovative recruiting (e.g., Axon Group, 1987; Commerce Clearing House, 1987; Merrill, 1987).

Recruitment activities (other than the interview). Market and vacancy characteristics are likely to affect a wide range of recruitment activities. Although a full review of these activities is beyond the scope of this paper, it is useful to consider a few examples and their potential impact on the interview.

As applicants become scarce, organizations implement a number of changes in their recruiting procedures. For example, they may turn to more (or more expensive) applicant sources (Malm, 1954; Commerce Clearing House, 1987), set lower position specifications (Merrill, 1987), recruit earlier and more frequently (Hanigan, 1987; Schwab et al., 1987), or select and train recruiters to make a better impression on applicants (Hanigan, 1987; Rynes & Boudreau, 1986). In general, these decisions will affect both the quantity and quality of applicants available for selection.

To the extent that these activities increase the size of the applicant pool, organizations would be expected to increase the attention given to screening and selection in the employment interview. Conversely, to the extent that they increase the general level of applicant qualifications, a greater recruitment emphasis would be expected, as the typical applicant would be both more difficult to attract, and less in need of screening.

The general point is that the nature and scope of other recruitment activities are likely to have an impact on characteristics of the applicant pool, and hence the relative emphasis placed on selection versus recruitment in the interview. In addition, characteristics of interviewers themselves may be influenced by general recruitment activities (e.g., extent of interviewer training, selection of line versus staff recruiters).

Hypothesized Differences Between "Recruitment" and "Selection" Interviews

Although the issue has received little direct attention, it seems likely that interviews designed primarily for recruitment purposes might differ substantially from those intended to screen or select. Specifically, interviewers are expected to modify both their nonverbal and verbal behaviors in accordance with changes in recruitment versus selection priorities.

Evidence for these propositions comes from research on the effects of initial impressions of applicants on interviewer behaviors (Dipboye, 1982). Interviewers with favorable first impressions have been found to talk more (Anderson, 1960), to interrupt more frequently and respond more quickly (Matarazzo & Weins, 1972), and to exhibit fewer long pauses (Feldstein, 1972) and errors of speech (Word, Zanna & Cooper, 1974) during the interview. In a slightly different context, teachers were found to lean farther forward, nod and smile more frequently, and display more consistent eye contact when interacting with students whom they had been led to believe were bright (Chaiken, Sigler, & Derlega, 1974).

In general, the preceding studies suggest that interviewers are likely to modify their behaviors in line with prior impressions of specific candidates. Whether they similarly adjust their behaviors in response to other, less personal conditions hypothesized to increase the importance of recruiting (e.g., general labor shortages, less attractive vacancies, use of sources with minimal prescreening) remains to be demonstrated.

The content of what is discussed in the interview may also change in response to recruitment priorities. One plausible prediction is that as recruitment increases in importance, interviewers spend relatively more time discussing the vacancy rather than the applicant (e.g., Dipboye, 1982; Taylor & Sniezek, 1984). Consistent with this hypothesis, Sydiaha (1961) reported that the interviews of eventual selectees were characterized by fewer interviewer questions and more attempts to solve candidate problems.

Recruitment priorities may also lead to more favorable (not just more frequent) discussions of vacancy characteristics. It has long been alleged that interviewers tend to downplay the negative, and emphasize the positive, features of vacancies (Schneider, 1976). What is not clear, however, is whether this tendency is correlated with the relative urgency of recruitment versus selection needs. Although such a relationship seems plausible, there is little evidence to substantiate it. Indeed, the practitioner literature suggests that the so-called "marketing" approach (as opposed to "realistic" recruiting) is favored by most recruiters, regardless of market tightness or vacancy attractiveness (e.g., Krett & Stright, 1985; Stoops, 1984).

Another hypothesis claims that the type of screening questions asked of applicants may change as interview priorities change. For example, it is possible that interviewers who are under strong recruitment pressures may ask fewer questions that are likely to disqualify applicants from further consideration. Although this hypothesis has not been directly tested, Carlson, Thayer, Mayfield, and Peterson (1971) reported that inexperienced managers who were instructed to assume they were "behind quota" evaluated applicants less stringently than those who were ahead of quota or had no quotas.

A final prediction is that interviewers who place a high priority on recruitment give the applicant more explicit information about the organization's postinterview decision processes, and initiate earlier contacts following the interview (Hanigan, 1987). Although research has suggested that earlier contacts and repeated follow-ups may favorably influence applicant decisions (e.g., Arvey, Gordon, Massengill, & Mussio, 1975; Ivancevich & Donnelly, 1971; Soelberg, 1967), there is no firm evidence that organizations with a strong recruitment orientation adopt these practices to a greater extent than others.

In summary, as the importance of the recruitment function increases, employment interviewers are hypothesized to: (1) exhibit more positive verbal and nonverbal behaviors, (2) place relatively more emphasis on vacancy rather than applicant characteristics; (3) describe vacancies in more favorable terms, (4) ask questions that are less likely to lead to candidate disqualification, and (5) pursue more aggressive postinterview follow-up practices.

Effects of Recruitment on Applicants

Effects on Applicant Behavior Within the Interview

Several researchers have speculated that the initial orientation of the interviewer can have an effect on the applicant's subsequent performance in the interview (e.g., Dipboye, 1982; Eder & Buckley, 1988; Schmitt, 1976). Specifically, it is hypothesized that the positive (or negative) orientation of an interviewer is quickly conveyed to the interviewee, who in turn responds with similar affective and behavioral responses.

Thus, in a sort of "self-fulfilling prophecy" (Dipboye, 1982), applicants who receive positive early treatment are hypothesized to respond with greater confidence and more effective verbal and nonverbal presentations. Moreover, Dipboye (1982) hypothesized that these effects are likely to be strongest in cases where the interview is unstructured, the interviewer very confident of his or her initial impression, and the applicant unsure of how well he or she is likely to perform. However, the important point is that the postinterview reactions of both the interviewer and interviewee are likely to be influenced by the results of these social interaction processes.

Effects on Applicant's Postinterview Impressions and Decisions

Although it has been widely assumed that recruitment practices are indeed capable of influencing applicant's decisions (e.g., Glueck, 1973; Stoops, 1985), most theories of job choice ignore recruitment as a relevant variable. Economists, for example, view choices as driven by market distributions of job attributes (e.g., salaries) and individual job search patterns (e.g., search intensity, systematic versus random search; see Lippman & McCall, 1976). Vacancy characteristics have also dominated most expectancy theory (e.g., Vroom, 1964) and policy capturing (e.g., Zedeck, 1977) research.

Thus, it is not immediately obvious how recruitment practices contribute to applicants' decisions, over and above the impact of vacancy characteristics per se. The present chapter addresses two possibilities, each of which depends on the presence of uncertainty in the job search and choice process (Schwab, 1982). Specifically, it is hypothesized that recruitment influences job choices through its impact on applicants' expectancy and valence perceptions.

Expectancy effects. The first hypothesis is that recruitment practices influence job seekers' expectations of receiving job offers (Vroom, 1964; Rynes et al., 1980). Because job seekers are frequently uncertain about their marketability, they have been hypothesized to grasp at any available information that might help them estimate their chances of receiving offers. Thus, interviewer behaviors may become a source of clues as to whether or not a job offer is likely to be forthcoming.

There is some evidence that interviewers do in fact influence applicants' expectations of receiving job offers. For example, Schmitt and Coyle (1976) collected college students' descriptions of recruiter behavior in their most recent campus interviews. These descriptions were then correlated with a variety of dependent variables, including applicants' expectations of receiving a job offer. Perceived likelihood of receiving an offer was significantly associated with recruiter personality and recruiter familiarity with the applicant and the job in question. These same variables were also correlated with applicants' self-perceptions of performance in the interview, as well as the likelihood that they would further explore job possibilities with the company.

Interpretation of these results is complicated, however, by the fact that all measures were based on applicant perceptions. As such, common method variance may account for many of the observed correlations. Additionally, the data do not permit causal inferences.

In an attempt to circumvent these problems, Rynes and Miller (1983) obtained college student reactions to a series of experimentally controlled videotaped interviews. Tapes were varied in terms of recruiter affect, specificity of recruiter-provided job information, and attractiveness of job attributes. Recruiter affect had a sizeable impact on subjects' perceptions of the applicant's performance and whether or not the applicant would receive a second interview.

It should be noted that in the preceding study, applicant behaviors were held constant across videotapes. As such, the study did not address the self-fulfilling prophecy prediction that interviewer behavior may also affect applicants' *objective* interview performance (e.g., Dipboye, 1982; Schmitt, 1976).

Even if interviewers do affect applicant expectancies, however, additional processes are required to explain how differing expectancies might translate into different job choices. One possibility is that applicants with high expectancy perceptions are more motivated to actively pursue alternatives

(Vroom, 1964). Increased pursuit, in turn, increases the likelihood of actually receiving an offer (Schwab et al., 1987), which in turn enhances the probability that the job will ultimately be chosen.

Another possibility is that expectancy perceptions may have a direct impact on perceived job valence. Indeed, there is some evidence that jobs that are perceived as attainable may benefit from cognitive distortions that increase their perceived attractiveness (Soelberg, 1967). Conversely, jobs that are viewed as unattainable may suffer from a "sour grapes" phenomenon.

Valence perceptions. Interviewers may influence job choices not only through their effect on applicant expectancies, but also through their impact on perceived job attractiveness. Previous research suggests that valence perceptions may be altered either through indirect (*signaling*) or direct (*marketing*) processes.

The signalling hypothesis suggests that interviewer behaviors are interpreted by applicants as "cues" concerning unknown organizational or job characteristics (Rynes et al., 1980). Although attributes such as starting salary or location may be quite obvious at the time an offer is extended, other characteristics (e.g., promotion opportunities, considerate supervision) can only be inferred or estimated. Thus, for example, interviewers might be viewed as symbolic of the "typical" company employee in terms of friendliness, competence, formality, and other characteristics.

There is some evidence that interviewer behaviors do affect applicant perceptions of organizational attractiveness, at least in the early stages of the recruiting process. For example, Schmitt and Coyle (1976) found significant relationships between recruiter personality and informedness on the one hand, and perceived increase (or decrease) in organizational favorability and likelihood of offer acceptance on the other. However, interpretation is clouded by the correlational nature of the data, as well as the inability to determine precisely which recruiter behaviors are associated with what organizational characteristics.

These difficulties were at least partially overcome in Rynes and Miller's (1983) laboratory experiment. There, manipulations of recruiter affect (eye contact, nodding, smiling) were found to have a positive effect on perceptions of how the company treats employees, but not on overall job attractiveness or beliefs about how well the company rewards employees.

Finally, Taylor and Bergman (1987) correlated three sets of interview characteristics (recruiter descriptions of interview processes, applicant descriptions of recruiter behaviors, and recruiter demographics) with applicant perceptions of job attractiveness and probability of job offer acceptance. The degree of interview structure (as reported by recruiters) was significantly associated with applicants' probabilities of accepting job offers. In addition, applicants' (but not recruiters') perceptions of recruiter empathy were positively associated with perceived organizational attractiveness and likelihood of accepting an offer.

Several recruiter demographic characteristics (being older, female, and from the personnel department) were negatively associated with perceived organizational attractiveness. In addition, being interviewed by a recruiter with a bachelors (rather than masters) degree decreased the stated probability of job offer acceptance. These results, combined with similar experimental findings (for age and job title) by Rogers and Sincoff (1978), suggest that there may be a "status" element associated with certain interviewer demographics.

In sum, interviewer characteristics were significantly associated with applicant perceptions of organizational attractiveness in each of the above studies. However, they did not explain a high proportion of overall variance, particularly at later stages of the recruitment process (Taylor & Bergmann, 1987) and in studies where the impact of job attributes was also examined (Rynes & Miller, 1983; Taylor & Bergmann, 1987).

In addition to possible signalling effects, interviewers may also exert a more deliberate influence on valence perceptions through their choice of recruitment "marketing" strategies. Specifically, decisions about what (and what *not*) to tell applicants, in combination with applicants' lack of detailed organizational information (e.g., Reynolds, 1951; Taylor & Bergmann, 1987), may cause job seekers to make choices they might not otherwise make. Indeed, the whole "realistic job preview" literature is predicated on this assumption. Thus, the opportunity exists for manipulation of applicant decisions through selective interviewer presentation, interpretation, or withholding of organizational information.

Meta-analytic evidence suggests that "realistic" recruiting messages (i.e., those that include larger proportions of negative and neutral information) do in fact have a negative effect on applicants' propensities to accept job offers (Premack & Wanous, 1985). However, realistic recruiting has also been associated with longer tenure among those who do accept offers (McEvoy & Cascio, 1985).

Methodological difficulties preclude precise understanding of the processes responsible for these findings, as well as the net utility to employers of providing realistic rather than marketing treatments. For example, one possible explanation for the higher retention of "realistic" recruits is that the most marketable applicants disproportionately self-select out of the recruiting process when confronted with negative information. If so, the higher retention rates of acceptees who receive realistic previews may be due to the fact that they reflect a less marketable subset of the original applicant pool.

Apart from the issue of accuracy and detail, applicants may also be influenced by the relative attention devoted to various attributes in the recruitment process. Unfortunately, scores of "attribute importance" studies have not yet provided definitive answers as to which attributes are of greatest concern to applicants in job choice (e.g., Lawler, 1971; Schwab et al., 1987).

Schwab et al. (1987) and Rynes (in press) have hypothesized that a number of general factors are likely to influence the relative importance of attributes in the job choice decision. These include the extent to which the attribute can be known with certainty prior to choice (e.g., location versus promotional opportunities), the extent of attribute variability across alternatives (e.g., high variability in hours but low variability in pay for nurses), and the extent to which the attribute is directly comparable across alternatives (e.g., pay versus developmental opportunities). Others hypothesize that the relative importance of different attributes varies as a function of applicant demographics (e.g., Lawler, 1971), personality characteristics (e.g., Whyte, 1955) or work experience (e.g., Ullman & Gutteridge, 1973).

The professional literature suggests that recruiters believe they could recruit much more effectively if they only knew "what applicants are *really* looking for" (e.g., Krett & Stright, 1985, Stoops, 1985). Unfortunately, little is known about how recruiters answer this question, how their answers affect what they tell applicants, and finally how variations in those messages influence applicants' decisions.

Other Influences on Applicant Decisions

As Figure 9.1 illustrates, there are a variety of factors other than the interview that influence recruitment success. These include the state of the labor market (e.g., Schwab, 1982), vacancy characteristics (e.g., Hanssens & Levien, 1983; Taylor & Bergmann, 1987), applicant characteristics (Thurow, 1975), and recruitment practices other than the interview (Boudreau & Rynes, 1985).

A full review of the impact of these factors on applicants' attitudes, job choices, and post-hire behaviors is outside the scope of this chapter (for more detailed treatments see Rynes, in press, or Schwab et al., 1987). However, it is important to keep in mind that some of these factors, particularly vacancy characteristics, have been shown to have strong effects on applicant attitudes and decisions.

Indeed, in cases where vacancy and recruitment variables have been studied simultaneously, vacancy characteristics have strongly dominated recruitment in terms of variance explained in job attractiveness, likelihood of job acceptance, and actual job choice (e.g., Powell, 1984; Rynes & Miller, 1983; Taylor & Bergmann, 1987). The implication, of course, is that recruitment practices in general, and the interview in particular, are limited in the extent to which they can influence job acceptance and post-hire behaviors.

Future Research

If correct, the model suggests that the recruitment effects of employment interviews cannot be evaluated in a vacuum. As a practical matter, it makes little sense to scrutinize the impact of interviewers' nonverbal behaviors on applicants' postinterview impressions if applicant decisions are "swamped" by labor market conditions and vacancy characteristics. Thus, researchers are urged to follow the lead of Taylor and Bergmann (1987) in studying multiple aspects of attraction at various recruiting phases.

A good deal of basic descriptive research is needed to validate, modify, or disconfirm the model. For clarity of exposition, research questions suggested by the model will be categorized according to *content* and *process* issues.

Content Questions

1. Do labor market variables and vacancy characteristics influence the perceived importance of recruitment? The model hypothesizes that factors such as general labor shortages, low wages, or high turnover rates increase the priority attached to recruitment. If true, these conditions should be associated with (a) higher recruiting priorities among organizational executives (both line and human resource managers) and (b) increased expenditures on recruitment (e.g., percent headcount or budget devoted to recruiting).

Therefore, future researchers might attempt to establish relationships between hypothesized exogenous variables (e.g., labor market conditions, organizational characteristics) and the degree of emphasis placed on recruitment. Measurement of these exogenous factors would benefit from the use of data bases not generally associated with recruitment research (e.g., IRS Statistics of Corporate Income, Bureau of Labor Statistics Employment and Earnings Data, Bureau of the Census Population Industrial Characteristics, and consulting firm data). By using sources such as these, researchers could avoid the common method variance associated with typical recruitment surveys, where all data are obtained from the same (subjective) sources (e.g., organizational recruiters or placement directors).

2. Does perceived importance of recruitment influence organizational recruitment practices? The model suggests that a strong recruitment emphasis should translate into such activities as careful selection and training of organizational representatives, increased scrutiny of applicant decision processes, and more extensive evaluation of recruiting outcomes. Future researchers should attempt to determine whether strong recruiting priorities do in fact translate into the kinds of practices believed to improve recruiting effectiveness (e.g., Boudreau & Rynes, 1985; Rynes & Boudreau, 1986).

3. Do the recruiting priorities of top-level executives "filter down" to individual recruiters and hiring managers? Presumably, recruiting effectiveness will not improve unless those involved in actual recruitment and hiring procedures also adopt a recruitment priority mentality. Research is needed to determine whether, and how, recruitment priorities can be successfully instilled in operating managers and recruiters. Possibilities include increased communications regarding recruitment objectives and successes, or special training to sensitize interviewers as to how their actions might influence applicant decisions.

4. Do recruiters and hiring managers who place a high priority on recruitment behave any differently than those who do not? The model suggests that interviewers who place a high priority on recruiting will display a more positive affect toward applicants, be better informed concerning vacancy and applicant characteristics, spend more time trying to solve applicant problems, and pursue applicants more aggressively, both prior to and following the initial interview. To date, little is known about whether this is actually the case. A related question concerns whether or not recruiters are able to implement these tactics on their own, or whether specific training is required to induce these behaviors.

5. Do recruiters induce "self-fulfilling prophecy" behaviors on the part of applicants? Although there is evidence that prior information about applicants can exert a biasing effect on interviewer behaviors and decisions, there is no direct evidence that interviewer behaviors cause distortions of applicant behavior. Such evidence might be obtained by confronting applicants with different kinds of interviewer behaviors (e.g., positive versus negative nonverbal cues, little versus extensive knowledge of the applicant's resume), and observing how applicants respond under the various conditions (e.g., effectiveness of verbal and nonverbal presentation, time spent talking, and so on). At least initially, such research would probably best be pursued in experimental settings, where close control could be exerted over recruiter behaviors.

At issue is the question of how much information interviewers should have at their disposal prior to the interview. On the one hand, research has shown that recruiters who demonstrate more knowledge of an applicant's background leave a better impression on the applicant (e.g., Schmitt & Coyle, 1976). On the other hand, Dipboye (1982) and others have suggested that unfavorable information about an applicant could cause a recruiter to exhibit negative, rather than positive, behaviors.

To date, most of the evidence suggesting positive reactions to extensive interviewer information has come from field studies. As such, it is possible that selection bias may partially account for the results. That is, recruiters may only take the time to address questions of applicant-vacancy "fit" when the applicant's resume has already created a favorable impression.

6. What interviewer characteristics are most likely to "signal" organizational attributes? The model hypothesizes that recruiter characteristics and behaviors (e.g., attire, affect, question content) may signal general organizational characteristics (formality, employee relations climate, attitudes toward minorities and women) to applicants. To date, little is known about which interviewer characteristics create inferences about particular organizational characteristics.

7. To what extent is the information that applicants receive about organizational and job characteristics accurate? Previous research has clearly shown that perceived job and organizational attributes dominate applicant job choices. However, this research has relied almost exclusively on applicants' self-reports of perceived vacancy characteristics. It should be recognized that these perceptions are, at least in part, a function of interviewers' marketing "pitches" as well as actual vacancy characteristics. Research has shown that new employees consistently experience reductions in perceived valence once they actually begin working (e.g., Vroom, 1966). To the extent that interviewer recruiting strategies exert an independent influence on valence perceptions, over and above true vacancy characteristics, some of the variance previously attributed to job characteristics might more appropriately be attributed to recruitment.

Process Questions

A general contribution future researchers might make is to disentangle the processes responsible for a number of commonly observed empirical findings. For example, most field research has found significant correlations between subjects' descriptions of recruiter behaviors, perceptions of job attractiveness, and behavioral intentions. However, these studies have not determined the extent to which perceptions of attractiveness arise from true vacancy characteristics, interviewer representation of those characteristics (marketing effects), or subject inferences or assumptions about those characteristics (signalling or halo effects). Similarly, despite two meta-analyses of realistic job preview research, the processes through which prehire information affects posthire attitudes and behaviors are still not well understood (Premack & Wanous, 1985).

A second process contribution would be to delineate the likely effects of selection bias and sample attrition on recruitment research findings. For example, it is not known whether differences in results across early versus late recruitment stages (e.g., Taylor & Bergmann, 1987) reflect differences in the effects of recruitment variables, or selection biases due to non-responses from sample "drop-outs."

Similarly, most realistic job preview research has been based only on "selectees." Even where differences in job acceptance rates have been reported across conditions, no attempt has been made to correct for potential selection and self-selection biases. Thus, there is a need for more careful tracking of applicant pools over time, and more extensive measurement of applicant characteristics (beyond basic demographics) so that appropriate adjustments can be made for sampling bias.

This kind of research would appear to be particularly important in that the practical implications of good versus poor recruitment may not be well reflected in measures such as "change in R^2" or "omega^2." The detrimental effects of poor recruitment (e.g., negative applicant self-selection) will be underestimated to the extent that only volunteers from the "survivor" population are represented in results.

Finally, experimental research in field settings would be particularly helpful in delineating the potential benefits of improved recruitment practices. There is a great need to determine whether recruiting effectiveness can in fact be improved by following normatively prescribed practices. For example, large organizations could train recruiters in the use of applicant-sensitive interview techniques, and then measure whether or not any improvements are noted in applicant feedback, second interview acceptances, and the like. Similar studies could be done for other aspects of recruitment as well (e.g., choice of recruiting sources, modified timing of campus visits). Studies of this type are already well-developed in the armed services, where attempts have been made to determine what effects recruitment activities and expenditures have on enlistments, holding other factors (e.g., unemployment rates, military to nonmilitary pay ratios) constant (e.g., Hanssens & Levien, 1983).

In sum, much work remains to be done before a fuller understanding will be achieved of the recruitment aspects of employment interviews. However, these effects cannot be examined in isolation from a variety of other factors (other recruitment practices and labor market, applicant, and vacancy characteristics) likely to have an impact on both interview processes and outcomes.

PART V

Interview Content:
Information Search Strategies

Unless the employment interview is entirely extemporaneous, the interviewer will likely engage in some form of preparation before meeting with the applicant. Interviewer preparation produces an information search strategy that has a substantial bearing on interview content, interviewer conduct, and the ultimate criteria against which judgments of job suitability are rendered. Activities typically include (1) review of the job description, job specifications, and historical performance difficulties, (2) determination of weighted rating factors, preferably on a scored interviewer report form, which are reflective of important job requirements, (3) development of a set of questions designed to tap the rating factors, (4) review of interview content and process to remove any potential charges of unfair discrimination, (5) arrangement of questions to insure that the same key question areas are covered for all applicants, and (6) review of completed application forms and resumes to follow up on omissions or inconsistencies.

Considerable research has been directed toward enhancing interview predictive validities by structuring interview content to maximize the job relevancy of questions asked and judgment criteria employed. The following four chapters collectively provide considerable optimism for improving interviewer practice. It is quite likely that ongoing research efforts will accelerate in the years ahead to better understand how "structured interviewing" affects interviewer-applicant behavior and decision making processes.

Feild and Gatewood examine the role of job information in the development and application of a selection interview, describing one method that may prove advantageous, namely the Job Content Method. The method integrates job task data (i.e., information on the required knowledge, skills, and abilities) and critical incidents data. The method's comprehensive coverage of job and employee specifications (a) lends itself to the development of other selection methods, (b) emphasizes behavioral correspondence between interview content and job task requirements, and (c) supports a content validation strategy for selection methods for which such a validation model is appropriate.

The next two chapters are authored by the leading proponents (Tom Janz and Gary Latham) of the two more popular, researched, and efficacious structured interviewing formats: respectively, the patterned behavior description interview (PBDI) and the situational interview. In structuring their chapters, each author was asked to follow the same format to highlight the similarities and differences between the two approaches. This format includes discussion of theoretical foundations, review of relevant empirical literature including new unpublished findings, description of the approach's advantages over traditional interview techniques and other structured interviewing approaches, and suggestions for future research.

The final chapter by Schuler and Funke describes the development and initial testing of a structured multimodal interview approach that includes both past behavior-based questions and situational interviewing. The target job in this study is a bank clerk apprentice position in a large West German bank, where user acceptance of a new selection technique takes precedent over predictive validity. The study may prove to be instructive on how to test the contrasting and combined effects of different interview content structuring approaches.

10

Development of a Selection Interview: A Job Content Strategy

Hubert S. Feild
Auburn University

Robert D. Gatewood
University of Georgia

Selection interviews may differ in any number of ways, but they all have at least one common characteristic—the use of interview questions. Questions asked in the selection interview are important in that they affect an interviewer's evaluation of an applicant's ability to successfully perform a job. Ultimately, these questions and their answers have an impact on the effectiveness of selection decisions based on the interview.

One key assumption in the use of interview data in selection decision-making is that an applicant's performance in the interview is predictive of performance on the job. Because an applicant's performance in the interview is in part a function of the questions posed, a related assumption is that interview question content is also job related. With respect to this last assumption, there have been mixed opinions as to the source of interview question content. Some writers have implied that interview questions might simply be developed from a pool of questions. For instance, Stewart and Cash (1974, pp. 152-154) suggested questions such as the following be used in interviewing prospective job candidates: "What kind of people do you enjoy being around the most?" "If you could control what people said behind your back, what would you like for them to be saying about you?" Rather than employing different questions for different jobs, the practice of using the same or very similar questions for hiring in a wide variety of jobs is apparently widespread. Lindquist (1988), for instance, has published a listing of the 50 questions most frequently used by college recruiters in employment interviews. Yate (1988) has also prepared such a listing of questions and answers for use by an applicant in a selection interview. The principal difficulty in simply selecting and using existing interview questions for an assortment of jobs is their questionable relevance and relationship to job performance. To use the same questions for every job is to assume that these jobs require the same knowledge, skills, and abilities for job success.

To better insure the job relatedness of interview content, other writers (e.g., Campion, Pursell, & Brown, 1988; Zima, 1983) have called for a different strategy in choosing interview questions. Rather than selecting existing questions, they have recommended the use of job analysis in developing interview content. They have argued that a study should be made of the job for which the interview will be used. Questions should then be based on the important requirements of the job. But few publications have documented how job analysis results should be employed to systematically develop interview content. This chapter examines the use of job information in the development of the selection interview; specifically, the role of job analysis in developing interview content is discussed, and one means for incorporating job analysis information into the content of the interview is outlined.

Role of Job Analysis Data and Interview Content

There are two principal reasons for employing job analysis data to develop a selection interview. These data are used to (a) enhance the effectiveness of the interview as a selection tool, and (b) comply with legal guidelines required of measures used in personnel selection.

Enhancement of Interview Effectiveness

The questions that are asked by an interviewer elicit a sample of applicant behavior in the form of answers to these questions. On this behavioral sample rests a significant portion of an interviewer's evaluation of an applicant. If the questions asked are not job related, the answers given may not provide a representative sample of relevant behavior in the applicant. Lowered interview validity with consequent errors in predicting an applicant's future job performance will likely result.

In an unstructured interview, an interviewer is given free rein in choosing questions. The opportunity for nonjob-relevant factors (e.g., applicant characteristics such as sex or race) to affect the choice of questions is high. In such a situation, the probability of an interviewer asking questions, receiving answers, and then making evaluations of the applicant that are not job related is also high. The lack of systematic coverage of job-relevant information and the impact of nonjob-relevant factors on interviewer evaluations are two factors that appear to contribute to the low validity of the interview. Thus, for improving interview reliability and validity, the use of a structured interview based on job content is frequently recommended.

Research has shown that job information incorporated into the interview can improve the effectiveness of the interview. Langdale and Weitz (1973) concluded that the reliability of interviewers' evaluations of job applicants increased as the interviewers were given more information about the job to be filled. Similarly, Wiener and Schneiderman (1974) reported less impact of nonjob-relevant factors on selection decisions with the availability of more job opening information. In addition, Osburn, Timmrick, and Bigby (1981) and Vance, Kuhnert, and Farr (1978) noted higher interviewer accuracy when applicants were rated on scales keyed to specific behavioral job dimensions. More recent research by Arvey, Miller, Gould, and Burch (1987), Janz (1982), Latham and Saari (1984), Latham, Saari, Pursell, and Campion (1980), Orpen (1985), and Weekley and Gier (1987) have documented that when job information is used to develop interview questions as well as to evaluate applicant answers, interview validity can also be enhanced. Overall, these research results suggest that incorporating job information is an effective strategy for interview development and use. Job analysis is the first step toward incorporation of this information.

Compliance with Legal Guidelines

The adoption of the *Uniform Guidelines on Employee Selection Procedures* (Federal Register, 1978) by the federal government accorded substantial importance to the role of job analysis in the use of tests and other measures for personnel selection purposes. These guidelines generally require that job analysis be performed as part of the development, application, and validation of employee selection devices. In the *Uniform Guidelines*, a selection procedure includes "the full range of assessment techniques from traditional paper and pencil tests, performance tests, training programs . . . through informal or casual interviews and unscored application forms" (p.38308). Similar definitions of a selection device can be found in the *Standards for Educational and Psychological Testing* (1985: 4-5) and the *Principles for the Validation and Use of Personnel Selection Procedures* (1987: 1).

When the *Uniform Guidelines'* definition of a selection device is coupled with the Supreme Court's implied support of job analysis in *Griggs v. Duke Power Co.* (1971) and its stated endorsement of job analysis, as well as the EEOC's *Uniform Guidelines on Employee Selection Procedures* in *Albemarle Paper Co. v. Moody* (1975), it would seem that job analysis is one essential ingredient for legal compliance in selection interview use.

However, the linkages between the *Uniform Guidelines*, landmark legal cases such as *Griggs* or *Albemarle*, and the selection interview are not as clear as they may first appear. The legal issues surrounding the application of job analysis and a subjective selection device, such as an interview, are too complex to address in detail here, but a brief overview may be helpful.

In the past, many courts have typically applied disparate *treatment* analysis rather than disparate *impact* analysis in reviewing the legality of the selection interview in employment discrimination cases (Jones, 1987; Lamber, 1985). As a result, employers have not been required to provide the same psychometric evidence on the interview, namely validity evidence, that has been required on other selection measures in disparate impact cases. Instead, employers have been required to provide a legitimate, non-discriminatory explanation of the job relatedness of the selection interview. In contrast, objective selection measures, such as ability tests, have more often been examined under disparate impact analysis. The courts have generally held the view that objective selection criteria can be clearly identified, applied equally to job applicants, and scientifically evaluated through a validation study. From their perspective, subjective employment criteria, such as an interview, involve judgments and opinions about job applicants and cannot be similarly evaluated (Larson & Larson, 1986, pp. 15-82-15-85). This view, however, has recently been challenged. For example, the American Psychological Association (1987) has filed an *amicus* brief with the Supreme Court arguing that the validation requirements in the *Uniform Guidelines*, the *Principles*, and the *Standards* that apply to objective selection measures should apply to subjective ones as well (see also American Society for Personnel Administration, International Personnel Management Association, & Employment Management Association, 1987). If the courts' view of validation requirements for subjective criteria changes, employers will be mandated to validate their selection interviews. The first step in legal compliance will be to incorporate job information into the interview. Job analysis will provide the vehicle for achieving this; its presence (or absence) in developing a selection interview will likely have an effect on the outcome of an employment discrimination case (Thompson & Thompson, 1982).

Development of Interview Content from Job Analysis Data

Developing job-related interview questions begins with a thorough analysis of the job for which the interview will be used as a selection measure. When job analyses have been implemented in recent studies of the selection interview, the method of choice has been the critical incidents technique (e.g., Latham & Saari, 1984; Weekley & Gier, 1987). Using this method, job analysts ask supervisors, job incumbents, or other key observers to describe specific incidents of effective or ineffective behavior that have occurred on a job. Literally hundreds of incidents may be produced for a job. Because all incidents produced cannot be incorporated into interview content, they are reduced to a manageable number. (A 10:1 ratio of incidents discarded to those retained is not unusual [Orpen, 1985].) For this reason, Schwab, Heneman, and DeCotiis (1975) have noted that the substantial number of incidents discarded is a major limitation of the critical incidents process. Most studies developing interview content from critical incidents data do not completely explain the rationale used for discarding behaviors. As a consequence, the job content domain being sampled may not be fully covered by the selected behavioral incidents. If a content validation strategy were adopted, it would be difficult to document with empirical data that the job content domain had been covered adequately.

One method, the Job Content Method, for documenting the translation of job analysis results into interview content is summarized in this paper. The method blends job analysis data produced from a technique described by Gatewood and Feild (1987) with critical incidents data. The method was chosen for several reasons. First, it builds selection measure content so as to reflect workers' knowledge, skills, and abilities (KSAs) as well as other characteristics essential for successful job performance. These KSAs are derived from the tasks that compose the job. Coupling KSAs with critical incidents data helps to insure that interview questions reflect job content.

Second, the method lends itself to the development of other selection measures as well, for example, tests. Often, a variety of selection measures, including the interview, must be developed from the same job analysis data to provide a complete selection program. Thus, it is necessary that the job analysis method employed be amenable to developing a diversity of selection measures. The approach described appears to be useful in meeting this need.

Third, the method is consistent with Wernimont and Campbell's (1968) proposal for a point-to-point correspondence between predictors and criteria. Latham et al.'s (1980; 1984) work on the situational interview has shown that when interview content is behaviorally consistent with job task requirements, an empirically valid selection interview can be produced. The present method begins with identification of job tasks and the KSAs needed to perform them. Critical incidents are then tied to these tasks and KSAs. Behavioral consistency is emphasized by keying interview questions to the incidents derived from the job tasks and the KSAs necessary for task performance.

Finally, the method lends itself to a content validation strategy. It is not being suggested that a content validation strategy be used to validate the selection interview. That decision will depend upon the attributes being assessed by the interview as well as the particular validation situation. However, the use of a content validation strategy can facilitate the development or construction of a selection measure (Tenopyr, 1977). For those measures for which a content validation strategy is appropriate, job analysis data with proper documentation can support such a strategy.

The Job Content Method: Job Analysis

The objective of a job analysis is to identify the critical job tasks and the KSAs required to perform them. These identified tasks and KSAs represent the job domain from which the selection interview and other measures are developed. A series of steps are involved in the job analysis process; the major ones are summarized below.

Identifying and Rating Job Tasks

The first step in the proposed job analysis process is identification of important work behaviors performed on the job. These behaviors serve as the basis for developing the selection interview as well as other selection measures. Task statements are used to describe work behaviors by incorporating (a) what the worker does, (b) to what or to whom a behavior is directed, (c) upon what instructions, (d) how the behavior is performed, and (e) why the action is taken. An example of a task statement for an engineering technician's job is as follows:

> Inspects systems monitoring equipment using calibration devices and following user manuals in order to comply with manufacturers' maintenance requirements of the monitoring equipment.

Task statements can be developed through any number of methods including the use of questionnaires, interviews, observation, or combinations of these. One method is to use small groups of job incumbents who serve as subject matter experts (SMEs). SMEs work with a group leader to develop task statements which reflect the major activities performed on a job.

Once the tasks have been specified, the next step is to identify those most critical to job performance. Numerical ratings provided by the SMEs are used to isolate these tasks. Task ratings are made on the basis of rating scales involving several criteria or dimensions such as the following: frequency of task performance, importance of the task to successful job performance, and necessity for a new employee to be able to perform the task upon entry into the job. Each task is scored on all of the rating criteria. Normally, a task is scored by arithmetically combining each of the numerical ratings. Unit weights can be used simply by adding the dimension ratings given for each task (Cascio & Ramos, 1986), or differential weights can be employed to reflect relative importance of the dimensions (Levine, 1983; Schmitt & Ostroff, 1986). The total scores of the task ratings serve as the basis for defining the most important job content. This job content is in turn the basis for defining the questions to be asked in the selection interview.

Identifying and Rating KSAs Necessary for Task Performance

Once a job's critical tasks have been identified, the KSAs necessary to perform these tasks must be determined. KSAs can be defined as follows:

Knowledge—A recognized body of information that is required for successful job performance.
Skill—A competence, with a specific measurable level of performance, that enables an incumbent to perform the job.
Ability—A more general, lasting capability of an incumbent to perform the job.

A rating panel of SMEs is used to identify the necessary KSAs. This panel may be the same as that used to derive the task statements, or it may be composed of other individuals who are knowledgeable of the job.

In addition to specifying the KSAs, the panel also rates the importance of these KSAs in successfully performing the job. The interview and other selection measures should reflect the relative importance of the KSAs for the job (i.e., those KSAs most important for successful job performance should account for more of the selection measure content than those considered less important).

KSAs are rated in much the same way as the job tasks; namely, panelists use rating scales to judge the identified KSAs. Most of these scales consist of criteria such as the importance of a KSA for acceptable job performance, whether or not a newly-hired employee must possess a KSA, and the degree to which a KSA distinguishes between superior and adequate performance of a newly-hired employee. This step is important since the KSAs are the basis for inferences about the nature and content of selection measures.

Linking KSAs to Critical Job Tasks

For KSAs to serve as a source for selection measure content, they must be required for the successful performance of critical job tasks. Thus, it must be determined whether the identified KSAs are necessary for at least one important task. KSAs can be linked to tasks in any one of several ways. One common means is to employ a job task by KSA rating matrix. Critical tasks are listed vertically on one side of the matrix, and KSAs are listed horizontally across the top. For each cell in the matrix (i.e., each task–KSA combination), job analysts (e.g., SMEs or KSA rating panelists) judge the importance of each KSA for successful task performance.

So far, the critical job tasks, KSAs needed to perform the job, and relationships among these KSAs and critical job tasks have been identified. The next step in job analysis is to select those KSAs that should be reflected in the selection instruments. The job task and KSA rating information described earlier is used to choose the most relevant KSAs. Those chosen are typically required to meet each of several different rating criteria. For example, each KSA must be (a) rated by the SMEs as important for job success, (b) acknowledged by a majority of the SMEs as essential for a newly-hired employee upon job entry, and (c) linked to the performance of at least one critical job task. KSAs meeting *all* of these screening criteria ultimately define the content of the interview as well as other selection measures.

Choosing Selection Measures

After the KSAs necessary for job performance have been identified, measures for assessing them can be chosen. This process is a judgmental one. Upon reviewing these important KSAs, inferences and judgments determine which type of selection device is best for measuring each important KSA. This process results in a selection plan that shows the techniques to be used to measure the important KSAs of a job. In addition, it reflects the relative emphasis of the KSAs that should compose the content of the selection measures. Table 10.1 displays part of a selection plan that was developed for a public assistance clerk position in state government. From application of the previously described steps, five KSAs were judged most important to successful performance of critical job tasks. The weights assigned to these KSAs were based upon the ratings given by the KSA rating panel in the job analysis. The assigned weights were used in determining the relative emphasis on the content areas of the selection instruments.

Of importance here is the selection interview shown in the selection plan.

TABLE 10.1. A Selection Plan for the Position of Public Assistance Clerk

		Selection Method		
KSA[a]	KSA Weight	Work Sample Test	Selection Interview	Written Test
1. Knowledge of basic business styles for typing correspondence.	15%	10		5
2. Knowledge of arithmetic to include addition, subtraction, multiplication, and division.	15%			15
3. Skill in typing letters and narrative reports at 50 words per minute (corrected for errors).	35%	35		
4. Ability to interact tactfully with agency clients on a face-to-face basis.	20%		20	
5. Ability or willingness to help coworkers, without being told by a supervisor, when client requests are high.	15%		15	
KSA/Selector Method Weight	100%	45%	35%	20%

[a]Knowledge, skills, and abilities.

It was judged that the interview could be used to measure two KSAs: (a) ability to interact tactfully with agency clients face-to-face and (b) ability or willingness to help co-workers, without being told by a supervisor, when client requests are high. Interview data were judged to compose roughly one-third (35%) of the total assessment data to be collected on applicants for the public assistance clerk position.

The Job Content Method: Interview Content

A job analysis and selection plan identify the major content categories of the interview and other selection measures in the form of KSAs. For the interview, what remains is to translate the appropriate KSAs into specific interview questions. One source of these questions is KSA and job task information specified through the job analysis. This information gives a broad frame-of-reference for phrasing the questions. But more specific, detailed information about job incumbent behaviors would help develop not only the questions but also a means for judging applicant responses. Latham et al. (1980; 1984), Janz (1982), and others have shown that the use of critical incidents provides these job behavior details. Critical incidents are more explicit descriptions of job behaviors than task statements. A number of incidents may be associated with any one task statement. If these incidents can be isolated, a clearer, more detailed picture of task performance can be obtained.

Critical incidents are collected in the present interview development method with one important modification: the specification of the job content domain for which the incidents are developed. When critical incidents have been employed in earlier approaches to interview development, SMEs were asked to describe effective and ineffective job behaviors. As discussed earlier, this strategy may result in some important aspects of a job not being adequately covered by the incidents retained. With the present method, SMEs are asked to produce critical incidents in the context of important job tasks and KSAs identified through a preliminary job analysis. Interview questions are then developed from these incidents. To illustrate this process, reference is made to Latham and Wexley's (1981) discussion of critical incidents, and the previous example of KSAs identified for the public assistance clerk position.

Developing Critical Incidents
for Selection Interview KSAs

Critical incidents are descriptions of effective and ineffective job behaviors performed during the recent past. Because they deal with specific job behaviors, critical incidents can be used as a basis for developing interview questions. A series of steps is needed to identify these incidents; these are outlined as follows:

1. A panel of SMEs who have had the opportunity to observe individuals performing the job is assembled. The SMEs review the KSAs to be assessed by the interview as well as the job tasks associated with the KSAs. Then, they are asked to develop a list of effective and ineffective job behaviors they have seen occur which reflect these KSAs and associated tasks.

2. A second group of SMEs is given a listing of the KSAs and associated job tasks as well as a separate listing of the incidents developed in the previous step. They are asked to read each incident and allocate it to the one KSA they believe the incident best illustrates. Incidents that are not allocated to the same KSA by a certain percentage of the judges (e.g., a minimum of 75%) are eliminated.

3. The incidents retained from step 2 are rewritten in the form of questions. In the situational interview, these questions are descriptions of situa-

tions that describe an important behavior on the job. The applicant is asked "How would you handle this situation?" or "What would you have done in this situation?" Sometimes the incidents developed require job experience to deal with them. Schmitt and Ostroff (1986) have provided an example of the preparation of incidents so that job candidates have the experience or knowledge necessary to address them.

4. Panelists are then asked to think of persons whose performance on the job they would rate as outstanding, average, and poor, and to estimate how those persons would respond to each question. Panelists' ratings of the possible answers are made as to whether they represent answers of persons with poor performance (scored 1) or those with outstanding performance (scored 5) records. Ratings of answers with a high degree of interjudge agreement are retained as anchors for a rating scale. The rating scale is used by interviewers in judging applicants' answers to the situational questions.

Translating KSAs into Interview Questions: An Example

Table 10.2 illustrates the translation of a KSA and critical incident into an interview question. The type of question developed is like that used as part of the situational interview. It was formed simply by having SMEs (a) study the relevant tasks associated with the KSA and (b) identify critical incidents that represent the tasks and KSA. Then, a question was phrased to reflect an incident suggested by the SMEs. Other questions could be similarly formed to depict additional incidents developed for the KSA.

The rating scale shown in Table 10.2 represents a means for scoring applicants' responses to the question. Low ratings on the continuum represent less effective responses to the question than do high ratings. As with the question itself, the scoring points were based on SMEs' ratings of answers to the question.

Summary and Future Research Needs

Job analysis has played and will continue to play an important role in the development of effective selection measures. Recent evidence on the selection interview has shown that when job data can be incorporated in the development and application of the method, its effectiveness can be significantly enhanced. An important issue for future research is how job information can best be assimilated to develop an interview.

TABLE 10.2.   Example of an Interview Question and Rating Scale
Developed from Job Task, KSA, and Critical Incident Data
for the Position of Public Assistance Clerk

Important Job Task	Important KSA[a]	Interview Question	Rating Scale
Meets with and assists agency clients through personal contacts in the completion of agency forms, determination of public assistance checks, and interpretation of agency eligibility requirements in order to facilitate distribution of public assistance funds from the state.	Ability to interact tactfully with agency clients on a face-to-face basis.	A client of your state agency walks up to your desk. She says she was told that a check she was due from the agency was sent 5 days ago. She claims she has not received the check. She says she has bills to pay, and no one will help her. She is very angry. How would you handle this situation?	1—Tell her you will try to find the person with whom she talked and you will have that person call her. 2— 3—Apologize and tell her you will have to check into the problem and call her in a day or two. 4— 5—Try to calm her and investigate the problem while she waits.

NOTE: The critical incident on which the interview question was developed is not shown due to space limitations. The interview question itself is an edited version of a description of the incident.

[a]Knowledge, skills, and abilities.

Critical incidents data have provided the job analysis method of choice for those publishing research on interview development. It has been suggested in the present paper that a more complete coverage of the important aspects of a job might be obtained by blending critical incidents data with information on the critical job tasks, as well as the KSAs required for task performance. The Job Content Method is an example of such an approach. With appropriate modifications, the method may also be suitable for other structured interview techniques where critical incidents data have been employed (e.g., the pattern behavior description interview, Janz, 1982).

Future research needs to examine whether the Job Content Method or some other means captures job information important for interview question development that is unaccounted for by other methods. One such project would be to compare the extent of coverage of critical KSAs by the questions developed through the Job Content Method versus those produced by other methods, such as the critical incidents technique. Questions would first be prepared by both methods for the same job. Then, KSAs for that job would be identified by another method, for example, the Job Element Method (Primoff, Clark, & Caplan, 1982). A group of selection specialists could then rate the adequacy of coverage of each KSA by the questions produced by each process. These ratings would then be statistically compared.

Other research should investigate the psychometric properties of the Job Content Method. Inter-interviewer reliability in the evaluation of applicants is of basic importance. A possible method for examining this issue would be to develop questions for a specific job and train a group of interviewers in their use. In a controlled data gathering session, a group of applicants would be interviewed such that each applicant would be individually interviewed by multiple interviewers. Reliability of applicant ratings by the multiple interviewers could then be calculated for the applicants. A variation of this approach could use trained interviewers observing a video-taped replay of an interview. Each interviewer would then independently evaluate the applicant appearing in the film. The validity of evaluations based upon the use of questions from this method should be investigated with a predictive format. A concurrent validity strategy would seem infeasible because of the possible effect of work experience on question responses. In the predictive study, it would seem imperative to use criteria collected for job tasks that require the specific KSAs measured in the interview rather than an overall performance measure.

11

The Patterned Behavior Description Interview: The Best Prophet of the Future Is the Past

Tom Janz
University of Calgary

Personnel professionals and line managers give the interview a strong vote of confidence, both in terms of the frequency and the importance to which it is accorded (Glueck, 1978). Yet, as noted recently (Janz, 1987), almost all the widely used personnel textbooks and over 30 years of academic reviews criticize and even condemn the selection interview as lacking reliability and validity. It leads one to wonder how science and common sense could be so far apart over such an extended period.

One answer draws on the power of meta-analysis (Hunter, Schmidt & Jackson, 1982). When all studies of the interview were lumped together, the average uncorrected validity was .25 for Wagner's 27 studies (Wagner, 1949) and .27 for Wiesner and Cronshaw's 143 studies (Wiesner & Cronshaw, 1988). Wagner and others, without the benefit of recent statistical techniques, concluded that the interview lacked predictive accuracy. With meta-analytic corrections for range restriction and criterion unreliability, Weisner and Cronshaw's population corrected validity rose to a respectable .48. Furthermore, Wiesner and Cronshaw found several important moderators. The most important was interview structure, with population corrected validities of .29 for unstructured and .62 for structured interviews.

This chapter reviews the literature on one particular type of structured interview, the patterned behavior description interview (PBDI), discusses two unpublished studies which compare two specific types of interview content—opinions versus behavior descriptions, and expands on the theoretical arguments for PBDI. Distinctions are made between maximum and typical performance, as introduced by Cronbach (1970), to explain the substantial validity of PBDIs (see Cronshaw and Weisner, this volume).

Behavior Description Theory

Lord Byron coined the phrase "The best prophet of the future is the past" in 1823. In spite of this, research found that both seasoned interviewers (Janz, 1988), and students trained in traditional interview techniques (Janz, 1982), focused mostly on applicant opinions and generalities as opposed to what the applicant's had actually done in the past. The PBDI zeros in on what applicants have accomplished (or failed to accomplish), and how they went about doing it, in situations similar to ones they will face on the job.

An interview information taxonomy developed by Lowell Hellervik (Janz, Hellervik, & Gilmore, 1986, Chapter 3) forms the basis for PBDI. This taxonomy identifies four key types of interview information: (1) credentials—objective verifiable information about the applicant that predicts performance, (2) experience descriptions—surface descriptions of applicants normal or usual duties, capabilities, responsibilities, or practices, (3) opinions (including self-perceptions and hypothetical questions)—applicants' thoughts about their strengths, weaknesses, plans, goals, and intentions, and (4) behavior descriptions—detailed accounts of actual events from applicants' job and life experiences.

Behavior description theory holds that of the four key types of interview information, only behavior descriptions offer practical, clear data on which to base predictions of future performance. Credentials also predict future performance, as research on biodata clearly shows (Hunter & Hunter, 1984), but it can be gathered more efficiently using the application form. Time in the interview is too precious to be taken up by "closed-ended" factual questions. Experience descriptions do expose areas for deeper probing, but do not reveal how well the applicant performed the duties or practices described. Opinions allow the applicant to create a good impression by telling the interviewer what the applicant thinks the interviewer wants to hear. Applicants with above average verbal and inductive reasoning abilities may outshine applicants with lesser such abilities but whose job performance would be more valuable to the organization in the long run.

Behavior descriptions reveal specific choices applicants have made in the past, and the circumstances surrounding those choices. The interviewer probes the details of the situation and what the applicant did in that situation, or what the applicant did the next time that same situation arose. Only then can the interviewer independently judge how well the applicant performed in that situation. From that basis, the interviewer can then check the typicality of this particular set of circumstances and actions to build a picture of the applicant's behavior patterns. The more recent and the more long-standing the applicant's behavior pattern in the past, the more likely it will predict behavior in the future.

Single Study Research:
Behavior-Based Structured Interviews

The research trail leading to the development of patterned behavior description interviewing originated with an article by Mass (1965). He argued for critical incident analysis as the basis for asking better interview questions. Mass suggested that the scaled behavior expectation procedure created for measuring job performance be applied to developing benchmark answers against which to rate an applicant's interview answers. He reported high interviewer agreement in two data sets.

Latham, Saari, Pursell, and Campion (1980) carried the behavior-based notion a step further. They turned critical incidents—stories of effective and ineffective job behavior—into interview questions. They called their approach "situational interviewing." For example, one incident described an employee who called in sick because his wife was away and his child came down with the flu. Latham et al. turned this into an interview question by asking applicants what they would do if their spouse was away visiting parents and their 8 year old child came down with the flu.

The situational interview approach develops benchmark answers to these open-ended questions. Continuing the example, an answer like "I would stay home with my kid" is benchmarked low on the response scale whereas an answer like "I would phone a neighbor and ask her to check in on my kid so I could make my shift" is benchmarked at a high score. Latham et al. (1980) reported high interviewer reliabilities (.71 and .67) and significant correlations with job performance measures (.46 and .30).

The situational interview asks the applicant "what would you do IF." In contrast, the patterned behavior description interview (PBDI) asks the applicant "what did you do WHEN" (Janz, 1982; Janz et al. 1986). PBDI interview patterns start with the same pool of critical incidents as the situational interview. Instead of forming questions that ask the applicant to provide hypothetical responses, the PBDI asks the applicant to recall the most satisfying, most disappointing, most frustrating or most recent time in the applicant's past similar to the situation described in one of the critical incidents. The situational interviewer asks applicants, "What would you do IF your spouse was away visiting her parents and your 8-year-old child came down with the flu?" A PBDI interviewer asks "Tell me about the most recent time you had to miss work and stay at home. What was the reason? What did you do?"

The situational interview is an improvement (see also Latham & Saari, 1984) over unstructured interviews or even structured interviews that dwell mainly on applicant opinions. Still, applicants with above average verbal reasoning, fluency, and inductive reasoning should respond with greater agility to the hypothetical questions posed by the situational interview. Thus their stated intentions could well depart from their ultimate job behavior. The applicant may know what to do, but will he or she do it when the time comes? Worse yet, in spite of reasonable human efforts to keep the bench-marked answers a secret, this author has learned that after a few months the answers often leak out, reducing the validity of situational interview predictions. On the positive side, situational interviews do not require that the applicant has past experience that samples future settings, an advantage for some applicants.

Two research studies directly support the validity of the PBDI method. Janz (1982) compared traditional, unstructured interviews with behavior description interviews. One group of eight senior undergraduate business students was trained in traditional interview techniques (i.e., establishing rapport, active listening, and so on). Another group of students was trained in PBDI interviewing. The position studied was Teaching Assistant. The criterion was the TAs student performance rating administered at the end of the semester. Forty-five of the 60 interviews were successfully tape recorded and analyzed. While the traditional interviewers obtained PBDI answers about 4% of the time, PBDI interviewers raised that percentage to 33%. Traditionally trained interviewers obtained experience descriptions (generalities) and opinion answers to 80% of their questions.

The traditional interviewers showed higher inter-rater agreement (.71 versus .46), indicating that when two traditionally trained interviewers rated the same applicant, their assessments correlated more highly with each other than when two PBDI trained interviewers were rating the same applicant. However, PBDI interview predictions of the teaching assistant's end-of-term student ratings (validity) was both statistically and substantially higher (.54 versus .07). This result confuses readers, since reliability and validity are often thought to go hand in hand. Of course, they need not. Reliability does not set an upper limit on the correlation of a variable with another variable, but that upper limit is the square root of the reliability.

Janz (1982), sifting through the data, suggested that the traditional interviewers agreed more often because they operated with a simple stereotype of a successful business administration teaching assistant—a stereotype based mainly on "downtown experience." The PBDI trained interviewers, operating with a more complex process, agreed less often, but their disagreements more often bracketed the TA's ultimate student rating—the criterion in this case. TAs with business experience looked more like business people, but were less willing to communicate with students and guide them through the problems they were there to solve.

The relatively small sample size (30 interviews), the academic setting, and the non-random assignment of subjects to interview conditions weakened the Janz (1982) study. Orpen (1985) corrected these deficiencies in a replication of the Janz (1982) design conducted for predicting life insurance sales success. He randomly assigned potential interviewers to two conditions: (1) behavior description training, and (2) traditional interview training. He ensured that both training programs took the same length of time and offered similar opportunities to practice. Orpen measured two job criteria: (a) value of insurance sales, and (b) supervisor's ratings. The results echoed the Janz (1982) finding, and offered even stronger support where they differed.

For the criterion of supervisor's ratings, Orpen (1985) reported the PBDI validity at .56 versus .08 for traditional, unstructured interviews. For the criterion of the dollar value of policies sold, Orpen found a PBDI interview validity (i.e., average of two PBDI ratings) of .72 versus .10 for unstructured interviews (i.e., average of two traditional interview ratings).

Opinions Versus Behavior Descriptions: Two Studies

To investigate the effects of interview content separate from the effects of interview structure, two studies were conducted to directly compare the validity and the current usage of structured questions that tap applicant opinions versus questions that tap behavior descriptions (Janz, 1988). The core independent variable was type of interview question—opinion versus behavior description.

In the first study, fourteen human resource (HR) professionals reviewed and rated the importance they would place on each of eight questions (4 opinion, 4 behavior description) for interviewing a secretary/receptionist, and then watched two videotapes of an applicant actually responding to the eight questions. As hypothesized in Janz (1988), the opinion questions were rated as more popular and important to interview judgment by the HR professionals. When ratings of the videotaped applicants were correlated with actual performance ratings of job incumbents, the behavior description question composite correlated .64 with the supervisor's ratings while the opinion composite correlated .56. The greater validity falls to behavior description questions, though this difference did not reach significance at the .05 level. Interestingly though, HR professionals who placed greater importance on behavior description questions had interview ratings that were significantly ($P \leq .01$) closer to the clerical supervisor's performance ratings than HR professionals who placed more weight on opinion questions.

One post hoc explanation for the lack of significant difference in opinion versus behavior description question validities may be the applicant role played by each secretary. In an attempt to achieve stimulus person variation, the author sought out stimulus persons to represent the high and low end of the performance scale, based on general performance reputation. As it turned out, the stimulus persons differed in more than just performance, with the low scoring person talking slower, evading the questions more often, and appearing distinctly less attractive than the high end target person. Consequently, the strength of the independent variable (i.e., type of interview information) was confounded with other differences between the stimulus persons.

As a follow up to this study, Janz (1988) employed a similar methodology with the following modifications: (1) five stimulus persons representing varying levels of performance were taped and three were selected to represent top, middle and bottom third sectors, avoiding extreme scores in either direction based on pre-tests, (2) the stimulus persons were senior business students video taped while interviewing for paid teaching assistant positions, (3) the subjects were 27 senior business students enrolled in a personnel management class in workforce planning, (4) the average rating on a 5 point percentile scale over all interview questions for each applicant made by two senior teaching assistants and two professors formed the criterion scores.

The average inter-correlation among expert ratings which formed the criterion was .84, and the mean student rating correlated .89 with the mean expert rating. In study two the range of stimulus person performance was reduced. Thus, with normal ranges of stimulus variance, study two presented a more powerful setting to examine the relative predictive strength of opinion versus behavior description answers. The expert-rated criterion score correlated .45 ($p \leq .01$) with the sum of the behavior description question ratings and .03 (ns) with the opinion composite.

Taken together, these two studies revealed that human resource professionals currently make greater use of, and place greater weight on, opinion based versus behavior-based questions; yet, opinion questions proved less predictive of criterion ratings. These results call for a major shift away from opinion questions (Janz, 1982), and toward a greater emphasis on behavior description questions. Still, some interview time should be retained to probe applicant credentials, general experiences, and opinions.

Current Theories and Future Research

Why do PBDIs predict job performance well when traditional, unstructured interviews do not? When should the situational interview's validity meet or exceed the validity obtainable by PBDIs? When should carefully constructed PBDIs achieve higher or lower validity than a carefully constructed battery of cognitive ability tests? When will combining PBDI and ability assessments prove more effective, than using either one alone? These practical questions require a good theory to supply answers.

In this volume, Cronshaw and Weisner describe a model for selection validation originally introduced by Schwab (1980). They offer convincing arguments in support of strong I - I′ and I - C links for PBDIs, particularly when one distinguishes between maximum and typical performance (Cronbach, 1970). Maximum performance captures how effectively people perform mental, interpersonal, or psychomotor tasks when they are highly motivated to achieve their best. Typical performance captures how people choose to perform under prevailing motivational conditions. In other words, maximum performance focuses on competencies, whereas typical performance focuses on choices.

The maximum versus typical performance distinction applies to both the I (independent) and C (criterion) sides of the causal model. The relative strength of maximum versus typical variance components at the criterion construct level needs to be reflected in the operational measures of the criterion, otherwise the predictor-criterion relationships will not reflect the ultimate criterion.

On the criterion (C) side, the construct or ultimate criterion for a selection decision remains the expected value of annual performance contributions that would be rendered to the organization by each applicant. Variance among applicants' true scores on the ultimate criterion could be decomposed by the following model (all terms in standard score metric):

$$Y(C) = MAX(C)*Wt1 + TYP(C)*Wt2 \text{ where:}$$

$Y(C)$ is the applicant's true ultimate criterion score in standard score metric,
$MAX(C)$ is the applicant's true score on a composite of job relevant maximum performance dimensions,
$Wt1$ is the beta weight for $MAX(C)$,
$TYP(C)$ is the applicant's true choice pattern on a composite of job related choice scenarios, and
$Wt2$ is the beta weight for $TYP(C)$.

The ultimate criterion construct reflects how much value the applicant actually produces. For some jobs such as computer programmer, geophysicist, designated hitter, TV evangelist, or concert pianist, scoring high on the ultimate criterion likely places a heavier weight on competencies—be they cognitive, interpersonal, or psychomotor. For other jobs less demanding of maximum performance, such as taxi driver, cabin attendant, department store sales staff, or data entry operator, the ultimate criterion probably depends more heavily on behavioral choice consistencies.

Operationally, empirical measures of the ultimate criterion can load heavily on either maximum or typical components of the criterion. Immediate supervisor's performance ratings, especially when gathered using clearly defined dimensions and averaged over two or three rating occasions, likely come closest to capturing the true, long-term value added by an employee (Meyer, 1987). Paper and pencil tests of job knowledge following new hire training programs or the new "hands on" measures of performance on complex physical tasks (e.g., army tank crew drills) likely load heavily on maximum performance or competency variance. Thus, these criterion measures capture what people can do when motivation to perform is high, but fail to include what people will choose to do under more typical motivational conditions.

Stated another way, the operational measures of the ultimate criterion can distort the true weights Wt1 and Wt2, if the operational measures load too heavily on either maximum or typical performance. As a result, one might presume to have captured all of the predictable job performance with a given class of predictor (e.g., cognitive abilities), when in actuality one has succeeded only in measuring the criterion construct too narrowly.

All of this concern over decomposing criterion measures into maximum versus typical variance components would be much ado about nothing if maximum performance correlated highly with typical performance. A recent study by Sackett, Zedeck, and Fogli (1988) has suggested they do not. They developed highly reliable measures of both maximum and typical performance for supermarket cashiers who used the new laser scanning cash registers. Measures of maximum performance were gathered with investigators present using direct observation, thus maximizing motivation. Then, unobtrusive measures of scanning speed were collected by the scanning computer, allowing for the direct comparison. While reliabilities for both measures were high, the correlation for new employees was .16 and for seasoned cashiers was 0.36—both low enough to warrant substantial caution in assuming that criterion measures loading only on maximum performance adequately tap the ultimate criterion construct.

Why Traditional Interviews Poorly Predict
Actual Job Performance

First, Cronshaw and Wiesner suggested in this volume that one reason for the poor performance of traditional interviews lies in a poorly executed link between the interviewers' constructs (or lack of any clear constructs) and the actual measure of those constructs. While many interviewers seek to assess an applicant's technical competence and ability to work with existing staff (via matching the personalities of applicants to existing key staff), research suggests that what they actually do in interviews (i.e., probe applicants typical experiences and opinions) has little value for measuring these constructs. Thus, a weak I - I' relationship undermines the validity of traditional interviews.

Beyond this, the objective of assessing applicant personality fit represents an operational construct that, even if traditional interviews measured validly, may not weigh heavily on the ultimate criterion. After all, the new-hire will work with the hiring supervisor only for a period of time, and then will move on to work for and with other organizational members. Certainly, a poor or abrasive fit between the hiring supervisor and the new-hire would not facilitate the delicate process of new-hire orientation and acculturation. This paragraph has argued that applicants with strong abilities, congruent values, and needed skills should not be screened out simply because their personalities differ from the hiring supervisor.

Also, traditional interviewers may often focus on the "here and now"—how well the applicant responds to the stresses and demands of the interview itself (Janz, 1982). Because the ultimate criterion is long term value added, such a focus is too narrow. Thus, the criterion constructs of some interviewers may further undermine traditional interview validity by weakening the I - C causal link.

Cognitive Ability Tests and Interviews:
When Each Pays Off

Cognitive ability tests get at maximum performance, and they do it efficiently. Costs of administering and scoring the tests fall far below the costs of developing, conducting, and scoring PBDIs. If the true weight for maximum performance dimensions dominates the ultimate criterion (Wt1 0.70), then ability tests likely represent the best initial payoff, if tests versus interviews were the only two choices.

However, unless Wt2 falls very low, it may still make economic sense to use a two-stage combination of ability tests and interviews. Paper and pencil tests of some maximum performance factors (e.g., basic cognitive abilities) can be administered effectively and efficiently to groups, and thus serve a valuable screening function. Screening decisions form a critical intermediate step between the initial pile of resumes and the 4-6 people advanced to the short list for hiring decisions. McDaniel and Schmidt (1985) found that even systematic training and experience ratings based on resumes yielded only a .17 meta-analytic validity. Raising the validity of screening decisions through a cognitive ability screen would allow the interview to focus on the typical performance topics not captured by tests. The result should yield higher overall selection validity and pay off to the extent that typical performance factors weigh in the ultimate criterion.

By probing specific past accomplishments for demonstrated competencies as well as choice patterns, PBDIs can tap both maximum and typical criterion variance. Thus, perfectly conducted PBDIs should always be able to outperform ability tests, since tests don't tap typical performance. Of course, neither PBDI's nor cognitive ability tests obtain perfect reliabilities, but the reliability of cognitive ability tests over different test administrators likely exceeds the reliability of PBDI interviews over different interviewers.

Though it is too early to speculate on how large the typical performance weight (Wt2) needs to be before PBDIs pay off, future research will establish guidelines for specific job families. PBDIs often cost more to administer than tests, so they must outperform tests by a large enough utility margin to cover their increased costs. Also, as mentioned above, ability tests likely obtain higher reliabilities. Both factors suggest the Wt2 needs to exceed some threshold value before PBDIs can add to the prediction of performance beyond what can be obtained from ability tests alone. New exhaustive studies of performance criteria will clarify what the relative weights of maximum versus typical performance are in the ultimate criterion of job performance value. The larger the weight of typical performance in the ultimate criterion, the more likely PBDIs will yield a better net after-tax present value than maximum performance tests.

Three PBDI Research and Development Needs

First, replications of the Janz (1982) and Orpen (1985) studies with a wider range of occupations from routine to managerial jobs are needed. In addition to the variables examined in the Janz and Orpen designs, researchers should determine the maximum versus typical performance structure of the jobs they study, choosing jobs that represent different levels of Wt1 and Wt2.

Second, clear and direct comparisons of situational versus PBD interviewing are needed across jobs that sample a range of maximum versus typical performance weightings. Where maximum performance dominates the ultimate criterion, situational interviews should do as well as PBDIs. As the weight for typical performance rises, the theory advanced above suggests an advantage for PBDI, since situational interviews likely load more heavily on verbal and inductive reasoning abilities than do PBDIs. Also, research should investigate the use of benchmark answers, a situational interview concept, in PBDIs. Once an initial round of PBD interviews has been completed, the interviewer's notes could be assessed to determine high, average, and low answers to questions from the BD pattern. These benchmark answers would be useful for improving the reliability of PBDI answer ratings, and for training new interviewers.

Third, basic research is needed into the memory, attentional, and physiological processes associated with applicant responses to opinion versus behavior description questions. It might be hypothesized that applicants draw on entirely different attentional processes when responding to an opinion versus a behavioral description question. Physiological measures, and measures of attentional load, may show a high level of mental processing throughout an opinion answer (i.e., the applicant is figuring out how to say what the interviewer wants to hear). Attentional load during PBDI answers may be high initially, while the applicant is trying to locate the incident in memory, but should then fall off during recall. Also, mean applicant response delays to subsequent probes should be short for BD answers, but much longer for opinions.

12

The Reliability, Validity, and Practicality of the Situational Interview

Gary P. Latham
University of Washington

One of the first exhaustive literature reviews on the selection interview appeared in 1949 (Wagner, 1949). The evidence showed that the interview lacked both reliability and validity. In the next two decades, seminal research (e.g., Webster, 1964) was conducted to understand why this was the case. Among the findings were that applicants were not asked the same questions, and when they were asked the same questions, the questions were often not job related. When the same job related questions were asked, the "correct" answers were usually transparent to the applicant. When the correct answers were not obvious to applicants, they were usually not obvious to the interviewers either. Thus, two decades later, literature reviews of the interview showed that the reliability and validity of the interview were still low (Mayfield, 1964; Ulrich & Trumbo, 1965).

The research by Webster (1964) and his colleagues was particularly helpful in identifying observation-judgmental errors that interviewers make when evaluating others. This research was seminal in that it stimulated investigations on ways to train people to increase their objectivity in evaluating others (e.g., Hedge & Kavanagh, 1988; Latham, Wexley, & Pursell 1975; Wexley, Sanders, & Yukl, 1973). However, the results of these subsequent studies affected performance appraisal practices far more than they did the selection interview (Latham, 1986, 1988; Latham & Wexley, 1981). Thus by the end of the 1970s, there was no appreciable improvement in the reliability and validity of the interview (Arvey & Campion, 1982). In 1980, the first study on the situational interview appeared in the empirical literature (Latham, Saari, Pursell, & Campion, 1980). The method was shown to be both reliable and valid (Tenopyr & Oeltjen, 1982).

AUTHOR'S NOTE: The author wishes to thank Dawn Winters and Terence Mitchell for their critical review of this chapter. Preparation of this chapter was made possible by Ford Motor Research Affiliate funding to the author.

The purpose of the present chapter is fivefold. First, a behind-the-scenes view of the history that led to the development of the situational interview is presented. Second, the procedure for developing the situational interview is given. Third, research on the reliability and validity of the technique and the extent to which it is biased is summarized. Fourth, the practicality of this method relative to unstructured and structured interviews is examined. Finally, future research streams emanating from the situational interview are identified.

History

Skinner (1956) has argued that meaningful research findings are often obtained serendipitously. For example, laboratory apparatus breakdowns revealed the effects of previously unknown reinforcement schedules on animal behavior. Serendipity, through a snowstorm and a missed airplane, contributed to the development of the situational interview.

In December, 1975, Weyerhaeuser Company was considering the purchase of a sawmill in the South. Late on a Friday afternoon, in Tacoma, the present author was told to be in the South by early Monday morning to assist a Weyerhaeuser team in determining which hourly sawmill employees should be retained. It was suggested that the insights that this author could provide as the company's staff psychologist would prove helpful. However, one person's insights, even if those of the company's staff psychologist, are probably no better than the next person's. What to do?

On Sunday evening, stranded in a St. Louis airport due to a snowstorm, this author longed for the days with the American Pulpwood Association where critical incident studies of pulpwood producers were conducted (Latham, 1969), and goal setting techniques had been successfully applied to increase productivity (Latham & Kinne, 1974; Ronan, Latham, & Kinne, 1973). Whether it was serendipity or a replication of the problem solving ability of Kohler's (1927) insightful chimpanzees, the situational interview suddenly took shape: present people with critical incidents from a job analysis where the answers are not obvious and the questions are job related. In this way their intentions would be discerned. Get interviewers to develop a scoring guide for evaluating the answers to these questions. Put the scoring guide in writing under each question so all the interviewers play by the same rules. Pray that no one notices the nervousness of the psychologist who has had his Ph.D. for less than 2 years.

Situational Interview

To the author's knowledge, the situational interview is among the very few, if not the only, interview technique grounded in theory. The theory, goal setting (Locke, 1968; Locke & Latham, 1984), states that intentions or goals are the immediate precursor of a person's behavior. The purpose of the situational interview is to identify a potential employee's intentions by presenting that person with a series of job-related incidents, and asking what he or she would do in that situation. The steps for developing a situational interview are as follows:

(1) Conduct a job analysis using the critical incident technique (Flanagan, 1954).

(2) Develop an appraisal instrument such as behavioral observation scales (Latham & Wexley, 1977, 1981) based on the job analysis.

(3) Select one or more incidents that formed the basis for the development of the performance criteria (e.g., cost consciousness) which constitutes the appraisal instrument.

(4) Turn each critical incident into a "what would you do if . . ." question.

(5) Develop a scoring guide to facilitate agreement among interviewers on what constitutes a good (5), acceptable (3), or an unacceptable (1) response to each question. If a 2 and 4 anchor can also be developed, do so.

(6) Review the questions for comprehensiveness in terms of covering the material identified in the job analysis and summarized on the appraisal instrument.

(7) Conduct a pilot study to eliminate questions where applicant/interviewees give the same answers, or where interviewers cannot agree on the scoring.

(8) Conduct a criterion-related validity study when feasible to do so.

As noted in step 4, critical incidents are the basis of the situational question. An example of a critical incident is the following:

> The company was trying to bring about a culture that valued team playing. The manager hurt his own bottom line for the quarterly review by cooperating with a peer who badly needed some of his resources. Specifically, the manager sold the product internally to the peer for a much lower cost than would have been obtained on the external market.

Literary license is taken with an incident to turn it into a situational question where the wording is not biased against people who are unfamiliar with internal company operations. A scoring guide is developed which contains acceptable answers illustrating a 5, 3, and 1 response. The result with regard to the above incident is shown in Table 12.1. The applicants are not shown the scoring guide, nor are they informed of the dimension that is being assessed.

The interview is conducted by a panel of two or more people. One person reads the question. All members of the panel record the answers. A typical panel consists of two managers of the job for which the applicant is applying, and a person from human resources.

Reliability and Validity

At least eight studies have examined the psychometric characteristics of the situational interview. Three studies were conducted by Latham et. al. (1980), two by Latham and Saari (1984), one by Weekley and Gier (1987), one by Maurer and Fay (1988), and another by Campion, Pursell, and Brown (1988). The data on reliability and validity are shown in Table 12.2.

TABLE 12.1. An Example of a Situational Question and Scoring Guide

You are in charge of truck drivers in Philadelphia. Your colleague is in charge of truck drivers 800 miles away in Atlanta. Both of you report to the same person. Your salary and bonus are affected 100% by your costs. Your buddy is in desperate need of one of your trucks. If you say no, your costs will remain low and your group will probably win the Golden Flyer award for the quarter. If you say yes, the Atlanta group will probably win this prestigious award because they will make a significant profit for the company. Your boss is preaching costs, costs, costs as well as cooperation with one's peers. Your boss has no control over accounting who are the score keepers. Your boss is highly competitive, he or she rewards winners. You are just as competitive, you are a real winner!

Explain what you would do?

Record answer:

_____

_____

_____

_____

Scoring Guide
(1) I would go for the award. I would explain the circumstances to my buddy and get his or her understanding.
(3) I would get my boss' advice.
(5) I would loan the truck to my buddy. I'd get recognition from my boss and my buddy that I had sacrificed my rear-end for theirs. Then I'd explain the logic to my people.

The criteria used in the validity studies included behavioral observation scales (BOS) in both the Latham (Latham et al., 1980; Latham & Saari, 1984) and the Campion et al. (1988) studies, and hard criterion measures, namely sales volume, in the study by Weekly and Gier (1987). The samples included unionized hourly workers, applicants for a sales position, and first line supervisors. The validation studies were conducted separately for whites and nonwhites, and males and females (Latham et. al., 1980). Campion et al. (1988) evaluated test fairness using a moderated regression strategy, which assessed equality of intercepts and slopes. Intercept differences were tested by adding race to the equation, and the slope differences were tested by adding the race by interview interaction to the equation. A similar analysis was conducted for the applicant's sex. The results indicated a significant intercept difference for race, but a plot of the separate regression lines indicated a common line slightly over-predicted (i.e., was not unfair) for minority applicants. No slope or intercept differences were obtained for sex.

At least five conclusions can be drawn from Table 12.2. First, the situational interview has adequate interobserver reliability and internal consistency. The high interobserver reliability coefficients are undoubtedly a result of the behaviorally-based scoring guide. The term scoring guide, rather than key, is used because an applicant need not state literally what is written in the guide to receive a specific numerical evaluation. The internal consistency estimates would undoubtedly be higher if the overall interview score were not treated as a composite, but rather the questions were broken into subscales corresponding to the specific criterion that each is trying to predict. If this were done, the number of scales would increase dramatically and internal consistency should increase as well. Thus the extant evidence for reliability is probably a conservative estimate.

Values from the Maurer and Fay (1988) study are not shown in Table 12.2 because their data were reported in terms of standard deviations. In brief, the authors showed that variability was significantly lower among interviewers who used the situational rather than a conventional interview.

Second, investigations are needed on the method's test-retest reliability. The correlation of .04 in the Latham and Saari (1984) study was not significantly different from zero. Nevertheless, this value yielded a meaningful conclusion serendipitously. The predictive validity coefficient in that study was .14. This coefficient is identical to the value obtained by Hunter and Hunter (1984) in their meta-analysis of the interview literature.

An investigation was undertaken to learn why the validity coefficient was low relative to other research studies of the situational interview. The initial step involved assessing the test-retest reliability of the technique. The r of .04 led to intensive debrief interviews of the interviewers. The inter-

TABLE 12.2. Reliability and Validity of the Situational Interview by Employee Type

Study	Sample Type	N	Internal Consistency	Reliability Inter-observer	Test-Retest	Concurrent Validity	Predictive Validity	Construct
Latham et al. (1980)	Union Sawmill Workers							
	(Males)	49	.71	.76		.46		
	Supervisors	63	.67	.79		.30		
	Union Pulp Workers							
	Blacks	56	.70	.87			.33	
	Females	30	.78	.82			.39	
Latham & Saari (1984)	Clerical	29	.73	.81				
					(Supervisors)	.39		
					(Peers)	.42		
	Newsprint Hrly. Empl.	157					.14	
		29		.90	.04	.40		
Weekley & Gier (1987)	Retail Sales Applicants	54	.61	.84			.45	
Mauer & Fay (1988)	Managers	42						
Campion et al. (1988)	Union Pulp Mill Workers	149	.72	.88			.34	
	Blacks	57						
	Females	30						
Lin & Manligas (1988)	Custodians			.96				
	Whites	61						
	Blacks	825						
	Hispanics	274						

viewers had followed the steps outlined above for developing a situational interview. However, they did not use the scoring guide for evaluating the response to each question. Instead, they simply recorded their overall impression of each applicant.

This finding underscores the importance of a behaviorally-based scoring guide. When the scoring guide is not used to evaluate each response to each question, the situational interview is no better than other interview techniques evaluated by Hunter and Hunter (1984). The retesting of the applicants for whom the scoring guide was used properly yielded a concurrent validity coefficient of .40. Subsequent research should identify whether it is the tapping of behavioral intentions, the use of a behavioral scoring guide, or the job relevancy of the questions, or all three that make the situational interview reliable and valid.

A third conclusion that can be drawn from Table 12.2 is that significant validity coefficients can be obtained with relatively small sample sizes. This is one indicator of the procedure's practicality. Most criterion-related validity studies require sample sizes in excess of 100 people to obtain significant coefficients (see also Schmidt & Hunter, 1983). This requirement is simply infeasible for all but very large organizations.

One reason why the validity of the situational interview has been easy to demonstrate is that most investigators have adhered to Wernimont and Campbell's (1968) plea to develop predictors that are not only realistic samples of behavior, but are as similar to the criteria as possible. In seven of the eight studies reviewed here, the performance criteria have consisted of observable behaviors derived from the same job analysis used to develop the situational questions (see Feild and Gatewood, this volume).

An exception to the use of behavioral criteria is the study by Weekley and Gier (1987). The danger in using only hard criterion measures (e.g., cost related outcomes or economic constructs) is the possibility of committing a Type II error, namely rejecting the hypothesis that there is a significant relationship between the predictor and the criterion when one actually exists. This danger exists because hard criteria are often contaminated in that they are affected by factors beyond the control of the individual employee (Campbell, Dunnette, Lawler, & Weick, 1970; Latham, 1986).

A fourth conclusion is that studies are needed on the construct validity of this interview technique. To what extent is the situational interview tapping cognitive abilities, interpersonal skills, or both? The implicit hypothesis of this technique is that the underlying construct being measured is behavioral intentions. That is, to the extent that applicants cannot discern the answer the interviewer desires, they are presumably forced to state their true intentions. Intentions correlate significantly with behavior. It is likely that these intentions are affected by, or related to, certain cognitive abilities and sociability skills. Cognitive abilities should certainly account for situational questions of a technical nature (e.g., "What would you do if one gauge in the nuclear plant showed 'x' and two others showed 'y' ?"). Thus, cognitive ability tests might explain why some people do better in situational interviews than others.

A fifth conclusion that can be drawn from Table 12.2 is that criterion-related validity studies have been done with relatively low level jobs. This undoubtedly reflects the sample size constraints that exist with high level jobs. This problem could be overcome in industry-wide consortium studies. In addition, the situational interview could be included as a component of assessment center studies where the average validity of the latter ranges from .30-.49 (Cohen, Moses, & Byham, 1974). Where neither is possible, many companies that use the situational interview for selecting executives take steps to show the content validity of the procedure. Precedent for this can be found in *Harless v. Duck* (see also Arvey, 1979), where 43% of the female applicants failed the interview compared to 15% of the males. The police department successfully defended their case by showing that they used a structured interview which consisted of hypothetical questions simulating situations likely to be encountered on the job. The department also showed that the questions focused on dimensions exemplified through a job analysis that differentiated among persons who would be better patrol officers than others.

Freedom from Bias

Thorndike (1949) posited four criteria for evaluating a measurement instrument, namely validity, reliability, freedom from bias, and practicality. With regard to freedom from bias, Maurer and Fay (1988) found that training designed to reduce rating errors such as halo (e.g., Fay & Latham, 1982) was not necessary for reducing variability among interviewers who used the situational interview. In another study, Maurer and Fair (in press) found the situational interview exhibited interobserver reliability that was resistant to such rating errors as similar-to-me, first impressions, positive and negative leniency, and contract effects.

Lin and Manligas (1988) found that, relative to a traditional structured interview, the "situational interview had a positive impact on reducing rater race effects in the interview process" (p. 14). Hispanic applicants received significantly lower interview scores ($X = 78.43$) than white ($X = 83.52$) and black applicants ($X = 82.57$), but this was due to their difficulty in comprehending English. And as was noted earlier, Campion et al. (1988) found that the technique was not biased in favor of race or sex of the applicant.

Practicality

With regard to an instrument's practicality, it is not known whether researchers, journal editors, or both have ignored this issue. There is, however, a paucity of studies on this subject. The necessity of accounting for practicality was cogently pointed out by Dreher and Sackett (1983). An industry consortium had commissioned the development and validation of a selection battery for a given job. After the validity of the battery had been demonstrated, it was not used because aspects of the tests did not "make sense" to the key decision makers in those companies.

From the applicant's perspective, Sackett and Dreher (1982) have also found that the face validity of a selection device affects the decision of college students regarding the fairness and appropriateness of the device. The issue of fairness has implications for the probability of lawsuits being filed based on Title VII of the 1964 Civil Rights Act.

The potential for lawsuits is particularly a problem with the use of a selection interview due to the frequent findings of low reliability and validity (Arvey, 1979). This problem may be exacerbated when an unstructured interview is used, and applicants perceive that different people are asked different questions. The problem may be exacerbated even when a structured interview is used if applicants perceive that they are asked the same questions, but that their responses to the questions are evaluated differently. Thus, there is a need for researchers to know how their selection instruments are perceived by applicants as well as by users.

In summary, the purpose of a selection interview, as with any selection instrument, is threefold. First the procedure must consistently identify people who can do the job. Second, the method used in making selection decisions must be able to withstand legal challenges. Third, the method must be viewed as practical if it is to avoid being discarded by managers. Consequently, Latham and Finnegan (1987) conducted a study to identify the practicality of the unstructured, structured or patterned, and situational interviews as perceived by users and applicants, and to identify the reasons for their perceptions. Practicality was defined as the ease or likelihood with which each group perceived that their objectives would be obtained using a given interview method.

Users were defined broadly as falling into one of three categories. First, interviewers who have used each of the three interview methods were identified in two international companies. The job titles included line vice presidents and personnel managers. The second group of users were managers who had no experience with the situational interview, but who did do unstructured and patterned interviewing of applicants. Thus, these individuals were categorized as potential users of the situational interview. These people were included in the study specifically to determine the salability (Smith, 1976) of the situational interview relative to the two alternatives.

The second user group were potential applicants (i.e., college students in a senior-level management and organization class). These people were selected because they would be interviewing for jobs upon graduation. A second group of applicants consisted of people who worked for a company that uses unstructured, patterned, and situational interviews. These individuals were selected because they had actually experienced, as applicants, the three interview formats. The third user group consisted of attorneys who practice Title VII related litigation in the Seattle metropolitan area. Attorneys were defined as users because they are called upon by clients to defend the method used to make a selection decision.

The results showed that both groups of managers preferred the patterned interview to the unstructured interview, and they viewed the situational interview as significantly better than the patterned interview in meeting their needs. Specifically, both groups rated items above 4.0 on a 5-point scale having to do with the situational interview allowing them to appear organized and prepared to the applicant, determining whether the applicant has the ability to perform the job, being able to compare the applicants on an objective basis, and being able to hire or reject the applicant on solely job related reasons. The situational interview received the lowest rating relative to the patterned and unstructured interviews on ease of preparation. This is because the situational interview does in fact require at least one day to develop, in contrast to an unstructured interview which can be done on the spur of the moment.

The employee hires did not view one interview method as preferable to another, but college students rated the unstructured interview as significantly more appealing than the patterned and situational interviews, ostensibly because the unstructured interview allowed them to say everything they wanted to say. Thus, they viewed the interview experience as a personal selling opportunity. Moreover, if this opportunity was not to be realized, they indicated that the use of an unstructured interview would more likely enable them to win a lawsuit.

Practicality for attorneys was defined in terms of ease of supporting a client's decision in court. Attorneys rated the situational interview as most easy to defend, and the unstructured interview as least easy to defend in the courtroom. They stressed the importance of being able to show that the questions were based on a job analysis, and representative of the types of occurrences that the applicant would encounter on the job, that the evaluation was unaffected by the biases of the interviewers, and that all applicants were asked the same questions. On all items, the situational interview was rated by the attorneys as significantly better than the two alternatives.

The value of presenting utility analyses to executives as questionable (Guion & Gibson, 1988; Latham, 1986, 1988). For example, Tenopyr

(1987) reported that managers are unimpressed with utility estimates. Nevertheless, Campion et al. (1988) estimated the gain in utility from using the situational interview over random selection based on formulas suggested by Schmidt, Hunter, McKenzie, and Muldrow (1979). Their conclusion was:

> Relevant data included interviewer time and administrative costs of $30 per applicant, selection ratio of .62, average standard score on the interview of those selected of .42, and validity coefficients of .34 uncorrected and .56 corrected. The standard deviation of job performance in dollar terms was estimated at $5,000 per year by supervisors using the Schmidt et .al direct estimate technique. This value was 33% of annual mean wages, which was slightly below the 40% estimate often discussed in utility research (Schmidt & Hunter, 1983; Outerbridge & Trattner, 1986). Using these figures, the one-year utility from the 149 hires was estimated at approximately $100,000 using the uncorrected validity. Assuming a 10% annual interest rate and no separations (Boudreau & Berger, 1985), the estimated gain in 10 years would be over $1 million in net present value in the year 1980. Precise development costs were unknown, but they would be small compared with this gain in utility (e.g., $20,000 to $30,000 in salaries). (Campion et al., 1988, p. 34)

Discussion

In summary, these ten studies collectively showed that properly developed situational interviews were relatively valid, free from bias, reliable, and practical. Moreover, the evidence suggests both test fairness and cost/benefit utility. Why is this the case when other interview methods have fared so poorly? In part, the answer lies in the fact that the method is based on theory, the questions are based on a job analysis and are, hence, job related, the questions are sufficiently abstruse that applicants cannot determine the desired answer, and hence, must state their true intentions, the interviewers have a scoring guide for each item, and the predictors and the criteria are similar so that one is using "apples to predict apples rather than oranges."

A major problem potentially affecting the development of situational interviews is the development of the scoring guide, which was noted by Pursell (1988). Specifically, care must be taken to ensure that a 1 anchor guide is not so ridiculous that no one would even utter it during an interview, or that the 5 anchor is too idealistic. The scoring guide must reflect the reality experienced by practicing interviewers.

A second problem, common to any selection test, is that the scoring guide may become known to the applicants. This problem is minimized in many companies by including "dummy questions" that are not scored.

Future Research

A number of research issues have been addressed in this chapter. For example, the need to conduct studies on the test-retest reliability and construct validity of this technique has been raised, as well as the need to determine the value of a scoring guide for other interview techniques. This was attempted unsuccessfully (Latham & Saari, 1984) in using questions advocated by Ghiselli (1966), where the focus was on past behavior. However, the method section of Ghiselli's article did not permit exact replication.

Research is also needed on the criterion-related validity of the technique in predicting the job behavior of people in upper-level jobs. Research should also be done on the extent to which the interview questions measure cognitive abilities, and therefore, the extent to which concurrent validity coefficients are good approximations of predictive validity (see also Barrett, Phillips, & Alexander, 1981).

Research should also be done on the value of the situational interview as a realistic job preview (Wanous, 1973, 1978). Many companies that use the situational interview inform candidates, prior to the interview, that the questions presented to them are based on issues that are encountered on the job. Wanous has shown that realistic previews can reduce employee turnover.

Finally, research should be conducted on the relative advantages of situational and patterned behavior description interviews (PBDI) (see Janz, this volume). As can be seen from Table 12.3, both methods are not only based on a job analysis, but on the same job analysis, namely the critical incident technique. Both have drawn on the same literature to guide research (e.g., Flanagan, 1954; Maas, 1965; Wernimont & Campbell, 1968). Thus, both emphasize a focus on behavior, and both have obtained evidence of reliability and validity.

The two methods differ in that PBDIs are not based on theory but rather on the well-founded empirical truism that past behavior predicts future behavior. This focus on the past rather than the future results in questions being phrased as "what did you do when?" rather than "what would you do if?" Because there is no behavioral guide for the PDBI, and because the same questions are not asked of each applicant, a number of issues need to be addressed.

First, the issue of social desirability needs to be examined. In developing a situational interview, questions that all pilot study subjects answer correctly are discarded. Because this is not, and perhaps cannot be, done with the PBDI, due to its relative lack of structure, the issue of social desirability in the form of applicants altering or exaggerating the truth

TABLE 12.3. Similarities and Differences Between Situational Interviews and Patterned Behavior Description Interviewing (PBDI)

	Situational	PBDI
1. Characteristics based on theory	X	—
2. Job Analysis: CIT	X	X
3. Client/customer writers and asks questions	X	—
4. Psychologist or trained interviewer prepares and asks questions	—	X
5. Same questions asked of all applicants	X	—
6. Probing allowed/encouraged	—	X
7. Scoring guide for interviewers	X	—
8. Questions emphasize past	—	X
9. Questions emphasize future	X	—
10. Emphasis is on behavior	X	X
11. Check for social desirability	X	—
12. Evidence of reliability	X	X
13. Evidence of validity	X	X
14. Evidence of test fairness	X	—
15. Evidence of practicality	X	—
16. Evidence of utility	X	X

becomes problematic. This is especially true in an era where applicants are aware that there are legal barriers to thorough reference checking.

Second, the PBDI's sole focus on the past may inadvertently affect women and minorities adversely because of their relative lack of opportunity to enjoy experiences traditionally reserved for white Anglo-Saxon males. Thus, the question that needs to be addressed is which method has the least adverse impact on sectors of our society.

Third, the very fact that PBDI does not require that each person be asked the same questions should be investigated in terms of its advantages and disadvantages relative to the situational interview from the standpoint of validity, reliability, freedom from bias, and practicality. Moreover the legality of the latter needs to be probed.

Fourth, in a workshop, Janz stated that his research has been limited to questions that he himself has developed and administered (Hellervik & Janz, 1988). This is in stark contrast to the situational interview, where the questions, administration, and scoring guide are developed by job incumbents. Thus, the relative advantages and disadvantages of these two approaches need to be explored.

Nevertheless, it is instinctively appealing to focus effectively on both past behavior and future intentions. Because Janz (see Chapter 11, this volume) has been able to show the value of PBDI, the following questions now need to be addressed:

(1) Are there some behaviors or constructs that are tapped more readily by one method versus another?

(2) To what extent do the situational interview and PBDI yield results that correlate with one another (i.e., yield corroborating conclusions)?

(3) What is the incremental validity of including the PBDI with a situational interview?

Answers to these questions are likely to result in interview techniques that are comparable, if not superior psychometrically, to pencil and paper tests, and as acceptable, if not more acceptable, to the public than are conventional testing procedures.

13

The Interview as a Multimodal Procedure

Heinz Schuler
University of Stuttgart-Hohenheim
Uwe Funke
University of Stuttgart-Hohenheim

Employment interviews can be conceived as being more than global assessment instruments. Looking at them closely can reveal that they have the two properties which constitute multimodal assessment procedures (Fahrenberg, 1987). An interview can consist of multiple methods, such as different question types, and it can measure multiple dimensions, such as different abilities or behavior domains. Thus, multimodal interviews are oriented towards different dimensions, and corresponding dimensions are operationalized by different methods.

Recent reviews have noted the likely influence of interview method on predictive validities (Wiesner & Cronshaw, 1988; McDaniel et al., 1987). Wiesner and Cronshaw reported a mean validity coefficient of $r = .13$ for unstructured interviews and $r = .40$ for structured interviews. McDaniel et al. reported a mean validity coefficient of $r = .30$ for job related interviews and $r = .21$ for traditional psychological interviews with performance ratings as the criterion. Within job related interviews there was another small influence of interview method; namely, the mean validity coefficient for structured interviews was $r = .32$ and $r = .26$ for unstructured interviews. The higher validity coefficients of about $r = .40$ for special methods of interviewing such as situational interviews (Latham & Saari, 1984; Latham, Saari, Pursell & Campion, 1980; Weekley & Gier, 1987) and biographical interviews (Ghiselli, 1966; Janz, 1982; Orpen 1985), raises questions about selection interview validity generalization when there may exist significant interview method effects.

Construct-oriented research on the employment interview is sparse. With regard to multiple interview dimensions, Hunter and Hirsch (1987) emphasized that "the question of the construct measured by the interview is clearly the key issue for the interview" (p. 330). Hunter and Hirsch (1987) projected that interview ratings correlated $r = .20$ with general cognitive ability, and argued that it would be much higher for structured interviews because

183

they tend to resemble verbally administered intelligence tests, job knowledge tests, or work sample tests. For example, Campion, Pursell, and Brown (1988) reported a multiple correlation between structured interviews and four aptitude tests of $R = .75$ (corrected for range restriction).

Discussing multiple methods within a single interview, Janz (1982) reported the results of a content analysis of 45 tape-recorded interviews. Standard interviews followed Fear's (1973) suggestion that interviews include three typical categories of questions: (a) credentials (factual, qualitative details); (b) experience descriptions (surface descriptions of past experience); and (c) self-perceptions (self-assessment of strengths, weaknesses, likes, dislikes, and hypothetical questions). Janz' biographical interview, called Patterned Behavior Description Interviewing (PBDI), focused on applicant descriptions of specific job-relevant events in the applicant's past. Latham and Saari (1984) combined 20 situational and 5 biographical questions in their interview. Another example of multiple methods is the structured interviewing technique Campion et al. (1988) employed. In their study, they combined situational questions with questions of job knowledge, worker requirements, simulation questions, and job samples.

Multidimensionality of single interviews can emerge from basing question development on a broad spectrum job analysis. Explicitly condensed into dimensions, job analysis data can contain incidents that are specific to a performance dimension or required ability (see Feild and Gatewood, this volume). For example, the patterned behavior description interview used by Janz (1982) and Orpen (1985) included six behavior dimensions derived from critical incidents. In the situational interview, Latham et al. (1980) and Latham and Saari (1984) selected questions representative of performance factors such as attendance, interaction with peers, and so forth.

In none of these studies was an effort made to deal with the different dimensions systematically. Instead, a simple unidimensional structure was adopted in the analysis of these interviews, enhancing the likelihood of greater internal consistency across judgments. In the studies by Latham et al. (1980), Latham and Saari (1984), Weekley and Gier (1987), and Campion et al. (1988) a total of eight coefficients of internal consistency (Cronbach's alpha) was reported, ranging from $r = .61$ to $r = .78$. Since a shortcoming of alpha as an index of dimensionality is its tendency to increase as the number of items increases, Cronbach (1951) proposed that an indication of inter-item consistency could be obtained by applying the Spearman-Brown formula to alpha, thereby estimating the mean correlation between items. The results of this computation for the four studies cited above are mean item-intercorrelations from $r = .05$ to $r = .26$, and a mean across all eight coefficients of $r = .15$, indicating quite heterogenous interviews. One implication of these results, in accordance with Weekley and Gier's (1987) suggestion, is to construct interviews to reflect an a priori dimensional structure and thereby test whether applicant job potential can be evaluated accurately on independent dimensions.

This chapter describes a research effort to construct a multimodal interview procedure, and then to analyze items and scales representing different methods and dimensions. Two interrelated research questions were investigated. First, the effects of an explicit use of different methods in one interview are examined. Distinctness or overlap of methods is analyzed. Furthermore, different methods are compared against psychometric properties and expert judgments. Second, the effects of an explicit use of different dimensions in an interview are examined. In order to identify dimensions and/or constructs, parts of the interview are correlated with construct-related external criteria of cognitive ability and social skills. Whether different dimensions or constructs in the interview actually can be differentiated is analyzed by means of a multitrait-multimethod (MTMM) matrix (Campbell & Fiske, 1959) of items operationalizing different methods and dimensions.

Multimodal Interview Development

Objectives of the Interview

The target job was an entry-level, bank clerk apprentice position within a large bank in West Germany. The bank uses a cognitive ability test for preselection which has predicted grades in the final apprenticeship examination with a validity of $r = .48$. However, the bank is also interested in selecting for marketing (i.e., sales ability), and social skills in interacting with customers and colleagues.

The task of devising a suitable employment interview is complicated in West Germany by the legal emphasis (i.e., codetermination by staff councils) and social expectation that employer selection techniques must first and foremost be acceptable to applicants and the unions that potentially would represent them. Some years before, the bank had commissioned consultants to construct a biographical inventory. However, members of the union opposed this instrument, so the bank decided to abstain from its use in order to avoid a possible conflict. Again, West German courts consider acceptability of selection procedures and the presumed reactions of applicants towards the selection tests to be most important. At the same time, comparatively lower importance is given to test validity and fairness.

Recent studies suggested that employment interviews could fulfill the need for acceptability. Interviews were evaluated by applicants as significantly more acceptable than ability tests (Fruhner & Schuler, 1987), and the same questions were evaluated by members of the staff council as more acceptable in interviews than in biographical inventories (Stehle, 1983). To increase the acceptability of any new interview procedure all relevant groups were surveyed to collect information on legal aspects, expectancies, and willingness to accept different interview methods. From this survey supplementary conditions emerged. Interview questions would need to be preselected for acceptability. The interview could not be completely standardized, but rather it must give the interviewers some choice between equivalent questions. Finally, lawyers agreed that no element of the planned multimodal interview would be in violation of West German law.

Main Features of the Interview

The multimodal interview under pilot exam included: (a) content predicated on a thorough job analysis, (b) dimensions/abilities corresponding to social skills in behavior towards customers and colleagues, (c) questions with high face validity/acceptability, (d) rating scales that are behaviorally-anchored, (e) structured interview format, but with choices between parallel interview questions), (f) inclusion of exactly defined, unscored, "isles" of free conversation (preferred by applicants as well as by interviewers), (g) rules for aggregating ratings, (h) interviewer training in job requirements, and social perception processes, interview conduct, question formulating, and performance-referenced feedback to the interviewer based on interviewer practice with volunteers.

Steps in Interview Development

Workshops were organized to conduct job analysis and develop situational questions in accordance with Latham's methodology (Latham et al. 1980). Six half-day workshops with job incumbents (N = 40) and supervisors (N = 40) were held. The critical incident technique (see also Schwind, 1977), yielded 845 incidents concerning social situations with customers and colleagues. Workshop participants formulated approximately 120 nonredundant situational questions with appropriate behavioral anchors. Questions were screened for dimensionality, quality, and acceptability. Initially, twenty-one behavior dimensions were identified by consensus of three organizational psychologists. The situational items and a list of the dimensions were sent to participants of the workshop and to other subject experts, totalling 109 persons, who rated the dimensions and each question on importance and acceptability. A final set of 45 situational questions, evenly spread across nine dimensions, was agreed upon. Dimensions included: (1) dealing with customer objections and criticisms, (2) exchange and transmission of information, (3) taking one's own initiative, (4) dealing with mistakes in service, (5) mutual assistance and support, (6) working conscientiously, (7) consulting skillfully, (8) attending politely to customers, and (9) being flexible in complying with customer needs.

Next, biographical questions were selected. The existing biographical questionnaire, which was not in use, formerly had been factor analyzed. Seven of the biographical factors appeared to match up with seven of the nine dimensions. Two factors, calmness and verbal expression, which proved to be important in the questionnaire, were added. The items were selected on the basis of factor loadings and former tests of acceptability. Items that dealt with parental home, family, private activities, and state of health were omitted. For the resulting nine dimensions, 45 items, five per dimension, were chosen in a manner parallel to that used for selecting situational questions. About half of the biographical items resembled Janz's (1982) category of self-perception questions; the other half were more like past behavior description questions. However, descriptions of specific work-related past events were deemed unacceptable for candidates applying for the entry-level apprentice program.

In addition to the situational and biographical questions, a self-presentation part of the interview was developed based on prior assessment center experience in selecting sales people (see also Thornton & Byham, 1982). Six behaviorally anchored rating scales included three formal dimensions (i.e., expression, self-confidence, and liveliness) and three content dimensions (i.e., completeness, realistic self-perception, and attitude toward work). Vocational interest and choice questions, which are usually asked, were also given behavioral anchors. In the final step five parallel and completely standardized experimental versions were compiled out of the pool of questions in order to test all questions. However, the self-presentation section was the same for all five versions.

Interview Structure

Interviewers each followed the same structured process: small talk introduction, candidate self-presentation, vocational interest and choice questions, free interviewer question period, biographical questions, a realistic job preview, situational questions, and applicant questions. A sample biographical question was:

Did you get better grades at school for written or for oral achievement?

    2 points Oral;   1 point No differences;   0 points Written

A sample situational question was:

A customer has a very special demand. You are not well versed in this banking transaction. What would you do?

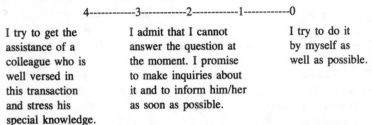

4------------3------------2------------1------------0		
I try to get the assistance of a colleague who is well versed in this transaction and stress his special knowledge.	I admit that I cannot answer the question at the moment. I promise to make inquiries about it and to inform him/her as soon as possible.	I try to do it by myself as well as possible.

Analysis of Initial Use of Multimodal Interview

At the time this chapter was written, no job performance data had been collected against which to correlate interview ratings. As interim criteria measures, a cognitive ability test that had high criterion-related validities for predicting clerical aptitude, and a consensus judgment by six observers of each applicant's social skills were recorded on dimensions of contact, influence, emotional stability, activity, cooperation, and argumentation. During this test phase, 307 applicants for the bank clerk apprenticeship position were interviewed.

Table 13.1 contains the intercorrelations between the four question types. The overlap of the methods is moderate. Internal consistency and interrater reliability of the four question types are shown in Table 13.2. Cronbach's alpha and the derived mean item intercorrelations are low. This is especially the case with mean item intercorrelations for biographical and situational questions. Situational questions have slightly lower interrater reliabilities than the biographical and vocational choice questions. The interrater reliability for self-presentation, which was the least structured interview method, is very low.

Cognitive Ability and Social Skill Criteria

The four questioning methods were correlated with the cognitive ability test and independent assessments of applicant social skills. In Table 13.3,

TABLE 13.1 Intercorrelations Between Question Types

Method	2	3	4
1. Self presentation	.33	.36[a]	.39[a]
2. Vocational choice	—	.28	.23
3. Biographical questions		—	.34
4. Situational questions			—

NOTE: Results of the five interview versions were combined by meta-analysis. Correlation coefficients are weighted average correlations.

[a]Variance of correlations not completely explainable by sampling error.

the four question methods collectively correlated more with assessments of social skills than with cognitive ability, which was the objective of interview development. The strongest predictors, in order, were self-presentation, situational, biographical, and vocational questions. These high correlations hold even if cognitive ability is partialled out. There were no significant differences limited to applicant gender.

Interviewer ratings of the applicant's answers to biographical and situational questions were correlated within each dimension to produce a multitrait (seven dimensions) multimethod (two question types) matrix. Analysis of the MTMM matrix suggested that ratings across dimensions, regardless of method, are intercorrelated, especially for situational questions. This suggests the presence of halo error in interviewer rating, lack of a priori dimension independence, or true interrelatedness across dimensions across applicants. For whatever reason, the result is higher convergence across dimensions within methods (heterotrait-monomethod) than convergence within dimensions across methods (monotrait-heteromethod). With the exception of criteria dimensions of skillful consulting and mutual assistance, applicant responses to biographical and situational questions did not converge to a greater extent than inherent dimension intercorrelatedness on five of the seven dimensions.

Implications

Interview Methods

Applicant responses to the four question methods are modestly intercorrelated. The correlation of .34 between situational and biographical questions is more than twice the .15 reported by Latham and Saari (1984). This could be due to the construction of both question types directed at comparable dimensions. Internal consistency and mean item intercorrelations

TABLE 13.2. Internal Consistency and Interrater Reliability
of Four Question Types

Question Type	Internal Consistency[a]			Interrater Reliability[b]	
	n of Items	Alpha	Mean Item Intercorr.	Items	Scales
Self presentation	6	.77[c]	.13	.40	.32
Vocational choice	3	.32[c]	.11	.73	.90
Biographical questions	9	.43[c]	.05	.77	.83
Situational questions	9	.68	.08	.65	.71

NOTE: [a]Results of the five interview versions were combined by meta-analysis.

[b]Interrater reliabilities as mean pairwise Pearson-correlations of raters, using Fisher's Z; for items, pairwise interviewer ratings were correlated over applicants; for scale, pairwise interviewer ratings were correlated over items. Interrater reliabilities were available for three versions (5 pairs of raters, 72 candidates) and averaged.

[c]Variance of coefficients not completely explainable by sampling error. This is mainly due to extremely low coefficients in version five for self presentation and biographical questions.

of situational questions are at the lower limit of results reported by Latham et al. (1980) and Weekley and Gier (1987). The objective of uncovering internal consistency measures for the biographical questions are not inconsistent with prior research (Owens, 1976).

Interrater reliabilities of situational questions are lower than those of biographical questions, which corresponds with Latham and Saari's (1984) results. Results for situational questions are slightly lower than reported elsewhere (Latham et al. 1980; Latham & Saari 1984; Weekley & Gier, 1987). The lower interrater reliabilities for situational questions, in comparison to biographical questions, may be the result of rater tendency toward the mean in the three-point scales of biographical items compared to the five-point scales of situational items. The gain in interrater reliability by structuring the interview is in sharp contrast with the self-presentation part of the interview, which was only partly structured.

Yet, the self-presentation part of the interview correlated more strongly with both social skill assessments and cognitive ability, in comparison with situational or biographical questions. One explanation may be the inadequacy and subjectivity of the intermediate criterion measures chosen. Actual objective, independent measures of job incumbent performance would be preferable. Also, all the interviews began with self-presentation. It is possible that if interviewers were making decisions early in the interview (i.e., primacy effect), then the remainder of the interview for many applicants may have been simply an exercise in confirming the interviewer's initial evaluation (see Rowe, this volume). Randomly placing each question method within the interview would control for this potential order ef-

TABLE 13.3. Correlations of Question Types with Cognitive Ability, Social Skills, and Gender

Question Type	Cognitive Abilities		Social Skills		Gender	
	$\bar{r}$	$\bar{r}$ Corrected	$\bar{r}$	$\bar{r}$ Corrected	$\bar{r}$ Partial	$\bar{r}$
	Items					
Self presentation	.12	.22	.46	.53	—	—
Vocational choice	.01	.02	.13	.15	—	—
Biographical questions	.06	.10	.19	.22	—	—
Situational questions	.11	.20	.27	.31	—	—
	Scales					
Self presentation	.18[a]	.33	.63[a]	.73	.63	−.05
Vocational choice	.03	.07	.24	.28	.22	−.08
Biographical questions	.14	.26	.40[a]	.47	.40[a]	.02
Situational questions	.19	.34	.52[a]	.60	.52[a]	−.09
Total interview	.21[a]	.37	.60[a]	.69	.60[a]	−.10

NOTE: Results of the five interview versions were combined by meta-analysis; $\bar{r}$ = weighted average correlation; $\bar{r}$ corrected = with cognitive ability corrected for unreliability of criterion test (r_{yy} = .90) and for range restriction (u = .56), with social skills corrected for unreliability of group discussion (r_{yy} = .75); $\bar{r}$ partial = weighted average correlation if cognitive ability partialed out.
[a]Variance of correlations not completely explainable by sampling error.

fect, but may be impractical if user and applicant acceptance of the entire interview process is of paramount concern.

The tentative results of this multimodal interview method suggest that biographical and situational questions may be practically combined with incremental informational value for the interviewer. The fairly low correlation of situational and biographical question with measures of cognitive abilities appears to contradict the findings of Campion et al, (1988).

The MTMM analysis does not support a clear dimensional structure of the construct of social skills in the interview. Biographical and situational questions, which belong to the same dimension, should be more highly correlated than questions belonging to different dimensions, although an appropriate magnitude of correlations cannot be unequivocally determined as an indicator of convergent and discriminant validity. The resulting heterotrait-monomethod and monotrait-heteromethod correlations, which with few exceptions are not higher than the heterotrait-heteromethod correlations, cast doubt on any systematic dimensional effects.

Does the missing support for the operationalization of particular dimensions disconfirm dimensionally based interview construction? Certainly not, because the realization of the interview dimensions could have been misdirected in retrospect: Subdimensions of the global construct "social skills" supposedly could not have been confirmed because they were too similar to be differentiated. The results of a content validation of biographical and situational questions by 25 interviewers showed that 90% of the items had a positive content validity ratio (Lawshe 1975) but in only 29% of the ratings of biographical questions and 12% of the ratings of situational questions, the highest content validity ratings were purely on the convergent dimensions. Besides, the diffuse set of too many dimensions could be overcome by combining and reducing dimensions, and better matching the biographical items with the dimensions to prevent low convergent validities.

Although a final predictive validation study is not yet realized, benefits of constructing interviews as multimodal procedures could be demonstrated. But the strategies for the construction of dimensions and dimension-related questions must be quite sophisticated. There has been little systematic research concerning interview components. For future investigations, researchers should give priority to experimental variations of question types and dimensions, aiming at optimal coverage of job demands and criterion relatedness. Perhaps, the attempt reported in this chapter will encourage others to try. In principal, it is promising to conceive the employment interview not as a unit, but as a rather unspecified cover which can be decomposed into different construct-related and criterion-related components.

PART VI

Applicant Strategies

If one assumes that what happens in the interview discussion plays a significant role in determining the interviewer's ultimate judgment, than clearly there is a second independent set of strategies brought to the interview event; namely, the applicant's. The relative success or failure of particular applicant strategies is both insufficiently understood in the employment interview literature and likely to be unknown even to applicants, beyond their intuition of how well they did. The two following papers suggest related lines of research on applicant strategies that are predicated on understanding organizational politics and impression management tactics.

Gilmore and Ferris investigate the role of organizational politics and impression management theory on the organizational entry process, by formulating research questions to develop a more informed understanding of the interpersonal political dynamics of the employment interview. Applications of specific impression management strategies and tactics are discussed.

Also building upon an impression management framework, Baron empirically demonstrates in two separate studies that, up to a point, such tactics may induce positive affective reactions among interviewers, and thereby enhance the ratings assigned to applicants. However, beyond this point such tactics may become excessive, and lead interviewers to perceive their users as manipulative or insincere, and in such cases result in lower interviewer ratings of applicants. A theoretical model is proposed on the impact of affective states on cognitive processes.

14

The Politics of the Employment Interview

David C. Gilmore
University of North Carolina at Charlotte

Gerald R. Ferris
University of Illinois at Urbana-Champaign

Politics permeates virtually all aspects of organizational life. Like it or not, there is increasing anecdotal, popular press, and systematic empirical evidence that people in organizations behave opportunistically for purposes of self-interest maximization (e.g., Bowes, 1987; Ferris & Kacmar, 1988; Kanter, 1977). Furthermore, recent arguments have been made for the importance of organizational politics in human resources management (Ferris, Fedor, Chachere, & Pondy, 1989; Frost, 1987), extending from organizational entry to organizational exit decisions. Within this area, much of the research activity has focused on politics in goal setting, performance appraisal, pay increase, and promotion decisions (Ferris, Buckley, Yee, & West, 1988; Eder & Fedor, in press-a; Ferris & Porac, 1984; Longenecker, Sims, & Gioia, 1987) as well as in career management and mobility (Gould & Penley, 1984; Greenhaus, 1987). Interestingly, whereas one can readily recognize the potential for opportunistic behavior to emerge in the organizational entry process, relatively little is known about the interpersonal political dynamics of personnel selection. The present chapter focuses on the selection process to examine the politics of the employment interview.

Theoretical Background

To understand the nature of political or opportunistic behavior in organizations it is necessary to integrate several previously independent streams of theory and research. Over the past twenty-five years or more, sizable knowledge bases have emerged within the field of social psychology in areas such as ingratiation, self-presentation, and impression management (e.g.,

195

Jones & Pittman, 1982; Schlenker, 1980; Tedeschi, 1981). Concomitantly, organizational scientists have been investigating political behavior in organizations from a number of perspectives, ranging from the more microanalytic to the more macroanalytic (e.g., Burns, 1961; Gandz & Murray, 1980; Mayes & Allen, 1977; Pettigrew 1973; Wood & Mitchell, 1981).

A common theme that seems to characterize much of this work is that organizational politics refers to the opportunistic behavior of some entity (i.e., individual, group, or organization) that is engaged in for purposes of self-interest maximization (Ferris & Kacmar, 1988), and thus represents an important social influence process (Ferris & Mitchell, 1987). Research has largely proceeded along two lines: one identifies the antecedents of, or conditions under which people behave opportunistically, and the other examines the effects of, or instrumental nature of political behavior. Only recently have scholars begun to examine antecedents and consequences of perceptions of politics, an endeavor which has interesting implications in at least two ways. Political behavior is often exhibited to manage an image/perception or to create/modify a reality. Lewin (1936) suggested that people respond on the basis of their perceptions of reality, not reality per se and more recently, Porter (1976) argued that perceptions are important to study and to understand, even if they are misperceptions of actual events. Thus, the extent to which images, perceptions, and realities are effectively created or managed in various organizational contexts is an area in need of systematic investigation.

A specific focal context that provides a good opportunity to examine such behavior and its effectiveness is the employment interview. In such situations, impression creation and manipulation are practiced by both the interviewer and the applicant. Taking perhaps an extreme position in observing such interpersonal dynamics, one might conclude that at some point "objective reality" ceases to be an issue, because competence, ability, and so forth are subjectively created realities influenced in large part by the active efforts of the actor toward the observer or recipient. In such cases, impression management potentially could overshadow actual job-related skill or competence in influencing a selection decision.

Antecedents and consequences of perceptions of political behavior are of interest in another way as well. The foregoing discussion suggests that an actor's political behavior toward an observer can achieve the desired result (e.g., job offer, and so on), primarily due to the observer's failure to define the actor's behavior as politically motivated. What happens to the actor when such behavior is perceived by the observer as an active manipulation attempt? The employment interview might here again provide a useful context for investigation.

Whereas political behavior in organizations has been studied with respect to a number of decisions, actions, and activities, little attention has been focused on the organizational entry process in general, or the specific context of the employment interview. The employment interview provides an interesting opportunity for the investigation of political behavior for a number of reasons. For one thing, the employment interview encourages opportunistic behavior by job applicants if they are at all interested in the job in question. Second, the employment interview is typically characterized by high ambiguity and uncertainty, which are conditions conducive to the effective demonstration of political behavior (Ferris et al., 1988; Ferris & Kacmar, 1988). Factors that contribute to the degree of contextual ambiguity or uncertainty include the definition and nature of the job in question (e.g., there is typically more uncertainty interviewing candidates for a managerial or professional position than for a sales or production/machine operator position), the degree of experience and training the interviewer has had, and the amount and type of information the interviewer has about the focal job (Eder & Buckley, 1988).

It seems clear that political behavior in organizations is a fact of life, and that it is incumbent upon organizational scientists to pursue and develop a more informed understanding of the dynamics underlying these processes. Very important and costly decisions are made in the employment interview concerning who gains entrance to organizations, yet little effort has been made to date to investigate the politics of the interview (Baron, 1986; Eder & Buckley, 1988; Gilmore & Ferris, 1988; Gilmore, Ferris, & Kacmar, 1988).

Literature Review

Considerable research (Arvey & Campion, 1982; Hakel, 1982; Eder & Buckley, 1988; Gilmore & Ferris, 1980; Schmitt, 1976) has investigated the impact of a variety of variables, such as applicant sex, physical appearance, type of job, applicant qualifications, stereotypes, order of information, interview context, and contrast effects on overall evaluations of applicants. Although these variables may influence interview outcomes, limited knowledge is available concerning the specific type of interactions that occur within the interview (Arvey & Campion, 1982; see Tullar, this volume). Both the interviewer and the applicant attempt to present positive images to each other so that the interviewer attracts the best applicant and the applicant gets the best job offer. Applicants must appear interested in the interview and answer the interviewer's questions, but the subtle techniques employed by applicants to create positive impressions on the interviewer have received little research attention (Baron, 1986; Gilmore & Ferris, 1988; Gilmore, Ferris, & Kacmar, 1988).

Most of the early interview research attempted to establish relationships between interviewer-applicant characteristics (i.e., sex, physical appearance) and interviewer ratings, but much less is known about what actually happens in the interview process. The intervening process of what applicants say and how they respond to the interviewer, how interviewers phrase questions, and listen to applicants, and what influences the interaction between the applicant and interviewer have not been well explored. Binning, Goldstein, Garcia, Harding, and Scattaregia (1988), McDonald and Hakel (1985), and Sackett (1982) have explored the questioning strategy employed by interviewers, but the subtle ways by which applicants influence interviewers is still not well understood.

Interpersonal Politics and Impression Management

One approach to investigating the interviewer-applicant interaction is to examine the subtle ways applicants and interviewers present themselves in an interview. Jones and Pittman (1982) and Tedeschi and Melburg (1984) have developed theoretical approaches for the systematic study of social influence processes. Jones and Pittman identified a number of self-presentation techniques that can be used to shape attributions including ingratiation, intimidation, self-promotion, exemplification, and supplication. To achieve likability, people use ingratiation techniques, such as self-description and self-enhancement, which are very prevalent in employment interviews. To enhance attributions of competence, applicants can use self-promotion techniques in which the applicant claims responsibility for prior performances and accomplishments. Intimidation, while an option for applicants, may be imprudent in most interview situations. The exemplifier seeks to be respected for his or her moral values or saint-like qualities, but must be careful not to overdo self-presentation in a brief interview. Supplication, or exploiting one weaknesses, could be used by an applicant who is looking for help from the interviewer, but this strategy is unwise in most interview situations. Thus, there are a variety of techniques that applicants could employ to enhance their image in an employment interview using the typology of Jones and Pittman.

Tedeschi and Melburg (1984) built upon this work and developed a more complete model of impression management. Their taxonomy distinguishes between assertive and defensive self-presentations. Assertive behaviors are used to actively enhance one's image as is typically done by an applicant trying to make a good impression in an employment interview. Defensive behaviors are used by individuals in situations where negative or undesirable attributions might be made about them. By making excuses, offering explanations or other defensive behaviors, the individual may be able to maintain a positive image. Tedeschi and Melburg also distinguish between tactical and strategic impression management. Tactical behaviors are directed at immediate, short-term issues such as a conversation with a stranger. Strategic behaviors are directed at more "long-term interests of the individual" (p. 33), and establish the person's reputation and character. Individuals' school records, job assignments, and assistance to others eventually lead to a reputation based upon their "track-record," or list of accomplishments. Tedeschi and Melburg developed a 2x2 taxonomy of impression management behaviors which incorporates the assertive-defensive and tactical-strategic distinctions.

Assertive tactical behaviors, such as claiming responsibility for positive events, promoting one's accomplishments, ingratiation, and to a certain extent intimidation, are commonly employed by applicants in most interviews. Supplication, or revealing weaknesses in order to gain help from someone such as an interviewer, may not be employed frequently but certainly occurs in some interviews. Intimidation can be used by applicants in an interview, but this would generally seem to be a risky tactic. All of these assertive tactical behaviors serve the short-term goal of influencing the interviewer in that social situation. How often applicants use such tactics, and how interviewers are influenced by them, is not well understood.

Assertive strategic impression management behaviors that establish one's reputation are very salient in the employment interview, but are more enduring characteristics of the applicant which are not easily modified in the interview itself. The prestige of an applicant's background, his/her competence, status, credibility, and attractiveness are assessed by interviewers, but are difficult to manipulate within the interview.

Defensive tactical behaviors, such as making excuses, justifications, and apologies, do occur in the interview particularly when the applicant perceives himself to be in a predicament. Applicants may be forced to use these behaviors, but too much reliance on them can certainly sway an interviewer's judgment about the applicant's fitness for a job. Defensive strategic behaviors that are long-term adjustments to failures are usually avoided by applicants who desire to make favorable impressions on interviewers. Using poor physical health, alcoholism, or mental illness as a justification for one's prior performance may maintain some degree of self-esteem, but does not enhance one's chances for employment.

An examination of prior research on the employment interview (Schmitt,

1976; Gilmore & Ferris, 1980) suggests that considerable attention has been focused on the impact of what Tedeschi and Melburg (1984) would label assertive strategic behaviors. These "reputational" characteristics include the applicant's background, attractiveness, and competence. For example, physical attractiveness appears to influence interview outcomes (Beehr & Gilmore, 1982; Dipboye, Arvey, & Terpstra, 1977; Gilmore, Beehr, & Love, 1986); and Schmitt (1976) concluded that attitudinal similarity has some influence on interviewer decisions. The prestige of an applicant's background, competence (esteem), status, and credibility are usually job relevant characteristics that are assessed in the interview. It appears that these factors do influence the decisions made by interviewers. The other type of strategic impression management techniques—defensive strategic behaviors such as mental illness—may occur in the interview, but seem to have strongly negative consequences. Little systematic research exists on the impact of these behaviors, but common sense would seem to dictate the probable outcome.

The area most in need of further examination involves tactical impression management behaviors. The dynamics of the social interaction between applicant and interviewer needs to be investigated in a systematic fashion. In particular, how applicants influence interviewers in subtle ways by using what Tedeschi and Melburg (1984) label as tactical assertive behaviors deserves more attention.

Most job seekers try to present their positive qualities in an interview, with self-enhancing statements intending to create a good impression. Statements that suggest positive qualities or traits, if credible, should positively influence the interviewer. This somewhat obvious ingratiation technique is employed frequently by applicants seeking to bolster their image in an interview. Another ingratiation technique that involves tactical assertive behaviors is other-enhancing communication (Tedeschi & Melburg 1984). Applicants who flatter or praise the interviewer directly ("You're a good interviewer," "You're a nice person") or indirectly ("You work for a great company") are enhancing the interviewers' esteem. This should result in increased liking of the applicant and possibly the granting of favors such as improved chances of being hired. This flattery must not be indiscriminate or it may be discounted by the interviewer, and the praise must appear genuine if it is to have the intended effect. Overuse of praise or flattery can backfire on an applicant if the interviewer perceives it to be insincere and/or an active manipulation attempt.

Applicants also ingratiate themselves by appearing to have beliefs and attitudes similar to that of the interviewer. Research has demonstrated that attitude similarity is linked to interpersonal attraction (e.g., Berscheid &

Walster, 1978; Schmitt, 1976). Applicants who listen carefully to the opinions expressed by interviewers, or who have prior knowledge about the organization's culture, can express opinions consistent with that information so that they appear to "fit in" well. Interpersonally sensitive applicants can sense the social climate of a situation and can influence the interviewer's perception.

Another tactical assertive technique which could be used in an interview is exemplification (Tedeschi & Melburg, 1984). By explaining how the applicant was virtuous or morally principled in a situation, the applicant can provide an example for the interviewer to follow. The applicant may influence the interviewer to be forgiving by relating how the applicant has forgiven others in the past.

Supplication, presenting oneself as helpless or dependent, may coax the interviewer to rescue the "poor applicant." By selectively revealing ones' weaknesses the applicant may be able to influence the interviewer to become partially responsible for his or her success in a job search. The interviewer may champion an applicant who may not be best qualified for a job, but who needs a break. This may occur when a chivalrous male interviewer tries to assist a female applicant who portrays stereotypic sex-related characteristics.

Another tactical assertive technique is taking credit for, or enhancing the value of, positive events in a person's past. Tedeschi and Melburg (1984) have labeled these tactics as entitlements and enhancements. In an interview, applicants may promote their background by claiming sole or major responsibility for positive events to which their real contribution was minimal. Potential employers often attempt to verify applicant claims through reference and background checks or letters of reference because of the possibility of misrepresentation. Of course, applicants realize that many claims made in the interview are difficult to substantiate.

Thus, applicants have at their disposal a number of techniques that can be used to influence interviewers. Clearly, there are differences in which techniques are used, how frequently they are used, in what situations, and how effectively they influence interviewers.

Management of Impressions in the Interview Process

Interviewers often form first impressions of applicants very early in the interview (Springbett, 1958). In practice, interviewers usually have prior information about the applicant from an application blank or a resume. This information often predisposes the interviewer even before the applicant has been seen (see Dipboye, this volume). In impression management terminology, this prior information (i.e., application blank or resume) available to the interviewer is typically strategic impression management data. Self-reports of prior experience and education all operate to enhance or detract from the applicant's reputation. Applicants who present themselves well on paper at this stage enter the interview at a decided advantage. Poor presentation in the resume or application may result in rejection even before the interview begins.

If information from application blanks or resumes does, in fact, result in a first impression which is difficult to overcome, it may be that tactical impression management that occurs in the actual face-to-face meeting between applicant and interviewer has relatively little influence except in borderline cases. That is, tactical impression management behaviors may be influential only in situations where the applicant's credentials and background are viewed as neither extremely good nor extremely bad. It should be noted that much of the research on the employment interview process has not actually studied live interviews, but has used "paper people" to study selection decision making. It is likely that several subtle forms of tactical impression management behaviors, such as ingratiation, require a face-to-face interview research context. Not much data exist concerning how tactical behaviors influence interviewers.

It is a distinct possibility that the type of job for which one is interviewing determines the relative influence of strategic and tactical impression management. For technical jobs with clearly defined requirements such as accounting or engineering, interviewers may be influenced heavily by the applicant's background, and will only be influenced by the tactical impression management required to make fine distinctions among candidates. In jobs where technical background is less important and interpersonal skills are more salient, as in a sales position, interviewers may unwittingly evaluate candidates on their tactical impression management skills. Interviewers have implicitly been doing this for years, but it may be beneficial to delineate these tactical behaviors so that interviewers can better understand what they are doing.

Impression management behaviors may also be employed differentially by applicants depending upon their information about the job and organization. In the conduct of the interview, it is commonplace for the interviewer to question the applicant before explaining the specifics of job and organization. Applicants who have relevant information about the job and organization either from outside sources or because the interviewer informs them early in the interview may be able to alter impressions so that they appear to fit in well. For example, if it is known that cooperation and teamwork are valued in the organization, the applicant could employ tactical impression management such as conforming to the interviewer's opinions rather than engaging in self-enhancing communication.

Research Implications

Using the conceptual underpinnings derived from organizational politics and impression management as a framework, it may now be possible to study the subtle forms of interaction that occur in interviews. Better conceptual development and subsequent theory-driven research is needed in this area in order to more effectively advance the existing limited knowledge base concerning interviewer-applicant political dynamics.

One approach that researchers could take would to follow Schlenker's (1980) advice and identify individual differences that predispose applicants to use impression management techniques. Measures of interpersonal sensitivity (i.e., Snyder's Self-Monitoring Scale, 1974), social desirability (Crowne & Marlow, 1964), Machiavellianism (Christie & Geis, 1970), and possibly levels of self-esteem could be examined to identify applicants who are more or less likely to influence interviewers. The same individual differences could be used with interviewers to determine their sensitivity to social influence attempts. Furthermore, a line of research that investigates questioning strategies in the interview (Sackett, 1982; McDonald & Hakel, 1985; Binning et al., 1988), coupled with the impression management strategies suggested here, could help develop a more informed understanding of what actually happens in the employment interview. Research needs to examine more closely what happens within the interview if this nearly universal selection technique is to be improved. Research designed from an impression management perspective should ultimately help to provide insights that may be used to improve interview effectiveness.

The foregoing analysis and discussion focused on the efforts of job applicants to manage impressions and behave opportunistically. Research needs to investigate further the antecedents and consequences of the political behavior of interviewers, as well as other organizational decision making events. Beer, Spector, Lawrence, Mills, and Walton (1984) recently have suggested that managers frequently become actively involved in interviewing and decision making processes to exercise control over what types of people (e.g., skills, ideas, ways of thinking, and so on) are hired, in efforts to increase their own influence or power base. Obviously, much more needs to become known about such manifestations of the internal organizational politics of selection.

15

Impression Management by Applicants During Employment Interviews: The "Too Much of a Good Thing" Effect

Robert A. Baron
Rensselaer Polytechnic Institute

Despite repeated criticism of its accuracy, reliability, and validity, the employment interview remains in widespread use (Arvey & Campion, 1982). As such, it often constitutes the first contact between persons seeking employment and a wide range of organizations. Because many applicants recognize the importance of this initial contact, they engage in strenuous efforts to assure that it yields a positive outcome. In short, they use every skill and tactic at their disposal to induce positive reactions among interviewers, and so "tip the balance" in their favor. Such tactics are generally described as "impression management" (Jones & Pittman, 1982; Schlenker, 1980). More formally, this term refers to a process by which individuals change or manage several aspects of their behavior in order to create a positive impression on other.

Many different techniques and actions are used for inducing positive affective reactions among target persons. Recent research has clarified the nature of several of these tactics. For example, in one revealing study, Godfrey, Jones, and Lord (1986) assigned subjects, meeting a stranger for the first time, the following goal: induce this person to like you as much as possible. Subjects' behavior was then observed during brief conversations with the stranger. These observations revealed the use of several distinct strategies. Subjects frequently engaged in ingratiation, offering compliments and undeserved praise of the target person. They demonstrated interest in this individual, and expressed agreement with his or her views. Finally, they emitted many positive nonverbal cues (e.g., smiles, nods, eye contact), and made frequent use of humor and self-deprecation. Not surprisingly, these tactics were quite successful. Subjects who made frequent use of these procedures were liked by their partners to a greater extent than subjects who used them to a lesser degree.

Do such impression management tactics also succeed in employment interviews? Results from several studies suggest that they do under some circumstances (e.g., within the context of brief, informal interviews). Several investigations have indicated that interviewers' reactions to job candidates are strongly influenced by applicants' appearance (e.g., style of dress, physical attractiveness, use of grooming aids). Persons judged to be attractive, or appropriately groomed and attired, generally received higher ratings than ones judged to be unattractive or inappropriately dressed (Cash, 1985; Forsythe, Drake, & Cox, 1985). Moreover, attractive persons actually seemed to attain higher levels of success in their careers than persons judged to be unattractive (Dickey-Bryant, Lautenschlager, Mendoza, & Abrahams, 1986).

Similarly, other studies have indicated that the emission of a high level of positive nonverbal cues can enhance ratings of applicants by interviewers (Imada & Hakel, 1977; Rasmussen, 1984). Presumably, such tactics generate positive affect and this, in turn, elevates subsequent ratings (Cardy & Dobbins, 1986).

On the basis of such evidence, it is tempting to conclude that where impression management during job interviews is concerned, a simple principle prevails—the more the better. That is, the greater the number of tactics employed, the more favorable the reactions induced among interviewers. As anyone familiar with university employment centers well knows, many job applicants (or at least relatively inexperienced ones) seem to accept this principle as accurate. On days when popular companies are conducting interviews, young men and women undergo what can only be described as major transformations in their mode of dress, grooming, and manners. Is it true then that "more" equals "better" where impression managements during interviews is concerned? Careful consideration of the nature of the processes occurring in this context suggests the need for caution with respect to this suggestion.

Perhaps the most telling weakness of a simple "more equals better" approach is the fact that a key process in social interaction is ignored—namely, attribution (Ross & Fletcher, 1985). Attribution refers to efforts by individuals to understand the causes behind others' behavior; that is, to understand precisely why other persons have behaved in specific ways. Such attributional analysis occurs in a wide range of social settings, but it seems especially relevant to employment interviews, where the interviewer has the assigned role of evaluating the applicant. Since evaluation involves assessment of applicant traits and characteristics, attributional analysis would appear to be a highly salient feature of the interview context.

To the extent interviewers engage in such efforts to understand the causes behind applicants' words or actions, they may become acutely aware of applicants' use of various tactics of impression management. To a degree, such tactics are expected, and may be viewed as an acceptable part of the interview process (see Tullar, this volume). Beyond some level, however, they may appear excessive. When they do, they may induce negative reactions among interviewers, and so tend to reduce rather than enhance applicant evaluation. Instead, moderation may be a more appropriate strategy where efforts at impression management during job interviews are concerned. In slightly different terms, it is hypothesized that tactics which, when used alone, induce positive reactions among interviewers, may, when used together, "boomerang," and produce opposite effects. This might be the case because, in combination, such tactics lead interviewers to perceive applicants who use them as manipulative, insincere, or merely unaware of what is appropriate in a job interview context. Such attributions may then generate negative affect which, in turn, reduces the ratings assigned to applicants.

Effects of the type suggested here have recently been observed by Weiner, Amirkhan, Folkes, and Verette (1987) in a somewhat different context—namely, excuse giving. In several studies on this topic, Weiner et al. arranged for subjects to be kept waiting by another person (actually an accomplice). When the accomplice finally arrived, the tardy individual supplied either a very weak excuse ("I ran into some friends in the hall") or a much stronger one ("My last class ran away over time"). As expected subjects exposed to a weak excuse rated the accomplice lower on a number of traits (e.g., dependability, sensitivity), and also reported more negative emotional reactions (e.g., greater anger and irritation) than subjects exposed to the relatively strong excuse. Inappropriate behavior on the part of another person apparently led to negative attributions about the accomplice with accompanying negative emotional reactions.

On the basis of these findings, plus the reasoning outlined above, excessive applicant efforts at impression management during a job interview may sometimes be "too much of a good thing." The possible existence of such effects has been investigated in two related studies by the present author. The first examined the impact of two distinct tactics of impression management on first impressions, while the second focused directly on the effect of such strategies on the outcomes of simulated employment interviews.

Impression Management in a Social Context: Effects of Dress and Grooming on First Impressions

"First impressions," it is often said, "last." To some extent, this adage is supported by the results of empirical research. Once individuals have formed an overall evaluation of another person, it is often difficult to alter that impression (Wyer & Srull, 1986). In part, cognitive representations of others, once formed, serve as filters for incoming information; input consistent with existing impressions is noticed, stored, and retrieved more readily than information inconsistent with such impressions (Fiske & Taylor, 1984). Whatever the basis for such effects, most individuals are aware of the importance of first impressions, and often engage in active steps to render them as favorable as possible.

In one study (Baron, 1981), male subjects interacted with a female stranger (actually an accomplice of the researcher) who engaged or did not engage in two different tactics of impression management (described below). Following exposure to the accomplice, subjects evaluated her on a number of different dimensions. In accordance with the reasoning outlined above, it was predicted that when used alone, each tactic would enhance evaluations assigned to the accomplice. In combination, however, a "too much of a good thing" effect would occur, and evaluations would be reduced.

Procedure

When male subjects arrived for their appointments, they found another person (a female accomplice) already present. Both were then informed that the study was concerned with the manner in which people form first impressions of others. To study this topic, the experimenter asked each participant a series of questions. Both persons listened to their partner's responses, and on this basis formed a first impression of the individual.

For each question, the accomplice responded first. Her answers, which had been prepared in advance, where both simple and noncontroversial. For example, the first question was: "What factors made you choose to come to this university instead of another one?" The accomplice's response, which was identical for all subjects, was: "Gee, I don't know. Several, I guess. It's pretty close to home so I can get back there on weekends, and it's got a good reputation. A lot of my friends came here, too, so that was one reason. I guess all those things together." Her replies to the remaining three questions ("What are your career plans or goals? "What are your favorite hobbies or leisure time activities?" "What do you think is the most serious problem facing the U.S. today?") were of a similar nature.

After the accomplice responded to each question, the subject, who was seated directly next to her, gave his reply. Following the last question, the accomplice and subject were taken to different rooms where they indicated their first impressions of the other person on a special form. Partners were rated on twenty personal trait dimensions (e.g., conceited-modest, warm-cold, shy-bold). In addition, subjects rated the extent to which their partner was attractive and well-groomed, and how much they liked her. Subjects' responses to these items (which were all made on seven-point scales) constituted the major dependent measures in the study.

To determine whether tactics of impression management would affect evaluations of the accomplice, the following procedures were used. First the accomplice did or did not make use of one grooming aid—artificial scent. This was accomplished by having her place (or not place) a measured amount of perfume behind each ear prior to the day's sessions. (The perfume employed lingered noticeably for several hours.) Second, the accomplice dressed either in an informal manner (jeans and sweatshirt), or in a neat manner (blouse, skirt, hose). A factorial design was employed, so that male participants were exposed to one of four conditions: perfume-informal dress, perfume-neat dress, no perfume-informal dress, no perfume-neat dress.

Results

Analyses of variance were performed on subjects' ratings of the accomplice's attractiveness and their liking for her. These analyses yielded significant interactions between scent and style of dress, $F(1, 93) = 11.01$, 13.36, $p \leq .002$, $p \leq .001$, respectively. The means involved in these interactions are shown in Table 15.1. As is apparent from this table, liking for the accomplice was highest when she employed only one of the two tactics of impression management (i.e., she used perfume *or* dressed neatly). Ratings were lower when she made use of both tactics.

Additional analyses were performed on subjects' ratings of the accomplice's personal traits. Here, too, significant interactions between scent and style dress were obtained for two items: warm-cold, unromantic-romantic, $F(1, 93) = 8.77$, 4.80, $p \leq .005$, $p \leq .03$, respectively. The form of these interactions was identical to that shown in Table 15.1. The accomplice was rated as warmer and more romantic when she either wore scent or dressed neatly than when she employed both of these tactics.

TABLE 15.1. Mean Ratings of Liking for the Accomplice and the Accomplice's Attractiveness as a Function of Use of Artificial Scent and Mode of Dress

	Liking For Accomplice		Accomplice's Attractiveness	
Mode of Dress	No Scent	Scent	No Scent	Scent
Informal	5.09$_a$	5.87$_b$	4.87$_a$	5.50$_b$
Neat	5.58$_b$	5.00$_a$	5.67$_b$	4.91$_a$

NOTE: For each dependent measure (liking, attractiveness), means that do not share a subscript differ significantly ($p \leq .05$).

Discussion

The results of this study supported the hypothesized "too much of a good thing" effect; single use of an impression management tactic enhanced evaluations, while use of two tactics reduced these ratings. Moreover, comments provided by subjects suggested that the attributional mechanisms described above may have contributed to this pattern of findings. Specifically, several individuals in the perfume-neat dress condition reported that they had reached negative conclusions about the accomplice and the causes of her behavior (e.g., "She's conceited—that's why she's so dressed up." "She's all dolled up for someone else—I'd be wasting my time to even try.")

In sum, it appeared that in the context of informal "get acquainted" meetings between strangers of the opposite sex (i.e., meetings that resemble informal recruitment interviews), two techniques of impression management were definitely *not* superior to only one in terms of inducing positive reactions toward the users. Would such effects also occur in the context of employment interviews, where much more is at stake than simply making a favorable impressions on a potential romantic partner? A second investigation was conducted to address this issue.

Impression Management in Employment Interviews: Effects of Grooming and Nonverbal Cues on Evaluations of Applicants

One tactic of impression management that is frequently used by job candidates, and which sometimes enhances their ratings, is the emission of positive nonverbal cues (e.g., Imada & Hakel, 1977). Smiles, head nods, leaning forward, a high level of eye contact, and so forth, convey interest in and positive reactions toward the interviewer (Buck, 1984). In a second study, the use of such cues was combined with a second tactic (the use of artificial scent) to determine whether, in combination, these diverse strategies would generate negative rather than positive reactions among interviewers. On the basis of the previous results, it was hypothesized that this would indeed be the case. Specifically, it was predicted that applicants would receive higher ratings when they either emitted positive nonverbal cues or wore artificial scent than when they employed both of these tactics together.

Procedure

Male and female students played the role of a personnel manager and conducted brief, simulated employment interviews with another person (i.e., a female accomplice). The job in question was described as an entry-level management position requiring participation in a wide variety of activities. During the interview, subjects read a series of questions to the applicant (i.e., the accomplice). The questions were typed on index cards and were quite straightforward (e.g., "What are the major goals you are seeking in your career?" "How would you feel about a transfer to an office far from your home state?"). The accomplice's responses to each question were prepared in advance and thoroughly memorized. They were uniformly simple and noncontroversial in nature.

Following the final question, subjects rated the applicant in terms of job related (e.g., motivation, potential for success) and personal (e.g., attractiveness, friendliness) characteristics. In addition, a measure of recognition memory for information presented during the interview was also included. This measure was employed to determine whether efforts at impression management by the accomplice would interfere with accurate encoding or retrieval of social information (Fiske & Taylor, 1984).

A factorial design based on two tactics of impression management was employed. For half the participants, the accomplice wore perfume, while for the remainder she did not. In addition, for half of the subjects in each of these conditions, the accomplice emitted a high level of positive nonverbal cues (e.g., smiling, leaning toward the interviewer); for the remainder, she emitted a low level of such cues. The accomplice was carefully trained until she could readily emit contrasting levels of these cues in the two conditions (neutral or positive nonverbal cues).

Results

A multivariate analysis of variance on subjects' ratings of the applicant along job-related dimensions yielded a significant main effect for nonverbal cues, $F(5.61) = 6.02$, $p \leq .005$. This effect stemmed from the fact that subjects rated the accomplice more favorably on all of these measures when she emitted a high rather than low level of positive nonverbal cues. In addition, the three-way interaction between sex of subject, nonverbal cues, and use of artificial scent closely approached significance $F(5, 61) = 1.98$, $p \leq .07$. Follow-up univariate analyses revealed that this interaction was significant for ratings of the applicant's potential future success, $F(1, 65) = 3.90$, $p \leq .05$, and approached significance for ratings of intelligence, $F(1,65) = 2.76$, $p \leq .10$. Mean ratings of potential for job success are shown in Table 15.2. As can be seen from this table, the predicted "too much of a good thing" effect appeared among male interviewers but not among females. Male interviewers assigned higher ratings to the accomplice when this person either emitted positive nonverbal cues or wore artificial scent, than when the female accomplice employed both impression management tactics. Similar effects were not observed among female interviewers.

A multivariate analysis of variance performed on the data relating to personal characteristics of the accomplice (i.e., applicant) yielded a significant main effect for nonverbal cues, $F(4, 62) = 7.80$, $p \leq .005$, and a significant interaction between scent and sex of subject, $F(4,62) = 3.06$, $p \leq .025$. Follow-up univariate analyses indicated that subjects assigned higher ratings to the accomplice for personal grooming, $F(1, 65) = 3.82$, $p \leq .025$ and friendliness, $F(1, 65) = 29.25$, $p \leq .001$, when she emitted many rather than few positive nonverbal cues. The interaction between scent and sex of subject stemmed from the fact that male interviewers rated the accomplice as more attractive when she wore perfume ($M = 6.00$) than when she did not ($M = 5.33$, $p \leq .05$). In contrast, female interviewers rated the accomplice as equally attractive whether she wore perfume ($M = 5.38$) or did not ($M = 5.40$).

Subjects' memory of accomplice responses to scripted questions was assessed by six questions pertaining to this information. Answers were scored as correct (1) or incorrect (0) and these data were then subjected to an analysis of variance. This analysis yielded a significant three-way interaction between scent, nonverbal cues, and sex of subject $F(1, 65) = 4.27$, $p \leq .05$. The means involved in this interaction are presented in Table 15.3. As can be seen from this table, males remembered more information presented by the accomplice when she either emitted positive nonverbal

TABLE 15.2.   Mean Ratings of Accomplice's Potential for Success as a Function
of Nonverbal Cues, Sex of Subject, and Use of Artificial Scent

| | No Scent | | Scent | |
Sex of Subject	Neutral Cues	Positive Cues	Neutral Cues	Positive Cues
Male	4.50_{ac}	5.50_{bd}	5.29_{bcd}	4.90_{bc}
Female	4.80_{acd}	5.70_{bd}	3.89_{a}	5.67_{bd}

NOTE: Means that do not share a common subscript differ significantly ($p \leq .05$).

cues or wore artificial scent than when she employed both of these tactics
of impression management. Again, a similar pattern was not apparent among
females.

Discussion

The results of this study provide additional evidence for the hypothesized
"too much of a good thing" effect. Among male interviewers (but not among
females), the accomplice was rated as possessing greater potential for future
success and as more intelligent when she either wore artificial scent or
emitted positive nonverbal cues than when she demonstrated both of these
tactics. Similarly, males remembered more of the information presented
by the accomplice during the interview when she wore perfume or emitted
positive nonverbal cues than when she employed both tactics in combination. Together, these findings support the suggestion that where impression management during employment interviews is concerned, moderation
may indeed be the best course.

Contrary to predictions, however, similar findings were not observed
among females. One possible explanation for this unexpected sex difference
may be that males are less adept at ignoring various aspects of applicants'
personal appearance than females. Previous research has indicated that males
are aware of their own shortcomings in this respect; they realize that they
are more "susceptible" to appearance-related factors (Baron, 1983). As
a result, when confronted with attempts at impression management, males
may react more negatively than females. This is because they realize that
they will experience difficulty in coping with such tactics, and that this difficulty, in turn, may adversely affect their performance as interviewers.
The result is that males react more negatively than females to the use of
these types of impression management tactics, and so tend to downrate applicants who use such procedures. Further evidence on the accuracy of these

TABLE 15.3. Mean Recognition Memory for Information Presented by Accomplice as a Function of Nonverbal Cues, Sex of Subject, and Use of Artificial Scent

	No Scent		Scent	
Sex of Subject	Neutral Cues	Positive Cues	Neutral Cues	Positive Cues
Male	5.33ac	5.70bc	5.63bc	4.78a
Female	5.80bc	5.80bc	5.56bc	5.56bc

NOTE: Means that do not share a common subscript differ significantly ($p \leq .05$).

suggestions can be obtained in future studies specifically designed to compare the abilities of males and females to ignore irrelevant personal characteristics of others when evaluating their performance or future potential.

Impression Management, the "Too Much of a Good Thing" Effect, and Social Cognition: A Theoretical Integration

Taken together, the findings of the two studies described above, plus those of related investigations (Baron, 1987; Cardy & Dobbins, 1986), suggest that efforts at impression management during employment interviews can indeed go too far. Beyond some point, they may backfire and reduce rather than enhance the ratings assigned to their users. Previous research, however, has not directly addressed a crucial question: Why, precisely, do these effects occur? More generally, why do tactics of impression management enhance applicants' ratings when used in moderation, but reduce them when employed to excess? One possible explanation is suggested by recent research concerned with the impact of affective reactions upon social cognition (Isen, 1987).

Such research suggests that positive and negative affect, induced by a wide variety of events, can exert strong effects upon memory, the cognitive organization of information, decision making, the propensity to take risks, and even creativity (Isen, 1987; Isen, Daubman, & Nowicki, 1987; Park, Sims, & Motowidlo, 1986). It has been found that (1) information consistent with current affective states (i.e., mood) is often recalled more accurately than information inconsistent with such reactions; (2) the interpretation of ambiguous stimuli is shifted in a positive or negative direction by

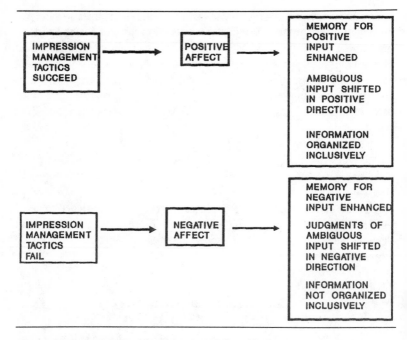

Figure 15.1. Impression Management and Cognition

NOTE: Theoretical model of the impact of impression management tactics used by job applicants upon interviewer's affective states, cognitive processes, and evaluations of applicants.

positive and negative affect, respectively; and (3) individuals who experience positive affect organize information more inclusively than persons who do not experience such an affect (e.g., they perceive more and richer relationships between diverse stimuli).

Applying these findings to the role of impression management during job interviews, the following predictions are suggested. When such tactics produce their intended effect (i.e., when they induce positive affective states among target persons), subsequent evaluations of applicants through the above mechanisms (e.g., recall of positive information about such persons) are enhanced, judgment is "tilted" in a positive direction, and the breadth of such key cognitive categories as "acceptable" is increased. In contrast, when such tactics are perceived as excessive, and negative affective responses are induced (see also Weiner et al., 1987), opposite effects will follow (e.g., recall of negative information about applicants will be increased, judgments will be "tilted" in a negative direction, and the breadth of key cognitive categories will be reduced). These predictions are represented in Figure 15.1.

To summarize, it is suggested that tactics of impression management produce their effects upon subsequent evaluations of job candidates by inducing varying degrees of positive or negative affect among interviewers. Such affect, in turn, influences cognitive processes which play a key role in the appraisal process that is, presumably, the central goal of employment interviews. Depending on the nature of the affect generated by efforts at impression management, enhancement or reduction of such evaluations may result.

One final question remains: what factors determine whether efforts at impression management will generate positive or negative affect among interviewers? To date, little direct evidence on this issue exists (see also Godfrey et al., 1986). However, it seems likely that a wide range of factors involving applicants' skill in the use of such tactics all play a role (e.g., their apparent appropriateness to the interview context, the extent to which they appear to represent intentional efforts at manipulation (Weiner et al., 1987), and interviewers' degree of prior exposure to them). Future research is needed to delineate the nature and impact of such factors, as well as to extend the "too much of a good thing" effect beyond the confines of laboratory simulations.

PART VII

Interpersonal Dynamics

Although considerable research has been conducted on the post-interview reactions of interviewers and applicants to the employment interview, limited research attention has been directed toward understanding the dynamics of the interview event itself. Research on interview process dynamics requires a theoretical perspective that captures the dyadic level of analysis between applicant and interviewer, not just the information processing of each separately. The following two chapters offer both theoretical and methodological frameworks from which promising interview process research can be conducted.

Liden and Parsons summarize research from organizational communications and psychology which is relevant to the dyadic interaction between interviewer and applicant. They apply this research to the study of the employment interview within an organizational behavior context. The authors summarize the major analytic techniques designed to assess reciprocal dyadic interaction.

Tullar offers script analysis, a useful theoretical framework for understanding the employment interview. His chapter shows how the notion of the cognitive performing script explains interview variations and provides an explanation for the vagaries of interviewer recall of applicant information. Tullar also examines the subsequent effects of script following and breaking on mindful and mindless interview behaviors. Research strategies for studying the interview from a scriptal perspective are suggested.

16

Understanding Interpersonal Behavior in the Employment Interview: A Reciprocal Interaction Analysis

Robert C. Liden
Georgia Institute of Technology

Charles K. Parsons
Georgia Institute of Technology

Considerable research on interviewer reactions to applicants (e.g., Jablin & McComb, 1984), and applicant responses to interviewers and the interview process (e.g., Rynes, Heneman, & Schwab, 1980) has been conducted on the employment interview. However, few researchers have examined both interviewer and applicant reactions within the same study. Especially rare in the organizational behavior and human resource management literatures are studies of the interview process (Arvey, 1979; Dipboye, 1982; Tengler & Jablin, 1983). Here, process signifies here the dyadic social interaction that takes place between interviewer and applicant in the employment interview setting. Perhaps the lack of consistency across studies of interviewer and applicant reactions to the interview can be explained by investigating this dyadic interaction (Street, 1986). Understanding interviewer and applicant reactions to an interview may require examination of the way in which interviewer behavior influences the applicant during the interview, and vice-versa.

A conceptual model is proposed and presented in Figure 16.1 in an attempt to organize research that relates to the interview process. In general, the model presents preinterview impressions, the interview process, and postinterview reactions from both interviewer and applicant perspectives. Individual characteristics are presented as influencing all three components of the model. Although "the interview itself" component contains the reciprocal dyadic interaction between the interviewer and applicant that is the focus of this chapter, inclusion of the other components illustrates the way in which the interview process issues are embedded in the existing literature on the employment interview. More detail on these "other components" is provided in models by Arvey and Campion (1982), Dipboye (1982), and Schmitt (1976).

Preinterview Impressions

To understand the initial verbal and nonverbal exchange that takes place between the interviewer and applicant at the beginning of the interview, it may be important to consider preinterview impressions. Interviewers may form impressions from resumes, application blanks, reference letters, and the like (see Dipboye, this volume). Applicants may develop preinterview perceptions based on knowledge of the organization from published records or friends who work for the organization.

Interviewers

There appears to be conflicting evidence on the extent to which preinterview information influences the types and patterns of questions asked by the interviewer (e.g., Binning, Goldstein, Garcia, & Scattaregia, 1988; Dipboye, Fontenelle, & Garner, 1984). Negative preinterview information might exacerbate negative information received during the interview (see also Rasmussen, 1984). Or, negative preinterview information might simply be combined in a linear fashion with additional negative information received during the interview.

Some insight on the effect of preinterview information may be provided in work by Snyder and Swann (1978). They suggested that interviewers ask questions that confirm their preinterview impressions of an interview applicant (see also Dipboye, 1982). Although initial tests of this hypothesis within the context of an employment interview were not supported with samples of students (McDonald & Hakel, 1985) or actual recruiters (Sackett, 1982), Binning et al. (1988) argued that this lack of support may be due to a methodological flaw. In both studies interviewers were asked to select questions from a list designed to elicit either positive or negative information about the applicant. Binning et al. (1988) instead asked subjects to write their own questions, which were later coded as "positive" or "negative" questions. With this strategy, it was found that interviewers who interviewed applicants with unimpressive resumes and applications asked significantly more negative questions than did interviewers in the impressive resume and application blank condition. Although not assessed by Binning et al. (1988), it appears that interviewer nonverbal behavior may also have been influenced by preinterview impressions (Dipboye, 1982).

Preinterview impressions may be formed by interviewers on the basis of the applicant's sex, race, age, or ethnic background (derived from the

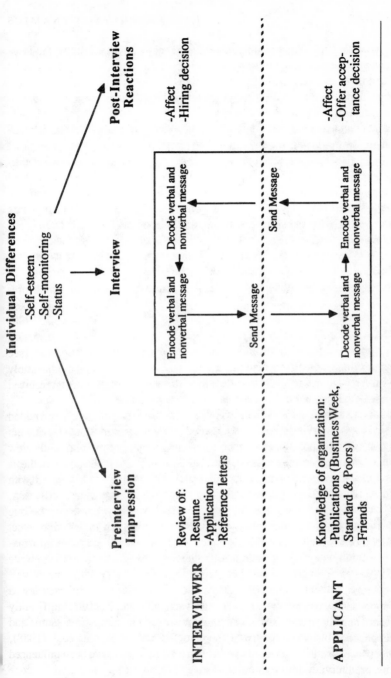

Figure 16.1. Model of the Employment Interview Process

person's name). For example, an interviewer who is racially prejudiced may start off an interview with dominating verbal behavior and corresponding nonverbal behavior (e.g., forward lean, little eye contact, stern, no smiling) in an attempt to confirm the assumption that this is not a good applicant (see also Dipboye, 1982; Snyder & Swann, 1978). If the applicant is indeed intimidated by the interviewer's initial behavior, the applicant's performance during the interview may suffer.

It is also possible that interviewer bias based on applicant individual characteristics may surface at the outset of the interview. For example, the present authors know of a student who felt that the best way to find an organization that he would feel comfortable working for would be to wear blue jeans, a flannel shirt, and boots, and to keep his long hair and beard when interviewing for a job. Over 90% of the time, after the interviewer realized that he was the applicant, the interviewer immediately cancelled the interview. In less extreme cases, the interviewer's behavior during the interview may be influenced by the first impression of the applicant.

Applicants

Applicants may also form impressions of what the interview will be like. For example, based on reading articles in *Business Week* or discussions with friends, an applicant may decide to dress very formally for an interview with IBM, but much more casually for an interview with Apple Computer. Similarly, an applicant may find out that a particular organization uses stress interviews, and this knowledge might be important in guiding the applicant's preinterview impressions and strategy for behaving in the interview. Research by von Baeyer, Sherk, and Zanna (1981) provides an interesting example of the effect that preinterview impressions can have on applicants. Female students, playing the role of job applicants, presented themselves in a more feminine way (i.e., both verbally and nonverbally, including physical appearance) when led to believe that they were being interviewed by a traditional (chauvinist) male interviewer as compared with a nontraditional male interviewer.

It has been suggested that people organize their perceptions of an upcoming dyadic interaction (such as an interview) according to either offensive or defensive psychological sets (Swann, Pelham, & Roberts, 1987). Offensive chunking involves framing an interaction in "my action–partner's action" units whereas "partner's action–my action" units are used in defensive chunking. Swann et al. (1987) argued that applicants typically use defensive psychological sets, and that this type of chunking makes applicants feel that their behavior is not influencing the interviewer's behavior. Their mind set is such that they do not consider the influence that they could have on the interviewer. Although this may be true for some applicants, the impression management literature (Liden & Mitchell, 1988) indicates that many people may form offensive psychological sets and strive to present the desired image (see Gilmore and Ferris, this volume). In fact, applicants may be quite aggressive in attempts to influence the interviewer (Dipboye & Wiley, 1977, 1978). An aggressive applicant may use a number of strategies in order to impress the interviewer: Walk purposefully into the interview room, use a firm handshake, maintain eye contact, sit with upright posture, speak forcefully and with confidence, make flattering comments about the interviewer and/or the organization, and so forth.

In most cases it is unlikely that the applicant will know about the interviewer's individual characteristics prior to the interview. So preinterview impressions will probably not be influenced by interviewer sex, race, age, and other individual characteristics. More important will be the individual characteristics of the applicant. For example, individuals who are high in self-esteem will be more confident of performing well in the interview (Ellis & Taylor, 1983), and high self-monitoring individuals will likely form a strategy for presenting themselves in the interview based on what they know about the organization (von Baeyer et al., 1981).

In summary, both interviewer and applicant appear to form preinterview impressions that can presumably influence the verbal and nonverbal behavior of both parties at the outset, and perhaps for the duration of the interview.

The Interview Process

An examination is now made of the interview process portion of Figure 16.1, which involves the interaction that takes place between interviewer and applicant. This is the component of the model that has received virtually no attention in the organizational behavior and human resource management literatures (Arvey, 1979). Although several researchers have conducted studies consistent with Arvey and Campion's (1982) suggestion for interview research to examine such variables as person perception (e.g., Liden & Parsons, 1986; Schmitt & Coyle, 1976), attribution, and impression management (Dipboye & Wiley, 1977, 1978), this research has focused on the separate effects these variables have on interviewer and applicant postinterview reactions. The current authors are not aware of studies in organizational behavior that have examined the effect of such variables on interviewer and applicant behavior *during* the interview, and how this behavior influences the other individual.

In fact, at a more general level, behavioral scientists have tended to ignore message sequences when studying verbal and nonverbal behaviors.[1] The unit of analysis is typically the individual or group, and the *interaction* between individuals is ignored (Cappella, 1981). Although research has shown that verbal and nonverbal messages affect outcomes, such as interviewer reactions to an applicant and hiring decisions, these messages or cues may also influence the interviewer's own verbal and nonverbal behavior during the interview. This may, in turn, affect the behavior of the applicant, and so on. In essence, the interviewer and applicant may be constantly processing verbal and nonverbal cues from each other, and using this information to adjust their behavior during the interview.

As shown in Figure 16.1, the interview process is conceptualized as a hybrid of the Katz and Kahn (1978) role model and the basic communication model (Shannon & Weaver, 1948; Schramm, 1953). The steps of the interview process shown in the figure should not be interpreted as following a step-by-step sequence, but rather as a constant, simultaneous encoding and decoding of verbal and nonverbal behavior by both the interviewer and the applicant.

Reciprocation and Compensation

After a verbal or nonverbal cue has been decoded, individuals may respond either by reciprocating or compensating (Cappella, 1981). A reciprocal response involves matching increases and decreases in the other person's verbal and/or nonverbal behavior. For example, the disclosure-reciprocity effect found in a number of studies involves an individual making a self-disclosure after the other person has made a self-disclosure (Davis, 1977; Miller & Kenny, 1986). Reciprocity may also occur with nonverbal behaviors. For example, an interviewer who smiles and maintains eye-contact may induce an applicant to do the same, and if the interviewer becomes more serious later in the interview, the applicant may reciprocate by being more serious as well.

Compensation occurs when a person reacts to a partner's verbal and/or nonverbal behavior either by increasing or decreasing the amount of that behavior. For example, an applicant who addresses the interviewer by his/her first name may prompt the interviewer to become more formal during the interview. It appears that compensation does not always involve the identical verbal or nonverbal behavior. For example, applicant responses to interviewer questions tend to be shorter when the interviewer does not maintain eye contact with the applicant (Kleinke, 1986).

Although support has been found for both the reciprocal (e.g., Matarazzo & Wiens, 1972) and compensation (Cappella & Planalp, 1981) hypotheses, Patterson (1982) noted that inconsistencies abound in this literature. In an attempt to reconcile these inconsistencies in the empirical studies,

Patterson claimed that arousal states will determine whether reciprocation or compensation will occur. In a positive state, where an individual feels good about the other person and would like to receive more intimate nonverbals (e.g., smiles, eye contact, touching), the individual will reciprocate these behaviors. In a negative state, Patterson (1982) hypothesized that compensation will occur.

Positive states may develop from perceived similarity with the other person. For example, Street and Brady (1982) postulated that receivers hold speech stereotypes whereby such noncontent aspects as rate, inflection, and accent are related to beliefs about the speaker's competence as well as social attractiveness. Although past research had found a linear relation between speech rate and perceived competence, Street and Brady hypothesized that speech rates that are similar to a receiver's will be perceived as being more favorable. They tested this proposition by presenting audio taped passages to undergraduates. The subjects also had their speech rate computed. Results showed that there was a linear relation between speech rate (i.e., on the stimulus tape) and the perceived competence and social attractiveness. There was also an interaction between listener's and speaker's speech rate on perceived competence: faster speaking listeners rated faster talkers as more competent and judged slower talkers as being less competent. No interactions were found for social attractiveness.

Ambiguity in Encoding

So far it has been assumed that both the interviewer and applicant have no difficulty decoding messages. Sometimes, however, there may be ambiguity interpreting the verbal and/or nonverbal messages of the other individual (e.g., Hall, 1978). For example, Leathers (1979) was interested in how listeners interpret the speaker's basic attitude when verbal and nonverbal channels communicate inconsistent meanings. Although some studies have shown that nonverbal cues are weighted more heavily, some researchers have hypothesized that receivers weight the channel that is seen as most believable. Leathers (1979) had discussions video and audiotaped. A trained confederate manipulated the independent variables of interest. Four different scripts were presented: (1) positive nonverbal, positive verbal (NV+, V+); (2) NV+, V−; (3) NV−, V+; and (4) NV−, V−. The videotapes were then coded, and results were interpreted. First, receivers relied more heavily on nonverbals than verbals to communicate their response to inconsistent messages (NV+, V− or NV−, V+). Second, inconsistent messages had a disruptive effect on the decoding of nonverbal cues; receivers spent much time searching for additional cues. And third, responses to inconsistent messages resulted in confusion, the search for more cues, and outright withdrawal. The most negative reactions occurred in response to NV+, V− messages.

Exploring a related theme, Rasmussen (1984) investigated the interaction of verbal and nonverbal behavior. Specifically, he had undergraduate students view one of four videotapes of an actor playing the role of an applicant. The four tape scripts were based on combinations of high/low nonverbal behaviors (i.e., eye contact, smiling, hand gesturing, and head nodding) and appropriate/inappropriate verbal responses. Interestingly, high nonverbal behaviors positively influenced the qualification rating when the verbal content was good. However, high nonverbal behaviors had a negative influence when the verbal content was bad. It appears that the interpretation of nonverbals is influenced by the appropriateness of the verbal content. Rasmussen (1984) suggested that nonverbals may enhance the magnitude of the effects of verbal content but not the direction.

It is also relevant to better understand the role that nonverbals play in the interpretation of verbal behavior. Woodall and Folger (1985) demonstrated, in a videotape study, that hand gestures affect a listener's recall of a partner's verbal behavior. Specifically, they found that gestures that carry some semantic meaning associated with the verbal message (referred to as emblematic) provide much greater recall of the verbal message even after one week than do emphasizing gestures (e.g., pounding the table) or no gesturing. Different (manipulated) instructions given to subjects prior to viewing the videotape did not produce any significant effects; results were the same whether subjects were specifically asked to look for associations between verbal and nonverbal behavior or were asked simply to watch the tape carefully. Though not empirically examined, the authors suggested that in situations where the verbal communication is unclear or uninterpretable, the listener/observer may have observation goals that emphasize the encoding of more nonverbal features and may use these cues differently in reconstructing a memory trace. It may be that when interviewers are confronted with verbal communications that are meaningless in terms of distinguishing good from poor applicants, they will attempt to encode semantic meaning from gesturing and other nonverbal behaviors which accompany the verbal behavior. This encoding may then create the selective recall of certain verbal behavior to be used in judgment.

Relational Control

An emerging stream of research in communications has attempted to categorize verbal behavior in dyadic interactions in terms of dominance, submission, and equivalence (Rogers & Farace, 1975). This approach has been used in examining communication patterns in different types of dyads such as leader-subordinate (Fairhurst, Rogers, & Sarr, 1987; Watson, 1982), police officer-citizen (Glauser & Tullar, 1985), and interviewer-applicant (Tullar, 1986). In general, these studies have shown that relational control measures, such as the total number of dominant verbal messages in a conversation, are related to outcomes such as satisfaction with the interaction. For example, Fairhurst et al. (1987) were interested in the correspondence between dominance demonstrated by leaders and subordinates during a typical work interaction, and self-report measures of the leader-member relationship. Correlations were found between dominance indices for leaders and reports of general decision-making involvement by subordinates.

In another study, Tullar (1986) videotaped 61 college undergraduates who were being interviewed by potential employers. Tapes from 14 applicants who were eventually given second interviews, and 14 applicants who were not, were coded for dominance, structuring, equivalence, and submissiveness on the part of both interviewer and applicant. The behavior patterns were modeled through Markov matrices. It was found that successful applicants show more dominance and equivalence behavior in response to an interviewer's structuring utterances than do unsuccessful applicants.

Although some studies have explored the effect of the relational control of verbal messages on the relational control aspects of the other individual's verbal response, data have been analyzed on an aggregate basis. For example, the number of times that a dominant verbal behavior is followed by submissive verbal behavior is recorded. In future research, it is recommended that the effects relational control may have on each person's verbal behavior *during* the interview be investigated. For example, will an interviewer's use of dominant verbal behavior at the outset of an interview preclude applicant dominance later in the interview?

Individual Differences

According to the model in Figure 16.1, individual differences such as sex, race, and personality may influence the interview process. For example, Street and Murphy (1987) were interested in how a construct called "Interpersonal Orientation" (IO) influenced communication behavior during the conversation. Conversations were coded for turn duration, vocalization duration, internal pause, response latency, speech rate, interruptive simultaneous speech, and non-interruptive simultaneous speech. It was found that high IO people routinized some of their communication behaviors such as gesturing and vocal behavior, and could thus focus their cognitive resources on monitoring the other person's responses, choosing content, and the like. These findings relate to the literature on automatic processing of social information (e.g., Bargh & Pietromonaco, 1982).

Individual differences such as personality influence both interviewer and applicant first impressions as well as initial communication exchanges between interviewer and applicant. These initial exchanges at the outset of the interview, in turn, alter the pattern of subsequent interaction (e.g., Dipboye, 1982; Taylor & Sniezek, 1984; Tullar, 1986).

Postinterview Reactions

What takes place early in an interview influences the behavior of both interviewer and applicant for the duration of the interview, which in turn affects the overall interviewer-applicant reactions each forms about the other after the interview is completed. It can safely be assumed that interviewer reactions to the applicant (e.g., Amalfitano & Kalt, 1977; Arvey, 1979; Arvey & Campion, 1982; Eder & Buckley, 1988; Imada & Hakel, 1977; Jablin & McComb, 1984; Kinicki & Lockwood, 1985; Parsons & Liden 1984; Sterrett, 1978) and applicant responses to the interviewer (e.g., Downs, 1969; Ellis & Taylor, 1983; Fisher, Ilgen, & Hoyer, 1979; Harris & Fink, 1987; Jablin & McComb, 1984; Liden & Parsons, 1986; Powell, 1984; Rynes, Heneman, & Schwab, 1980; Rynes & Miller, 1983; Schmitt & Coyle, 1976) are largely determined by the interview process. Research is now needed to examine the way in which the nature of the dyadic interaction between interviewer and applicant during the interview translates into postinterview reactions.

As indicated in Figure 16.1, individual differences may further complicate the interview process. Although the effect of such individual differences such as race, sex, age, and personality may influence interviewer (e.g., Dipboye, 1978; Jackson, Peacock, & Smith, 1980; Parsons & Liden, 1984) and applicant reactions to the interview (e.g., Liden & Parsons, 1986; Rynes et al., 1980), the effects tend to be small or insignificant (Graves & Powell, 1988; Powell, 1987). Future research should examine individual difference main effects and interactions that may occur between interviewer and applicant during the interview.

Data Analysis for Interviewer-Applicant Interactions

As dyadic interactions are more closely analyzed, more attention by organizational scientists is being paid to the statistical methods used for deriving meaning from the data. Various approaches have been suggested in the literature, with some corresponding controversies, which provide guidelines for the choices that researchers must make in this area. Because of the evolving nature of this area, no claim is intended here to be comprehensive.

The first approach uses a relational coding scheme that yields data concerning patterns of communication that are interpreted as dominance, deference, restriction, and so forth. These data can be used to provide a "trait" characterization of each partner in the interaction. For example, Tullar (1986) used the proportion of each type of utterance in an employment interview by each partner as indicating that partner's contribution to the interview as a whole. These individually based variables can be correlated with other variables of interest (e.g., the correlation between applicant dominance behavior and the interviewer's overall impression of the applicant's qualifications). However, in order to better analyze the communication interactions, each incident of interviewer-applicant (or applicant-interviewer) communication needs to be recorded in such a way that two-way contingency tables results. Here, tables are created that represent applicant behavior as antecedent and interviewer behavior as subsequent, and vice-versa. The transitional matrices are then treated as Markov matrices (see for comparison Faraone & Dorfman, 1987; Gottman, 1979). An example of a transitional probability would be as follows: given that the applicant provides a dominant utterance, what is the probability that the interviewer will provide a submissive utterance. The transition matrices then characterize the pattern of interviewer-applicant communication behavior. Statistical tests exist that allow a comparison between the matrix from interviews where the applicant is judged unsuccessful, and a matrix from interviews where the applicant is judged successful.

A second approach also analyzes dyadic interactions from the relational communication perspective, but adopts a different coding scheme (Rogers & Farace, 1975). This approach defines the "interact" between two people as being the unit of analysis (as opposed to the behavior of two individuals). The coding of "interacts" provides a sequential pattern of "interact" types which can be interpreted. For example, when a large proportion of interacts is characterized by one of the partners asserting definitional rights, followed by the other partner's acceptance of this definition, the asserting partner is characterized as "dominant." When there are few changes in the type of "interact" throughout the communication episode, it is characterized as rigid. These interaction "trait" measures then form continuous variables, which can be analyzed with either standard univariate or multivariate data analysis methods (e.g., correlation, multiple regression). An alternative approach to analysis would be to examine the time series of interacts to observe discontinuities that might be attributable to factors of interest.

The similarity of different relational coding schemes was studied by O'Donnell-Trujillo (1981). Coders were trained to use either the Rogers and Farace (1975) scheme or the Ellis (1979) scheme. Transcripts from 1 minute discussions by marital dyads were coded by two groups of coders. Then, reliability of coding was estimated using Cohen's kappa statistic. Reliabilities across scheme were .12 to .27 for 3 categories of communication. Within scheme, the reliability between raters was quite high (.71 to .89 for the Ellis system and .72 to .92 for the Rogers and Farace system).

To give the reader some idea of the amount of time and effort involved in this type of analysis reference, reference is made to the study by Fairhurst et al. (1987). In this investigation, audiotapes were coded at the level of communication transaction and frequencies determined. The authors reported that the information culled from 30 minute audiotapes resulted in over 14 pages of transcription per tape, and the number of transactions per dyad ranged from 128 to 743. Similarly, in the Tullar (1986) study, the coding required a great deal of effort as evidenced by the three months taken by two full-time coders.

One assumption implicit in the above approaches is that "interact" is characterized by the temporally contiguous behaviors of two people. That is, a partner's dominance is measured by the proportion of times that his/her statement of definitional rights is immediately followed by the acceptance of such rights by the other person. Other researchers have relaxed this assumption in order to allow for the testing of hypotheses where the dependence of one person's behavior on the other's may not be immediately manifested. The general category of statistical methods here concerns testing for "lagged dependence" of one person's behavior on another's (e.g., Budescu, 1984).

The data used for these techniques comes from dividing up a behavioral episode between partners into time intervals (for instance, 1 minute). Each time interval is then observed and coded as to whether each partner in a dyad exhibited a behavior or not (i.e., assuming a categorical variable). Each partner's data then represent a pattern of 1's and 0's with as many observations as there are time intervals. If X represents the interviewer's behavior and Y represents the applicant's behavior, then X_t and Y_t represent the presence or absence of the behavior of interest in time interval t. One way to approach the estimation of lagged dependence is to state the null hypothesis that:

$$P(Y_{t+1} = 1 | X_{t=1}) - P(Y_{t=1}) = 0.$$

where $P(Y_{t+1} = 1 | X_{t=1} = 1)$ is the conditional probability that the applicant's behavior occurred at time $t+1$ given the interviewer's behavior occurred at time t, while $P(Y_t = 1)$ is the unconditional probability of the applicant's behavior occurring at time $t+1$. Various statistics have been derived that are assumed to be normally distributed under the null hypothesis. However, the assumptions and limitations underlying these statistics await further clarification (Allison & Liker, 1982; Dumas, 1986).

Alternative approaches to analyzing the contingency tables that can result from dyadic interactions have been suggested. For example, Feick and Novak (1985) have recommended the use of log-linear models as mechanisms for examining more finely the structure of the dependence. Dillon, Madden, and Kumar (1983) have suggested that a latent structure analysis might also allow the testing of different causal hypotheses in sequential interaction data.

Several approaches to gathering and analyzing data from dyadic interaction episodes, such as the employment interview, have been presented. At this point, it is premature to suggest which of these methods is superior. Comparison of several approaches within the same empirical study is recommended.

Summary

In this chapter, the literatures in organizational communications and psychology were advanced as offering useful insights for studying the employment interview. Acquiring a better understanding of the process dynamics of what actually transpires between an interviewer and applicant during an interview may initially appear to be a basic interpersonal relations research problem, one with few direct applications to employment decisions. Although this may partially be true, the present authors believe that better understanding of the interview process may uncover additional factors that contribute to the interview's historically low predictive validity (Zedeck, Tziner, & Middlestadt, 1983), and may help greatly in the design of more effective training programs for interviewers (Gatewood & Feild, 1987) and applicants (Campion & Campion, 1987).

In addition to practical considerations, there are numerous implications for future research. It has been stressed that more empirical studies of the interview process (i.e., the dyadic interaction between interviewer and applicant) is sorely needed. Beyond this, the incremental effect that these interaction dynamics have on postinterview affect, and decisions of both interviewers and applicants, needs to be specified. How much additional variance in interviewer and applicant postinterview reactions can be explained by the interview process (that is not already captured by individual and organization level variables which have already been researched extensively)? Answers to these questions should not only enhance the employment interview literature, but may also be generalized to other types of dyadic exchange (e.g., supervisor-subordinate; employee-customer) which regularly occur in organizational settings.

Note

1. Throughout this chapter, a distinction is made between verbal and nonverbal behaviors to reflect their separate treatment in empirical studies and the finding in several studies suggesting that verbal and nonverbal components of messages do not always have consistent meaning (e.g., Leathers, 1979; Woodall & Folger, 1985).

17

The Employment Interview as a Cognitive Performing Script

William L. Tullar
University of North Carolina at Greensboro

Following the lead of studies in social cognition (e.g., Abelson, 1981; Schank & Abelson, 1977; Sims & Gioia, 1986), this chapter conceives of the employment interview as a cognitive performing script. Using this starting point, this chapter attempts a full conceptualization of the employment interview as a scripted event, explaining the functions of both interviewer and applicant scripts. This then leads to a discussion of the psychometric failure of the interview in scriptal terms, shows how microanalytic study results may be explained in terms of scripts, and culminates in suggestions for research that may help to improve the employment interview.

The interview as a cognitive performing script allows a framework to better understand the dynamics of interviewing in at least four ways: (1) It provides a system for analyzing the applicant-interviewer interaction; (2) it provides a vocabulary to describe a number of important aspects of interview structure; (3) it suggests reasons why interviewer information processing may be defective; and (4) it suggests that allowing only standard script performance on the part of the applicant may not be an efficient use of time.

The Script Concept

The script concept has been suggested as a potential explanation for a number of different phenomena in organizations (Gioia & Poole, 1984; Gioia & Manz, 1984; Sims & Gioia, 1986). The script, as delineated by Abelson (1981), is a schema that mediates social behavior in common, well-understood situations. Unlike more abstract schemata, scripts are well-structured and allow for a more focused analysis and investigation of social activity. More specifically, Abelson (1976) defined the script as "a coherent sequence of events expected by an individual, involving him either as a participant or as an observer'' (p.33).

Gioia and his colleagues at Penn State explored the development of scripts in organizational settings. Poole (1984) noted that as an organization develops, one way participants can render the experience meaningful is to develop scripts. Such scripts allow participants to engage in coordinated behavior which they believe is situationally appropriate. In new situations, people must attend closely to what is going on. But gradually, as a task or situation becomes more familiar, people develop scripts to deal with it. According to Mangham (1978), organization participants seek to reduce the equivocality in their organizational world by arriving at mutually satisfying accommodations with others. Two or more individuals, involved in activity for which interaction is required to accomplish a task, can create interlocking behaviors that are reciprocal, repetitive, and contingent, that is, they perform according to a script.

A well formulated script is composed of several major scenes. Each scene is a principle activity that occurs with each repetition of a particular script. In the restaurant script discussed by Schank and Abelson (1977), the major scenes include entering the restaurant, ordering the food, eating the food, and leaving the restaurant. While a variety of behaviors may occur within the major scene of a script, the major scenes nearly always occur in each run through of the script and in some sense hold the script together.

Abelson (1981) suggested that three conditions must be met for scripted behavior to occur: (1) the script must be a stable and efficient knowledge structure for the individual; (2) an evoking context, or header, for the script must occur; and (3) the individual must enter the script. Script stability is determined by two factors: internal coherence and external similarity. Internal coherence refers to the probability that a common core of major scenes occurs across separate experiences of the same script. A script will have high internal coherence when the same major scenes can be expected to occur in nearly all the run throughs of the script. For instance, the interview has high internal coherence because of its core scenes of introduction and small talk, interviewer questions about the applicant's background, applicant questions about the organization, and customary leave-taking behavior. High internal coherence comes not just from the scenes, but also from the content of the interaction within the scenes. Many questions and answers occur only in this script.

A second factor in script stability is external similarity. External similarity refers to the extent that major scenes occur in situations other than the one governed by the script; the kinds of topics discussed in an employment interview, and indeed the whole character of the interaction, are different than those found in any other script. The lower the external similarity, the more stable and efficient the script. It seems safe to say that few situations in life closely resemble a job interview. Overall script stability is the maximization of the ratio of internal coherence to external stability. A script will be stable and have significant impact on behavior if it has high internal coherence and low external similarity. Given this requirement, the employment interview qualifies as a stable and efficient script.

Another precondition for scripted behavior is that it must be called up by a header or evoking condition (Schank & Abelson, 1977). Three types of headers make strong predictions that scripted behavior will occur. A *precondition header* is a condition or state that must occur before the script can be enacted. In order for the interview script to be enacted, one person must be (ostensibly) seeking employment, and one employer must be (ostensibly) seeking to hire someone. A header that makes stronger predictions about scripted behavior is the *instrumental header*. An instrumental header is a specific event that occurs just prior to the script. In an interview situation, this might be walking down to the placement office on campus or driving out to the company plant. A third type of header, the *locale header*, makes the strongest predictions of scripted behavior. Locale headers involve arriving at the time/place where the script is to be enacted. If the script is a stable and efficient knowledge structure and the appropriate headers have been presented, the script will be "called up" and enacted as the individual enters the first major scene.

One of the problems of script enactment is the possibility that the script will be performed without much conscious attention to details. Langer, Blank, and Chanowitz (1978) demonstrated that what appears to be thoughtful, consciously mediated action sometimes turns out to be quite mindless. Abelson (1981) argued that mindful behavior occurs in scripts in several ways. First, some scripts have major scenes that require thinking. In Abelson's (1981) restaurant example, one must decide what food to order. However, one can easily imagine how the food order becomes automated. Many people (the author included) have a tendency to order the same thing for lunch each day. In any case, a script may have a header in it which tells the person: "Now you must think ." However, in the repetition of interviews for an entry level management job, many interviewers will talk to fifty or sixty candidates before they settle on the five or ten they really want. Is not the interviewer's part of the interaction likely to be relatively mindless for many of the fifty or sixty? The script framework suggests that there are various places in the interview where the interviewer is cued: "Now you must gather data and remember it." This may explain, in part, Blakeney and McNaughton's (1971) finding that the temporal placement of unfavorable information in the interview had a substantial effect on interview judgement.

Abelson (1981) argued that there are eight factors that make one run-through of a script different from another: tracks, scene selection, variables, free behaviors, equifinal actions, paths, interferences, and distractions. Each of these is examined in turn to assess their implications for the employment interview.

Tracks refer to ways in which the major scenes can be embellished. Thus, an interviewer who conducts interviews for different positions will have a track for each different position. That is, the major scenes of the interview still include preinterview preparation, greeting and small talk, interviewer questioning, applicant inquiries, and interviewer wrap-up. However, these major scenes can be enacted in a number of different ways. The preinterview preparation is likely to be longer in an interview for a managerial position than it is in an interview for a clerical job. In addition, the small talk would be different, as would the questions asked during the questioning scene. Different tracks are necessary to make employment interviews relevant for the jobs for which they are used to select. However, different tracks can also serve to desensitize interviewers to information available in one track at a given scene, but not available in other tracks.

Scene selection is a second source of variation. In a weak script the major scenes are supposed to occur, but the order in which they occur may vary depending on the needs of the situation. In interviewing, it is possible to include hypothetical situations as separate scenes. The interviewer may use discretion as to how or when to introduce the hypothetical situation during the interview. Of course, scene selection is a source of variation in the interview script that is a major concern for equal employment opportunity. Unless minority candidates receive the same scenes in the same order, they will not be given the same opportunity in the interview. On the other hand, scene selection is one factor on which interviewers want to be able to use their professional judgment. If the applicant had already convinced the interviewer that he or she is inappropriate for the job, the rest of the interview is just grinding through the balance of the script. There is evidence that interviewers tend to make negative decisions early on in the interview and then abbreviate the rest of the script (Tullar, Mullins, & Caldwell, 1979; Tullar, 1986). Even with the abbreviation of the script, they still enact all of the major scenes, but they reduce the number of interacts in those scenes.

Variables are objects that remain constant during one enactment of a script, but differ in consecutive run-throughs. In a given interview track, the questions asked are the same, and are received in the same order during the questioning scene, but the question wording varies in consecutive run-throughs, even in the most standardized of interviews. Even in those cases where an interviewer follows a standardized form or template, the question wording will vary slightly from run through to run through.

Free behaviors are all the activities which can acceptably intermix with the events of the ongoing script. Free behaviors set bounds on what can and cannot be done. An interview could be conducted (or at least continued) while the interviewer takes the applicant on a brief tour of the plant, or shares a cup of coffee with the applicant in the cafeteria. However, the interviewer could not make romantic advances toward an applicant, such actions would exceed the accepted bounds of free behavior.

Equifinal actions are various communicative behaviors which can produce the same desired result within a given major scene. There are a number of ways of asking an applicant about experience the applicant had gained in a previous position. Some phrasings are more direct and some more obtuse, but as long as they elicit the desired information from the applicant, they are equifinal actions.

Script paths arise when one must choose between alternatives to normal procedures within a script. Thus, an interviewer may choose when to begin a line of questioning. Paths are thus branch points where decisions must be made as to which of several alternatives one should follow: alternatives available at branch points usually comprise a set of equifinal actions. Generally, paths have been employed in interviews when further probing is necessary to access certain kinds of information. For instance, an applicant's resume may show a gap in employment that the applicant is reluctant to discuss. The interviewer may have to take the path of asking several direct questions to uncover what the applicant was doing during the employment gap.

These first six factors produce variations a script and thus may necessitate thinking. However, acceptable variations are most likely learned and stored along with the script. Individuals may come to paths in scripts, make decisions, and then apply acceptable behaviors rather mechanically. Thus, scripted behavior may consist of chains of stimulus-response sequences, where some stimuli promote conscious cognitive mediation which in turn gives way to automaticity of performance. Therefore, stable scripts may promote both mindful and mindless behavior. Interviews as stable, efficient scripts also produce both mindful and mindless behavior. The fact that interviews involve mindless behavior on the part of the interviewer may explain the faulty information processing that recent studies (e.g. Arvey & Campion, 1982; Hakel, 1982; Reilly & Chao, 1982) have held to be the root problem with interviewing as a selection device.

The Interviewer Script

Virtually all literature reviews on the employment interview have called for more structure on the part of the interviewer. This notion has permeated the practitioner literature through a myriad of books, articles, and training manuals (e.g. Goodale, 1982; Mullins & Davis, 1982; Stewart & Cash. 1978). Even if interviewers have not read any of these "how to" publications, most receive some on-the-job training in interviewing principles and practice which probably incorporates these structuring suggestions. In addition, since the *1978 Uniform Guidelines* on selection were issued by the EEOC, many interviewers have become aware that the interview is regarded as a test by the EEOC. Hence, there is a need to standardize the interview in order to conform with the *Guidelines*. It is quite likely that after repetitive interviewing experience, the interviewer simply finds a script with which he or she is comfortable.

Figure 17.1 depicts the major scenes of the interviewer and applicant scripts. After the three types of headers have occurred (preconditional, instrumental, and locale), the interviewer is ready to enact Scene 1, Precontact Preparation. This scene occurs just prior to meeting the applicant. Here interviewers complete last minute preparations for the interaction to follow (e.g., prepare setting, review applicant's resume, go over reference check material). During this scene, interviewers also select the track to follow. For example, the interviewer may have a secretarial track, a clerical track, and a sales representative track. Although the activities that embellish the major scenes may vary somewhat due to differences across jobs, the major scenes will remain the same for most interviews. Various tracks are most likely learned by interviewers over time.

Though interviewers select the track to follow, little scene selection is available to them. Though a variety of equifinal actions can produce the same desired outcomes for each major scene, the specific major scenes and the order in which they occur are fairly well fixed. The Disengagement Scene, for example, cannot be enacted until the question and answer scenes have occurred. Likewise, the question and answer scenes cannot occur until the applicant has been greeted and rapport has been established.

The activities of Scene 2, Greeting and Establishment of Rapport, are highly standardized. Script paths do arise during small talk, however, because most interviewers have a variety of strategies to put applicants at ease (e.g., discussing the weather, sports, business news, common experiences). These topics represent equifinal actions for building rapport. Such actions are a subset of the free behaviors that are socially acceptable for interviewers. Most interviewers probably have a clear understanding

Scene	Applicant Script	Interviewer Script
1: Precontact Activities	• Check appearance/dress • Enter locale • Announce arrival • Review notes while waiting	• Review resume • Review interview guide • Make note of questions • Prepare setting
2: Greeting & Establish Rapport	• Shake hands • Sit when asked to • Make good impression in small talk	• Shake hands • Seat applicant • Relax applicant with appropriate small talk
3: Ask Job Related Questions	• Provide educational history • Provide details of work history • Detail personal skills and abilities • Try to demonstrate proper motivation for the job	• Ask educational background • Seek relevant details about work history • Discuss special skills and abilities • Get to applicant's motiva- tion to work
4: Answer Applicant Questions	• Ask about pay & benefits • Ask about opportunities for advancement • Ask about organization culture—work norms, etc.	• Answer applicant ques- tions putting face on organization • Try to create positive impression about organization
5: Disengagement	• Wait for interviewer cue that interview is over • Discuss next step • Stand up and shake hands • Exit	• Show that interview is about to conclude • Suggest what the next step will be • Stand up and shake hands • Show applicant out

Figure 17.1. Applicant and Interviewer Scripts

of what behaviors are appropriate. An interviewer may place his or her feet on the desk to convey casualness and informality, but he or she cannot make romantic advances toward an applicant in an attempt to build rapport. The set of free behaviors for the interviewer is quite different from the set of free behaviors for the applicant. Though it may be acceptable for an interviewer to be late, put his feet on the desk, and so forth, and applicant displaying these behaviors would be exceeding the set of free behaviors in his script.

After rapport has been established, interviewers are ready to initiate Scene 3, Ask Job Related Questions. More branch points arise during this scene than in any other, because the interviewer can to select from a variety of equifinal actions the specific paths to follow to acquire the desired information. The specific information needed is generally derived from a job analysis, but the interviewer has great freedom in how the information is to be obtained. The interviewer may use open-ended questions, direct questions, hypothetical probes, and so forth. Most likely interviewers have, within a given track, one set of equifinal actions to elicit educational history, another to attain work history, and so on. When the needed information is acquired, the interviewer will allow relational control to pass briefly into the applicant's hands for Scene 4, Applicant Asks Questions.

Even though control is relinquished to the applicant during Scene 4, interviewers probably have a well rehearsed set of answers to most common questions. Since the applicant is a script variable that remains constant throughout one enactment of the script, but changes from one interview to the next, this scene can vary considerably depending upon the information needs of the applicant. However, as with most of the rest of the script, repeated enactments protect the participants from embarrassment or social ambiguity: The experienced interviewer has fielded almost all possible questions before and has pat answers for them. Even for questions that the interviewer cannot answer, most interviewers have discovered that "I don't know about that because it's out of my department, but I can find out and get back to you . . ." is also a satisfactory answer.

Scene 5, Disengagement, is probably the most standardized of all the major scenes in the interview. Here the interviewer displays leave-taking behaviors to indicate that the interview is over. Discussion of the next step, standing up, shaking hands, and seeing the applicant out follows the classic sequence, and even the most persistent applicant gets the hint that the interview is over after a hand shake and a gentle guide toward the door.

The interview script is a stable and efficient knowledge structure for interviewers. Because the major scenes occur in almost every run though of the script, and since the order of scenes is well fixed, the interviewer script has high internal coherence. The interviewer script also has low external similarity, since the major scenes seldom occur in situations other than employment interviews. Thus, the ratio of internal coherence to external similarity is quite high, which means that the interviewer script should be a strong predictor of interviewer behavior.

As Gioia (1986, pp. 58-59) has noted:

> Script processing provides for efficient, but not necessarily effective, cognitive processing . . . information that has been incorporated into a script

has necessarily been transformed by the script. Recall is therefore based on the script, not necessarily on events actually experienced.

The script protects the interviewer from embarrassment and allows the interviewer to get through the day without becoming exhausted. If the interviewer actually had to attend carefully to each thing said by each applicant, every day would be a mentally exhausting experience similar in nature to taking the SAT's for the first time. However, just as the script protects, it also insulates. This insulation causes the interviewer to miss certain pieces of information, or at least not to process them properly. This is at least one reason for the psychometric failure of the interview.

The Applicant Script

The applicant is also guided by a cognitive performing script. Although the interview may occur less frequently for the applicant, it is an extremely significant event. The importance of the interview encourages most applicants to prepare thoroughly for its enactment. Individuals may thus expend more effort learning the applicant script than they do learning more commonly occurring scripts. High schools, technical schools, colleges, and universities abound with short courses in interviewing techniques. In most instances, some sort of organized role play of the interview is used to teach it. New graduates are also encouraged to interview with a number of different organizations before they interview for the job they really want.

Needing a job, securing an appointment, and arriving at the place of the interview are headers that lead to the enactment of the applicant script. Scene 1, Precontact Activities, probably occurs just after arriving at the location of the interview, but prior to greeting the interviewer. During this scene, applicants check their appearance (e.g., comb hair, check make-up, straighten tie), then report to the receptionist/secretary at the specific interview setting. While waiting, applicants likely review the mental or written notes they have made while preparing for the interview.

Scene 2, Greeting and Establishment of Rapport, is orchestrated largely by the interviewer. However, it is important for the applicant to appear able to discuss a number of different topics and to be sociable and likeable. Most training done on how to be successful in the interview emphasizes the importance of making a good impression in the first few minutes of the interview.

After a relatively short time the interviewer asks the first job related question, which serves as the header for Scene 3, Ask Job Related Questions. Though the applicant is not able to predict the specific questions to be asked, the applicant probably knows approximately the content of the questions. During this scene, a well prepared applicant watches the interviewer carefully to make sure that the answers follow the line that the interviewer is looking for. Often applicants supply information during Scene 3 that is not specifically requested; they do so because they have come to associate it with Scene 3 performance. Thus, applicant behavior in Scene 3 may be characterized by some ''semimindlessness'' (i.e., mindfully assessing, then mindlessly responding).

After exhausting the list of job-related questions, the interviewer allows the applicant to gain control of the conversation in Scene 4, Applicant Asks Questions. This scene varies greatly depending on the applicant. Commonly, the applicant wants more information about pay and benefits, developmental/promotional opportunities, work climate, and organizational norms. Here again, applicants have been taught that it is important to ask informed questions about the organization. Most applicants understand that taking control and asking some intelligent sounding questions is not optional. When the applicant has asked what seems to be a reasonable number of questions for Scene 4, the interviewer will seize control of the conversation as a header for Scene 5. The applicant's role in Scene 5 is minimal since the applicant is being dismissed.

The applicant's performing script is learned from a variety of sources, probably rehearsed many times, and enacted in several other interview settings. As with the interviewer script, internal coherence is moderately high for the applicant and external similarity is low. Thus, the applicant script should be a strong guide for applicant behavior.

Scripts and Validity

It has become customary to begin papers on interviewing with a recitation of the litany of failure of the employment interview as a valid and reliable selection device. New evidence on cognitive and aptitude tests has indicated that they are more generally valid than was previously thought (Hunter & Hunter, 1984). In addition, recent studies have indicated that biodata and work samples are more valid than the interview (e.g., Arvey & Campion, 1982; Hakel, 1982; Reilly & Chao, 1982). Reviewers have concluded that the reason for poor interview validity is the many information processing errors made by interviewers.

Earlier reviews (e.g., Wagner, 1949; Mayfield, 1964; Ulrich & Trumbo, 1965) concluded that the cure for the problem was more structure in the interview. Although structure has been shown to improve interrater reliability in interviews (Carlson, Schwab, & Heneman, 1970; Mayfield, 1964; Schwab & Heneman, 1969), a corresponding impact on validity has not been documented (Heneman, Schwab, Huett, & Ford, 1975). While increasing the amount of structure in interviews may help interview validity and reliability, problems occur when one attempts to operationalize structure. Usually, structure has meant some sort of a pattern or standard set of questions which are meant to be asked in a standard order. Anyone who has tried to interview from a prescribed structure can attest to the fact that knowing the questions and their order does not guarantee that applicants going through the same interview have the same interview experience. In fact, in order to be able to describe the structure of an interview fully, it is necessary to discuss it as a scripted event where the interviewer's lines and gestures are fixed as in a play, and the only variables are the applicant's verbal and nonverbal behavior.

There is at least some data to support the notion that effective script enactment is a good predictor of positive interview outcomes. Studies of nonverbal behavior have shown that certain applicant behaviors do affect interviewer perceptions (Washburn & Hakel, 1973; Amalfitano & Kalt, 1977; Young & Beier, 1977; Forbes & Jackson, 1980). Forbes and Jackson (1980) showed that eye contact, facial expression, and head movements varied systematically across applicants who were accepted, reserved for further consideration, or rejected. Their results are similar to the results one might expect at the end of any applicant training program: Accepted applicants make more direct eye contact, smile more, and nod their heads in agreement more.

In a somewhat different approach, Tullar (1986) examined the relational control or dominance aspect of verbal behavior in actual job interviews. The study found three principle differences between successful and unsuccessful interview interactions. First, unsuccessful applicants received much less interaction with the interviewer; less than two-thirds the number of utterances were given to successful applicants. Second, successful applicants dominated more than unsuccessful ones. Third, successful applicants responded to interviewer dominance and interviewer structuring differently than did unsuccessful applicants. Successful applicants responded to interviewers dominance with more dominant and structuring responses, and fewer submission responses. Successful applicants responded to interviewer structuring with more dominance and more equivalence. Also, successful applicants did not return structure for structure as often as unsuccessful applicants did.

Taken together, these studies indicate that cues other than what is said have a strong influence on the outcome of interviews. These other cues have to do with how the applicant script is enacted by the applicant. It is useful here to recall Gioia's (1986) point that recall is based on the script, not necessarily on events actually experienced. Interviewer information processing is strongly influenced by the scripts being enacted. In pilot studies with students, the author has found that students actually do gap-filling and regression of displaced events (see also Bower, Black, & Turner, 1979; Galambos & Rips, 1979) when asked to recall a specific interview after they have experienced five or six interviews.

Interviewers probably are not good processors of the verbal information transmitted in the interview. This is due to the processing of this information through the medium of the script and also due to the fact that the interviewer is attending to more than just the verbal cues presented by the applicant.

Research Implications

Script theory and indeed the whole area of social cognition suggests a rethinking of much of the interviewing research. First, script theory suggests that there is a need to demonstrate that scripted behavior is occurring. The methods used to study gap-filling, regression of displaced events, and mindless behavior might be utilized to examine the specific knowledge structures interviewers and applicants possess which are relevant to interview behaviors (Bower et al., 1979; Galambos & Rips, 1979; Graesser, Wall, Kowalski, & Smith, 1980; Langer et al., 1978).

Second, script theory suggests that there is a need to study interview expectations. Both interviewers and applicants could be asked to write stories about upcoming interviews. Using various category systems, the frequency of certain events and their timing in recalled stories would demonstrate the commonality of interview expectations among interviewers and applicants. Sequential statistical techniques such as Markov Analysis or Lag Sequential Analysis (see also Anderson & Goodman, 1957; Sackett, 1978; 1979) could be used to determine the sequential ordering of various events. These procedures could help verify the existence and stability of interview scripts. In addition, the techniques available from cognitive causal mapping (e.g., Weick & Bougnon, 1986) might be helpful in understanding how interviewers and applicants see their actions as causing actions in the other. Causal maps might capture some of the major idiosyncratic features of the applicant script. This might be useful in counseling applicants who have a problem with the interview script. The applicant's causal map might also be useful in finding places in the script where the applicant could be nudged away from the script for some time with minimal disruption and anxiety.

Third, as noted above, it is possible to get applicants away from their scripts. While this may generate some anxiety in applicants, if it is done carefully, script breaking or script avoidance may help interviewers to focus on scripts more allied with doing the work. For example, the Latham, Saari, Pursell, and Campion (1980) situational interviewing technique likely pulls the applicant away from the interviewing script. They found predictive validities for situational interviewing to be from .30 to as high as .46. Thus, situational interviewing, in part, may prove more effective than traditional interviewing procedures, because the interview both breaks and avoids applicant scripts, and compels the applicant to enact work specific scripts.

Fourth, applicant reactions to script breaking and script avoiding interviews should be examined for the effects they produce in the applicant. The cognitive performing script is a protective umbrella for an otherwise anxiety-provoking situation: the applicant is given the once over to see if he or she is suitable. Script breaking and script avoiding may enhance interview validity, but this may be achieved at the expense of the applicant. Research in the area of applicant anxiety and stress when the script is broken or avoided is necessary to prevent unnecessary psychological discomfort for the applicant (see Latham on the practicality of the situational interview, this volume).

Summary and Conclusions

Script analysis suggests a whole new framework from which to examine what happens in employment interviews. With the current expansion of interest in the area of social cognition, there will doubtless be many studies with paradigms and/or results that will apply to employment interview research. Just understanding that both applicants and interviewers are working from a cognitive performing script may change the way organizational scientists and practitioners look at data generated from the employment interview.

It is clear that the cognitive performing script enacted in the interview situation is a far cry from the cognitive performing scripts enacted on the job. Applicant script enactment is often completely unrelated to job behavior, but the interview persists as the central deciding factor in who is hired and who isn't. Pursuing the research directions suggested above can help to promote better interviewer information processing for better interviewing decisions.

PART VIII

Employment Interview Validity

In recent years, employment interview research has come full circle, returning to its original concern over predictive validity. In part, this development has resulted from recent developments in meta-analytic techniques for quantitative reviews of the empirical literature. The following two papers reflect recent meta-analytic and conceptual efforts to understand the full multi-dimensionality of interview outcomes, and the factors that likely influence judgment validity.

Dreher and Maurer examine the quality of employment interview validity evidence. The authors argue that validity estimates are likely to be sensitive to a variety of contextual and methodological factors which have been largely ignored in previous research. Recent literature on these factors is reviewed, and a research agenda is provided that will be needed if future validation studies are to be taken seriously by practicing managers.

Cronshaw and Wiesner examine two aspects of employment interview validity. First, results of a comprehensive meta-analysis of the interview are reported that contradict two "received doctrines" concerning the criterion-related validity of the interview. These are, the belief that the interview is generally invalid, and the belief that many social psychological process variables moderate the validities of unstructured interviews. Second, the issue of interview validity is restated in more comprehensive models of construct validity and substantive research (see also Schwab, 1980). It is recommended that researchers use these conceptual models to drive future research on interview validity.

18

Assessing the Employment Interview: Deficiencies Associated with the Existing Domain of Validity Coefficients

George F. Dreher
Indiana University, Bloomington

Steven D. Maurer
Washington State University—Vancouver

Questions related to the validity and usefulness of the employment interview have received nearly seventy years of research attention. Published empirical investigations on the employment interview date back to the 1920's (e.g., Hollingworth, 1923; Snow, 1928). In one of the more current textbooks, Heneman, Schwab, Fossum, and Dyer (1986) summarized the validity research on the interview: "Intrarater reliability is typically quite high; interrater reliability is moderate to low; and the validity of the typical interview is very low" (p. 320). This literature is unique, not only in terms of its size and continuity, but also in terms of how persistently it has been ignored by practicing managers.

Taking the contrary view, this chapter will suggest that practicing managers are likely to be correct when they conclude that the existing literature does not relate well to operational employment practices. They are correct because a variety of important issues have not received systematic research attention and because much of the existing validity evidence is flawed by potentially serious methodological deficiencies.

In many ways, this chapter simply builds upon and develops further the concluding section of Arvey and Campion's (1982) review of the employment interview literature, in which the authors addressed the issue of why the interview is still in widespread use in view of the discouraging empirical evidence. Particular attention is devoted here to the possibility that the interview is "really" valid, at least within certain selection contexts.

There seems to be no other area of managerial practice where a large academic research literature has been as systematically ignored as it has been in the area of employee selection. When one reviews the available validity evidence associated with alternative predictors of job performance, a clear pattern emerges (Hunter & Hunter, 1984). The validity coefficients associated with cognitive ability tests, work samples, and assessment center exercises consistently reach useful levels; validity coefficients associated with such things as college GPA, the employment interview, and personality tests are consistently disappointing. Finally, for other classes of predictors (e.g., informal reviews of application materials, reference checks, and letters of recommendation), little validity evidence currently exists.

When one reviews surveys describing the selection techniques most commonly used by companies making hiring decisions, a very different pattern emerges. According to an ASPA (1983) survey, the most frequently used selection procedures include references and record checks, and unstructured interviews. Only 20 percent of the responding firms reported using cognitive ability tests when hiring outside applicants, and only 10 percent reported using cognitive ability tests when making internal promotion decisions. The unstructured interview was used by 81 percent of the responding firms when making external hiring decisions and by 70 percent when making promotion decisions. Firms seemed to use procedures for which little current validity information exists or for which the validity evidence is very disappointing.

Given the persistence with which individuals in organizations disregard prescriptions from the academic literature, perhaps certain informal interviewing practices add value to the firm that is not well understood in the academic literature. From a rational perspective, if alternatives are really superior to the unstructured interview, reasonable people would likely use them. Recent theoretical and empirical work devoted to utility analysis has suggested that the rates of return associated with investing in more valid selection techniques are very favorable when compared to other investment options (see also Schmidt, Hunter, McKenzie, & Muldrow, 1979; Schmidt, Hunter & Pearlman, 1982). If these models are correct, firms investing in improved selection procedures would possess a clear competitive advantage over their less well informed counterparts. Something is seriously wrong. Either the validity estimates are incorrect or the utility models are under-specified or conceptually inappropriate.

In this chapter, the focus is on the quality of the validity evidence associated with the employment interview. A variety of methodological and contextual factors that can affect the magnitude and accuracy of validity estimates are reviewed. The chapter concludes with a research agenda that suggests what is needed if present validity research is to be taken seriously by practicing managers.

Validity Estimates: Some Complications

Employment interview validity estimates are likely to be sensitive to a variety of contextual and methodological factors. Particular attention in this literature review is given to work published since Arvey and Campion's (1982) review, which is summarized in Table 18.1. In Table 18.1, relevant contextual and methodological factors are listed, factor specific articles identified, and related findings described.

Validation Study Design

As noted in Table 18.1, few articles have focused on this issue. The prevalent data analytic method used to validate employment interview judgments has included aggregating judgments across multiple interviewers. Both concurrent and predictive designs have been used, but virtually all studies have reported that multiple interviewers provide independent judgments about job candidates, and that these ratings are then combined to form one analysis sample. Dreher, Ash, and Hancock (1988) reviewed the domain of employment interview validity studies published in the *Journal of Applied Psychology*, *Personnel Psychology*, and the *Journal of Occupational Psychology* up through the Spring of 1987. In their review of 28 studies, they observed that only five of the studies from this domain considered, in any manner, validity at the level of the individual interviewer (Dougherty, Ebert, & Callender, 1986; Ghiselli, 1966; Heneman, Schwab, Huett, & Ford, 1975; Yonge, 1956; and Zedeck, Tziner, & Middlestadt, 1983), and two of these five did so by virtue of having involved only one interviewer in the validation study (Ghiselli, 1966; Yonge, 1956).

In most of these 28 studies insufficient descriptions were provided of the specific procedures to allow for replication. Across most of these studies, the total number of interviewers was not reported, little information was given concerning the rating tendencies or rating distributions of the individual interviewers; and there was rarely any information regarding the degree of range restriction resulting from the study's design. Furthermore, the manner in which interview ratings were operationalized received little attention in these studies (i.e., almost nothing is reported about how multiple interview ratings were combined, how interviewers reached consensus about candidates, or about the degree to which interview ratings were considered along with other predictor scores).

The typical employment interview validation study presents three classes of problems that interfere with the usefulness of much of the existing

TABLE 18.1.   Contextual and Methodological Factors Related to the
                  Accuracy and Magnitude of Validity Estimates: A Post-1982
                  Summary of the Employment Interview Literature

Factor	Source	Summary
Study Design	Dougherty, Ebert, & Callender (1986)	Substantial differences among three interviewers were observed in an actual field setting. Judgments of one interviewer correlated significantly with a variety of job performance ratings, while the judgments of the other two interviewers failed to correlate with any of the criteria. Also, interviewers differed in their constant tendencies to make favorable or unfavorable ratings.
	Dreher, Ash, & Hancock (1988)	A general review of the existing literature revealed that individuals are likely to differ in their ability to provide accurate predictions of employee behavior, and that interviewers often differ in their constant tendencies to make favorable or unfavorable ratings. A review of published validation studies showed that most researchers fail to consider these tendencies and therefore may be inappropriately collapsing data across multiple interviewers. The authors conclude that reviews of the existing domain of validity studies underestimate the validity of the typical employment interview and therefore confuse comparisons with alternative selection procedures.
	Schneider & Schmitt (1986)	These authors discuss the usefulness of conducting validity studies at the level of the individual interviewer (pp. 390-391, 394). They also provide an illustration of the type of study needed to investigate interviewer validity.
	Zedeck, Tziner, & Middlestadt (1983)	These authors provide evidence that interviewers differ in their constant tendencies to make favorable or unfavorable ratings. They also provide indirect evidence that interviewers are differentially valid.
Deficient Criteria	Hunter & Hunter (1984)	In this review of the validity and utility of alternative predictors, the validity of the interview is estimated for three separate criteria (performance ratings, training success, and turnover/tenure). The average correlations across these three cri-

TABLE 18.1. (continued)

Factor	Source	Summary
		terion variables are .14, .10, and .03 respectively. However, this review makes it clear that criteria other than rated job performance or training success have received very little attention when evaluating the validity of the interview.
Occupation/ Job	Arvey, Miller, Gould, & Burch (1987)	Based on job analysis evidence of a significant interpersonal skill (e.g., friendly, outgoing, energetic) requirement in retail sales clerk positions, these authors found that an inteview designed largely to detect interpersonal skills yielded uncorrected correlations of .34 and .51 in samples of clerks hired in successive holiday seasons. Note that the high validity may be due to apparent similarity between behaviors sampled in the interview and those exhibited on the job. It is suggested that in those job situations where relevant job behaviors cannot be assesed, interview validity will diminish.
	Eder & Buckley (1988, p. 90)	"The more complex the job the greater the difficulty in adequately assessing candidates' qualifications, and hence, the more reliance is placed on the interviewer's cognitive skills to form a valid judgment."
	McDaniel, Whetzel, Schmidt, Hunter, Maurer, & Russell (1987)	In a meta-analysis of 91 validity coefficients, divided into police and non-police studies, corrected mean population estimates of .11 for police, and .24 for non-police jobs were reported.
	Maurer (1983)	Conducted meta-analysis of subsample of McDaniel et al. data. Corrected correlations for non-management jobs (.26) were not significantly different than for management jobs (.15).
Capacity/ Motivation	Wright, Pursell, Lichtenfels, Kennedy (1987)	These authors noted that capacity and motivation are measured in structured interviews through three classes of questions commonly included in such interviews: job knowledge and job sample/simulation questions (i.e., capacity inquiries) and willingness to perform tasks (i.e., motivation inquiries).

TABLE 18.1. (continued)

Factor	Source	Summary
	Zedeck, Tziner, & Middlestadt (1983)	These authors argue that research has not investigated factors such as motivation, adjustment, and similar factors that may be assessed in the interview. They provide evidence indicating that personal qualities such as oral communication, decisiveness, and manner of self-preservation are what is detected in the interview.
	Schneider & Schmitt (1986, p. 387)	The point is made that interviews may be most effective for assessing "applicant interests, motivation, or affinity for a particular job" and that these assessments may not be related to productivity criteria.
Interview Setting	Eder & Buckley (1988, p. 76)	These authors offer an interactionist approach to interview research and note that because the interview is conducted under conditions that "can best be called variable" greater effort should be devoted to studying the effects of situational factors on interview outcomes. They also propose that judgments (and hence, validity) may be affected by operational factors such as: —Whether the purpose of the interview is attraction or selection. —The perceived amount of risk in making an error. —Whether the interview is used to produce a summative rating, comparative ranking, or simple accept/reject decision. —The accountability of interviewers for their decisions.
	Wiesner & Cronshaw (1988)	Board and individual interviews were analyzed as moderators in a meta-analysis of interview validity. They found no differences between the two basic approaches, but did find greater validity for board ratings reached by consensus than for board ratings based on a statistical combination procedure.
	Dreher, Ash, & Hancock (1988)	These authors suggest that in settings in which judgments of multiple interviewers are pooled through a consensus process the resultant decision may be superior to individual judgments.

TABLE 18.1. (continued)

Factor	Source	Summary
Interview Format	Latham, Saari, Pursell, & Campion (1980)	Using a behaviorally based "situational interview" format, these researchers reported concurrent validity coefficients of .46 and .30 for samples of hourly workers and foremen respectively; .39 and .33 for female and black samples, respectively, of entry level pulp mill workers. They also noted that interviews based on overt behavior are more likely to be valid than those based on traits which tend to be ambiguous and therefore unpredictable.
	Janz (1982)	Behaviorally based "patterned behavior description" (PBD) interviews were compared to "standard unstructured interviews." It was observed that interviewers trained in use of one or the other of these methods produced correlations significantly greater using the PBD format (.54) than the unstructured format (.07).
	Orpen (1985)	In this study the predictive validities of Patterned Behavior Description (PBD) interviews were compared to those of unstructured interviews. The validities of the PBD interviews were significantly greater than those achieved using unstructured formats (.61 and .48 versus .08 and .05).
	McDaniel et al. (1987)	In this meta-analysis, mean correlations with job related criterion were .27 and .22 for structured and unstructured formats respectively. Corrections for criterion unreliability and range restriction increased mean estimates to .50 and .40.
	Wiesner & Cronshaw (1988)	In this meta-analysis (based on studies different than those studied by McDaniel et al.) mean correlations (corrected for criterion unreliability and range restriction) were .62 and .31 for structured and unstructured methods respectively.
	Wright et al. (1987)	These authors conducted a meta-analysis of ten situational interview studies, including four studies performed in a large manufacturing corporation and not reported in earlier research. The mean correlation (corrected for predictor and criterior unreliability) with graphic and be-

TABLE 18.1. (continued)

Factor	Source	Summary
		havioral rating criteria was .36. The authors note that the 95% confidence interval (SD = .09) indicates a significant difference from the estimate of .14 computed by Hunter & Hunter (1980) for traditional unstructured interviews.
	Latham & Saari (1984)	An interview comprised of 20 situational questions and 5 "past history" questions reported in studies by Ghiselli (1966) was used to conduct a concurrent validation study among 29 office workers. Situational question correlations with supervisor and peer BOS ratings were .39 and .42, while past history correlations were .14 and .15 with these same criteria. A follow-up study using a 21 item situational interview to hire 157 entry level utility workers in a newsprint mill yielded a correlation of .14.

literature. First, problems are associated with evidence that individuals are likely to differ in their ability to provide accurate predictions of employee behavior, and that interviewers often differ in their constant tendencies to make favorable or unfavorable ratings. These tendencies, noted in Dreher et al.'s (1988) review of the literature, leads to errors in interpretation when aggregated samples are analyzed in validation research. Through analytic argument, Dreher et al. demonstrated that the use of aggregate analysis samples will underestimate the validity of the typical employment interview, and that the degree of underestimation is likely to be appreciable. Thus, reviewing the current domain of validity studies leads to conservative point estimates which confuse comparisons with alternative selection procedures.

A second set of problems is represented in the full meta-analytic reviews that are beginning to appear. The most favorable review to date is that of McDaniel, et al. (1987). The mean validity coefficient was .22 when job performance was used as the criterion. After correcting for unreliability in the criterion, the estimated mean (p) increased to .29, and after adjusting for range restriction (p) increased to .41. Meta-analytic reviews suggest a basic failure in past validity studies to make important statistical adjustments. The range restriction problem is the most obvious. When describing their range restriction adjustments, McDaniel et al. stated: "While the mean and standard deviation of the distribution appear reasonable, we do not place great confidence in the representativeness of the distribution because it is based on so few observations" (p. 20). Furthermore, the existing domain of validity studies is generally deficient with regard to other forms of descriptive information—failure to describe the content of the interview and often failure to discuss the construct of interest (i.e., does the interview focus on the willingness to perform or the capacity to perform?).

The final point to be made regarding the research designs or data collection procedures used when studying employment interview validity concerns what can be referred to as the low degree of ecological validity displayed in this literature. Almost nothing is known about the distribution, range, intensity, and frequency of interviewer behavior in actual organizational settings. It is important to learn more about how the interviewing process is distributed in natural systems. Simply observing, counting, measuring, tallying, and classifying everyday interviewer behavior perhaps represents to some a commonplace, mundane activity. However, for research to be relevant to practicing managers, it must focus on the proper phenomena. With the current state of knowledge there is no assurance that the forms of employment interviewing that have received research attention are representative of common managerial practice.

Deficient Criteria

Validation studies have used a variety of job performance measures as the criterion variable. Though few data describe the frequency with which various purposes are served by the typical interview, it is likely that important purposes include being able to identify candidates possessing the willingness to (1) accept job assignments, (2) attend work regularly, and (3) remain with an employer. Therefore, it is surprising that more research has not focused on a wide range of criteria which represent this class of purposes. Measures of turnover, job satisfaction, absenteeism, commitment, and loyalty are simply not adequately represented in this research domain.

Beyond behavioral outcomes of the type just described, employment interviews are used for other critical purposes. Arvey and Campion (1982) argued that one reason managers continue to use the interview is because it does other things well. Important non-selection purposes mentioned include selling the job to the candidate, answering unique candidate questions about the job, and using the interview as a public relations tool. First, because the employment interview represents for many job candidates their first exposure to members of the recruiting firm, it serves as a form of contact likely to influence first impressions and ultimately job acceptance rates. Hence, it is logical to consider how the interview compares to alternative selection procedures in terms of influencing candidate job offer acceptance (see Rynes, this volume). To date, research has focused on the effects of interviews on applicant choice (see also Rynes & Boudreau, 1986), but has yet to compare interviews to other procedures in terms of applicant predispositions toward employers.

The second non-selection purpose is the use of the employment interview as a means of informing candidates about other aspects of the employing company. Currently, many organizational theorists are suggesting that to be effective management systems must be internally consistent and congruent with the primary objectives of the firm. For example, Staw (1986) has proposed that systems of variables must be manipulated in concert if they are to have powerful effects on employee behaviors. Staw's ideas translate into specific personnel practices. Certain selection procedures will be more or less congruent with the various systems of organizational change proposed by Staw. For example, for Staw's Group-Oriented System, panel interviews conducted by members of semi-autonomous work teams will be congruent with other components of the management system. In this instance, interviews will likely focus on values, needs, and the willingness to conform to group norms. The typical selection interview would seem inappropriate for this.

Finally, there is the goal of courting a positive public image perception of the organization from the manner in which the interview is conducted. In Dreher and Sackett's (1983, pp. 93-95) critique of current utility and decision-making models, they pointed out that standard utility models disregard the rejected applicant, and that there are substantial costs associated with negative employment decisions. What is suggested here is that different selection procedures will differentially affect these costs. For example, when an applicant is inappropriately rejected (i.e., a false negative employment decision is made) the costs to the firm and to the rejected candidate may vary as a function of the selection procedure in place.

Occupational/Job Differences

In part, interview validities vary across occupational groups, based on assessments of applicant attributes such as verbal skills, interpersonal skills, and intelligence (see also Arvey & Campion, 1982; Mayfield, 1964; Ulrich & Trumbo, 1965) that are of varying importance to success across these occupations. This ability to evaluate factors that are of varying importance to success in various jobs suggests that interviews may well exhibit occupational differences analogous to those demonstrated for other selection methods, such as mental ability tests (Ghiselli, 1973; Hunter & Hunter, 1984) and biographical data (Reilly & Chao, 1982).

Despite the appeal of considering interview validity in terms of an occupational typology, Table 18.1 reveals relatively few references to this subject in recent research. Moreover, the few references that do exist offer conflicting signals on the wisdom of this approach. For instance, a recent meta-analytic study by McDaniel et al. (1987) yielded no evidence of enhanced interview correlations for jobs requiring high social interaction skills, whereas Arvey, Miller, Gould, and Burch (1987) demonstrated high correlations (.34, .51) in two studies of an interview process specifically aimed at assessing the interpersonal skills needed by sales clerks in customer interactions.

Another difficulty presented by existing research is that the empirical reviews conducted to date have been inconclusive and somewhat remiss in their analysis of job categories as moderators of validity. For instance, McDaniel et al. (1987) only divided coefficients into those for police and nonpolice (i.e., all other) occupations, and found that the interview's validity in predicting performance of police officers was only half that for other jobs. On the other hand, Maurer (1983) found, contrary to expectations, that the interview's validity for non-management jobs was no different than that for managerial jobs. Unfortunately, three other empirical reviews conducted since Arvey and Campion (1982) (i.e., Hunter & Hunter, 1984; Reilly & Chao, 1982; Wiesner & Cronshaw, 1988), did not choose to analyze correlations based on job or occupational differences. Hence, available empirical evidence is inconclusive regarding arguments that validity may be affected by factors such as job complexity (see Eder & Buckley, 1988), level of interpersonal skills required in the job (Arvey et al., 1987), or verbal skills (Rasmussen, 1984).

Capacity/Motivation

Interview validities may differ according to whether the interview is intended primarily to assess the applicant's job-related abilities (i.e., capacity) or his/her willingness to perform (i.e., performance motivation). Although the distinction between these objectives is seldom made clear in research studies, elements of each are usually assumed in statements of the interview's validity as a predictor of job performance.

The summary of comments and evidence shown in Table 18.1 argues for each of these purposes in interview evaluations. On the one hand, Zedeck et al. (1983) suggested that intrinsic qualities of the applicant such as motivation, decisiveness, and ability to adjust might be validly assessed in the interview process. In contrast, others lend both logical and empirical support to the premise that interviews are most effective when job dimensions are well known to the interviewer, and the goal of the interview is to assess the candidate's knowledge, skills, and abilities against the salient features of the job. Eder and Buckley (1988) suggested that both of these may operate in practice and may vary in importance as interviewers adjust information search strategies (i.e., seek information concerning either job skills or applicant motivation) in accordance with fluctuations in perceived goals and expectations during the interview process.

Conspicuous by its absence in recent research is evidence of any real effort to study the type of information sought through the interview process. This dearth of effort implies a corresponding lack of concern with interview content and reveals an uncomfortable consistency with Guion's (1987) criticism that classical personnel selection efforts are more directed to the question of "does it work?" rather than "what is measured?" Narrowly defining the interviewer's judgment as the applicant's capacity to perform may well overlook and undervalue the interview's contribution to the total hiring process.

Interview Setting

In Table 18.1, the term "setting" refers to the varying conditions, purposes, and procedures that affect interview practice. Included in this definition are factors, other than the interviewer or applicant, that comprise the environment in which interviews are conducted. Arvey and Campion (1982) proposed that interview decision processes may well be affected by such items and emphasized that the lack of studies investigating situational factors was an "important hole" in interview research. Eder and Buckley (1988) commented on this neglected topic by proposing research attention on situational factors such as interview purpose and decision making accountability within an interactionist perspective. If these assertions and preliminary indications are correct, then additional investigation of specific validity/situational factor pairings should enhance understanding of the determinants of interview effectiveness, and as a result enable practitioners to improve the outcomes of the interview process through administrative actions under their control. Regrettably, recent research reveals little in the way of systematic inquiry into the role and effect of situational factors (see Eder, this volume).

Interview Format

A consistent theme throughout reviews of interview research is that validity increases as the interview becomes more structured (Arvey & Campion, 1982; Ulrich & Trumbo, 1965; Wagner, 1949). In recent years, this theme has been reinforced by empirical reviews which revealed greater estimates of predictive validity for structured than for unstructured methods (see also McDaniel et al., 1987), and by an impressive number of studies that have consistently demonstrated high validity coefficients using highly structured interview methods (see also Latham & Saari, 1984).

Contemporary research as to the effect of format on interview validity has been marked by two developments. First, based on evidence of a clear relationship between interview structure and validity, researchers have designed and tested new, more highly structured interview methods (see also Campion, Pursell, & Brown, 1988). Second, it is evident that much contemporary research has focused on behaviorally-based interviews aimed at the applicant's job-related behavioral intentions (see also Latham & Saari, 1984; Latham et al., 1984) or experiential record (see also Janz, 1982). Although the emphasis on better structures and the promise of behaviorally-based methods are encouraging from a validity perspective, there remain a number of practical considerations surrounding the development and use of such methods that should not be ignored. Thus far, issues such as development costs, face validity of structured methods, user or applicant reactions to increasing interview structure, and the relationship between interview structure and other activities (e.g., interviewer training), have received only scant attention (e.g., Latham & Finnegan, 1987).

Some Needed Research

In this final section, some directions for future research are outlined which in many ways are a call for what has historically been neglected. It is the present authors' view that early research on interview validity often was methodologically deficient, or neglected fundamental issues. This flawed research base was then used to prematurely conclude that the standard employment interview failed to meet its primary objectives, thus setting the stage for decades of "process" research devoted to decision making, and the identification of factors related to overall interviewer judgments. Researchers abandoned studying the accuracy of these judgments. The present authors urge a return to the systematic evaluation (with a focus on validity) of the selection procedures used by the majority of managers and staffing practitioners.

Study Design

The most pressing need is for studies of interviewer validity, not the validity of "the interview." Schneider and Schmitt (1986) made this same suggestion and outlined what would be required to investigate the accuracy of interviewers' judgments. Such a study was actually conducted by Dougherty et al. (1986), and can serve as a model for future research. In this study, three employment interviewers, working as employment professionals for a large firm, each interviewed multiple candidates from a common applicant pool using the same company-provided rating instruments for predicting future job performance. For each interviewer, some subset of candidates was eventually hired and criterion data collected. The relative validity of the different interviewers was then estimated by calculating interviewer specific validity coefficients. This predictive design not only complies with accepted research standards, but is also likely to have practical appeal to employers since it renders individual-level results useful for maintaining and providing needed feedback to employment specialists.

Even when sufficient data are not available for interviewer specific analyses, there is value in simply studying the typical interview while paying attention to standard validation principles. A properly conducted study, even when based on an aggregate analysis sample, can make a contribution to this literature if record keeping practices allow for accurate range restriction adjustments; and there is evidence that the extent of the constant rating error problem is not extensive.

Finally, more information is needed on how interviewing practices are naturally distributed in organizational settings. Descriptive research focusing on the types of questions asked, the attributes of interviewers, what interviewers do before and after conducting an interview, and the uses of interview data is needed so that validation efforts address the concerns of employment specialists. There is a need to focus on proper phenomena and address the validity of data collection and evaluation procedures as represented in natural settings. Perhaps the place to begin is simply to ask "what do employment specialists do?" The use of a variety of observational and self-report measures would be appropriate here. This methodology could then be applied to studying the interviewing behaviors and settings associated with managers and professionals outside the employment function.

Deficient Criteria

Researchers need to expand the set of criteria used in standard validation efforts. Measures of turnover, job satisfaction, absenteeism, commitment, instrumentality perceptions, and loyalty all represent appropriate criteria measures if the interview is being used to assess motivational states. One particularly interesting strategy might be to focus on the degree to which interview ratings predict person/job congruence. Using a predictive design, persons hired through an interview could complete (after an appropriate time interval) a measure like the Minnesota Importance Questionnaire (MIQ). Their supervisor or some subset of co-workers could complete the Occupational Reinforcer Pattern (ORP). The MIQ and ORP are measures developed by the Work Adjustment Group at the University of Minnesota. The MIQ assesses the importance or desirability of twenty job characteristics to the target employee. The ORP describes the degree to which these job characteristics are present on the job. A measure of congruence could be constructed from these two measures and used as a criterion measure in validation research focusing on interviews designed to assess motivational attributes of candidates.

Researchers could also compare interviews with alternative selection procedures in terms of other objectives and outcomes (e.g., applicant acceptance rates and perceptions of fair treatment). Of particular interest would be studies that capture applicant reactions to being rejected for a job. The model provided by Dreher and Sackett (1983, pp. 94-95) could serve as a useful guide. Experiments could be conducted where the employment process was simulated. The cognitive and affective responses of rejected candidates would serve as the dependent variables in these studies and selection procedure type would serve as the independent variable. One might predict that the belief that the rejection was due to a true attribute deficiency (versus a decision error), feelings of inequitable treatment, and a variety of behavioral intentions will systematically covary with the type of selection method experienced by the applicant.

Occupational/Job Issues

A logical first step in the investigation of occupational/job influences is to reconsider existing validity evidence in terms of identifiable and distinguishable job elements. Such inquiries might begin by forging a taxonomy of existing validity evidence according to various components of jobs reported in each study. A strategy for accomplishing this task might be to use the DOT descriptions for the jobs noted in each research report to categorize correlations according to the Functional Job Analysis (FJA) "data-people-things" components of each job. Using this approach, validity data could be categorized according to jobs having different requirements in dealing with data-people-and things. Work could then begin to assess which of the components of these categories is (or is not) successfully measured in the interview.

An alternative to the categorization scheme just described is suggested by Eder and Buckley's (1988) observation that job complexity may affect interview validity. This notion suggests a study approach similar to that described above except that instead of categorizing results across data-people-things jobs components, attention would be devoted to forging a taxonomy corresponding to a hierarchy of skills within a given component (e.g., comparing validities for jobs having a high "supervising" people component with those having primarily a "persuading" people component). For instance, a concurrent validity study in a large organization could be conducted where interviewers evaluate employees working in jobs that differ significantly along a particular work dimension (e.g., data, people, things).

Capacity/Motivation

Interviews may be used to measure either capacity (i.e., job related abilities) or motivation (interest, work motivation, work commitment) of applicants. Hence, it may be inappropriate to assume that work ability is the primary factor evaluated when in fact other factors, such as the ability of the employee to get along, the willingness to do the job, and the likelihood of turnover, might constitute the primary concerns of the interviewer. By making such distinctions, one could better assess the form of contribution made by the interview in the selection process and measure its validity in terms of the job consequences it is intended to predict.

One could begin to determine the degree to which capacity and motivational interests are pursued in the interview simply by observing actual interviews, and attempting to content-analyze questions and procedures according to their relevance to the capacity or motivation of the applicant. This could be accomplished by audiotaping employment interviews, categorizing questions into relevant categories, and conducting follow-up interviews with interviewers to determine the purpose of inquiries made of the job applicant. An alternative approach might be to employ information gained from interviewers in the conduct of a factor or discriminant analysis study. This exploratory analysis could yield the primary components investigated in interviews and their relative values. Such information could be then used to construct the categories for use in extending the capacity/motivation study suggested previously.

Interview Setting

This issue could be of the greatest practical value to increasing interview validity because many of the potentially important elements of the interview setting (e.g., the purpose of the interview, the amount of risk involved in interview decisions, the methods used to reach a decision) can be affected directly by the employer. Clearly, such issues are subject to change through administrative fiat or deliberate policy changes, whereas other factors are difficult for the employer to control (e.g., interviewer limitations and biases), or can be altered only through a major effort (e.g., development of a suitable structured interview). One task of future research, then, is to identify salient factors in the interview setting and determine the form and magnitude of their effect of the validity of assessment outcomes (see Eder, this volume).

Since the manner in which interview decisions are made appears to be a major setting variable, efforts should be made to contrast interview decisions based on different decision practices. For instance, it seems logical to compare decisions reached when interviewers are required to rate each applicant immediately after the interview against those made after interviewing a series of applicants and then developing ratings for each of the interviews. This analysis may prove especially useful to improving interview validity in situations where interviewers are required to perform multiple interviews (e.g., college recruiting).

Another factor noted in discussion of interview decision outcomes is the influence of the perceived purpose of the interview process (Eder & Buckley, 1988). In general, this issue is purported to affect decision factors such as the amount of time devoted to the interview, the degree to which applicant qualifications are pursued or weighted, and the allotment of time to selection versus recruiting discussions in the interview. Alteration of these factors allegedly affects the quantity and quality of selection related information obtained, and hence the potential validity of interviewer assessments of applicant potential. A beginning approach to analyzing the relationship between interview purpose and predictive validity might be to survey individual interviewers to determine the degree to which they have pursued selection versus recruitment issued in the interview process, and then to relate the scores on the survey measure to the validity of each individual's assessments. Such a study, based on use of both Likert and "constant sum" scales to gain absolute and relative importance scores, would seek to determine whether validities are greater among interviewers who placed greater emphasis on selection-related issues versus those that emphasized recruitment.

An intriguing situational factor noted by Eder and Buckley (1988) is the effect of the perceived amount of risk associated with making an error in interview validity. This issue directly relates to management actions in response to questions such as who should interview (Should managers who have the most to gain or lose from interview decisions conduct the "selection interview?"), the degree to which interviewers should be held accountable for their decisions (Should we evaluate interviewers according to the "quality" of their interview decisions?), the establishment of checks and balances designed to affect individual risks (Should we utilize panel interviews, successive multiple interviews, or rely on a single interview conducted by a trained interviewer?), and the use of interview results (Should interview outcomes be used in a compensatory, multiple hurdle, or multiple cutoff strategy?). If perceived level of risk does indeed influence interview validity, then corporate decisions concerning these questions should influence the quality of assessments to be expected in employment interviews.

To begin study in this area, it would be useful to ascertain the components of "risk" in interview decisions and relate these components to decisions made. For instance, Employment Office interviewers may define risk in terms of EEO concerns in the interview and may, as a result, deliberately avoid lines of questioning that though job related, may involve legally delicate inquiries. In contrast, a line manager more concerned with the risk of having to "live with" a bad hiring decision, may define risk primarily in terms of employment outcomes, and decide to pursue the same line of inquiry so cautiously avoided by the Employment Office interviewer. Because risk may be a multi-faceted construct, which operates in different ways in different settings, it may be necessary first to define the forms of risk under study and then relate these to various behaviors in interviewing interactions. Perhaps this line of inquiry could begin by attempting to relate definitions and behavioral consequences of risk provided by collective bargaining researchers (see also Walton & McKersie, 1965) to the behavioral dynamics and decision outcomes of the employment interview.

Once the components and form of risk are defined, it will become possible to study systematically its effect on interview outcomes. An obvious strategy would be to conduct lab studies in which experimental subjects are placed under risk and control subjects are not. If risk is defined primarily in terms of short-term outcomes, then decision experiments could be conducted among college students utilizing some short-term risk (e.g., part of a course grade) on decision characteristics (e.g., reliability, accuracy, leniency/severity, but not validity per se). These outcomes could be used to describe decision effects which may influence validity of interview decisions.

Interview Format

Recent studies of structured interview formats continue to show considerable promise for the positive effect of structured interviews on the validity of interview outcomes (see also Latham & Saari, 1984; Orpen, 1985). Because of the consistency of the interview structure/validity relationship, it is logical that researchers should begin to explore questions designed to delve further into structured formats and their impact on valid assessments. This inquiry could examine questions such as: How might interview formats be combined (if at all) to enhance validity?; how do various structured formats compare in their effect on factors likely to influence validity levels?; and how do structured interviews compare with other selection methods in terms of validity/utility tradeoffs?

An interesting approach would be to conduct a validity study based on an interview composed of both situational and conventional (i.e., previous experience oriented) components. Validity coefficients could be developed independently for the conventional and the situational components of the interview, thus allowing a direct comparison of validity of assessments based on each of the general approaches to developing structured formats. Further, a composite score could be developed, and a validity coefficient computed, to examine potential contributory and interactive effects of adding situational questions to a conventional interview.

Study of structured interviews and their effect on factors likely to influence interview validity ought to investigate the psychometric properties of various interview formats, as well as their impact on decision making tendencies of interviewers and the quality of information received from interviewees. To compare the psychometric properties of various interview structures, it would be useful to contrast formats based on their resistance to errors, influence on rating consistency, effect on rating accuracy, and sensitivity to problems such as "faking" or "false responses." Research of this type would isolate psychometric strengths and weaknesses affecting the validity of alternative formats.

As a complement to research on the psychometric effectiveness of various structured alternatives, it would be beneficial to examine "user" reactions likely to influence the consistency and efficiency of participants in the interview process. For instance, the high degree of structure inherent in behavioral formats (e.g., the situational interview) could induce boredom and drive down the interest and motivation of interviewers, especially in situations where they must conduct multiple interviews. Related to this inquiry would be questions concerning the face validity of highly structured formats and the impact of the perceived legitimacy of such methods on the behaviors of both interviewers and interviewees.

Summary

In this chapter, the focus has been on the quality of the validity evidence associated with the "typical" employment interview. The view of the present authors is that the current domain of validity coefficients is of limited value when attempting to evaluate the usefulness of this widely used selection technique. The existing domain is of limited value because it is largely based on a flawed methodology (i.e., collapsing judgments across multiple interviewers when creating analysis samples), and has failed to take into account a variety of other methodological and contextual factors that are likely to affect the magnitude of validity estimates. Instead of considering how to convince individuals in organizations to follow the prescriptions coming from this literature, there is a need to more fully consider the deficiencies associated with this literature which have led to its rejection by many practicing managers. Managers resist abandoning unstructured interviews because they are convinced that this class of techniques provides useful information about job candidates, and helps achieve other important organizational objectives. These objectives and perceptions should play a more integral part in future employment interview research.

19

The Validity of the Employment Interview: Models for Research and Practice

Steven F. Cronshaw
University of Guelph

Willi H. Wiesner
Concordia University

The validity of the employment interview has been the subject of controversy and debate for at least 50 years (compare Vitelles, 1932, with a recent review by Arvey & Campion, 1982). The conclusions reached about the criterion-related validity of the employment interview in reviews throughout those intervening years have been generally pessimistic (Mayfield, 1964; Schmitt, 1976; Ulrich & Trumbo, 1965; Wagner, 1949; Wright, 1969). Wiesner and Cronshaw (1988) referred to the resulting belief that interviews are generally invalid as the "doctrine of interview invalidity." Importantly, a recent meta-analysis of the employment interview by these two researchers yielded results which contradict the doctrine of interview invalidity, especially for so-called "structured" interviews (e.g., Pursell, Campion, & Gaylord, 1980).

A second accepted doctrine of the employment interview has also received a wide following in industrial/organizational psychology. This doctrine, which developed from the seminal Webster studies at McGill University in the 1950's and 1960's, holds that a large number of micro-based social psychological factors moderate the validity of the employment interview (particularly the unstructured interview). In fact, Webster (1964) originally developed his interview research program as an "indirect" approach to studying the reliability and validity of the employment interview; that is, he believed that the detailed study of social psychological and individual decision processes in the interview would help researchers to identify the moderators of interview reliability and validity.

Undoubtedly, some gains have been made in understanding the sources of interview invalidity through the large volume of research that followed in the McGill tradition. However, the large volume of fragmentary McGill research requires integration. It is surely time to reintroduce "direct" models of interview reliability and validity as a means of providing a broader conceptual framework for the integration of these findings. Even Webster himself has suggested recently that the primary focus of interview research must be to determine how interviewers can make accurate and valid interview decisions (Webster, 1982). Therefore, this paper advocates a shift of emphasis from the "indirect" study of miro-analytic interview processes to "direct" models of interview validity. The Wiesner and Cronshaw (1988) findings provide impetus for this work.

The remainder of this chapter is divided into two major parts. First, the meta-analytic findings that cast serious doubts on the dual accepted doctrines of interview invalidity and differential validity of unstructured interviews are reviewed. Second, interview validity is restated in terms of two related processes: construct validation and substantive research. This approach refocuses attention away from the diffuse approach of investigating the impact of innumerable micro-moderators on interview "decisions" (e.g., decision to accept or reject a job applicant), toward the investigation of methodological and substantive variables that have the greatest influence on interview validity. Given that key practical and legal concerns in using interviews as selection predictors revolve around whether the interview is valid, this approach offers a potentially larger return for research resources invested than do the scattered and uncoordinated research efforts investigating the seemingly endless number of social psychological moderators that might influence interview decisions. It is important to note that validity is not the only concern facing practitioners who use employment interviews. Certainly, other criteria exist against which the interview can be assessed (e.g., economic utility, bias in interview ratings). Nevertheless, personnel psychologists consider validation concepts as primary when establishing the defensibility and appropriateness of their assessment procedures.

Before reviewing research findings of Wiesner and Cronshaw (1988), the concept of "validity" must be clarified. When the empirical findings are reported in the next section of this chapter, the primary focus will be on criterion-related validation (i.e., the relationship between interview ratings and job-related criteria as summarized by a correlation coefficient). In retrospect, the statement of interview validity in this way is far too restrictive. In the second section of this chapter, the determination of validity is reconceptualized as a dual problem of construct validation and substantive research. Construct validation/substantive models are then presented to guide future research which may examine interview validity.

The Predictive Efficiency of the Employment Interview:
The Wiesner and Cronshaw Study

When the initial decision was made to examine the doctrine of interview invalidity, it was found that the empirical base on which this widespread belief rests is surprisingly thin. The pessimism about interview validity has developed from a series of narrative reviews of the interview literature which conclude that, at best, the interview has low predictive validity (Arvey & Campion, 1982; Mayfield, 1964; Milne, 1967; Reilly & Chao, 1982; Rodger, 1952; Schmitt, 1976; Ulrich & Trumbo, 1965; Wagner, 1949; Wright, 1969). As Hunter, Schmidt, and Jackson (1982) have pointed out, such narrative reviews are highly susceptible to reporting biases and do not take into account statistical artifacts that could reduce observed interview validities (e.g., predictor and criterion reliabilities, range restriction). Similarly, the doctrine that unstructured employment interviews are differentially valid could be based on mistaken substantive interpretations imposed on empirical validity data which are contaminated by the effects of sampling error, as well as by differences between studies in the extent of predictor/criterion reliability and range restriction. That is, many differences between the unstructured interviews that were attributed to micro-analytic social psychological moderators may in fact result from statistical artifacts.

Hunter et al. (1982) reported a technique called meta-analysis for quantitatively combining individual study validities, and adjusting quantitatively for the effects of statistical artifacts so that underlying patterns of validities emerge from numerous individual data-points. This technique was so well-suited to resolving some of the long-standing controversies concerning interview validity that it was decided to undertake a comprehensive meta-analysis of the existing interview literature. The meta-analysis reported here was conducted in a way that controlled for the major threats to the validity of meta-analytic inference that were discussed by Carson and Kinicki (1988). Most importantly, the researchers tested theoretically grounded hypotheses, searched out all available interview validity studies (published and unpublished) worldwide through a variety of sources, and obtained good inter-rater reliability on the scheme used to code the moderator variables.

In all studies included in the meta-analysis, the employment interview conformed to the definition of an ''interpersonal interaction of limited duration between one or more interviewers and a job applicant for the purpose of identifying interviewee knowledge, skills, abilities, and behaviors that may be predictive of important job criteria such as job performance, training success, promotion, and tenure.'' In the model of interview validity developed by Wiesner and Cronshaw (1988), it was proposed that between-setting differences in criterion-related validity would be moderated by two major factors: interview structure and interview reliability. Two interview types were identified on the basis of structure: *unstructured interviews* without predetermined questions and/or rating scales where, typically, interviewers are required to make a global, subjective rating of the interviewee on completion of the interview based on information obtained during the interaction; and *structured interviews* which consist of "a series of job-related questions with predetermined answers that are consistently applied across all interviews for a particular job" (Pursell, Campion, & Gaylord, 1980) with rating scales completed during the interview and the ratings for each interview question combined to obtain an overall interview rating.

Two additional interview types were identified on the basis of reliability: *individual interviews* which are conducted by a single interviewer and *board interviews* which are conducted by a panel of two or more interviewers (note that board interviews included both averaging of independent judgments of panel members and ratings obtained through member consensus after discussion). The difference between individual and board interviews was referred to as the "format" moderator. The hypotheses stated that interview validity would vary as a function of both format (with board interviews being more reliable and so more valid) as well as by interview structure. That is, the mean lowest validity coefficients would be found for the unstructured-individual interview, whereas the highest would be found for the structured-board interview.

The hypotheses were tested using the meta-analytic procedures developed by Hunter, Schmidt, and Jackson (1982). The results from Wiesner and Cronshaw (1988) that are of greatest relevance to this paper are recapitulated in Table 19.1. As can be seen, the results support the hypothesis that structuring has an important effect on the validity of employment interviews. Structured interviews (both individual and board) had substantially higher validities than did unstructured interviews. However, board format had no apparent advantage in validity over the individual format when the interviews were structured. Interestingly, the board (as opposed to individual) interviews were more predictive of job criteria when interviews were unstructured. Finally (and not surprisingly), interview reliability was correlated with validity at .48. This finding suggests that reliability has an important main effect on interview validity, even if the effect of format varies over interview structure. From the cumulative results, the following general conclusions was drawn: practitioners wishing to maximize prediction of job criteria must improve reliability to the maximum extent by structuring the employment interview.

TABLE 19.1. Meta-Analyses of the Predictive Validity of A Priori Interview Types

Interview Source	Total Sample Size[a]	Mean Validity Coefficient[b]	Observed Variance in Sample Correlations	Residual Variance Unexplained by Statistical Artifacts[c]	95% Confidence Interval of Validity Coefficient
All Studies	51,459(150)	.47(.26)	.093	.080	$-.08 \leqslant p \leqslant 1.00$
Unstructured/ Individual	2,303(19)	.20(.11)	.013	−.014	—
Unstructured/ Board	3,134(19)	.37(.21)	.013	−.008	—
Structured/ Individual	7,873(32)	.63(.35)	.070	.051	$.18 \leqslant p \leqslant 1.00$
Structured/ Board	2,104(15)	.60(.33)	.043	.017	$.34 \leqslant p \leqslant .86$

SOURCE: Adapted from Wiesner and Cronshaw (1988).
NOTE: Not all interviews were classifiable according to structure and format. The subset sample sizes therefore do not sum to the total for all studies.
[a]The number of coefficients contributing to the total sample is given in brackets.
[b]Means were corrected for direct restriction of range and criterion unreliability. Uncorrected values are given in brackets.
[c]Variance in corrected sample correlations was adjusted for the following statistical artifacts: sampling error, differences in range restriction, and differences in criterion reliability.

It is important to note that the mean validities of the structured interviews were substantial, especially where mean validities were corrected for range restriction and criterion unreliability. It is also highly instructive to examine the 95% confidence intervals of the true validities (see the last column of Table 19.1). Adjustment for statistical artifacts (most notably, sampling error) accounted for virtually all of the variance in the validities of the unstructured interviews, but not the structured interviews. This finding has two major implications. First, the continued search for a plethora of social psychological and individual decision moderators of validity in the unstructured interview is largely a useless exercise. Beyond the operation of statistical artifacts, there does not appear to be much variance in validities that remains to be explained by such moderators. Interestingly, Raza and Carpenter (1987) have found that demographic characteristics of interviewers and interviewees have at best a modest effect on unstructured interview outcomes (this result is of course consistent with the present validity findings).

The second implication is equally far-reaching. More specificity is required concerning what is meant by structure and there is a need to investigate this variable much more closely because considerable differences in validities are still found among the interviews classified as "structured." In fact, the rather general definition of "structure" used in the Wiesner and Cronshaw (1988) study still left considerable latitude for differences in interview validity to express themselves as unexplained variance in the distribution of true validity coefficients for the structured interviews (e.g., it was found that validity of the structured interview was highest when interview questions were based on a formal job analysis). However, it is a poor strategy to tackle the "structure" issue merely on the basis of the operational characteristics that structured interviews purportedly possess (e.g., the same questions are asked of all job applicants). Instead, broad-based conceptual models are required if the field of personnel psychology is to extend its scientific understanding of what determines interview validity, as well as improve organizational application of employment interviews.

The next section of this paper presents two models of interview validity in a broader theoretical and interpretive framework. It is shown that the issue of criterion-related validation, investigated in the above meta-analysis, is more appropriately viewed as a problem of construct validation and substantive research. It is then demonstrated how differences in the criterion-related validities obtained by three operational interview methods (i. e., the conventional unstructured interview, the Patterned Behavior Description Interview, and the Situational Interview) are best predicted and understood by applying two related investigative processes: construct validation and empirical validation.

Construct Validity-Substantive Research Models of the Employment Interview

This section begins with the assumption that any validation is a form of hypothesis testing where some substantive question has been posed (Landy, 1986). On superficial examination, it might appear that investigations of the criterion-related validity of employment interviews (e.g., the meta-analysis reported in the previous section) are sufficient to answer the most critical substantive and applied questions regarding the validity of the employment interview. However, the complete process of validation *cum* hypothesis testing makes somewhat greater demands on the researcher than a mere demonstration of statistical relationships between predictor and criterion. If it is to be understood why employment interviews do, or do not, predict work-related criteria, the problem of criterion-related validation must be reformulated in more comprehensive terms.

Schwab (1980) presented a model of construct and empirical validity that is comprehensive in the above meaning. According to this model, interview researchers are required to carefully develop and coordinate two aspects of substantive research: construct validity and empirical validity. Construct validity answers the following question: How well does an operational indicator (e.g., interview rating, criterion measure) correspond to the hypothetical construct which it is developed to assess? Empirical validity refers to the presence or absence of a substantive relationship between two or more constructs. The roles of construct and empirical validity are diagrammatically illustrated in Figure 19.1. Theoretically, construct validity is indicated by a high correlation between I and I′ or between C and C′; empirical validity is shown by a correlation between I′ and C′ which in turn suggests a relationship between the unobserved constructs I and C (Schwab, 1980).

When reporting criterion-related validities, researchers give correlations between observed interview (I′) and criterion (C′) ratings. In fact, the researcher often fails to invoke any constructs at all, instead relying entirely on the face validity of operational measures of interviewee qualifications and job criteria. However, the vital scientific question revolves around whether there is a substantive linkage between the constructs I and C. Without invoking constructs, no scientific basis exists for generalizing the results of interview validity research. However, even if the predictor and criterion constructs are conceptually defined, any conclusions about a substantive relationship between I and C may be erroneous if the operational measures lack construct validity. Therefore, *both* construct and empirical validity are necessary if strong scientific inferences are to be made on the basis of interview research data. Criterion-related validity (i.e., establishing an empirical linkage between I′ and C′) by itself cannot provide the basis for such scientific inferences.

How can the validity of employment interviews be studied using the conceptual framework illustrated in Figure 19.1? First take the example of the conventional unstructured interview. In the unstructured interview, the interviewer asks a number of unstandardized questions while seeking to form an overall impression of the interviewee's job suitability. The interviewer then makes an accept or reject decision. Under validation, an overall measure of applicant suitability or an accept/reject rating is correlated with one or more work-related criteria. In terms of construct and empirical validity, there is greatest interest in whether an impression-based psychological construct (e. g., a person prototype as discussed by Feldman, 1981), which is denoted as I in Figure 19.1, is related to a criterion construct (e. g., job performance), which is denoted as C.

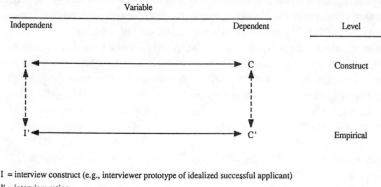

I = interview construct (e.g., interviewer prototype of idealized successful applicant)
I' = interview rating
C = criterion construct (e.g., job performance)
C' = operational criterion

Figure 19.1. Representation of Construct and Empirical Validity of the Employment Interview

SOURCE: Adapted from Schwab (1980).

The observed relationship (i.e., I' C') might be an inaccurate estimate of the true substantive relationship between I and C for at least one of the following three reasons: (a) statistical artifacts such as sampling error, range restriction, and predictor/criterion reliability enhance or attenuate the observed correlation between I' and C' (note that Wiesner & Cronshaw, 1988, controlled for these statistical artifacts in their meta-analysis); (b) I' lacks construct validity as a measure of I because of the influence of such biases in unstructured interview ratings as similar-to-me error (Baskett, 1973) and contrast effects (Wexley, Yukl, Kovacs, & Sanders, 1972); (c) C' lacks construct validity as measure of C or, in other words, is irrelevant as an operational criterion (Thorndike, 1949). Generally, the effect of (a) will attenuate the observed criterion-related validity coefficient and so underestimate the relationship between I and C. The effects of (b) and (c) may be either to inflate or to attenuate the observed criterion-related validity coefficient. In addition, the observed correlation between I' and C' may be attenuated simply because (d) there is a relatively weak substantive linkage between I and C.

Point (d) should be discussed in more detail because it is often overlooked in the highly pragmatic business of designing and conducting employment interviews. It will be assumed that unstructured interviews normally invoke a person prototype which serves as I (following on arguments made by

Sydiaha, 1959, 1961, and Bolster & Springbett, 1961). Are there a priori reasons for expecting such a prototype of an idealized successful applicant held by the interviewer to have a strong substantive linkage with a work-related criterion, C? Given the inherent ambiguity and imprecision of the prototype-matching process (Feldman, 1981), a strong I-C linkage seems unlikely. So even if the effects of the limitations discussed under (a), (b), and (c) are minimal, it is reasonable on substantive grounds to expect only a modest observed correlation between I' and C'.

The I construct of the unstructured interview is now compared to that proposed by two "structured" interviewing methods: the Patterned Behavior Description Interview (PBDI) and the Situational Interview (SI) (see Janz and Latham, this volume). The PBDI, as proposed by Janz and colleagues (Janz, 1982; Janz, Hellervik, & Gilmore, 1986), uses applicant self-reports of past job-related behavior (I') to predict corresponding dimensions of focal job behavior (C'). Therefore, the I construct is past job-related behavior corresponding to individual dimensions on the criterion, C.

Compared to the previous example of the unstructured interview, there are more compelling theoretical and empirical reasons for expecting a strong substantive relationship between I and C. On the theoretical side, many industrial psychologists indeed hold that "past behavior will predict future behavior." This doctrine has been labelled the "behavior consistency theory" (Wernimont & Campbell, 1968). On the empirical side, much evidence exists to demonstrate that past behavior predicts future behavior quite well. For example, McDaniel and Schmidt (1985) reported a mean true validity of .49 in their meta-analysis of behavioral consistency methods for scoring training and experience ratings.

Given the expectation of a strong substantive link between I and C for the PBDI, how does this interview method fare in terms of criterion-related validity (i.e., the I'-C' linkage)? Two studies (Janz, 1982; Orpen, 1985) reported PBDI validities ranging from .48 to .61. In both cases, the PBDI predicted substantially better than the standard unstructured interview. These empirical results are not surprising if one considers that the I-C linkage proposed by Janz is more direct and theoretically defensible than that proposed for the unstructured interview.

The SI, developed by Latham and colleagues (Latham & Saari, 1984; Latham, Saari, Pursell, & Campion, 1980), is based on the assumption that job-related behavioral intentions elicited from applicants in the interview will be predictive of corresponding criterion behaviors on the job. Again, considerable theoretical and empirical information already exists to support the contention that a relatively strong substantive linkage should exist between behavioral intentions and subsequent behavior. On the theoretical side, social psychologists have formulated well-known attitudinal models that conceptually link behavioral intentions to subsequent behavior (Ajzen & Fishbein, 1980). On the empirical side, organizational researchers have indeed shown that behavioral intentions predict behavioral outcomes. For example, a meta-analysis by Steel and Ovalle (1984) found a weighted average correlation of .50 between behavioral intentions and employee turnover.

Both theoretical and empirical reasons exist to support a relatively strong substantive relationship between I and C for the SI. The empirical findings on the SI once again are consistent with these expectations. In three studies (Latham & Saari, 1984; Latham et al., 1980; Weekley & Gier, 1987), criterion-related validity coefficients for the SI that range between .14 and .47 are reported, with all but one correlation exceeding .30. These correlations again generally exceed those found for unstructured interviews.

It is important to note that the improved predictive efficiency of PBDIs and SIs over the unstructured interview may be at least partially due to factors other than a stronger I-C linkage. In particular, the methodologies of these two interview methods almost guarantee improved reliability and construct validity of interview ratings (i.e., an improved I'-I linkage) over the unstructured interview. For example, the effects of cognitive biases on I' are minimized in both interview methods by using behaviorally-specific rating scales and requiring the interviewer to rate applicant responses as they are made. However, it is impossible to tell on an a priori basis what proportion of the increased prediction of the PBDI or SI over the unstructured interview is attributable to improved methodology (resulting in more reliable, construct valid interview ratings) and what proportion is attributable to a stronger substantive linkage of I with C. This question might best be answered by further meta-analytic work on the interview.

The three interview examples considered so far make reference to the construct/empirical validity model illustrated in Figure 19.1. In all of these examples, an independent variable (I' or I) is related to a dependent variable (C' or C). However, an interview at the extreme high end of "structure" might approximate the model found in Figure 19.2. Such an interview (restricted to jobs requiring primarily verbal skills) would require the applicant to provide a realistic behavioral facsimile of actual job requirements. In this case, the interviewer would assess the applicant on the criterion behavior itself rather than on a "sign" or "indicator" of criterion behavior (Wernimont & Campbell, 1968). The basic problem facing the practitioner is therefore how to obtain a reliable, construct valid indicator C' of the construct C.

The model represented in Figure 19.2 represents a situation qualitatively different from the first three because no independent variable is incorporated

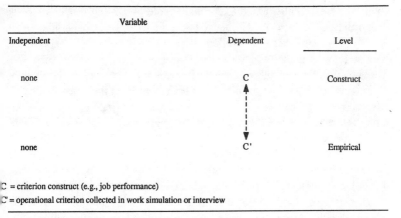

Figure 19.2. Representation of Construct and Empirical Validity of a Verbal Work Sample

SOURCE: Adapted from Schwab (1980).

into the model. An interview developed under this model should maximize the predictive efficiency achievable by the interview because it eliminates both the I'–I and I–C linkages. This type of interview is operationally feasible and, in fact, closely resembles verbal work samples which have already demonstrated a high degree of predictive efficiency (Asher & Sciarrino, 1974). If the practitioner requires a simple accept-reject judgment for selection purposes (as is common with other interview models), a cutoff score for the interview ratings could be established on rational grounds. The major drawback to this approach is that relatively few jobs are sufficiently verbal to justify the exclusive use of this interview model. Also, the C (and its corresponding C') would certainly be multi-dimensional for all but the simplest jobs. Therefore, greater practical demands would be placed on the practitioner attempting to establish the C'–C linkage than are suggested by the simplified unidimensional model in Figure 19.2

Implications for Future Research and Practice

This chapter reports findings of meta-analytic research that contradict two well-entrenched "received doctrines" (Barrett, 1972) of industrial/ organizational psychology—the belief that interviews are generally invalid and that the validities of unstructured interviews are importantly moderated by micro-analytic social psychological variables. However, this meta-analytic research also found that considerable variability remained in the true validities of "structured" interviews even when statistical artifacts such as sampling error were controlled. If research is to identify and control successfully for the methodological and substantive sources of this variability between criterion-related validity coefficients for "structured" interviews, the models of interview validity must be expanded to the domains of construct and empirical validity. Otherwise, research findings will soon accrete into a largely uninterpretable mass of empirical data as has so much past interview research.

The present authors believe that the argument over the criterion-related validity of unstructured interviews is moot. The Wiesner and Cronshaw (1988) meta-analysis suggests that although unstructured interviews do predict organization criteria, this prediction is somewhat poorer than that achieved with "structured" interviews. In addition, unstructured interviews do not differ greatly (if at all) among each other in predictive power. In fact, unstructured interviews may be so fatally flawed as assessment methods that no amount of micro-analytic research into interview decision processes will appreciably improve their criterion-related validity over the mean value reported by Wiesner and Cronshaw. Consequently, a moratorium is recommended on process research into the unstructured interview. Instead, these research resources should be devoted to investigating the moderators of validity for "structured" interviews (recognizing that the category of structured interviews as defined by Wiesner and Cronshaw is quite heterogeneous). In doing this, however, the mistake should not be repeated of fixating on interview "process" to the exclusion of the final validity outcome with which scientist-practitioners are most concerned.

The models of construct and empirical validity presented in this paper should help to coordinate and integrate research efforts into the structured interview. Most importantly, these models stress the need to be specific about the constructs being assessed with the interview (e.g., past job-related behavior, behavioral intentions). All too often, researchers embark on interview research, or organizational application, with a polyglot of measures developed purely on an operational basis without any thought given to construct validity. Such efforts offer absolutely no basis for understanding why or how interviews predict organizational criteria. The PBDI and SI offer a much better alternative. With these methods, the construct domains assessed by the respective interview procedures are clearly identified and substantively meaningful. Conversely, when practitioners develop operational indicators for a particular I construct (e.g., interview questions with corresponding rating scales), they should satisfy themselves that a reasonable a-priori rationale exists for expecting that I will be related to C.

At this point, a new definition is offered for the term "structure," at least as it applies to the employment interview. Structuring refers to any effort to improve the reliability and construct validity of I'. These efforts are mainly operational in nature as compared to the strategic and conceptual question of determining which I will be most highly related with C. Campion, Pursell, and Brown (1988) have outlined some important steps in operationally structuring the employment interview, including development of interview questions based on job analysis, asking the same questions of each interviewee, and anchoring interview rating scales with examples and illustrations. More empirical research is certainly needed to delineate the impact of such structuring dimensions on the criterion-related validity of the employment interview. However, it must be reiterated that structuring per se must remain subordinate to careful construct definition and theory building, which should be undertaken before the operational interview procedure is developed.

The stakes for industrial/organizational psychology in structured interview research are high. As the Wiesner and Cronshaw (1988) meta-analysis suggested, "better" structured interviews can indeed be identified (at least, "better" in terms of predictive efficiency). If organizations routinely use these maximally efficient structured interviews in selection, resulting productivity improvements, expressed as increased utility (Cronshaw & Alexander, 1985; Cronshaw, Alexander, Wiesner, & Barrick, 1987; Schmidt, Hunter, McKenzie, & Muldrow, 1979), may be very significant. However, the profession must proceed in a methodical and coordinated manner on this research in order eventually to make authoritative statements about how practitioners must best design their interviews to maximize prediction.

PART IX

Commentary

The final three chapters are commentaries on how the contributing chapters of this volume advance employment interview theory, research, and practice. Authors of the commentary section reviewed the chapters that comprise this edited volume according to the following guidelines: (1) highlight key contributions made, (2) note opposing perspectives, (3) fill in any gaps that may have been overlooked, and (4) discuss future challenges.

Hakel describes the shortcomings of current employment interview theory, notes recent developments that appear promising, and identifies areas in need of further development. Among the more promising areas are micro-analytic process models, interview structure, ideal applicant prototypes, script processing, unfavorable information, decision styles, incremental validity, attributions and context, recruitment and self-selection, and politics and impression management.

Buckley and Weitzel discuss the methodological developments and difficulties in conducting employment interview research. Particular attention is given to the multi-dimensional nature of the interview as a construct for study, threats to internal and external validity in research designs, the importance of incorporating situational variables into research designs to improve generalizability, and methodological innovations suggested by the chapters in this edited volume.

Goodale summarizes key principles and offers guidelines for more effective employment interview practice, founded both on the chapters in this edited volume and the author's considerable experience conducting interviewer training workshops. Major topics include interview structure, concepts examined in the interview, the types of questions to ask, and ways to evaluate applicants. Goodale suggests that the interviewer focus on assessing the applicant's potential and willingness to perform target job responsibilities by combining aspects of both Janz's patterned behavior description interview (PBDI) and Latham's situational interviewing techniques.

20

The State of Employment Interview Theory and Research

Milton D. Hakel

University of Houston and
Organizational Research and Development, Inc.

Looking back on 70 years of research about interviewing, and particularly this author's 25 years of participation in it, is both a humbling and a satisfying experience. It is humbling because the enormity of the task continues to be revealed, and satisfying because what appears to be meager progress *is*, nevertheless, progress. As shown in this volume, much has been learned that is useful, but too little of it has been put to use, and there remains so much more to learn.

Role of Theory

There is as yet no serviceable theory to guide research on interviewing. Simply put, a theory is just a model of a delimited set of phenomena together with rules that relate quantities in the model to empirical observations. A theory is good if it accurately describes a large class of observations while minimizing explanatory constructs, and it also yields specific predictions that can be validated against future observations.

Many researchers have advanced models of various facets of interviewing phenomena, and indeed, many of the chapters in this volume contain models or miniature models. Unfortunately, the domains they cover, the extent of their quantification, and their correspondence to observations are all extremely limited.

Beyond the models presented, each chapter in this book contributes to the list of sources of variance needed to adequately describe interviewing phenomena. A problem in all these efforts is that neither a comprehensive list of sources of variance nor the more specific models presented herein are stated precisely enough to yield predictions that can be tested empirically. Better measurement is needed, as is apparent from Buckley and Weitzel's review, and will help. Clearer conceptualizations and better differentiation and linkage of key constructs are also needed. As Kacmar, Ratcliff, and Ferris point out, research purposes need to be kept clearly in mind to provide the proper emphasis on issues of internal and external validity. Dreher and Maurer's discussion of research designs (pooling of data, incomplete reporting, ecological validity) also should inform future work.

The foremost challenge for interview researchers is to develop serviceable theory. There are adequate resources of creativity and attention to detail to succeed at this task, as can be seen in many of the chapters in this volume. Yet the standard needs to be raised; models alone aren't enough. There is a long way still to go. This volume will hopefully lead to both better theory and better practice. To get things started, and to provide context for commenting on some of the chapters, "microanalysis" and "process research" are briefly examined.

Reliability, Validity, and Microanalysis

Following Scott's initial reports (Scott, 1915, 1916), many studies were conducted during the first three decades of interview research. These were excellently summarized by Wagner (1949), who found that reliabilities ranged from .23 to .97 with a median value of only .57. Validities were disappointing and, of course, lower. The picture concerning reliability and validity hasn't changed appreciably in the following forty years, with a few exceptions noted later.

From the standpoint of contemporary understanding of interviewing, however, knowledge has increased immensely, as is clear from the historical review provided by Eder, Kacmar, and Ferris. Credit for this should go especially to Professor Edward Webster of McGill University. Webster (1964) reported on five dissertations conducted by his students, and also on several additional studies. He and his students observed that interviewers apparently make decisions by comparing job applicants with a stereotype of an ideal applicant, a finding that interviewing researchers may be once again ready to investigate (see Rowe and Tullar, this volume). Webster advocated what he called a decision-making approach to interviewing research (others have called it a microanalytic approach):

> There can be no question that the problems of reliability and validity are of fundamental importance to the interview, but there is an indirect as well as a direct approach to them. Until the factors which play a systematic role in determining the final decision of the interviewer are revealed, the limits of reliability and validity cannot be known. (Webster, 1964, p.2)

Webster's indirect route has been pursued through "process research" in the analysis of the many small and specific factors influencing interviewers' decisions. The goal was (and is) to redesign or reengineer the interview, taking into account the improved understanding of interviewing process brought about through microanalytic research. The McGill studies inspired hundreds of research studies.

There is skepticism, particularly among practitioners, about whether microanalytic lines of research will ever yield anything useful. A strong form of this skepticism is reflected in Cronshaw and Wiesner's recommendation that there should be a moratorium on process research into the unstructured interview. They warn that the mistake should not be repeated of fixating on interview "process" to the exclusion of the final validity outcome that most concerns scientist-practitioners. Webster himself (1982) apparently took a dim view of much of microanalytic research. His critique is clear and measured, and it draws attention especially to the motivational and experiential variables that differentiate subjects in most microanalytic research from practicing interviewers in the field. Parenthetically, it is both surprising and saddening that Webster's *Employment Interview: A Social Judgment Process* was cited by so few authors in this volume. The better the field understands Webster's viewpoint and arguments, the sooner practical improvements will be devised.

Attention now turns to some aspects of recent research, to see what has been learned and what this author believes needs to be studied next.

What to Research

Structure

Structured interviews are more valid than unstructured ones, as Cronshaw and Wiesner's (and others') meta-analyses show. This author disagrees with their definition of structure as anything that is done to "improve the reliability or validity of the interview," and with their call for a moratorium on process research on unstructured interviews. Researchers need to learn what it is about structuring that accounts for its superiority. Is it merely a consequence of greater reliability, that is, higher stability across time and interviewees, and also greater consistency within each interview? Does structuring increase interrater agreement? Does it result in more attention to applicant behavior? Are interview questions more job related? These are only a few of the possible factors causing the difference; direct research on them, following the lead furnished by Campion, Pursell, and Brown (1988), could be quite helpful in redesigning interviewing practices.

There are two difficulties in doing research on structure. First, it is difficult to define structure and then to manipulate it in an ordered set of operations ranging from low to high structure. Second, reliability varies over the range of structure, that is, the degree of structure and reliability are confounded. Thus, to make observations at a constant level of reliability, one would need greatly to increase relative sample sizes under low structure conditions. The reliability of unstructured interviews *is* greater than zero, but it is marginal, at least from the standpoint of practical psychometrics.

Can these two difficulties be surmounted? When one seeks to investigate a phenomenon that is marginally reliable, the need for creativity and methodological sophistication are especially great. Detecting signals in noisy data is always difficult, and that is what researchers on the interview have been trying to do. No wonder résumé studies, simulations, role playing, videotapes, and students as research participants have been so popular; each of these probably strengthens the signal. Yet each of these also probably introduces specific (but estimable) distortions. Some have lost patience with efforts to learn about how people make decisions based on résumés, arguing that such knowledge communicates nothing about how people make decisions based on face-to-face questioning. Generalizability is the issue, as Buckley and Weitzel pointed out. What is common to both experiments is the decision maker, the research participant. There are demonstrable regularities in the ways people process information; and if researchers concentrate on the "easy" mode of information transmission furnished by résumés, it is because they hope to understand what is happening in simpler situations before tackling more complex ones. There will, of course, be differences, and Webster (1982) has pointed out many of them. But patience and painstaking research are needed. This author agrees with Dreher and Maurer, that researchers ought to study what practicing interviewers actually do when they interview. However, as implied in the preceding paragraphs, this will not be an easy task; questionnaires and surveys won't come anywhere close to beginning the job. Neither the current theoretical conceptualizations nor research methods are yet adequate to the task.

Prototype and Schematic Processing

Earlier, it was noted that one of the central findings of the McGill studies was the importance of the stereotype, or in the current parlance, prototype, of the ideal applicant. The McGill findings were consistent with this interpretation, and many studies since are similarly consistent. However, as yet there have been no direct investigations of applicant stereotyping. Recent developments in social cognition, however, move closer to this possibility.

If one had to identify a single direction for future research (i.e., the one that would be most likely to provide usable knowledge), it is the one described by Tullar in this volume. Tullar ably reviews concepts and methodology from cognitive psychology and then describes implications for interviewing research. His research on relational control (Tullar, 1986) is a fine example of the kind of work that is urgently needed. It does not have immediate practical consequence, but in this observer's judgment it epitomizes the kind of research needed to develop theory that in turn will have practical consequences. It would be useful to know a lot more about cognitive performing scripts, schemas, and prototypes.

Fortunately, one is not constrained to make only one bet, and so this author would, in addition, call your attention especially to the work of Rowe, Schuh, and Dipboye.

Unfavorable Information

Rowe's chapter serves as a fine model of clarity of theoretical and conceptual thinking. Her discussion of explanations for why unfavorable information is more important than favorable information is especially fine; signal detection theory, reinforcement theory, and cost-benefit analysis are contrasted very effectively. Another nice touch in the Rowe chapter is the closing contrast between the interview as a search for unfavorable information, and the interview as a search for evidence supporting a hypothesis that the applicant is potentially a good worker (i.e., conforms to an ideal applicant prototype).

Decision Styles

Building on Webster (1982), Schuh describes probable consequences of variation in interviewer decision styles. The research needs he outlines are highly apt, but they will be tricky to execute because good methods do not yet exist for measuring decision styles. This author disagrees with his deemphasis of interrater agreement, but decision styles deserve much more research attention.

Incremental Validity

Yet another direction that deserves major attention is outlined by Dipboye. His emphasis on incremental validity is direct and to the point, but what is best about the chapter is the care with which many complicated issues underlying the interview's increment are brought into focus. There are even more to be considered.

Incremental validity is a key issue in personnel selection. One of the curiosities of employee selection is that interviewing continues to be used in spite of considerable evidence that it is unreliable (at least that reliability is below common psychometric standards), and its validity is surpassed by other techniques such as tests, application forms, and assessment centers. Nevertheless, the interview seems to be the technique of choice. One of the things that tests and application forms do not do effectively is measure applicants' skills in face-to-face communication. A commonly heard justification for interviewing is that managers want to know whether the applicant "has one or two heads," meaning that attributes not well measured by other techniques need to be scrutinized face-to-face. Nevertheless, appropriate justifications for the job-relatedness of "softer" dimensions such as communication skill, interpersonal effectiveness, cooperativeness, service orientation, and even neatness and grooming can be built. If a useful increment of validity is to be found, it will likely reside in measures of these (and similar) dimensions. Interviewers' impressions are multidimensional, even if the measures of their decisions are not.

Concern for incremental validity raises the issue of utility. Perhaps a suitable baseline for estimating the utility of techniques is their current level of usage in the marketplace. It is clear that interviewing is widespread and used far more frequently than any other preemployment selection technique. Regardless of what is said about it, managers believe in interviewing (evidently, applicants do also because less than one percent of the EEO charges filed between 1979 and 1987 involved the interview) (see Campion & Arvey, this volume). Interviewing must be judged to have value to the firms that use it because it is used even in the presence of less expensive, more reliable, or more valid techniques. Perhaps interview scholars have been remiss or ineffective in the marketing of superior techniques, including those described in this volume by Feild and Gatewood, Janz, Latham, and Schuler and Funke.

Another point needs to be made about baselines. Gathering data about empirical experience rates is preferable to using statistical calculations of what could be expected by chance. In statistical hypothesis testing, the observed effect is compared with what would be expected if the independent variable had no effect (i.e., the effect was determined at random). But all one need do to reject the null hypothesis is gather a large enough sample of data and it is guaranteed that practically trivial differences can become statistically significant. Part of the problem here is using chance as the baseline. Bayesian analysis, with its emphasis on prior probabilities, has not yet penetrated the working repertory of techniques in this area.

With respect to incremental validity, the concern is not with the increment beyond random prediction but, as Dipboye notes, with the increment beyond prediction achieved by techniques that are now in place. The above comments, however, suggest an additional and somewhat different perspective on the incremental validity question. From the standpoint of a manager, it is sensible to ask, "What can we usefully add to the interviewing that is already in place?" A true (corrected) validity for structured interviewing of .63 (Cronshaw & Weisner) is quite high. Given this high baseline to begin with, it would be difficult to show incremental validity for any other technique.

It is interesting to speculate about what the world would be like if the validity of the interview were 1.00. Most of the speculation will be left to the reader, but here are a few items to get things started. Surely tests, assessment centers, and application forms would not have been developed, because with perfectly valid interviewing there would be no need for them. Would applicants on the low end of the distribution ever get selected? Would some randomization procedure need to be introduced to allocate talent among firms?

Perfect validity implies perfect reliability, including interrater agreement. In practice interrater agreement is far from perfect. In the immediate future it would be interesting to see a meta-analysis of reliability coefficients (i.e., covering interrater agreements, internal consistencies and stabilities over time, sorted by rating dimensions). Although Schuh emphasizes accuracy and completeness of information, this author believes that interrater agreement is *the* key issue. Moreover, it is a convenient although somewhat unglamourous dependent measure for laboratory experimentation. There is a risk, of course, that the vigorous pursuit of interrater agreement might produce an interview that is so highly constrained that it has limited usefulness—for example, an interview that is nothing more than a self-reported work sample.

Construct validity is the basic issue here, specifically the problem of the tradeoff between bandwidth and fidelity. The interview is typically viewed as a wide-band, low-fidelity technique. Can it be transformed into a wide-band high-fidelity technique? Or will increasing the fidelity (i.e., interrater agreement, as a precursor to validity) necessarily extract a cost in the width of the band that is covered? This dilemma is another aspect of the problem of extracting signals from noisy data.

To repeat, interrater agreement should be a prime focus in future research. If interrater agreement in interviews can be improved, what is learned there should also be applicable in improving the reliability, validity, sensitivity, and accuracy of performance ratings made by managers, the most common criterion in validation research. What is learned on the predictor side of the equation will prove beneficial on the criterion side.

Attributions and Context

Herriott gives a particularly cogent account of attribution theory, where research on dispositional attributions will provide the greatest gains. Eder's review of contextual effects gives a clear and thorough account of the situationist and interactionist perspectives. The next step needed is to integrate these two perspectives into research activity. And Eder proposes several ideas that merit serious pursuit.

Recruitment and Self-Selection

Rynes neatly lays out issues on the interview as a recruitment device, taking a much more serious look from the applicant's perspectives at what occurs during interviews. Liden and Parsons take this another step and formally contrast interviewer's and applicant's perspectives in the preinterview, dyadic interaction (interview), and postinterview phases of contact. The authors of both these chapters point to the need for research on interviewing process, meaning the detailed analysis of the moment-to-moment interaction of interviewer and applicant. This is a suggestion that Tullar, especially, would likely endorse.

An additional research need must be mentioned here. It is the need to study applicant self-selection (see Rynes, this volume). Applicants don't appear for interviews randomly, but rather, sort themselves out quite consistently into various occupational fields. In recent years, women and minority group members have been more often selecting themselves into relevant pools, so there is a better mix of candidates from all races and both sexes. In any case, applicant pools are not random samples of the general population. The history of research on vocational interests shows clear and stable differentiation among many different career fields. Perhaps ideal applicant prototyping is operating at large in society and being sustained by the types of people who choose to present themselves as applicants for various jobs. Self-selection is largely unrecognized in interview research and deserves more attention.

Politics and Impression Management

The chapter by Gilmore and Ferris, and the chapter by Baron, get into domains that are far less researched, but which most would agree are quite important. Politics and impression management cover some of the most sensitive territory and interviewing phenomena. The interview is the place where the applicant must put his or her best foot forward. This means that the applicant's goal is, at least implicitly, to get the highest possible evaluation. Evaluation, after all, is what the interview is all about. Research covered in these two chapters gets the widest range of reactions from practicing interviewers and applicants alike. A common response from interviewers is, "So what?" with research-oriented interviewers pointing out that most of the effects here account for trivial amounts of variance (even though they are statistically significant). On the other hand, bookstores carry shelf after shelf of books and manuals on how to dress for success, how to write résumés, how to present oneself in interviews, and so forth. In looking at this welter of research and opinion, it would be easy to be pessimistic about building a science of one percent variance effects. But marginal effects are effective at the margin, which in the interview is at the cutting edge. Such effects by themselves may not be sufficient to alter radically the rank order of applicant suitability for jobs, but at the cutting edge, and in combination, they may make the critical difference.

One of the reasons why interrater agreement on postinterview ratings is so poor, perhaps, is that there is not a great deal of preinterview agreement on the favorability of the hundreds and thousands of cues that interviewers react to, such as whether the applicant's wearing of perfume is favorable (Baron) or the applicant's attempt to intimidate the interviewer is unfavorable (Gilmore & Ferris). Proper care and grooming may indicate conscientiousness to some and self-centeredness to others. What one interviewer might interpret as an attempt at intimidation may be viewed by another as a strong display of assertiveness and self-confidence. The point is that too little is known about the evaluative dimension. Though evaluation pervades the interview process, it has not been given the close attention that it deserves.

Concluding Comment

This book marks the first comprehensive collection of chapters on interviewing research and practice. It describes many variables and effects that need to be brought together in improved theoretical formulations. The legacy of this book should be stimulation. A clear and practical account is needed of how people gather information about others and how that information is used in making decisions about them. The immediate challenge is to build quantified, testable theories. It is an enormous challenge.

21

Comment on the Research Methodologies Used in Interview Research

M. Ronald Buckley
University of Oklahoma

William Weitzel
University of Oklahoma

Interview research methodologies have undergone considerable evolution since the earliest purely anecdotal, qualitative observations of the interview process (see Eder, Kacmar, & Ferris, this volume). The demarcation point for the change from a qualitative approach to a quantitative approach is usually considered the pioneering work of Edward C. Webster and his students at McGill University (Wright, 1969). Since that time, myriad methodological approaches to investigating the interview process have surfaced. In spite of (or maybe due to) this proliferation of approaches, progress has been made in attempts to understand the interview process, although not as rapidly as some like Guion and Gibson (1988) would like. They recently restated the selection interviewer's laments:

> Nor have repeatedly discouraging summaries . . . deterred the use of interviews. . . . Interviews will be used . . . and research on interviewing continues, whether in desperation or hope. (p. 367)

The selections in this volume tilt the scale more toward hope than toward despair for the future of research concerning interview effectiveness. The meta-analysis by Cronshaw and Wiesner in this volume reported that the interview is not as invalid as is usually believed and reported. From the potpourri of interview research outcomes, researchers are making constant, albeit slow, progress toward a more parsimonious understanding of the processes which occur in and during the interview process. The purpose of this chapter is to comment on the conceptualization of the interview process, the soundness of the strategies that have been used in interview research, the issues that should be of concern to researchers, the contributions of the chapters in this volume which have advanced interview research methodologies, and some of the problems that continue to bedevil research on the interview.

What Is *the* Interview?

Across the chapters in this volume and in the literature the employment interview has been operationalized in a number of different ways. In fact, it is equivocal to continue to refer to *the* interview. These different operationalizations have an effect upon the research questions that can be posed, the independent variables introduced for study, and the dependent variables measured in the research. In research on highly structured interview formats (i.e., situational interviews), the interview is operationalized primarily as a verbal cognitive ability test. No attempt is made to assess interpersonal skills, applicant interest and motivation to perform, or relevant training and experience. Based on this narrow definition, research might focus upon independent variables like the job relevance of questions, the social interaction between the applicant and interviewer, differences in verbal fluency, convergent/divergent thinking, or verbal reasoning. Possible dependent variables include encoding processes, judgment accuracy, the efficiency of the exchange process, and interviewer decision time.

From another perspective, the interview can be conceived of as a test of interpersonal skills. This connotation is frequently emphasized in recruitment interviews and for service-oriented positions. Investigations of this operationalization of the interview focus upon independent variables drawn from the interpersonal attraction literature, or on the communication styles of participants. The interview process becomes the research focus, and the affective responses of the participants to each other is one of the more important dependent variables assessed in an investigation of this type.

If the employment interview is considered a substitute assessment device to obtain information about job knowledge/ skill/ ability, then the structure and content of the interview questions become the focus of the independent variables developed for investigation. Long in-depth final interviews by supervisors/coworkers often look at the interview this way. Related issues include the sampling procedures that are used to develop important job requirements, job relevant question selection, and the appropriateness of the interview as a method for both evaluating and assembling information about the applicant. Focal dependent variables in studies of this type revolve around the accurate recording or recollection by the interviewer of applicant responses.

Others conceive of the interview as a general measure of manifest or long-term motivation (Ulrich & Trumbo, 1965). Depending upon the perceived operationalization of the interview, the interpersonal judgment task is both complex and multidimensional. Though all of these operationalizations tap important aspects of the processes which occur during the interview, it may become somewhat confusing when an attempt is made to integrate these variant research findings.

Just as there are multiple meanings for what is meant by interviewer judgment, there are multiple purposes toward which each interview type serves (see Rynes and Eder, this volume). Interviews can be for the purpose of, among others, recruiting applicants to comprise a large qualified applicant pool, attracting applicants to accept the position if offered, or selecting one preferred applicant from a number of final candidates. Different interview purposes will dictate different strategies for dealing with an applicant, and result in distinctly different process dynamics. As has been pointed out by Rynes, the dynamics of the interview change depending upon the purpose of the interview (i.e., selection or recruitment). Logically, researchers should not aggregate interview research which is confounded by purpose, nor that which reflects different operationalizations of the interview. Subsequent meta-analyses and more qualitative literature reviews should use the a priori categories of interview definition and purpose as moderator variables to summarize both process and outcome variables of interest.

Internal and External Validity of Interview Research

In order to successfully address the issues of internal and external validity in employment interview studies, sources of variance that have an influence upon those issues must first be identified. An earlier chapter in this volume by Kacmar, Ratcliff, and Ferris analyzes specific research designs in terms of their internal and external validity. What follows is a more general discussion of these issues which includes a number of ideas developed in that chapter.

From among the many different perspectives expressed by researchers concerning research settings and research questions, there is general agreement that the interview is an interaction between two or more individuals where an individual evaluative decision is occurring. This decision may be an applicant judgment about the quality of the interaction or an interviewer determination of the job suitability of an applicant. In the employment interview, the principle outcome of this focused interaction is an organization decision to employ/not to employ and an applicant decision to join/not join an organization.

Studies of various aspects of this interaction can be undertaken by means of participant observation (e.g., self-reports of applicant experiences) or through the observation of one or more of the participants by others (e.g., observers of videotaped interviews). There have been a number of ingenious approaches developed in order to test hypotheses concerning the interview process (see Gilmore & Ferris; Liden & Parsons; and Tullar this volume).

To be able to adequately determine why some studies appear to provide more useful answers and greater insights into the interview process than do others, it is necessary that the following five sets of variables be explained or controlled. This list also provides some insight into the question of whether a specific piece of research is capable of making a contribution to furthering what is understood about the interview process.

Setting

The setting for the study of the interview process can be in situ or in a field setting. Alternatively, it may be some approximation of an interview setting in an environment with varying levels of experimenter control. Studies conducted in the field are more likely to contain factors that may influence both the process occurring and the outcomes that arise from an actual job interview. A researcher interested in conducting field research, therefore, should measure critical dimensions of the setting (see Eder, this volume) and exercise some statistical control over their impact upon the endogenous variables that are of primary concern in a given study.

The purpose of a laboratory study is to emulate that which occurs in a field study. In a laboratory setting, key exogenous factors typically found in the interview context should be designed into the research. Each research design should attempt to measure the minimum variable set necessary to both generalize the findings and approximate the conditions which prevail outside of the laboratory. Kacmar et al. have discussed the problematic nature of this endeavor.

Individual Differences

Beginning with the earliest research inquiries, human judgment has been shown to be influenced by individual difference variables such as interviewer/applicant sex, age, education level, and intelligence, along with various other variables related to personal adjustment and personality. Studies of the interview process should account for the potential interactions of these variables in any complete explanation of research findings on the employment interview in field and laboratory research settings. One available option is to control for these variables either statistically or through randomization.

Experience/Training Regarding the Task

Participants in the interview process have varying amounts of experience within this type of social setting. Some have learned their style through trial and error, and have developed their own idiosyncratic approach. Others have developed their approach through a series of supervised experiences (i.e., training). However, what they do is only part of what is important. Also of relevance is how proficient these participants are in their own approach to carrying out the process. Some have had an abundance of opportunities to practice, whereas others are relative neophytes at interviewing. It is imperative to consider the existing levels of interviewer task experience and training among groups of participants in an interview research project so that the treatment effect is not confounded by preexisting levels of participant competence. This will necessitate that more of an ideographic approach to interview research be adopted in order to encourage more intensive study of individual interviewers.

Consequence of Interview Outcome to Participants

Research in an ad hoc interview situation, in which those involved have little stake in the outcomes or consequences of their actions, provides results which cannot be realistically compared to field research results where participants are heavily invested in the interview outcome. Eder's discussion of the role of perceived task clarity, rating purpose, decision risk, and accountability is particularly timely. In field settings, those seeking a position and those offering employment have a personal stake in the process and outcomes of the interview. The person who interviews a potential future subordinate or coworker is aware of the consequences of having to work with that person. Similarly, professional recruiters know that their reputation for spotting talent is under constant scrutiny by supervisors who receive their referrals. Applicants in real job search situations are also heavily invested in the interview process, and try to project the kind of image necessary to progress in the selection process (see Baron; Gilmore & Ferris, this volume). The applicant is also screening the organization from among possible job choices, anticipating what it would be like to work with the interviewer in that organization. Clearly, these mutual applicant-interviewer investments in the interview produce motivations, behaviors, and judgments that require careful replication in research designs alleging to have external validity.

Compare the aforementioned field setting with a role play laboratory setting involving participants who pretend that they are professional interviewers or that they are hiring someone to work alongside them on a hypothetical case or project. It is difficult to envision a comparable level of interviewer incentive value, potential for stress, or general motivational level between participants in a hypothetical interview situation, and managers who are interviewing and selecting their future colleagues.

Summary of These Sources of Variance

Each of the aforementioned sources of variance should be addressed and assessed by investigators studying employment interview processes. By recognizing both the importance and the pervasiveness of these sources of variance, more effective and insightful research streams can be developed. In addition, knowledge of the relationship of these sources of variance to the independent variables of the research will enable a clearer, more effective integration of research findings with those that have preceded (i. e., increase both the internal and external validity of the research). Failure to measure the impact of these sources of variance will result in deficiencies in study design as well as problems in interpreting research findings (see Kacmar, Ratcliff, & Ferris, this volume). Keeping these problems in mind, the authors of the papers in this volume have made numerous important methodological contributions to interview research.

Key Methodological Contributions in This Volume

Recognition of the Importance of Incremental Validity

In most studies, the interview and the selection decision are treated as interchangeable. In reality, the selection decision almost always includes a number of other data acquisition or data verification steps which are treated in a sequential and/or compensatory manner by the decision maker. Each step contributes to an overall evaluation of applicant suitability. Interview information is then combined with other predictor information to judge the fit of each applicant to the position. The rather myopic view that the employment interview is the sole information generation device in the selection process does not take into account other sources of information that also contribute to the final decision. The interview, as one predictor among many, must be judged in terms of its contribution to overall predictive efficiency.

Consistent with Meehl (1959), Sechrist (1967) pointed out that predictors are judged by their relative cost compared to that of alternative predictors. Also, a part of the evaluation process is the incremental gain achieved by the decision maker in terms of the improved validity of the predictions that are made. Cronbach and Glaser (1957) stated, "(predictors) should be judged on the basis of their contribution over and above the best strategy available, making use of prior information" (p. 31).

A recent study by Campion, Pursell, and Brown (1988) helps to point out one other factor to be considered with regard to incremental validity and the employment interview. They reported that some ability tests are equally effective and less costly predictors than are interviews for assessing applicant cognitive ability. An employment interview designed only as a surrogate cognitive ability test obviously adds little to the predictive power of the selection process. However, as stated earlier, employment interviews can measure more than just cognitive ability. Research should be designed so that incremental validity of different types of employment interviews may be easily assessed (see Dipboye, this volume). For example, this may be done by monitoring changes in R^2 associated with different selection components, or by determining whether the order in which selection components are configured affects the regression coefficients that are obtained when the dependent variables are regressed on the independent variable.

There are, in addition to incremental validity, other interview process dynamics that are of interest to researchers. For example, decision time may be a variable of interest in interview process research (Buckley & Eder, 1988). Or, the interview may be examined as a tool to aggregate data and integrate applicant information (Meehl, 1955). The role of the interview as an integrator of information from diverse sources seems to imply that the basis for doing a cost-benefit analysis of the interview must be broadened beyond its function as an information generating tool.

Movement away from Poorly Designed Laboratory Research

Laboratory research is an important part of any systematic research program. Research designs that are unleashed upon the field without prior pilot study in controlled conditions (i. e., adequate laboratory research) often lack sufficient internal and/or construct validity. The other side of the laboratory research issue is the serious shortcomings associated with generalizability of findings. Laboratory studies conducted within a "for research only" context disregard the decision accountability and responsibility that surely accompanies the task of the selection interviewer in an organizational context. Selection decisions that are obtained under role-enacted conditions simply do not generalize to interview decisions made in actual organizations.

Similarly, the stimulus materials (e.g., "paper people" and videotapes of stimulus personnel) which have been used in interview research have been less than optimal in some cases. Murphy, Herr, Lockhart, and Maguire (1986) corroborated the earlier work of Gorman, Clover, and Doherty (1978) in which the "paper people" approach resulted in systematically different outcomes from studies that utilized direct or indirect (videotapes) observation. Although audio- and videotape technology are superior to the "paper people" approach (see also Ilgen & Favero, 1985), viewing videotapes of interviews or listening to an audio playback of an interview is basically a passive activity. Research should be designed that carefully controls the implications/consequences of the subjects' decisions along with the nature of the information and the level of subject training/experience. The interview is an interactive interchange and a search for information. In actual interviews, it is possible to modify behavior, probe unexpected issues, and elicit additional information based on perceptions formed during the actual exchange. Audio- and videotapes, as a form of indirect observation, do not adequately capture the dynamics that invariably occur during the verbal and nonverbal exchanges in the interview. They control the stimulus presentation, but also force the subject into a strictly observational role that results in different causal attributions (see Storms, 1973) than when one performs the role of an actor. Thus, observed variation may be due to actor/observer differences and not to the independent variables under study. It is opined that studies that have been performed using the preceding methodologies have yielded limited insights into how interviews are actually performed in organizations.

This is not meant to be a denigration of all laboratory research that has been conducted on the interview. In fact, Paunonen, Jackson, and Oberman (1987) have presented data that supports the utility of laboratory simulations of the interview. It is intended, though, to take issue with those authors who have utilized methodologies that lack a way to relate their activities to in situ and other field settings. These lack, to some degree, both internal and external validity (see Cook & Campbell, 1976; Kacmar, Ratcliff & Ferris, this volume), which are required to answer those questions that will provide insight into the interview process. It is encouraging that, for the most part, researchers appear to be moving away from these relatively sterile designs to designs that more faithfully represent and adequately measure the salient variables surrounding the interview event (e.g., Eder; Liden & Parsons, this volume).

Recognition of the Importance of Situational Variables

Eder and Buckley (1988), and Eder (this volume) have suggested that interview judgment should be examined within its multidimensional context. There has been a movement to better capture these variables, evidenced by the Liden and Parsons chapter in this volume, which treats the interview process as a reciprocal interaction. Further, as Dreher and Maurer have pointed out in this volume, the fact that contextual and methodological factors have largely been ignored may be responsible for the relatively small validity coefficients which are reported for the interview. In conjunction with the report by Cronshaw and Wiesner in this volume, in which they gainsay the "received doctrine" that the interview is generally invalid, one can only conclude that this trend toward operationalizing the interview as a multidimensional process will be fruitful. In fact, the problem is probably not so much that the research was poorly done or invalid. Rather, it is more related to the notion that constructs under investigation were ill-defined, poorly measured and limited in dimension and scope (see Cote & Buckley, 1987, 1988 for a more detailed discussion of this problem).

Earlier, the importance of the setting in which research takes place was discussed. It was indicated that the differences between laboratory settings and field settings is that in the laboratory settings, all variables must be purposefully introduced. The implication of these earlier statements is that in field settings, by definition, all relevant moderating contextual variables are present. A researcher need only measure each variable to assure that the hypothesized results from the field study are capable of contributing to the existing body of knowledge. It is doubtful, though, that at this point in time all relevant contextual variables have been identified. For example, Gilmore and Ferris pointed out in their chapter on organizational politics in the interview that there are some variables which are very difficult to simulate in a laboratory (e.g., impression management). Perhaps this is because impression management is embedded in face-to-face situations which have an extensive and complex history within organizational and applicant lives.

The choice of laboratory or field research is driven by the variables of interest, not by the convenience of the sample or other secondary considerations. Field research and laboratory research must not be considered polar opposites. Their relationship should be interdependent. For example, some novel approach can be observed in the field and then investigated in the laboratory. Likewise, the appropriate laboratory work may yield novel, insightful interview strategies which can be implemented and tested by practicing interviewers.

It is likely, however, that in order to increase understanding of the more interesting variables (e. g., decision accountability) which occur in the interview process, in situ studies will need to be conducted in field settings. Variables such as the pressure to effectively manage impressions, the level of competition for a particular position, the consequences of making a correct/incorrect selection decision will most likely be present, to some extent, in all field studies. In addition, these variables may possibly interact with the knowledges, skills, and abilities required by the position, and with the individual differences of both the applicant and interviewer.

Opposing Perspectives in the Chapters

Inappropriate Expectations from Student Samples

To be sure, the use of student samples in interview research will likely continue. However, it is necessary to recognize the limitations of using a student sample. The demand characteristics associated with student samples are such that most students will attempt to perform almost anything that they believe the experimenter desires of them. Since the entire process is a form of a "pretend" activity, it may have limited utility, except as a pilot study of the design methodology intended eventually for field experimentation. For example, Rowe cites a number of studies, such as unpublished work by Mifsud, that have used inexperienced and untrained student subjects as interviewers. Research demand characteristics and experimenter expectations would need to be ruled out as alternative explanations for these studies' findings.

Students can, though, provide an acceptable sample in studies where the outcomes are relevant for them in ways analogous to the process dynamics that occur in an interview. For example, the selection of a roommate with whom the student must coexist for a year is analogous to the selection decision of an interviewer who must select a coworker. Students who are themselves interviewing for a position with a campus recruiter, or who are practicing and developing interviewing skills in anticipation of their interviews with a campus recruiter, are two additional examples in which student samples can be utilized in research on the interview process.

Using Inappropriate and Insufficient Research Settings

Less than optimal settings are still being utilized in employment interview research. The relatively sterile lab setting inhibits aspects of interview process dynamics that certainly occur in naturalistic field settings. The problem, though, is considerably more complex than this. Researchers have failed to sample across a variety of employment interview situations. For example, the situational interview (see Latham, this volume) is generally viewed as both more reliable and more valid than the traditional unstructured interview. The majority of the published research on this technique (except for Weekley and Gier, 1987) has utilized pulp workers for the subject sample. Although it is difficult to gainsay the positive results achieved thus far with the situational interview, this technique should be investigated utilizing a number of different samples across employment interviews with different objectives.

Related to this is the notion that researchers use subject or stimulus extremes while sampling minor situational variation (see Eder; Kacmar, Ratcliff, & Ferris, this volume). This results in a series of "unfair comparisons" (see Cooper & Richardson, 1986) which stack the deck, so to speak, in favor of a certain outcome. As Meehl (1982) has pointed out, researchers set up many situations in which research is destined to succeed (i.e., find a significant difference). The comparisons so made are not genuine comparisons at all; they are foregone conclusions. Researchers should include a larger sample of stimulus values in their research, and should attempt to use different research settings, which offer greater situational variability, in order to free their research from this criticism. This will result in more generalizable findings and will significantly reduce the number of "unfair comparisons" which are set up in interview research.

Related Problem Issues

There are a number of issues not addressed by the chapters in this volume which should be addressed in order to affect an improvement in employment interview research methodology. Initially, researchers need to develop more longitudinal studies of the interview process and its outcomes. There is a relative dearth of longitudinal validity studies of the interview. Virtually no attempts have been made to follow investigations through the careers of participants in the interview process. As Peters and Sheridan (1988) have pointed out, this one shot approach has a number of problems associated with it; namely, the right and left censoring of data points through historical factors associated with the attrition of individuals in organizations. By restricting the range of potential data points, a situation is facilitated in which problems occur with the varied statistical analyses used to analyze data that has been obtained on the interview process.

Further, the criteria used to assess the effectiveness of manipulations in the interview process may be deficient (see Dreher & Maurer, this volume for a more detailed explanation of this problem). For example, in a number of studies the dependent variable is dichotomous (accept/reject). This requires the formulation of an overall clinical judgment concerning each applicant, rather than more appropriate incremental judgments of the candidate's suitability across job-relevant knowledge, skill, and abilities. The major problem associated with this type of outcome measure is that it permits such a narrow range of response that it masks the decision variability that would otherwise occur. Using this type of dependent variable potentially leads to less precise inferences from data focused only on selection to a given position, and not on career success within the job cluster that the applicant is joining. In addition, there is some concern about the appropriate statistical analysis to use when the dependent variable is dichotomous. In some cases the general linear model is not appropriate. When measuring dichotomous variables, researchers would be wise to contemplate utilizing an econometric technique like logistic regression.

The addition of qualitative research design features may also enhance a better understanding of interviewer-applicant decision dynamics. Different approaches to research design, like participant observation and ethnomethodological approaches, have been largely ignored in employment interview research (see also Silverman & Jones, 1975). One consequence of this has been a limited notion of what constitutes an acceptable research design. Reducing behavioral observations to a series of numbers can lead to problematic conclusions, and a loss of a more complete comprehension of the subjective nature of behavioral responses. Quantitative methodology is, in comparison to the other available approaches, relatively simple, but the casualty of this simplicity is a failure to achieve the desired depth of understanding of certain phenomena.

Tullar's application of scripting theory from the organizational communications field is an excellent example of the benefits that may accrue from incorporating research streams from other disciplines. For example, one direction for study may be closer investigation of the language and syntactical structures that prevail in the interview. Likewise, perhaps interview researchers can borrow from clinical and educational psychology, and develop research technologies to study micro-behavioral phenomenon like those used to study interaction patterns in families or with individuals who have been clinically diagnosed and treated. The possibilities for this seem numerous.

Lastly, there is the problem of the misapplication of criteria from one type of operationalization of the interview to one with a different operationalization. The end result may be that many of the comparisons that have been made in research reviews should not have been made. It is difficult to speculate how much research suffers from this problem. This may be why some of the common sense generalizations that are held concerning the interview process may be untrue (see also Buckley & Eder, 1988). It is necessary that a common nomenclature and a series of operationalizations outlining the contents of the interview process be developed. This would serve both to facilitate and expand what is known about the interview process.

Future Challenges

Although great strides have been made in terms of the quality of the research methodology used to investigate the employment interview, there remain numerous challenges to be met. There is a need for methodology to catch up with research questions concerning the interview process. There have recently been some developments in multivariate time series analysis (Tiao & Box, 1981; Tiao & Tsay, 1983), which have extended the statistical capability to examine the interdependence of variables over some time interval. This would facilitate the inclusion of multiple variables into longitudinal interview research models. But, in a number of areas, methodology still must develop further in order to answer the research questions being posed. For example, in order to ascertain the precise decision time of an interviewer, there is a need to develop a methodology which is unobtrusive but that can measure the interviewer's internal decision point (assuming one exists). This may prove an impossible task, given the limits of the research methodologies currently available.

There is reason to be optimistic about the progress being made pertaining to what is understood about interview behaviors and judgments. While much has been learned, there is much still left to be explored and revealed. Hopefully, the collective result of the chapters in this volume will be a more cogent, unified, and insightful approach to the future of research concerning the interview process.

22

Effective Employment Interviewing

James G. Goodale
Philbrook, Goodale Associates
Houston, Texas

This edited volume represents a comprehensive, up-to-date summary of a wide range of theories and research findings about the strengths and weaknesses of the employment interview, and almost every author has included suggestions to practitioners. Some authors (e.g., Campion & Arvey) have restated the historical conclusion that the interview is less reliable and valid than other selection techniques. Dipboye and Herriot have even suggested that practitioners abandon the employment interview as a selection device, and use it primarily to promote good public relations and test the applicant's fit with the organization's culture.

Other contributors (Cronshaw & Wiesner; Feild & Gatewood; Janz; Latham; Schuler & Funke) have presented more respectable reliability and validity coefficients and have recommended structured, job-related approaches to interviewing. Finally, Dreher and Maurer have gone so far as to argue that practitioners may be correct in ignoring 60 years of research condemning the employment interview, and have suggested that researchers examine more carefully what practitioners actually do in their quest for valid selection decisions.

The purpose of this chapter is threefold. First, it presents observations about the current practices and needs of members of organizations who actually conduct employment interviews. Second, it summarizes and integrates the sometimes conflicting and potentially confusing research and theory included in this book. Third, it provides specific guidance for human resource professionals, line supervisors, and managers who interview job applicants.

Interviewer Practices and Problems

Several contributors called for research to examine the way employment interviews are conducted in organizations. This author strongly agrees and can offer preliminary trends that need closer examination with more structured research methods. Consultation with human resource professionals and hiring supervisors has produced considerable information about the way they conduct recruiting and selection interviews, and the problems they encounter. This sample is somewhat biased toward those who seek help in interviewing, although it contains many practitioners who have had previous interviewer training and many years of interviewing experience. Each workshop begins with discussions of participants' interviewing experiences, and over the years very consistent patterns have emerged from their comments.

Objectives and Approach

Most practitioners can clearly state their objectives and describe a definite approach to interviewing. As Dipboye, Rynes, Eder, and Dreher and Maurer pointed out in their chapters, interviews have multiple objectives. Practitioners usually list as major objectives collecting information to identify the best applicant, giving information to attract applicants, and checking whether the applicant will "fit in" with current members of the department. Although the first two have received considerable attention by researchers, the third objective has rarely been addressed in the literature.

Most practitioners use a semistructured approach with a small number of topics or prepared questions beyond which they probe as needed. Very few have resorted to a completely unstructured approach prior to this author's workshops. Highly structured approaches with long lists of prepared questions are also rare but are used most often in the public sector. Finally, a relaxed but professional atmosphere is preferred by the vast majority of practitioners surveyed.

Problems

Practitioners have also consistently raised the same types of problems, regardless of how much interviewing experience and training they have had. The most commonly mentioned problems reflect many of the topics discussed in this volume:

1. Uncertainty about the information they need to gather and how to ask questions to get it;
2. Not knowing how to get information without violating EEO guidelines;
3. Their own personal attitudes and stereotypes, first-impression biases, and early decisions;
4. Quiet, evasive, and polished applicants;

5. Lack of skill in breaking through the applicant's facade and prepared answers;
6. Not knowing how to evaluate what the applicant says; and
7. Not knowing how to make the hiring decision.

Human resource professionals also report problems with interviewing applicants for technical and professional jobs they do not understand, and with trying to evaluate applicants in terms that supervisors and other members of the hiring department can understand.

Professional Applicant/Untrained Interviewer

The sharp contrast between the quality of preparation of interviewers and applicants is startling. Literally thousands of practicing managers have said that they learned to interview through trial and error, with no instruction or coaching. Some individuals have had the opportunity to observe a more senior colleague in action, and are then turned loose on their own. Others receive even less guidance; many are simply told that they have staffing responsibilities and will need to interview applicants.

In contrast, interviewers report that the applicants they face, especially in campus recruiting, are well trained and rehearsed. Coaching offered by campus placement offices, professional résumé services, and articles and books (Beatty, 1986; Biegeleisen, 1984; Half, 1981; Ryckman, 1982; and Yate, 1987b) on how to pass an employment interview have led to the age of the "professional interviewee," who is trained in impression management techniques (see Baron; Gilmore & Ferris; Liden & Parsons, this volume) and has mastered a prepared script (Tullar, this volume). Thus, most practitioners are poorly prepared to deal with the increasingly sophisticated applicants they face.

Useful Research and Theory

This section describes key areas of research and theory contributed in this volume that are essential for improving interviewer practice: interview structure and the evaluation process. At the end, a set of integrated guidelines to help practitioners plan and conduct more effective employment interviews is provided.

In Pursuit of More Interview Structure

There can be little doubt that unstructured interviews are doomed to failure. Many contributors to this book have cited evidence that unstructured employment interviews produce low reliability and validity. In addition, they enable interviewers to confirm their own biases, stereotypes, and first impressions (see Dipboye; Rowe, this volume), and are therefore subject to charges of unfair discrimination (Campion & Arvey).

Increasing the degree of structure in employment interviews has some clear advantages. The reliabilities and validities cited in this volume by Feild and Gatewood, Janz, Latham, and Schuler and Funke make an impressive case for highly structured interviews. But it is also clear that the questions must be *job-related*. Unfortunately, many training courses and books (Drake, 1982; Fear, 1984; Lopez, 1975; Yate, 1987a) have proposed long lists of questions to probe ambiguous applicant traits of questionable job relevance (e.g., motivation, maturity, integrity, stability, character, emotional adjustment).

Structured questions on the wrong content are probably just as bad as no questions at all. For example, questions like "do you prefer to work alone or in a group, what are your greatest strengths . . . weaknesses, do you work well under pressure, do you make friends easily, where would you like to be in 20 years, (and from Feild and Gatewood's chapter) what kind of people do you enjoy being around the most, and if you could control what people said behind your back, what would you like them to be saying about you?" merely invite the applicant's prepared answers and probably provide little indication of the applicant's potential for successful job performance.

Several authors have provided sound guidance for how practitioners can structure their employment interviews. Janz's chapter made a strong case for emphasis on behavior descriptions. Latham argued with equal strength for situational questions that examine what the applicant might do when faced with a job-related situation, and both he and Feild and Gatewood offered extensive job analysis techniques for deriving the content to be covered. Schuler and Funke's ambitious field experiment in Germany combined a variation of behavioral description with situational questions.

Unfortunately, these highly structured approaches have major practical problems. First, practitioners resist spending the day needed for job analysis and preparation of situational questions. Second, applicants become aware of the situational question content through the grapevine, which undermines the technique's integrity. Third, applicants object to the limited opportunity in structured interviews to sell themselves, which has implications for applicant attraction (see Rynes, this volume). Finally, Tullar pointed out that the structured interview, with its predictable format, can lull interviewers into a mindless script that causes them to tune out answers.

How to Evaluate the Applicant

A topic that needs far more attention in both research and practice is the way interviewers evaluate the information they gather from applicants, and how they use those evaluations to reach a hiring decision. The evaluation process is central to interview effectiveness and has implications for (a) the concepts or "hypothetical constructs" being examined in the interview and the criteria used to measure them, (b) the information gathered from the applicant and probed during the interview, (c) the types of questions asked, and (d) the person who conducts the interview. Moreover, the structure and content of the interview can, and *should* be explicitly derived from points (a) and (b) above. Several chapters in this volume have presented diverse and sometimes conflicting views of the evaluation process, which are now summarized and integrated.

Concepts Examined and Criteria Used to Measure Them

What are practitioners trying to measure in the interview, and what can the interview measure well? This is the most important of the four points just mentioned, and has been addressed by several contributors. In their commentary chapter, Buckley and Weitzel listed four dimensions the interview has been used to measure: cognitive abilities; interpersonal skills; job-related knowledge, skills, and abilities (KSA's); and long-term motivation. Many practitioners also use the interview to measure a fifth category, personal traits. Personality assessment in employment interviews has been encouraged by many training programs and books, and by applicant evaluation forms on which interviewers rate initiative, maturity, personality, resourcefulness, reliability, and so forth. Several studies cited in this volume by Campion and Arvey used global impressions of the applicant's suitability. Finally, Janz and Latham have proposed highly job-related measures of the applicant's potential and intention to perform job responsibilities.

All these concepts fall into the following four categories (Goodale, 1982, in press): (a) *overall applicant suitability*, (b) *what applicants are* (e.g., personal traits), (c) *what applicants have* (e.g., intelligence, motivation, cognitive abilities, interpersonal skills, job-related KSA's), and (d) *what applicants can and will do* (potential and willingness to perform job responsibilities).

Let's begin with the first two categories. Practitioners and researchers alike have used global impressions of applicant suitability or ratings of personal traits to assess applicants. Many studies reporting low interview reliabilities and validities have relied on this type of measure. In addition, global criteria have commonly appeared in research demonstrating the dramatic impact of applicants' personal characteristics and interviewers' biases on interviewer judgments. For example, Campion and Arvey cited evidence of sex and racial bias in studies in which interviewers evaluated applicants in such general terms as favorability and "recommendation to hire." Similarly, Dipboye presented evidence that preinterview impressions formed from applicants' paper credentials strongly affected postinterview impressions, such as assessments of personal traits, "total" impressions, and hiring recommendations. Finally, Rowe cited research that indicated that people collect information in the interview to confirm the hypotheses they hold about the personalities of others.

This research strongly suggests that practitioners avoid global evaluations or ratings of ambiguous personal traits. When asked to assess applicants in these terms, interviewers resort to their stereotypes of ideal applicants. This is particularly true when interviewers are students who know little about the job to be filled. On a more positive note, Arvey and Campion also cited research showing that interviewers with more job information made evaluations that were less affected by preinterview impressions.

The key here is to examine and measure *job-related* factors in the interview. Researchers have proposed that the interview be used to measure what the applicant has, such as intelligence, motivation, general abilities, and job-related KSA's. For example, Eder cited research showing that the specificity of evaluation criteria helps interviewers discriminate among job applicants, and encouraged the use of behaviorally-specific criteria that are suggestive of key KSA's. This approach seems logical, because applicants' intelligence, motivation, KSA's, and so forth certainly affect job performance.

Dipboye has raised questions, however, about how well the interview measures these concepts, and about the incremental validity of interviews, when combined with other measures of the same concepts. For example, Dipboye cited research that interviewer assessments of motivation contributed less to the prediction of job success than did questionnaire measures of applicant motivation. Similarly, a highly structured interview predicted success of entry-level paper mill employees, but added little incremental validity when combined with scores on an ability test (see also Campion, Pursell, & Brown, 1988).

In sum, the assessment of concepts like personality characteristics, motivation, intelligence, and even KSA's may not be desirable or even necessary in employment interviews for two fundamental reasons. First, standardized measures of these concepts are often superior to the interview as a measuring device. And second, organizations hire employees not for knowledge, skills, personality characteristics, and so forth, but ultimately *to perform*. Although knowledge, skills, and personality affect job performance, the most job-related method for evaluating applicants is in terms of predicted performance. This leads to the fourth group of concepts to be measured in the employment interview; that is, what applicants can and will do (capacity and willingness to perform job responsibilities).

Several chapters have suggested that interviewers should focus on this category. As already noted, Janz proposed that interviewers examine applicants' descriptions of past job responsibilities, and Latham has concentrated on applicants' intentions to perform in the future. Building on Schwab (1980), Cronshaw and Wiesner (this volume) argued that the concepts examined in the interview *and the interviewer's assessment of the applicant* should be as similar as possible to the concepts reflected by the criterion, job performance (see Figure 19.1). They demonstrated that Janz's patterned behavior description interview and Latham's situational interview conform to this recommendation because they examine previous and intended job performance, respectively, as a measure of future job performance. In their discussion of construct and empirical validity, Cronshaw and Wiesner proposed that interviewers evaluate applicants in terms of future job performance (see Figure 19.2). Feild and Gatewood provided additional support for evaluating applicants in terms of future job performance in their discussion of Wernimont and Campbell's (1968) proposal for a point-to-point correspondence between predictors and criteria.

Information Gathered and Probed During the Interview

Janz's chapter summarized a taxonomy (Janz, Hellervik, & Gilmore, 1986) of four types of information available to interviewers (i.e., credentials, experience descriptions, opinions, and behavior descriptions). Janz argued that the first three are not useful sources of information, and called for emphasis on behavior descriptions. His patterned behavior description interview (PBDI) examines past performance to assess the applicant's potential to perform the responsibilities of the job to be filled. Although credentials and experience descriptions are a *springboard* for in-depth probing in the interview, superficial discussion of these items provides little information about the applicant's potential and willingness to perform specific job responsibilities, because applicants can (and sometimes do) claim to have any kind of background they want.

Janz also argued that the third category, opinions, offers little clear, practical data on which to base predictions of future performance because applicants are likely to give the opinions they think the interviewer wants to hear. Janz classified self-perceptions and hypothetical questions as opinions and listed in this category applicants' thoughts about their strengths, weaknesses, plans, goals, and intentions. Janz's method, then, opposes Latham's situational interview, which, by definition, consists solely of hypothetical questions. Latham's reports of impressive reliabilities and validities have clearly indicated that applicants' plans, goals, and intentions *can* predict future job performance. In their chapters, Janz and Latham included spirited arguments for the superiority of patterned behavior description interviews over situational interviews (and vice versa), but a dispassionate examination of preliminary data suggests that both approaches hold great promise. Later in this chapter, a suggestion is made for how these two approaches can be combined.

Types of Questions Asked

Interviewer questions should flow directly from explicit consideration of a) the job-related factors to be examined and the criteria used to assess them, and b) the information gathered from the applicant. A major reason for the failure of typical employment interviews is that practitioners do not derive questions this way. They either think up their questions on the spur of the moment in unstructured interviews, or even when they try to plan structured or patterned interviews, they consult books with inappropriate questions or make up their own questions without first asking what job-related concepts they want to measure, and what information they need to collect from the applicant to do so.

The Person Who Conducts the Interview

The choice of the interviewer is the fourth factor with important implications for interview effectiveness. Several chapters examined the information-collecting and decision-making processes in the interview, and offered suggestions for selecting and training interviewers. For example, Schuh suggested that interviewers should be selected on the basis of vocabulary, short-term memory, and ability to concentrate. Liden and Parsons argued that a better understanding of interview process may help in designing training programs for interviewers. Unfortunately, these suggestions and conclusions give little guidance to practitioners because they are based largely on research that used student "interviewers" making global evaluations of paper applicants or videotapes of simulated interviews. Kacmar, Ratcliff, and Ferris offered several parameters for assessing the quality of laboratory experiments on the employment interview and pointed out major problems in using student interviewers, not the least of which is that student subjects are unfamiliar with the job for which the candidate is applying. They concluded that external validity is critical in experiments designed to shed light on what occurs in employment interviews in organizations.

In his chapter, Eder presented the notion that interview effectiveness is a function of both interviewer and the situation, and argued convincingly against "myopic" theories that focus on how interviewers process information and make decisions, but ignore the context in which the interviewer functions. He also downplayed the usefulness of selecting and training interviewers as suggested by Schuh, and Liden and Parsons, arguing instead for engineering characteristics of the interviewing situation to help practitioners make more accurate assessments of job suitability. Eder listed task clarity, interview purpose, decision risk, and accountability as important situational factors, and stated, in particular, that practitioners need to be aware of the dual purpose of applicant attraction and selection (see Rynes, this volume). He emphasized the importance of clarifying interviewers' tasks by training them in how to perform those tasks effectively. Finally, he cited research showing that the primary effect of interviewer training is to enhance decision making *through increased task clarity*, which, in turn, increases interrater reliability when interviewers have more complete job information.

In summary, proposals to select or train practitioners to process information and make more valid interview decisions need stronger support from field experiments or more realistic laboratory research. A more fruitful strategy for increasing interviewer effectiveness would appear to lie in clarifying interviewer objectives and tasks. In particular, interviewers should be job knowledgeable individuals who question applicants on their potential and willingness to perform job responsibilities.

An Integrated Approach to Employment Interviewing

How can this book's key research results and recommendations be synthesized into a set of guidelines that human resource professionals, as well as line managers and supervisors, can understand and adopt? Practitioners need a systematic approach to help them design and conduct employment interviews. The following approach (Table 22.1) is based on key principles derived from several chapters in this book, as well as ideas this author has developed over the years (Goodale, 1976, 1981, 1982, in press).

Interview Objectives

An obvious place to start in planning an employment interview is with its objectives. Several contributors to this book have listed the dual objec-

TABLE 22.1. Recommendations for Designing and Conducting Employment Interviews

---

I. Before the Interview
   A. Identify major interview objectives
      1. Collect information for CAN DO and WILL DO
      2. Provide information
      3. Check personal chemistry
   B. Prepare interview content
      1. Identify major job responsibilities
      2. Write hypothetical situations
      3. Plan a format to meet interview objectives
   C. Review each applicant form or résumé for
      1. Previous related work or non-work experience, training, and education
      2. Hints of the applicant's work interests and career intentions
II. During the Interview
   A. Probe related work or non-work experience, training, and education to examine CAN DO; use hypothetical questions, if necessary
   B. Probe work interests and career intentions to assess WILL DO
III. After the Interview
   A. Use the Applicant Evaluation Form to record evaluations of CAN DO, WILL DO, and personal chemistry
   B. Record your level of interest in hiring each applicant on the Applicant Evaluation Form

---

tives of selecting and attracting applicants. Three fundamental objectives can be included in employment interviews.

Collect information. Interviewers need to gather information to answer the following two basic questions:

1. CAN the applicant DO the job? This involves the examination of previous work and non-work experience, training and education, and actual behavior during the interview to assess applicants' potential to perform specific job responsibilities.

2. WILL the applicant DO the job? As Dreher and Maurer note in their paper, researchers often overlook the applicant's willingness to perform. This part of the information-collecting objective involves the examination of applicants' preferences for and interest in the nature of the work to be done, their preferences for conditions of employment (e.g., salary, hours, travel), and the compatibility between their career goals and the organization's career opportunities.

Provide information. Interviewers also provide information to help the applicant make an informed choice. They present information about the company, department, job, and conditions of employment to attract the applicant. As Rynes points out in her chapter, realistic job previews lead to lower acceptance rates by applicants, but also to lower turnover rates in new employees.

Check personal chemistry. Finally, the interview allows both parties to assess each other's personal style and approach to work to determine whether they will enjoy working together.

These three objectives are fundamental to how the interview is designed and conducted, and it is important to place the proper emphasis on each. Characteristics of the labor market, employer, and vacancy affect the balance between the first two objectives (Rynes, this volume). All three require attention in all employment interviews (see Goodale, 1982, in press, for an interview format that ensures coverage of all three objectives). One major problem among practitioners is that they ask too few questions of the applicant, talk too much about the company and job, and are then forced to make their hiring decision on the basis of an overall impression of the applicant. Clearly, they need to put their primary emphasis on the first objective, determining whether the applicant CAN DO and WILL DO the job.

Evaluation Criteria

Guion (1965) made the fundamental point that the selection decision is based upon at least the implicit prediction of future job performance. When interviewers decide to hire an applicant, they are implicitly predicting that person's first performance appraisal. A useful starting point in designing and conducting interviews, therefore, is to clearly specify *desired job performance*.

Start with the job. There are practical problems with the elaborate procedures described by Feild and Gatewood, Janz, Latham, and Schuler and Funke to analyze jobs, write critical incidents and derive from them either situational questions or job dimensions, and identify job-related knowledge, skills, and abilities. As an alternative, a small group of managers and employees with good job knowledge can identify about ten major responsibilities that constitute the job to be filled (this is essentially a functional job description). They can also write a hypothetical situation—that is, a description of a problem that would challenge a potential hire—for each job responsibility. Examples for the job of Senior Systems Analyst in an MIS department appear in Table 22.2. This list of job responsibilities and hypothetical situations forms the basis for two key aspects of the employment interview: evaluating applicants and collecting information.

Establish job-related criteria. Interview ratings should be job-related and as similar as possible to the concepts being examined in the interview. Prac-

TABLE 22.2. Major Responsibilities and Examples of Hypothetical Situations for the Job of Senior Systems Analyst—MIS Department

1. Resolving application problems on a 24-hour basis during critical production cycles. Hypothetical situation: You learn one morning that a computer operator entered the wrong "system date" the previous night and your system used the incorrect date for four hours before the problem was discovered and you were alerted. How would you respond to correct the situation?

2. Developing written system/PGM specifications for other team members.

3. Developing and administering work plans for other team members, utilizing project management tools under imposed regulatory deadlines.

4. Analyzing requested modifications to existing systems.

5. Analyzing, designing, and implementing computer systems.

6. Communicating project status to end users and MIS management verbally and in writing.

7. Providing technical guidance to team members.

8. Directing the work of junior team members.

9. Sharing in programming responsibilities when necessary.

10. Setting priorities and scheduling your work and time under constantly changing conditions. Hypothetical situation: You have made plans for a six-month project based upon preliminary requirements established by management, but when the final requirements are issued, you learn that they have changed significantly and the completion date is one month sooner than you expected. What do you do?

titioners can base their applicant evaluations on the interview objectives already discussed, namely, collecting information to assess whether the applicant CAN DO and WILL DO the job, and checking personal chemistry (assessments of personal chemistry are recorded as Additional Comments). Figure 22.1 presents an Applicant Evaluation Form for doing so.

Employment interviewers can tailor Section A of the Applicant Evaluation Form to the specific job by writing in the major responsibilities of the job they plan to fill. Then during or immediately after the interview, they can *independently* evaluate each applicant's potential to perform specific job responsibilities. Rather than evaluating applicants in terms of *what they are* (e.g., personal traits) or *what they have* (e.g., intelligence, KSA's), interviewers can evaluate applicants in terms of *what they can do*. The result is a profile of ratings that can be compared among interviewers before a final decision is made. This approach is consistent with Eder's point about the innate multidimensionality of the evaluation task faced by employment

Applicant's Name	Interviewer

APPLICANT'S QUALIFICATIONS

Education_____

Years of Relevant
Work Experience _____

A. EVALUATION OF APPLICANT'S POTENTIAL TO PERFORM

Please Circle Your Evaluation

Major Responsibilities

	High				Low
1._____	5	4	3	2	1
2._____	5	4	3	2	1
3._____	5	4	3	2	1
4._____	5	4	3	2	1
5._____	5	4	3	2	1
6._____	5	4	3	2	1
7._____	5	4	3	2	1
8._____	5	4	3	2	1
9._____	5	4	3	2	1

B. APPLICANT'S WORK INTEREST AND CAREER DIRECTION

Please Circle Your Evaluation

	High				Low
1. Interest in Company	5	4	3	2	1
2. Interest in Position	5	4	3	2	1
3. Clarity of Career Goals	5	4	3	2	1

C. ADDITIONAL COMMENTS

_____

_____

_____

_____

D. INTERVIEW RESULT

Please Circle Your Evaluation

	Definitely Hire		Marginal		Reject
1. Recommendation for Hire	5	4	3	2	1

Figure 22.1. Applicant Evaluation Form

interviewers. It is also relevant to Dreher and Maurer's discussion about whether different interview evaluations should be combined according to a compensatory, multiple hurdle, or multiple cutoff strategy.

This author's preference is for a multiple cutoff model in which interviewers set some minimal level of potential for performing each major job responsibility. Each interviewer assesses all applicants on Section A of the form (CAN DO), and generates a profile for each applicant. Interviewers can then meet to discuss each applicant and decide who shows the most potential for performing the job responsibilities established before the interviewing process began. They can also compare their judgments in Section B (WILL DO), and their feelings of personal chemistry with the applicant (Section C). This Applicant Evaluation Form helps interviewers separate their assessments of whether the applicant can and will do the job as much as possible from the global assessment of personal chemistry. It also helps them separate the process of evaluating the applicant as much as possible from the process of reaching a hiring recommendation (Section D in Figure 22.1), and therefore helps prevent the "snap judgments" so common in employment interviews (see also Buckley & Eder, 1988).

Interview Content

In planning employment interviews, practitioners need to focus on a) the information they will gather from the applicant, and b) the types of questions they will ask. Although Janz and Latham propose highly structured interviews with prepared questions, this author prefers a semistructured approach with topics to be covered but without long lists of questions.

There are three reasons for this preference. First, applicants can anticipate prepared questions, and can plan and rehearse their responses. Second, highly structured interviews can appear to the applicant like an interrogation, and may place too much emphasis on the *selection* objective at the expense of the *attraction* objective (see Rynes; Latham, this volume). Latham noted that applicants don't like situational interviews because of the lack of opportunity to sell themselves. Third and most important, personal experience has suggested that interviewers can collect all the information they need by using the probing techniques that are discussed shortly, instead of prepared questions.

Information gathered and probed. There are three basic sources of information available to interviewers. They are:

1. Previous work and non-work experience (i.e., activities the applicant has performed in paid or unpaid settings that may be related to the responsibilities of the job to be filled).

2. Previous training and education (i.e., job-related activities the applicant has learned how to do).

3. Behavior demonstrated, preferences, and intentions expressed during the interview. The actual interview is a work sample for jobs involving such activities as dealing with pressure or expressing ideas orally. In addition, applicants can express their preferences for work activities and conditions of employment, and they can also state how they would respond to specific work situations.

Janz's patterned behavior description interview appears to focus on the first source of information, and Latham's situational interview appears to rely entirely on the third. Interviewers can make use of all three in the following way.

Types of questions to ask. The questions to be asked can and should be derived directly from interview objectives. The objective of checking personal chemistry really requires no questions at all (in spite of all the psychological questions recommended in interview books and training courses). This objective is covered automatically as interviewers and applicants interact and form impressions of one another.

The objective of collecting information to assess whether the applicant WILL DO the job requires probing into expressed preferences and intentions. Probing the applicant's reasons for leaving past jobs and applying for the current position, and questions about career goals and plans are useful. In addition, interviewers can inquire about the conditions of employment under which applicants have worked before (e.g., overtime, shift work, travel, pressure, changing priorities), and probe how well they dealt with those conditions. Questions can also be raised about applicants' preferences for specific work activities.

Of course, the most important objective of the employment interview is to collect information to determine whether the applicant CAN DO the job. A lively debate has emerged between Janz and Latham about whether behavior descriptions or behavioral intentions are the best predictors of future job performance. Fortunately, this debate can be resolved empirically, because it is possible to assess applicants' potential to perform specific job responsibilities by probing their past performance of those responsibilities as well as their intentions to perform them in the future.

Designing and Conducting the Employment Interview

In workshops, this author trains practitioners to prepare for employment interviews by identifying the job's major responsibilities and a set of hypothetical situations (Table 22.2). Prior to the interview, they can also review the application form or resume' to find the most clearly related previous job in the applicant's work history. Even when preparing to interview students, practitioners can often find related work experience. Students usually have some non-work experience, such as extracurricular activities or assignments and projects from their courses. The key to this preparation is to find something the applicant claims to have done before that overlaps with the responsibilities of the job to be filled.

Interviewers can use the following information-collecting sequence: initiate–listen–focus–probe (Goodale, 1982, in press). In brief, they initiate the discussion with an open-ended question, such as "I noticed on your resumé that you worked as a computer programmer for IBM. What were your major responsibilities on that job?" The interviewer listens for responsibilities that coincide with those of the job to be filled, focusing on each one systematically. For example, "you mentioned that you wrote software in COBOL and FORTRAN," would be a focusing statement for the job in Table 22.2 because it overlaps with the job responsibility of "sharing in programming responsibilities when necessary."

For each question set, a series of probing follow-ups are used to clarify the related experience: HOW, WHY, RESULTS, and if necessary, a hypothetical situation. Applicants are asked how they approached that part of their job (e.g., what was involved, what approach, what techniques, how), why the method was used and how well it worked, including specific results or evidence of effectiveness. At the bottom of this line of inquiry, they can also present the hypothetical situation for that job responsibility.

In essence, this combination of Janz's and Latham's approach permits the interviewer to conduct a more semistructured, conversational discussion with the applicant; it is neither too rigidly scripted nor focused on non-job-relevant questions. All interviews for the same job are *consistent*, however, because each interviewer covers all job responsibilities on the list prepared prior to the interview, and evaluates the applicant on his or her potential to perform each one.

If the applicant does not raise all the job responsibilities, the interviewer raises them. If the applicant has not performed a specific job responsibility in the past, the interviewer probes the applicant's training and education to examine whether the applicant has learned how to perform it. Finally, hypothetical situations can be used as an additional indicator of intention and potential to perform.

Unlike Latham, this author does not recommend score sheets with alternative answers to hypothetical situations. Personal experience has suggested that interviewers with good job knowledge can consistently evaluate the quality of applicants' responses. In-depth probing into the method, rationale, and results of previous work responsibilities, as well as applicant responses to hypothetical situations, provides ample information for interviewers to assess the applicant's potential to perform at the end of the interview, when comments and assessments are noted on the Applicant Evaluation Form.

How well does this approach work? This author developed it in 1971 when he began teaching a personnel management course at York University, and over the years it has been improved and refined. Although this approach was developed before most of the research in this book was published, it conforms with key principles reflected in the literature. Hundreds of workshops have produced evidence of learning and behavioral change taking place during the training. Practitioners have also sent reports of the usefulness of the training and their success in putting it into practice. But the approach needs additional examination, and this author would be pleased to collaborate with any researcher to test the reliability and validity of this approach to employment interviewing.

References

Abelson, R. P. (1976). Script processing in attitude formation and decision making. In J. S. Carroll & J. W. Wayne (Eds.), *Cognition and social behavior*. Hillsdale, NJ: Lawrence Erlbaum.

Abelson, R. P. (1981). Psychological status of the script concept. *American Psychologist*, *36*, 715-729.

Agee, M. H., Taylor, R. E., & Torgersen, P. E. (1976). *Quantitative analysis for management decisions*. Englewood Cliffs, NJ: Prentice-Hall.

Albanese, R., & Van Fleet, D. D. (1985). Rational behavior in groups: The free riding tendency. *Academy of Management Review*, *10*, 244-255.

Albemarle Paper Co. v. Moody, 422 U.S. 405 (1975).

Allison, P. D., & Liker, J. K. (1982). Analyzing sequential categorical data on dyadic interaction: A comment on Gottman. *Psychological Bulletin*, *91*, 393-403.

Ajzen, I., & Fishbein, M. (1980). *Understanding attitudes and predicting social behavior*. Englewood Cliffs, NJ: Prentice-Hall.

Amalfitano, J. G., & Kalt, N. C. (1977). Effects of eye contact on the evaluation of job applicants. *Journal of Employment Counseling*, *14*, 46-48.

American Psychological Asociation (1985). *Standards for educational and psychological testing*. Washington, DC: Author.

American Psychological Association (1987). American Psychological Association's amicus brief filed with U.S. Supreme Court in *Watson v. Fort Worth Bank & Trust. Daily Labor Report*, November 5, 1987, D1-D10.

American Psychological Association (1987). *Principles for the validation and use of personnel selection procedures*. Washington, DC: Author.

American Society for Personnel Administration, International Personnel Management Association, & Employment Management Association (1987). Amicus briefs with Supreme Court in *Watson v. Fort Worth Bank & Trust. Daily Labor Report*, December 29, 1987, D1-D20.

Anderson, C. W. (1960). The relation between speaking times and decision in the employment interview. *Journal of Applied Psychology*, *29*, 480-482.

Anderson, T. W., & Goodman, L. A. (1957). Statistical inference about Markov chains. *Annals of Mathematical Statistics*, *28*, 89-110.

Arvey, R. D. (1979). Unfair discrimination in the employment interview: Legal and psychological aspects. *Psychological Bulletin*, *86*, 736-765.

Arvey, R. D., & Campion, J. E. (1982). The employment interview: A summary and review of recent research. *Personnel Psychology*, *35*, 281-322.

Arvey, R., Gordon, M., Massengill, D., & Mussio, S. (1975). Differential dropout rates of minority and majority job candidates due to "time lags" between selection procedures. *Personnel Psychology*, *28*, 175-180.

Arvey, R. D., Miller, H. E., Gould, R., & Burch, P. (1987). Interview validity for selecting sales clerks. *Personnel Psychology*, *40*, 1-12.

Asher, J. J., & Sciarrino, J. A. (1974). Realistic work sample tests: A review. *Personnel Psychology*, *27*, 519-533.

ASPA-BNA Survey No. 45 (1983). *Employee selection procedures*. Washington, DC: Bureau of National Affairs.

Axon Group. (1987). How the colonel recruits. *Human Resource Executive*, *1*(3), 28.

Bailey v. Southeastern Apprenticeship Committee, 31 EPD 33,604 (1983).

Bales, R. F. (1950). *Interaction process analysis: A method for the study of small groups*. Reading, MA: Addison-Wesley.

Bargh, J. A., & Pietromonaco, P. (1982). Automatic information processing and social perception: The influence of trait information presented outside of conscious awareness on impression formation. *Journal of Personality and Social Psychology, 43*, 437-449.

Baron, R. A. (1981). The role of olfaction in human social behavior: Effects of a pleasant scent on attraction and social perception. *Personality and Social Psychology Bulletin, 7*, 611-617.

Baron, R. A. (1983). "Sweet smell of success?" The impact of pleasant scents on evaluations of job applicants. *Journal of Applied Psychology, 68*, 709-713.

Baron, R. A. (1986). Self-presentation in job interviews: When there can be "Too much of a good thing." *Journal of Applied Social Psychology, 16*, 16-28.

Baron, R. A. (1987). Interviewer's moods and reactions to job applicants: The influence of affective states on applied social judgments. *Journal of Applied Social Psychology, 17*, 911-926.

Barr, S. H., & Hitt, M. A. (1986). A comparison of selection decision models in manager versus student samples. *Personnel Psychology, 39*, 599-617.

Barrett, G. V. (1972). Symposium: Research models of the future for industrial and organizational psychology. 1. Introduction. *Personnel Psychology, 25*, 1-17.

Barrett, G. V., & Kernan, M. C. (1987). Performance appraisal and terminations: A review of court decisions since *Brito v. Zia* with implications for personnel practices. *Personnel Psychology, 40*, 489-503.

Barrett, G. V., Phillips, J. S., & Alexander, R. A. (1981). Concurrent and predictive validity designs: A critical reanalysis. *Journal of Applied Psychology, 66*, 1-6.

Baskett, C. D. (1973). Interview decisions as determined by competency and attitude similarity. *Journal of Applied Psychology, 57*, 343-345.

Beatty, R. H. (1986). *The five minute interview*. New York: John Wiley.

Beehr, T. A., & Gilmore, D. C. (1982). Applicant attractiveness as a perceived job-relevant variable in selection of management trainees. *Academy of Management Journal, 25*, 607-617.

Beer, M., Spector, B., Lawrence, P. R., Mills, D. Q., & Walton, R. E. (1984). *Managing human assets*. New York: Free Press.

Belec, B. E., & Rowe, P. M. (1983). Temporal placement of information, expectancy, causal attributions, and overall final judgments in employment decision making. *Canadian Journal of Behavioural Science, 15*, 106-120.

Bellows, R. (1961). *Psychology of personnel in business and industry* (3rd ed.). Englewood Cliffs, NJ: Prentice Hall.

Berkowitz, L., & Donnerstein, E. (1982). External validity is more than skin deep. *American Psychologist, 37*, 245-257.

Bernardin, H. J. & Buckley, M. R. (1981). Strategies in rater training. *Academy of Management Review, 6*, 205-212.

Bernstein, A. (1987, Oct. 19). Dispelling the myths about a higher minimum wage. *Business Week*, p. 146.

Bernstein, V., Hakel, M. D., & Harlan, A. (1975). The college student as interviewer: A threat to generalizability? *Journal of Applied Psychology, 60*, 266-268.

Berscheid, E. & Walster, E. H. (1978). *Interpersonal attraction* (2nd ed.). Reading, MA: Addison-Wesley.

Biegeleisen, J. I. (1984). *Make your job interview a success*. New York: ARCO Publishing.

Bierman, H., Bonini, C. P., & Hausman, W. H. (1986). *Quantitative analysis for business decisions*. Homewood, IL: Irwin.

Binning, J. F., Goldstein, M. A., Garcia, M. F., Harding, J. L., & Scattaregia, J. H. (1988). Effects of preinterview impressions on questionning strategies in same- and opposite-sex employment interviews. *Journal of Applied Psychology, 73*, 30-37.

Blakeney, R. N. & MacNaughton, J. F. (1971). Effects of temporal placement of unfavorable information on decision making during the selection interview. *Journal of Applied Psychology, 55*, 138-142.

Boileau, D. M. (1983). Listening: Teaching and research. ERIC Report, Speech Communication Module. *Communication Education, 32*, 442-447.

Bolster, B. I., & Springbett, B. M. (1961). The reaction of interviewers to favorable and unfavorable information. *Journal of Applied Psychology, 45*, 97-103.

Borman, W. C. (1982). Validity of behavioral assessment for predicting military recruiter performance. *Journal of Applied Psychology, 67*, 3-9.

Boudreau, J. W., & Berger, C. J. (1985). Decision-theoretic utility analysis applied to employee separations and acquisitions [Monograph]. *Journal of Applied Psychology, 70*, 581-612.

Boudreau, J. W., & Rynes, S. L. (1985). Role of recruitment in staffing utility analysis. *Journal of Applied Psychology, 70*, 354-366.

Bower, G., Black, J., & Turner, T. (1979). Scripts in text comprehension and memory. *Cognitive Psychology, 11*, 177-220.

Bowes, L. (1987). *No one need apply: Getting and keeping the best workers*. Boston: Harvard Business School Press.

Brody, W. (1947). Judging candidates by observing them in unsupervised group discussion. *Personnel Journal, 26*, 170-173.

Buck, R. W. (1984). *The communication of emotion*. New York: Guilford.

Buckley, M. R., & Eder, R. W. (1988). B. M. Springbett and the notion of the "snap decision" in the interview. *Journal of Management, 14*, 59-67.

Buckley, M. R., & Eder, R. W. (in press). The employment interview: Expecting a quick decision? *Personnel Administrator*.

Budescu, D. V. (1984). Tests of lagged dominance in sequential dyadic interaction. *Psychological Bulletin, 96*, 402-414.

Burns, T. (1961). Micropolitics: Mechanisms of institutional change. *Administrative Science Quarterly, 6*, 257-281.

Camara, W. J. (1988). Congress debates legislation to ban polygraph testing. *The Industrial-Organizational Psychologist, 25*, 45-47.

Campbell, D. T., & Fiske, D. W. (1959). Convergent and discriminant validation by the multitrait-multimethod matrix. *Psychological Bulletin, 56*, 81-105.

Campbell, D. T., & Stanley, J. C. (1967). *Experimental and quasi-experimental designs for research*. Chicago: Rand McNally.

Campbell, J. P. (1986). Labs, fields, and straw issues. In E. A. Locke (Ed.), *Generalizing form laboratory to field settings* (pp. 269-279). Lexington, MA: Lexington Books.

Campbell, J. P. (1982). Editorial: Some remarks from the outgoing editor. *Journal of Applied Psychology, 67*, 691-700.

Campbell, J. P., Dunnette, M. D., Lawler, E. E., & Weick, K. E. (1970). *Managerial behavior, performance and effectiveness*. New York: McGraw-Hill.

Campion, M. A., & Campion, J. E. (1987). Evaluation of an interviewee skills training program in a natural field experiment. *Personnel Psychology, 40*, 675-691.

Campion, M. A., Pursell, E. D., & Brown, B. K. (1988). Structured interviewing: Raising the psychometric properties of the employment interview. *Personnel Psychology, 41*, 25-42.

Cappella, J. N. (1981). Mutual influence in expressive behavior: Adult-adult and infant-adult dyadic interaction. *Psychological Bulletin, 89*, 101-132.

Cappella, J. N., & Planalp, S. (1981). Talk and silence sequences in informal conversations. III: Interspeaker influence. *Human Communication Research, 7*, 117-132.

Cardy, R. L., & Dobbins, G. H. (1986). Affect and appraisal accuracy: Liking as an integral dimension in evaluating performance. *Journal of Applied Psychology, 71*, 672-678.

Carlson, R. E. (1967a). Selection interview decisions: The effect of interview experience, relative quota situation, and applicant sample on interview decisions. *Personnel Psychology*, *20*, 259-280.

Carlson, R. E. (1967b). The relative influence of appearance and factual written information on an interviewer's final rating. *Journal of Applied Psychology*, *51*, 461-468.

Carlson, R. E. (1968). Selection interview decisions: The effect of mode of applicant presentation on some outcome measures. *Personnel Psychology*, *21*, 193-207.

Carlson, R. E., & Mayfield, E. C. (1967). Evaluating interview and employment application data. *Personnel Psychology*, *20*, 441-460.

Carlson, R. E., Schwab, D. P., & Heneman, H. G. (1970). Agreement among selection interview styles. *Journal of Applied Psychology*, *5*, 8-17.

Carlson, R. E., Thayer, P. W., Mayfield. E. C., & Peterson, D. A. (1971). Research on the selection interview. *Personnel Journal*, *50*, 268-275.

Carlston, D. E. (1980). The recall and use of traits and events in social inference processes. *Journal of Experimental Social Psychology*, *16*, 303-328.

Carson, K. P., & Kinicki, A. J. (1988). *Threats to the validity of meta-analytic inference*. Paper presented at the Academy of Management Meetings, Anaheim, CA.

Cascio, W. (1987). *Applied psychology in personnel management*. Reston, VA: Prentice-Hall.

Cascio, W. F., & Bernardin, H. J. (1981). Implications of performance appraisal litigation for personnel decisions. *Personnel Psychology*, *34*, 201-226.

Cascio, W., & Ramos, R. (1986). Development and application of a new method for assessing job performance in behavioral/economic terms. *Journal of Applied Psychology*, *71*, 20-28.

Cash, T. F. (1985). The impact of grooming style on the evaluation of women in management. In M. Solomon (Ed.), *The psychology of fashion*. New York: Lexington Press.

Chaikin, A. L., Sigler, E., & Derlega, V. (1974). Nonverbal mediators of teacher expectancy effects. *Journal of Personality and Social Psychology*, *30*, 144-149.

Christie, R., & Geis, F. L. (1970). *Studies in Machiavellianism*. New York: Academic Press.

Clark, E. L. (1926). Value of student interviews. *Journal of Personnel Research*, *5*, 201-207.

Cleveland, J. N., Festa, R. M., Montgomery, L. (1988). Applicant pool composition and job perceptions: Impact on decisions regarding an older applicant. *Journal of Vocational Behavior*, *32*, 112-125.

Cohen, B. M., Moses, J. L., & Byham, W. C. (1974). *The validity of assessment centers: A literature review* [Monograph II]. Pittsburgh: Development Dimensions Press.

Colon v. Sorensen, 45 EPD 37, 646 (1987).

Commerce Clearing House. (1987). Recruiting/hiring. *Ideas and Trends*, *148*, July, 119.

Conrad, H. S., & Satter, G. A. (1946). *The use of test scores and quality classification ratings in predicting success in Electricians' Mates School*. (OSRD No. 133290). Washington, DC: Department of Commerce.

Constantin, S. W. (1976). An investigation of information favorability in the employment interview. *Journal of Applied Psychology*, *61*, 743-749.

Cook, T. D., & Campbell, D. T. (1976). The design and conduct of quasi-experiments and true experiments in field settings. In M. D. Dunnette (Ed.), *Handbook of industrial and organizational psychology* (pp. 223-326). Chicago: Rand McNally.

Cook, T. D., & Campbell, D. T. (1976). *Quasi-experimentation: Design and analysis issues for field settings*. Boston: Houghton Mifflin.

Cooper, W. H., & Richardson, A. J. (1986). Unfair comparison. *Journal of Applied Psychology*, *71*, 179-184.

Cote, J. A., & Buckley, M. R. (1987). Estimating trait, method and error variance: Generalizing across seventy construct validation studies. *Journal of Marketing Research, 24*, 315-318.

Cote, J. A., & Buckley, M. R. (1988). Measurement error and theory testing in consumer behavior research: An illustration of the importance of construct validity. *Journal of Consumer Research, 14*, 79-83.

Crocker, J. (1981). Judgement of covariation by social perceivers. *Psychological Bulletin, 90*, 272-292.

Cronbach, L. J. (1951). Coefficient alpha and the internal structure of tests. *Psychometria, 16*, 297-334.

Cronbach, L. J. (1970). *Essentials of psychological testing.* (3rd. ed.) New York: Harper and Row.

Cronbach, L. J., & Gleser, G. C. (1965). *Psychological tests and personnel decisions* (2nd. ed.). Urbana: University of Illinois Press.

Cronshaw, S. F., & Alexander, R. A. (1985). One answer to the demand for accountability: Selection utility as an investment decision. *Organizational Behavior and Human Performance, 35*, 102-118.

Cronshaw, S. F., Alexander, R. A., Wiesner, W. H., & Barrick, M. R. (1987). Incorporating risk into selection utility: Two models for sensitivity analysis and risk simulation. *Organizational Behavior and Human Decision Processes, 40*, 270-286.

Crowne, D. P., & Marlowe, D. (1964). *The approval motive.* New York: John Wiley.

Daniels, H. W., & Otis, J. L. (1950). A method for analyzing employment interviews. *Personnel Psychology, 3*, 425-444.

Darley, J. M., & Goethals, G. R. (1980). People's analyses of the causes of ability linked performances. In L. Berkowitz, (Ed.), *Advances in experimental social psychology* (Vol. 13). New York: Academic Press.

Davis, J. D. (1977). Effect of communication about interpersonal process on the evolution of self-disclosure in dyads. *Journal of Personality and Social Psychology, 35*, 31-37.

de Beaugrande, R. (1982). General constraints on process models of language comprehension. In J. F. Le Ny & W. Kintsch (Eds.), *Language and comprehensive* (pp. 179-192). Amsterdam: North-Holland.

Deci, F. L., & Ryan, R. M. (1984). The dynamics of self-determination in personality and development. In R. Schwarzer (Ed.), *Self-related cognition in anxiety and motivation.* Hillsdale, NJ: Lawrence Erlbaum.

DeCotiis, T. A., & Petit, A. (1978). The performance appraisal process: A model and some testable propositions. *Academy of Management Review, 3*, 635-345.

DeNisi, A., Cafferty, T., & Meglino, B. (1984). A cognitive view of the performance appraisal process. *Organizational Behavior and Human Performance, 33*, 360-396.

Denzin, N. K. (1970) *The research act.* Chicago: Aldine.

Devine, T. G. (1978). Listening: What do we know after fifty years of research and theorizing? *Journal of Reading, 21*, 296-304.

Dickey-Bryant, L., Lautenschlager, G. J., Mendoza, J. L., & Abrahams, N. (1986). Facial attractiveness and its relationship to occupational success. *Journal of Applied Psychology, 71*, 16-19.

Diener, E., Emmons, R. A., & Larsen, R. J. (1984). Person x situation interactions: Choices of situations and consequence response models. *Journal of Personality and Social Psychology.*

Dillon, W. R., Madden, T. J., Kumar, A. (1983). Analyzing sequential categorical data on dyadic interaction: A latent structure approach. *Psychological Bulletin, 94*, 564-583.

Dipboye, R. L. (1982). Self-fulfilling prophecies in the selection interview. *Academy of Management Review, 7,* 579-586.

Dipboye, R. L., Arvey, R. D. & Terpstra, D. E. (1977). Sex and physical attractiveness of raters and applicants as determinants of resume evaluations. *Journal of Applied Psychology, 62,* 288-294.

Dipboye, R. L., & Flanagan, M. F. (1979). Research settings in industrial/organizational psychology: Are findings in the field more generalizable than in the laboratory? *American Psychologist, 34,* 141-150.

Dipboye, R. L., Fontenelle, G. A. & Garner, K. (1984). Effects of previewing the application on interview process and outcomes. *Journal of Applied Psychology, 69,* 118-128.

Dipboye, R. L., Fromkin, K. L., & Wiback, K. (1975). Relative importance of applicant sex, attractiveness, and scholastic standing in evaluation of job applicant resumes. *Journal of Applied Psychology, 60,* 39-43.

Dipboye, R. L., & Macan, T. M. (1988). A process view of the selection/recruitment interview. In R. S. Schuler, S. A. Youngblood, & V. L. Huber (Eds.), *Readings in personnel and human resource management* (3rd ed., pp. 217-232). St. Paul, MN: West Publishing.

Dipboye, R. L., Stramler, C. S., & Fontenelle, G. A. (1984). The effects of the application on recall of information from the interview. *Academy of Management Journal, 27,* 561-575.

Dipboye, R. L., & Wiley, J. W. (1977). Reactions of college recruiters to interviewee sex and self-presentation style. *Journal of Vocational Behavior, 10,* 1-12.

Dipboye, R. L., & Wiley, J. W. (1978). Reactions of male raters to interviewee self-presentation style and sex: Extensions of previous research. *Journal of Vocational Behavior, 13,* 192-203.

Dipboye, W. J. (1954). Analysis of counselor style by discussion units. *Journal of Consulting Psychology, 1,* 21-26.

Doe v. Syracuse School District, 25 EPD 31,696 (1981).

Dougherty, T. W., Ebert, R. J., Callender, J. C. (1986). Policy capturing in the employment interview. *Journal of Applied Psychology, 71,* 9-15.

Downs, C. W. (1969). Perceptions of the selection interview. *Personnel Administration, 32,* 8-23.

Drake, J. D. (1983). *Interviewing for managers: A complete guide to employment interviewing.* New York: AMACOM.

Dreher, G. F., & Sackett, P. R. (1983). *Perspectives on employee staffing and selection.* Homewood, IL: Irwin.

Dreher, G. F., Ash, R. A., & Hancock, P. (1988). The role of the traditional research design in underestimating the validity of the employment interview. *Personnel Psychology, 41,* 315-327.

Dumas, J. E. (1986). Controlling for autocorrelation in social interaction analysis. *Psychological Bulletin, 100,* 125-127.

Dunlap, J. W., & Wantman, M. J. (1947). *An investigation of the interview as a technique for selecting aircraft pilots.* (Report No. 50308). Washington, DC: U.S. Department of Commerce.

Eder, R. W., & Buckley, M. R. (1987). *The role of situation variables in the employment interview.* Paper presented at the annual meeting Academy of Management, New Orleans.

Eder, R. W., & Buckley, M. R. (1988). The employment interview: An interactionist perspective. In G. R. Ferris & K. M. Rowland (Eds.), *Research in personnel and human resources management* (Vol. 6, pp. 75-107). Greenwich, CT: JAI Press.

Eder, R. W., & Buckley, M. R. (1989). *Information source similarity, situational interviewing, primacy effects and interviewer judgment.* Unpublished manuscript.

Eder, R. W., & Fedor, D. B. (in press-a). Employee responses to supervisor feedback. In

R. A. Giacalone & P. Rosenfeld (Eds.), *Impression management in the organization*. Hillsdale, NJ: Lawrence Erlbaum.

Eder, R. W., & Fedor, D. B. (in press-b). Priming performance self-evaluations: Moderating effects of rating purpose and judgment confidence. *Organizational Behavior and Human Decision Processes*.

Eder, R. W., Fedor, D. B., Buckley, M. R. & Longenecker, C. (1988). *The role of supervisor intentions and power on employee reactions and responses to feedback*. Paper presented at the annual meeting Academy of Management, Anaheim, CA.

EEOC v. American National Bank, 21 EPD 30,369 (1979).

EEOC v. Rath Packing, 39 EPD 35,956 (1986).

EEOC v. Spokane Concrete Products, 28 EPD 32,624 (1982).

EEOC v. Tecumseh Products, 33 EPD 34,067 (1983).

Equal Employment Opportunity Commission, Civil Service Commission, Department of Labor, & Department of Justice. (1978). Adoption of four agencies of uniform guidelines on employee selection procedures. *Federal Register, 43*, 38290-38315.

Eiser, J. R. (1986). *Social psychology: Attitude, cognition, and social behaviour*. Cambridge: Cambridge University Press.

Ellis, D. G. (1979). Relational control on two group system. *Communication Monographs, 46*, 153-166.

Ellis, R. A., & Taylor, M. S. (1983). Role of self-esteem within the job search process. *Journal of Applied Psychology, 68*, 632-640.

Employment Practices Decisions (1979-1988, Vols. 18-46). Chicago: Commerce Clearing House.

Endler, N. S., & Magnusson, D. (1976). Toward an interactional psychology of personality. *Psychological Bulletin, 83*, 956-974.

Eppen, G. D., & Gould, F. J. (1984). *Introductory management science*. Englewood Cliffs, NJ: Prentice-Hall.

Fahrenberg, J. (1987). Multimodale Diagnostik—eine Einleitung [Multimodal assessment—an introduction]. *Diagnostica, 33*, 185-187.

Fairhurst, G. T., Rogers, L. E., & Sarr, R. A. (1987). Managers and subordinate control patterns and judgments about the relationship. In M. L. McLaughlin, (Ed.), *Communication Yearbook* (Vol. 10, 395-415). Beverly Hills, CA: Sage.

Faraone, S. V., & Dorfman, D. D. (1987). Lag sequential analysis: Robust statistical methods. *Psychological Bulletin, 101*, 312-323.

Farina, A., & Felner, R. D. (1973). Employment interviewer reactions to former mental patients. *Journal of Abnormal Psychology, 82*, 268-272.

Farr, J. L., & York, C. M. (1975). Amount of information and primacy-recency effects in recruitment decisions. *Personnel Psychology, 28*, 233-238.

Fay, C. H., & Latham, G. P. (1982). Effect of training and rating scales on rating errors. *Personnel Psychology, 35*, 105-116.

Fear, R. A. (1973). *The evaluation interview*. New York: McGraw-Hill.

Fear, R. A. (1984). *The evaluation interview* (3rd ed.). New York: McGraw-Hill.

Feick, L. F., & Novak, J. A. (1985). Analyzing sequential categorical data on dyadic interaction: Log-linear models exploiting the order in variables. *Psychological Bulletin, 98*, 600-611.

Feild, H, S., & Holley, W. H. (1982). The relationship of performance appraisal system characteristics to verdicts in selected employment discrimination cases. *Academy of Management Journal, 25*, 392-406.

Feldman, J. M. (1981). Beyond attribution theory: Cognitive processes in performance appraisal. *Journal of Applied Psychology, 66*, 127-148.

Feldstein, S. (1972). Temporal patterns of dialogue: Basic research and considerations. In
    A. W. Siegman & B. Pope (Eds.), *Studies in dyadic communication* (pp. 91-113). New
    York: Pergamon.

Ferris, G. R., Buckley, M. R., Yee, A. T., & West, C. K. (1988). *Performance evaluation
    systems in high technology firms.* Paper presented at the "Managing the High Technology
    Firm" conference, Graduate School of Business Administration, University of Colorado
    at Boulder.

Ferris, G. R., Fedor, D. B., Chachere, J. G., & Pondy, L. R. (1989). Myths and politics
    in organizational contexts. *Group & Organization Studies, 14,* 83-103.

Ferris, G. R. & Kacmar, K. M. (1988). *Organizational politics and affective reactions.* Paper
    presented at the 30th Annual Meeting, Southwest Division of the Academy of Manage-
    ment, San Antonio.

Ferris, G. R., & Mitchell, T. R. (1987). The components of social influence and their impor-
    tance for human resources research. In K. M. Rowland & G. R. Ferris (Eds.), *Research
    in personnel and human resources management* (Vol. 5, pp. 103-128). Greenwich, CT: JAI.

Ferris, G. R., & Porac, J. F. (1984). Goal setting as impression management. *Journal of
    Psychology, 117,* 33-36.

Fisher, C. D. (1984). Laboratory experiments. In T. S. Bateman & G. R. Ferris (Eds.), *Method
    and analysis in organizational research* (pp. 169-185). Reston, VA: Prentice-Hall.

Fisher, C., Ilgen, D., & Hoyer, W. (1979). Source credibility, information favorability, and
    job offer acceptance. *Academy of Management Journal, 22,* 94-103.

Fiske, S. T., & Taylor, S. E. (1984). *Social cognition.* Reading, MA: Addison-Wesley.

Flanagan, J. C. (1954). The critical incident technique. *Psychological Bulletin, 51,* 327-358.

Forbes, R. J., & Jackson, P. R. (1980). Nonverbal behavior and the outcome of selection
    interviews. *Journal of Occupational Psychology, 53,* 65-72.

Forcese, D. P., & Richer, S. (1973). *Social research methods.* Englewood Cliffs, NJ: Pren-
    tice Hall.

Forsythe, S., Drake, M. F., & Cox, C. E. (1985). Influence of applicant's dress on inter-
    viewer's selection decisions. *Journal of Applied Psychology, 70,* 374-378.

Frost, P. J. (1987). *Political influences on human resource management practice.* Distinguished
    speaker presentation at the International Personnel and Human Resource Management Con-
    ference, Singapore.

Fruhner, R., & Schuler, H. (1987). *Bewertung eignungsdiagnostischer Verfahren zur Per-
    sonalauswahl durch potentielle Stellenbewerber [Acceptability of personnel selection pro-
    cedures for candidates].* Paper presented at the 14. Kongre fur angewandte Psychologie,
    Mainz, West Germany.

Galambos, J. A. & Rips, L. J. (1979). *The presentation of events in memory.* Paper presented
    at the Midwestern Psychological Association, Chicago.

Gandz, J., & Murray, V. V. (1980). The experiences of workplace politics. *Academy of
    Management Journal, 23,* 237-251.

Gatewood, R. D., & Feild, H. S. (1987). *Human resource selection.* Hinsdale, IL: Dryden.

Geweke, J. (1982). Measurement of linear dependence and feedback between multiple time
    series. *Journal of American Statistical Association, 77,* 304-313.

Ghiselli, E. E. (1966). The validity of a personnel interview. *Personnel Psychology, 19,*
    389-394.

Ghiselli, E. E. (1973). Validity of aptitude tests in personnel selection. *Personnel Psychology,
    26,* 461-478.

Gifford, R., Ng, C. F., & Wilkinson, M. (1985). Nonverbal cues in the employment interview: Links between applicant qualities and interviewer judgments. *Journal of Applied Psychology, 70,* 729-736.

Giles, W. F., & Feild, H. S. (1982). Accuracy of interviewers' perceptions of the importance of intrinsic and extrinsic job characteristics to male and female applicants. *Academy of Management Journal, 25,* 148-151.

Gilbert v. City of Little Rock, 41 EPD 36,454 (1986).

Gilmore, D. C., Beehr, T. A., & Love, K. G. (1986). Effects of applicant sex, applicant physical attractiveness, type of rater, and type of job on interview decisions. *Journal of Occupational Psychology, 59,* 103-109.

Gilmore, D. C., & Ferris, G. R. (1980). Problems in the employment interview. In K. M. Rowland, M. London, G. R. Ferris, & J. L. Sherman (Eds.), *Current issues in personnel management.* Boston: Allyn & Bacon.

Gilmore, D. C., & Ferris, G. R. (1988). *The effects of applicant impression management tactics on interviewer judgments.* Unpublished manuscript.

Gilmore, D. C., Ferris, G. R., & Kacmar, K. M. (1988). The nature of employment interview decisions. In G. R. Ferris & K. M. Rowland (Eds.), *Human resources management: Perspectives and issues* (pp. 101-107). Boston: Allyn & Bacon.

Gioia, D. A. (1986). Symbols, scripts, and sensemaking. In H. P. Sims & D. A. Gioia (Eds.), *The thinking organization* (pp. 49-74). San Francisco, CA: Jossey-Bass.

Gioia, D. A. & Manz, C. C. (1985). Linking cognition and behavior: A script processing interpretation of vicarious learning. *Academy of Management Review, 10,* 527-539.

Gioia, D. A., & Poole, P. P. (1984). Scripts in organizational behavior. *Academy of Management Review, 9,* 449-459.

Glauser, M. J., & Tullar, W. L. (1985). Citizen satisfaction with police officer/citizen interaction: Implications for the changing role of police organizations. *Journal of Applied Psychology, 70,* 514-527.

Glueck, W. F. (1973). Recruiters and executives: How do they affect job choice? *Journal of College Placement, 34,* 77-78.

Glueck, W. F. (1978). *Personnel: A diagnostic approach.* Dallas, TX: Business Publications.

Godfrey, D. K., Jones, E. E., & Lord, C. G. (1986). Self-promotion is not ingratiating. *Journal of Personality and Social Psychology, 50,* 106-115.

Goodale, J. G. (1976). Tailoring the selection interview to the job. *Personnel Journal,* (February), 62-65, 83.

Goodale, J. G. (1981). The neglected art of interviewing. *Supervisory Management,* (July), 2-10.

Goodale, J. G. (1982). *The fine art of interviewing.* Englewood Cliffs, NJ: Prentice-Hall.

Goodale, J. G. (in press). *The manager's guide to effective interviewing.* Englewood Cliffs, NJ: Prentice-Hall.

Gordon, M. E., Schmitt, N., & Schneider, W. (1984). An evaluation of laboratory research on bargaining and negotiations. *Industrial Relations, 23,* 218-233.

Gordon, M. E., Slade, L. A., & Schmitt, N. (1986). The "science of the sophomore" revisited: From conjecture to empiricism. *Academy of Management Review, 11,* 191-207.

Gordon, M. E., Slade, L. A., & Schmitt, N. (1987). Student guinea pigs: Procine predictors and particularistic phenomena. *Academy of Management Review, 12,* 160-163.

Gordon, R. A. (1984). The effect of accountability on age discrimination in the employment interview. *Dissertation Abstracts International, 45,* 3113.

Gorman, C. D., Clover, W. H., & Doherty, M. E. (1978). Can we learn anything about interviewing real people from "interviews" of paper people? Two studies of the external validity of a paradigm. *Organizational Behavior and Human Performance, 22,* 165-192.

Gottman, J. M. (1979). Detecting cyclicity in social interaction. *Psychological Bulletin, 86,* 338-348.

Gould, S., & Penley, L. E. (1984). Career strategies and salary progression: A study of their relationships in a municipal bureaucracy. *Organizational Behavior and Human Performance, 34,* 244-265.

Graesser, A. C., Wall, S. B., Kowalski, D. J., & Smith, D. A. (1980). Memory for typical and atypical actions in scripted activities. *Journal of Experimental Psychology: Human Learning and Memory, 6,* 503-515.

Graves, L. M., & Powell, G. N. (1988). An investigation of sex discrimination in recruiters' evaluations of actual applicants. *Journal of Applied Psychology, 73,* 20-29.

Green v. USX, 46 EPD, 37,896 (1988).

Greenberg, J. (1987). The college sophomore as guinea pig: Setting the record straight. *Academy of Management Review, 12,* 157-159.

Greenhaus, J. (1987). *Career management.* Chicago: Dryden Press.

Griggs v. Duke Power Co., 401 U. S. 424. (1971).

Griffin v. Carlin. 36 EPD 35,600 (1985).

Guion, R. M. (1966). *Personnel testing.* New York: McGraw-Hill.

Guion, R. M. (1965). Recruiting, selection, and job placement. In M. D. Dunnette (Ed.), *Handbook of industrial and organizational psychology,* Chicago: Rand-McNally.

Guion, R. M. (1987). Changing views for personnel selection research. *Personnel Psychology, 40,* 199-213.

Guion, R. M. & Gibson, W. M. (1988). Personnel selection and placement. *Annual Review of Psychology, 39,* 349-374.

Hagafors, R. & Bremer, B. (1983). Does having to justify one's judgments change the nature of the judgment process? *Organizational Behavior and Human Performance, 31,* 223-232.

Hakel, M. D. (1971). Similarity of post-interview trait rating intercorrelations as a contributor to interrater agreement in a structured employment interview. *Journal of Applied Psychology, 55,* 443-448.

Hakel, M. D. (1982). Employment interviewing. In K. M. Rowland & G. R. Ferris (Eds.), *Personnel management* (pp. 102-124). Boston: Allyn & Bacon.

Hakel, M. D., Dobmeyer, T. W., & Dunnette, M. D. (1970). Relative importance of three content dimensions in overall suitability ratings of job applicants' resumes. *Journal of Applied Psychology, 54,* 65-71.

Hakel, M. D., Holleman, T. D., & Dunnette, M. D. (1970). Accuracy of interviewers, certified public accountants, and students in identifying the interests of accountants. *Journal of Applied Psychology, 54,* 115-119.

Half, R. (1981). *The Robert Half way to get hired in today's job market.* New York: Bantam.

Hall, C. S., & Lindzey, G. (1978). *Theories of personality,* New York: John Wiley.

Hall, J. A. (1978). Gender effects in decoding nonverbal cues. *Psychological Bulletin, 85,* 845-857.

Hamilton, D. L., & Zanna, M. P. (1972). Differential weighing of favorable and unfavorable attributes in impressions of personality. *Journal of Applied Psychology, 6,* 204-212.

Hanigan, M. (1987). Campus recruiters upgrade their pitch. *Personnel Administrator, 32,* 55-58.

Hanssens, D. M. & Levien, H. A. (1983). An econometric study of recruitment marketing in the U.S. Navy. *Management Science, 29,* 1167-1184.

Harless v. Duck, 22 EPD 30,871 (1980).

Harn, T. J. and Thornton, G. C. (1985). Recruiter counselling behaviours and applicant impressions. *Journal of Occupational Psychology, 54,* 165-173.

Harris v. Ford, 26 EPD 31,906 (1981).

Harris, M. M., & Fink, L. S. (1987). A field study of applicant reactions to employment opportunities: Does the recruiter make a difference? *Personnel Psychology, 40,* 765-784.

Hedge, J. W., & Kavanagh, M. J. (1988). Improving the accuracy of performance evaluations: Comparison of three methods of performance appraiser training. *Journal of Applied Psychology, 73,* 68-73.

Heider, F. (1958). *The psychology of interpersonal relations.* New York: John Wiley.

Heilman, M. E. (1980). The impact of situational factors on personnel decisions concerning women: Varying the sex composition of the applicant pool. *Organizational Behavior and Human Performance, 26,* 386-396.

Heilman, M. E. (1984). Information as a deterrent against sex discrimination: The effects of applicant sex and information type on preliminary employment decisions. *Organizational Behavior and Human Performance, 33,* 174-186.

Heilman, M. E., Martell, R. F., & Simon, M. C. (1988). The vagaries of sex bias: Conditions regulating the undervaluation, equivaluation, and overvaluation of female job applicants. *Organizational Behavior and Human Decision Processes, 41,* 98-110.

Heilman, M. E., & Saruwatari, L. R. (1979). When beauty is beastly: The effects of appearance and sex on evaluations of job applicants for managerial and nonmanagerial jobs. *Organizational Behavior and Human Performance, 23,* 360-372.

Hellervik, J. W., & Janz, J. T. (1988). *Behavior description interviewing.* Workshop presented at the third annual meeting of the Society for Industrial and Organizational Psychology, Dallas, Texas.

Henderson, J. C., & Nutt, P. C. (1980). The influence of decision style on decision making behavior. *Management Science, 26,* 371-386.

Heneman, H. G., Schwab, D. P., Fossum, J. A., & Dyer, L. D. (1986). *Personnel/human resources management.* Homewood, IL: Irwin.

Heneman, H. G., Schwab, D. P., Huett, D. L., & Ford, J. J. (1975). Interviewer validity as a function of interview structure, biographical data, and interviewee order. *Journal of Applied Psychology, 60,* 748-753.

Herriot, P. (1981). Towards an attributional theory of the selection interview. *Journal of Occupational Psychology, 54,* 165-173.

Herriot, P. (1988). Selection as a social process. In M. Smith & I. T. Robertson (Eds.), *Advances in personnel selection and assessment.* Chichester: John Wiley.

Herriot, P., & Rothwell, C. (1983). Expectations and impressions in the graduate selection interview. *Journal of Occupational Psychology, 56,* 303-314.

Hitt, M. A., & Barr, S. H. (1989). Managerial selection decision models: Examination of configural cue processing. *Journal of Applied Psychology, 74,* 53-61.

Hoffman, C., Mischel, W., & Mazze, K. (1981). The role of purpose in the organization of information about behavior: Trait-based versus goal-based categories in person cognition. *Journal of Personality and Social Psychology, 40,* 211-225.

Hogarth, R. M., & Makridakis, S. (1981). Forecasting and planning: An evaluation. *Management Science, 27,* 115-138.

Hollingworth, H. L. (1922). *Judging human character.* New York: Appleton-Century-Crofts.

Hollman, T. D. (1972). Employment interviewers' errors in processing positive and negative information. *Journal of Applied Psychology, 56,* 130-134.

Homans, G. C. (1961). *Social behavior: Its elementary forms.* New York: Harcourt Brace Jovanovich.

Honeck, R. P., Firment, M., & Case, T. J. S. (1987). Expertise and categorization. *Bulletin of the Psychonomic Society, 25,* 431-434.

Howard, G. S., & Dailey, P. J. (1979). Response-shift bias: A source of contamination of self report measures. *Journal of Applied Psychology, 64,* 144-150.

Huber, V. L., Neale, M. A., & Northcraft, G. B. (1987). Decision bias and personnel selection strategies. *Organizational Behavior and Human Decision Processes, 40*, 136-147.

Hunt, V. D. (1986). *Artificial intelligence & expert systems sourcebook.* New York: Chapman & Hall.

Hunter, J. E., & Hirsch, H. (1987). Applications of meta-analysis. In C. L. Cooper & I. T. Robertson (Eds.), *International review of industrial and organizational psychology* (pp. 321-357). Chichester: John Wiley.

Hunter, J. E., & Hunter, R. F. (1984). Validity and utility of alternative predictors of job performance. *Psychological Bulletin, 96*, 72-98.

Hunter, J. E., Schmidt, F. L., & Jackson, G. B. (1982). *Meta-analysis: Quantitative methods for cumulating research findings across studies.* Beverly Hills, CA: Sage.

Ilgen, D. R., & Favero, J. L. (1985). Limits in gerneralizaton from psychological research to performance appraisal processes. *Academy of Management Review, 10*, 311-321.

Ilgen, D. R., & Feldman, J. M. (1983). Performance appraisal: A process focus. In L. L. Cummings & B. M. Staw (Eds.), *Research in organizational behavior* (Vol. 5, pp. 141-197). Greenwich CT: JAI.

Imada, A. S., & Hakel, M. D. (1977). Influence of nonverbal communication and rater proximity on impression and decisions in simulated employment interviews. *Journal of Applied Psychology, 62*, 295-300.

Isen, A. M. (1987). Positive affect, cognitive organization, and social behavior. In L. Berkowitz (Ed.), *Advances in experimental social psychology* (Vol. 21). New York: Academic Press.

Isen, A. M., Daubman, K., & Nowicki, G. (1987). Positive affect facilitates creative problem solving. *Journal of Personality and Social Psychology, 52*, 1121-1131.

Ivancevich, J. M., & Donnelly, J. H. (1971). Job offer acceptance behavior and reinforcement. *Journal of Applied Psychology, 55*, 119-122.

Jablin, F. M., & McComb, K. B. (1984). The employment screening interview: An organizational assimilation and communication perspective. *Communication Yearbook* (Vol. 8, 137-163). Beverly Hills, CA: Sage.

Jackson, N., Peacock, A., & Smith, J. P. (1980). Impressions of personality in the employment interview. *Journal of Personality and Social Psychology, 39*, 294-307.

James, S. P., Campbell, I. M., & Lovegrove, S. A. (1984). Personality differentiation in a police-selection interview. *Journal of Applied Psychology, 69*, 129-134.

Janis, I. L., & Mann, L. (1977). *Decision making: A psychological analysis of conflict, choice, and commitment.* New York: Free Press.

Janz, J. T. (1982). Initial comparisons of patterned behavior description interviews versus unstructured interviews. *Journal of Applied Psychology, 67*, 577-580.

Janz, J. T. (1987). The selection interview: The received wisdom versus recent research. In S. Dolan & R. Schuler (Eds.), *Canadian readings in personnel and human resource management.* St. Paul, MN: West.

Janz, J. T. (1988). *Comparing the use and validity of opinions versus behavior descriptions in the employment interview.* Unpublished manuscript.

Janz, J. T., Hellervik, L. & Gilmore, D. C. (1986). *Behavior description interviewing: New, accurate, cost effective.* Newton, MA: Allyn & Bacon.

Johnston, W. B. (1987). *Workforce 2000: Work and workers for the 21st century.* Indianapolis: Hudson Institute.

Jones, S. M. (1987). Applying disparate impact theory to subjective employee selection procedures. *Loyola of Los Angeles Law Review, 20*, 375-419.

Jones, E. E., & Pittman, T. S. (1982). Toward a general theory of strategic self-presentation. In J. Suls (Ed.), *Psychological perspectives on the self.* Hillsdale, NJ: Lawrence Erlbaum.

Jung, C. G. (1971). A psychological theory of types. In *Collected works* (Vol. 6). Princeton, NJ: Princeton University Press.

Just, M. A., & Carpenter, P. A. (Eds.) (1977). *Cognitive processes in comprehension.* Hillsdale, NY: Lawrence Erlbaum.

Kane, J. S., & Lawler, E. E. (1979). Performance appraisal effectiveness: Its effectiveness and determinants. In B. M. Staw & L. L. Cummings (Eds.), *Research in organizational behavior* (Vol. 1, pp. 129-182). Greenwich, CT: JAI.

Kanouse, D. E., & Hanson, L. R., Jr. (1972). *Negativity in evaluations.* Morristown, NJ: General Learning Press.

Kanter, R. M. (1977). *Men and women of the corporation.* New York: Basic Books.

Kassin, S. M. & Hochreich, D. J. (1977). Instructional set: A neglected variable in attribution research? *Personality and Social Psychology Bulletin, 3,* 620-623.

Katz, D., & Kahn, R. L. (1978). The social psychology of organizations (Second edition). New York: John Wiley.

Kean, J. M. (1982). Listening. In H. E. Mitzel, J. H. Best, & W. Rabinowitz (Eds.), *Encyclopedia of educational research* (pp. 1102-1105). New York: Free Press.

Keenan, A., & Wedderburn, A. A. I. (1980). Putting the boot on the other foot: Candidates' descriptions of interviewers. *Journal of Occupational Psychology, 53,* 81-89.

Kelly, E. L., & Fiske, D. W. (1951). *The prediction of performance in clinical psychology.* Ann Arbor: University of Michigan Press.

Kelley, H. H. (1967). Attribution theory in social psychology. In D. Levine (Ed.), *Nebraska Symposium on Motivation* (Vol.15, pp. 192-238). Lincoln: Nebraska University Press.

Kelley, H. H. (1972). Attribution theory in social interaction. In E. Jones, D. E. Kanouse, H. H. Kelley, R. E. Nisbett, S. Valins, & B. Weiner (Eds.), *Attribution: Perceiving the causes of behavior.* Morristown, NJ: General Learning Press.

Kelman, H. (1967). Human use of human subjects: The problem of deception in psychological experiments. *Psychological Bulletin, 57,* 1-11.

Kerlinger, F. N. (1986). *Foundations of behavioral research.* New York: Holt, Rinehart, and Winston.

Kenagy, H. G., & Yoakum, C. S. (1925). *The selection and training of salesmen.* New York: McGraw Hill.

Kerr, S., Tolliver, J., & Petree, D. (1977). Manuscript characteristics which influence acceptance for management and social science journals. *Academy of Management Journal, 20,* 132-141.

Kilmann, R. H., & Herden, R. P. (1976). Toward a systemic methodology for evaluating the impact of interventions on organizational effectiveness. *Academy of Management Review, 1,* 87-98.

Kilmann, R. H., & Mitroff, I. I. (1976). Qualitative versus quantitative analysis for management science: Different forms for different psychological types. *Interfaces, 6,* 17-27.

Kinicki, A. J. & Lockwood, C. A. (1985). The interview process: An examination of factors recruiters use in evaluating job applicants. *Journal of Vocational Behavior, 26,* 117-125.

King v. TWA, 35 EPD 34,588 (1984).

Kintsch, W. (1982). Aspects of text comprehension. In J. F. Le Ny & W. Kintsch (Eds.), *Language and comprehension* (pp. 301-312). Amsterdam: North-Holland.

Klayman, J., & Ha, Y-W. (1987). Confirmation, disconfirmation, and information in hypothesis testing. *Psychological Review, 94,* 211-228.

Kleinmuntz, D. N. (1985). Cognitive heuristics and feedback in a dynamic decision environment. *Management Science, 31,* 680-702.

Kleinke, C. L. (1986). Gaze and eye contact: A research review. *Psychological Bulletin, 100,* 78-100.

Klitgaard, R. (1985). *Choosing elites.* New York: Basic Books.

Kohler, W. (1927). *The mentality of apes.* New York: Harcourt Brace.

338   THE EMPLOYMENT INTERVIEW

Kolodner, J. L. (1984). *Retrieval and organizational strategies in conceptual memory: A computer model*. Hillsdale, NJ: Lawrence Erlbaum.

Kraszewski v. State Farm, 36 EPD 35,219 (1985).

Kreftling, L. A., & Brief, A. P. (1977). The impact of applicant disability on evaluative judgments in the selection process. *Academy of Management Journal, 19*, 675-680.

Krett, K., & Stright, J. F. (1985). Using market research as a recruitment strategy. *Personnel*, (November), 32-35.

Lamber, J. (1985). Discretionary decision making: The application of Title VII's disparate impact theory. *University of Illinois Law Review, 1985*, 869-920.

Landy, F. J. (1986). Stamp collecting versus science: Validation as hypothesis testing. *American Psychologist, 41*, 1183-1192.

Landy, F. J., & Bates, F. (1973). Another look at contrast effects in the employment interview. *Journal of Applied Psychology, 58*, 141-144.

Langdale, J. A., & Weitz, J. (1973). Estimating the influence of job information on interviewer agreement. *Journal of Applied Psychology, 57*, 23-27.

Langer, E. J., Blank, A., & Chanowitz, B. (1978). The mindlessness of ostensibly thoughtful action. *Journal of Personality and Social Psychology, 36*, 635-642.

Larson, A., & Larson, L. K. (1986). *Employment discrimination*. New York: Matthew Bender.

Latham, G. P. (1969). *The development of job performance criteria for pulpwood producers in the Southeastern United States*. Atlanta: American Pulpwood Association—Harvesting Research Project.

Latham, G. P. (1986). Job performance and appraisal. In C. Cooper & I. Robertson (Eds.), *Review of industrial and organizational psychology*. Chichester: John Wiley.

Latham, G. P. (1988). Human resource training and development. *Annual Review of Psychology, 39*, 545-582.

Latham, G. P. & Finnegan, B. J. (1987). *The practicality of the situational interview*. Paper presented at the annual meeting of the Academy of Management, New Orleans.

Latham, G. P., & Kinne, S. B. (1974). Improving job performance through training in goal setting *Journal of Applied Psychology, 59*, 187-191.

Latham, G. P., & Saari, L. M. (1984). Do people do what they say? Further studies on the situational interview. *Journal of Applied Psychology, 69*, 569-573.

Latham, G. P., Saari, L. M., Pursell, E. D., & Campion, M. A. (1980). The situational interview. *Journal of Applied Psychology, 65*, 442-431.

Latham, G. P., Wexely, K. N. (1977). Behavioral observation scales for performance appraisal. *Personal Psychology, 30*, 255-268.

Latham, G. P., & Wexley, K. N. (1981). *Increasing productivity through performance appraisal*. Reading, MA: Addison-Wesley.

Latham, G. P., Wexley, K. N., & Pursell, E. D. (1975). Training managers minimize rating errors in the observation of behavior. *Journal of Applied Psychology, 60*, 550-555.

Lawler, E. E. (1971). *Pay and organizational effectiveness: A psychological view*. New York: McGraw-Hill.

Lawshe, C. H. (1975). A quantitative approach to content validity. *Personnel Psychology, 28*, 565-575.

Leathers, D. G. (1979). The impact of multichannel message inconsistency on verbal and nonverbal decoding behaviors. *Communication Monographs, 46*, 88-100.

Lepper, M. (1973). Dissonance, self-perception and honesty in children. *Journal of Personality and Social Psychology, 25*, 65-74.

Levin, I. P., & Schmidt, C. F. (1970). Differential influence of information on an impression-formation task with binary intermittent responding. *Journal of Experimental Psychology, 84*, 374-376.

Levine, E. L. (1983). *Everything you always wanted to know about job analysis*. Tampa, FL: Mariner Publishing.

Lewin, K. (1936). *Principles of topological psychology*. New York: McGraw Hill.

Lewin, K. (1951). Formalization and progress in psychology. In D. Cartwright (Ed.), *Field theory in social science*. New York: Harper.

Lexis. (1987). Mead Data Central.

Liden, R. C., & Mitchell, T. R. (1989). Ingratiatory behaviors in organizational settings. *Academy of Management Review, 13,* 572-587.

Liden, R. C., & Parsons, C. K. (1986). A field study of job applicant interview perceptions, alternative opportunities, and demographic characteristics. *Personnel Psychology, 39,* 109-122.

Lin, T. R., Manligus, C. L. (1988). *A comparative analysis of rater and rater race effects on employment selection interviews: Structured interview versus situational interview.* Paper presented at the annual meeting of the Academy of Management, Anaheim, CA.

Lindquist, V. R. (1988). Questions asked by employers. In *Career Opportunity Update* (p. 17). Fountain Valley, CA: Career Research Systems.

Lippman, S., & McCall, J. (1976). The economics of job search: A survey (Pt. 1). *Economic Inquiry, 14,* 155-190.

Locke, E. A., (1968). Towards a theory of task motivation and incentives. *Organizational Behavior and Human Performance, 3,* 157-189.

Locke, E. A., & Latham, G. P. (1984). *Goal setting: A motivational technique that works.* Englewood Cliffs, NJ: Prentice Hall.

London, M., & Hakel, M. D. (1974). Effects of applicant stereotypes, order, and information on interview impressions. *Journal Of Applied Psychology, 59,* 157-162.

London, M., & Poplawski, J. R. (1976). Effects of information on stereotype development in performance appraisal and interview contexts. *Journal of Applied Psychology, 61,* 199-205.

Longenecker, C. O., Sims, H. P., Jr., & Gioia, D. A. (1987). Behind the mask: The politics of employee appraisal. *Academy of Management Executive, 1,* 183-193.

Lopez, F. M. (1975). *Personnel interviewing* (2nd ed.). New York: McGraw-Hill.

Lucas v. Dole, 45 EPD, 37,624 (1987).

Lundsteen, S. W. (1979). *Listening: Its impact on reading and the other language arts* (2nd ed.). Urbana, IL: National Council of Teachers of English. (ERIC Document Reproduction Service No. Ed 169 537)

Lykken, D. J. (1984). Statistical significance in psychological research. In T. S. Bateman & G. R. Ferris (Eds.), *Method and analysis in organizational research* (pp.54-64). Reston, VA: Reston.

Maas, J. B. (1965). The patterned scaled expectation interview. *Journal of Applied Psychology, 49,* 431-433.

Macan, T. M., & Dipboye, R. L. (1985). *The college recruitment/selection interview: A dual process view.* Unpublished manuscript.

Macan, T. M., & Dipboye, R. L. (1987). *The effects of the application on processing of information from the employment interview.* Unpublished manuscript.

Macan, T. M., & Dipboye, R. L. (1988). The effects of interviewers' initial impressions on information gathering. *Organizational Behavior and Human Decision Processes.*

Maier, N. R. F. (1966). Sensitivity to attempts at deception in an interview situation. *Personnel Psychology, 19,* 41-53.

Maier, N. R. F., & Janzen, J. C. (1967). The reliability of reasons used in making judgments of honesty and dishonesty. *Perceptual and Motor Skills, 25,* 141-151.

Maier, N. R. F., & Thurber, J. A. (1968). Accuracy of judgments of deception when an interview is watched, heard and read. *Personnel Psychology, 21*, 23-30.

Malm, F. T. (1954). Recruiting patterns and the functioning of labor markets. *Industrial and Labor Relations Review, 7*, 507-525.

Mandell, M. (1940). Civil service oral interviews. *Personnel Journal, 18*, 373-382.

Markland, R. E. (1983). *Topics in management science*. New York: John Wiley.

Matarazzo, J. D., Suslow, G., & Matarazzo, R. G. (1956). The interaction chronograph as an instrument for objective measurement of interaction pattern during interviews. *Journal of Psychology, 41*, 347-367.

Matarazzo, J. D., & Wiens, A. N. (1972). *The interview: Research on its anatomy and structure*. Chicago: Aldine-Atherton.

Maurer, S. D. (1983). *The economic utility of the employment interview*. Unpublished doctoral dissertation, University of Oregon, Eugene.

Maurer, S. D., & Fair, B. L. (in press). Examination of rating agreement and rating error in the use of situational interviews. *Proceedings of the Southern Management Association*.

Maurer, S. D., & Fay, C. (1988). Effect of situational interviews, conventional structured interviews, and training on interview rating agreement: An experimental analysis. *Personnel Psychology, 41*.

Mayes, B. T., & Allen, R. W. (1977). Toward a definition of organizational politics. *Academy of Management Review, 2*, 672-678.

Mayfield, E. C. (1964). The selection interview: A re-evaluation of published research. *Personnel Psychology, 17*, 239-260.

Mayfield, E. C., Brown, S. H., & Hamstra, B. W. (1980). Selection interviewing in the life insurance industry: An update of research and practice. *Personnel Psychology, 33*, 725-739.

Mayfield, E. C., & Carlson, R. E. (1966). Selection interview decisions: First results from a long-term research project. *Personnel Psychology, 17*, 41-55.

McAllister, P. W., Mitchell, T. R., & Beach, L. R. (1979). The contingency model for the selection of decision strategies: An empirical test of the effects of significance, accountability, and reversibility. *Organizational Behavior and Human Performance, 24*, 228-244.

McArthur, L. A. (1972). The how and what of why: Some determinants and consequences of causal attribution. *Journal of Personality and Social Psychology, 22*, 171-193.

McCall, N. W., & DeVries, D. L. (1976). *Appraisal in context: Clashing with organizational realities*. Paper presented at the meeting of the American Psychological Association, Washington, DC.

McDaniel, M. A. & Schmidt, F. L. (1985). *A meta-analysis of the validity of training and experience ratings in personnel selection* (OSP-85-1). Washington, DC: U.S. Office of Personnel Management, Office of Staffing Policy, Examining Policy Analysis Division.

McDaniel, M. A., Whetzel, D. L., Schmidt, F. L., Hunter, J. E., Maurer, S., & Russell, J. (1987). *The validity of employment interviews: A review and meta-analysis*. Manuscript submitted for publication.

McDonald, T., & Hakel, M. D. (1985). Effects of applicant race, sex, suitability, and answers on interviewer's questionning strategy and ratings. *Personnel Psychology, 38*, 321-334.

McEvoy, G. M., & Cascio, W. F. (1985). Strategies for reducing employees turnover: A meta-analysis. *Journal of Applied Psychology, 70*, 342-353.

McIntyre, S., Moberg, D. J., & Posner, B. Z. (1980). Preferential treatment in preselection decisions according to sex and race. *Academy of Management Journal, 23*, 738-749.

McIntyre, R. M., Smith, D. E., & Hassett, C. E. (1984). Accuracy of performance ratings as affected by rater training and perceived purpose of rating. *Journal of Applied Psychology, 69*, 147-156.

Meehl, P. E., (1954). *Clinical versus statistical prediction*. Minneapolis: University of Minnesota Press.

Meehl, P. E. (1959). Some ruminations on the validation of clinical procedures. *Canadian Journal of Psychology, 13,* 102-128.

Meehl, P. E. (1965). Clincal versus statistical prediction. *Journal of Experimental Research in Personality, 63,* 81-97.

Meehl, P. E. (1978). Theoretical risks and tabular asterisks: Sir Karl, Sir Ronald, and the slow progress of soft psychology. *Journal of Consulting and Clinical Psychology, 46,* 806-834.

Merrill, P. (1987). Sign of the times. *Personnel Administrator, 32,* 62-65.

Meyer, H. H. (1987). Predicting supervisory ratings verus promotional progress in test validation studies. *Journal of Applied Psychology, 72,* 696-697.

Meyer, H. H., Kay, E., & French, J. R. P. (1965). Split roles in performance appraisal. *Harvard Business Review, 43,* 123-219.

Mifsud, S. M. (1988). *An attempt to alter cost orientation in personnel decision-making process.* Unpublished honours bachelor's thesis, University of Waterloo, Waterloo, Canada.

Miller, J. W. (1968). *A weighted averaging model for information integration in impression formation.* Unpublished doctoral dissertation, University of Waterloo, Walerloo, Canada.

Miller, J. W., & Rowe, P. M. (1967). Influence of favorable and unfavorable information upon assessment decisions. *Journal of Applied Psychology, 51,* 432-435.

Miller, L. C., & Kenny, D. A. (1986). Reciprocity of self-disclosure at the individual and dyadic levels: A social relations analysis. *Journal of Personality and Social Psychology, 50,* 713-719.

Milne, G. G. (1967). The interview: Let us have perspective. *Australian Psychologist, 2(2),* 77-84.

Mook, D. G. (1983). In defense of external invalidity. *American Psychologist, 38,* 379-387.

Moon v. Cook County Corrections Board, 44 EPD 37,560 (1987).

Moore, L. F., & Lee, A. J. (1974). Comparability of interviewer, group and individual interview ratings. *Journal of Applied Psychology, 59,* 163-167.

Moss, F. A. (1931). Scholastic aptitude tests for medical students. *Journal of Association of American Medical Colleges, 6,* 1-16.

Motowidlo, S. J. (1986). Information processing in personnel decisions. In K. M. Rowland & G. R. Ferris (Eds.), *Research in personnel and human resources management* (Vol. 4, pp. 1-44). Greenwich, CT: JAI.

Mullins, T. W. (1982). Interviewer decisions as a function of applicant race, applicant quality, and interviewer prejudice. *Personnel Psychology, 35,* 161-174.

Mullins, T. W., & Davis, R. G. (1982). A strategy for managing the selection interview process. *Personnel Administrator, 26,* 65-76.

Murphy, K. R., Herr, B. M., Lockhart, M. C. & Maguire, E. (1986). Evaluating the performance of paper people. *Journal of Applied Psychology, 71,* 654-661.

Murray, H. A. (1938). *Explorations in personality.* New York: Oxford University Press.

Nagi, S., McBroom, W. H., & Colletts, J. (1972). Work, employment and the disabled. *American Journal of Economics and Society, 31,* 20-34.

Newman, S. H., Bobbitt, J. M., & Cameron, D. C. (1946). The reliability of the interviewing method in an officer candidate evaluation program. *American Psychologist, 1,* 103-109.

O'Donnel-Trujillo, N. (1981). Relational Communication: A comparison of coding schemes. *Communications Monographs, 48,* 91-105.

Orne, M. T. (1969). Demand characteristics and the concept of quasi-controls. In R. Rosenthal & R. L. Rosnow (Eds.), *Artifact in behavioral research* (pp. 147-181). New York: Academic Press.

Orpen, C. (1985). Patterned behavior description interviews versus unstructured interviews: A comparative validity study. *Journal of Applied Psychology, 70,* 774-776.

Osburn, H. G., Timmerick, C., & Bigby, D. (1981). Effect of dimensional relevance on accuracy of simulated hiring decisions by employment interviewers. *Journal of Applied Psychology, 66,* 159-165.

Otis, J. L., Campbell, J. H., & Prien, E. P. (1962). Assessment of higher-level personnel: VII. The nature of assessment. *Personnel Psychology, 15,* 441-446.

Owens W. A. (1976). Background data. In M. D. Dunnette (Ed.), *Handbook of industrial and organizational psychology* (pp. 609-644). New York: John Wiley.

Park, O. S., Sims, H. P., & Motowidlo, S. J. (1986). Affect in organizations. In H. Sims & D. Gioia (Eds.), *The thinking organization.* San Francisco: Jossey-Bass.

Parsons, C. K. (1988). Computer technology: Implications for human resources management. In G. R. Ferris & K. M. Rowland (Eds.), *Research in personnel and human resources management* (Vol. 6, pp. 1-36). Greenwich, CT: JAI.

Parsons, C. K., & Liden, R. C. (1984). Interviewer perceptions of applicant qualifications: A multivariate field study of demographic characteristics and nonverbal cues. *Journal of Applied Psychology, 69,* 557-568.

Patterson, M. L. (1982). A sequential functional model of nonverbal exchange. *Psychological Review, 89,* 231-249.

Paunonen, S. V., Jackson, D. N., & Oberman, S. M. (1987). Personnel selection decisions: Effects of applicant personality and the letter of reference. *Organizational Behavior and Human Decision Processes, 40,* 96-114.

Peters, L. H., & Terborg, J. R. (1975). The effects of temporal placement of unfavorable information and of attitude similarity on personnel selection decisions. *Organizational Behavior and Human Performance, 13,* 279-293.

Peters, L., O'Connor, E. J., & Eulberg, J. (1985). Situational constraints: Sources, consequences, and future considerations. In K. M. Rowland & G. R. Ferris (Eds.), *Research in personnel and human resources management,* (Vol. 3, pp. 79-114). Greenwich, CT: JAI.

Peters, L., O'Connor, E. J., & Rudolf, C. J. (1980). The behavioral and affective consequences of performance-relevant situational variables. *Organizational Behavior and Human Performance, 25,* 79-96.

Peters, L. J., & Sheridan, J. E. (1988). Turnover research methodology: A critique of traditional designs and a suggested survival model alternative. In G. R. Ferris & K. M Rowland (Eds.), *Research in personnel and human resources management* (Vol. 6, pp. 231-262). Greenwich, CT: JAI.

Pettigrew, A. (1973). *The politics of organizational decision making.* London: Tavistock.

Phillips v. Placquemines School Board, 465 So. 2d 53 (1985).

Phillips, A., & Dipboye, R. L. (1989). Correlational tests of predictions from a process model of the interview. *Journal of Applied Psychology.*

Piaget, J. (1974). *Understanding causality,* New York: Norton.

Ponder, D. G. (1987). Testing the generalizability of bias in teacher selection ratings across different modes of screening. *Journal of Educational Equity and Leadership, 7,* 49-59.

Poole, P. P. (1984). *Organizational script development.* Unpublished manuscript.

Porter, L. W. (1976). *Organizations as political animals.* Presidential address, Division of Industrial/Organizational Psychology, 84th Annual Meeting of American Psychological Association, Washington, DC.

Posner, M. I., & McLeod, P. (1982). Information processing models: In search of elementary operations. *Annual Review of Psychology, 33,* 477-514.

Powell, G. N. (1984). Effects of job attributes and recruiting practices on applicant decisions: A comparison. *Personnel Psychology, 37,* 721-732.

Powell, G. N. (1986). Effects of expectancy-confirmation processes and applicants' qualifications on recruiters' evaluations. *Psychological Reports, 58,* 1003-1010.

Powell, G. N. (1987). The effects of sex and gender on recruitment. *Academy of Management Review, 12,* 731-743.

Premack, S. L., & Wanous, J. P. (1985). A meta-analysis of realistic job preview experiments. *Journal of Applied Psychology, 70,* 706-719.

Primoff, E. S., Clark, C. L., & Caplan, J. R. (1982). *How to prepare and conduct job element examinations: Supplement.* Washington, DC: Office of Personnel Management.

Pursell, E. D., Campion, M. A., & Gaylord, S. R. (1980). Structured interviewing: Avoiding selection problems. *Personnel Journal, 59,* 907-912.

Pushkin v. University of Colorado, 26 EPD 32,096 (1981).

Pursell, E. D. (1988). *Structured interviewing: Improving reliability, validity and relevance of selection interviews.* Symposium presented at the third annual meeting of the Society for Industrial and Organizational Psychology, Dallas, TX.

Putney, R. W. (1947). Validity of the placement interview. *Personnel Journal, 26,* 144-145.

Ramaprasad, A. (1987). Cognitive process as a basis for MIS and DSS design. *Management Science, 33,* 139-148.

Ramaprasad, A., & Mitroff, I. I. (1984). On formulating strategic problems. *Academy of Management Review, 9,* 597-605.

Rand, T. M., & Wexley, K. N. (1975). Demonstration of the effect, "similar to me," in simulated employment interviews. *Psychological Reports, 36,* 535-544.

Rasmussen, K. G. (1984). Nonverbal behavior, verbal behavior, resume credentials, and selection interview outcomes. *Journal of Applied Psychology, 69,* 551-556.

Raza, S. M., & Carpenter, B. N. (1987). A model of living decisions in real employment interviews. *Journal of Applied Psychology, 72,* 569-503.

Regan, D. R., & Totten, J. (1975). Empathy and attribution: Turning observers into actors. *Journal of Personality and Social Psychology, 32,* 850-856.

Reid, P. T., Kleiman, L. S., & Travis, C. B. (1986). Attribution and sex differences in the employment interview. *Journal of Social Psychology, 126,* 205-212.

Reilly, R. R., & Chao, G. T. (1982). Validity and fairness of some alternative employee selection procedures. *Personnel Psychology, 35,* 1-62.

Reynolds v. Sheet Metal Workers, 22 EPD 30,739 (1980).

Reynolds, L. G. (1951). *The structure of labor markets.* New York: Harper.

Robinson, F. P. (1955). The dynamics of communication in counseling. *Journal of Counseling, 2,* 163-169.

Rodger, A. (1952). The worthwhileness of the interview. *Occupational Psychology, 26,* 101-106.

Rogers, D. P., & Sincoff, M. Z. (1978). Favorable impression characteristics of the recruitment interviewer. *Personnel Psychology, 31,* 495-504.

Rogers, L. E., & Farace, R. V. (1975). Analysis of relational communication in dyads: New Measurement procedures. *Human Communication Research, 1,* 222-239.

Ronan, W. W., Latham, G. P., & Kinne, S. B. (1973). The effects of goal setting and supervision on worker behavior in an industrial situation. *Journal of Applied Psychology, 58,* 302-307.

Rosch, E. (1975). Cognitive representations of semantic categories. *Journal of Experimental Psychology: General, 104,* 192-233.

Rosen, B., & Mericle, M. F. (1979). Influence of strong versus weak fair employment policies and applicants' sex on selection decisions and salary recommendations in management simulation. *Journal of Applied Psychology, 64,* 435-439.

Rosenthal, R. (1969). Interpersonal expectations effects of the experimenter's hypothesis. In R. Rosenthal & R. L. Rosnow (Eds.), *Artifact in behavioral research* (pp. 182-279). New York: Academic Press.

Ross, M., & Fletcher, G. J. O. (1985). Attribution and social perception. In G. Lindzey & E. Aronson (Eds.), *Handbook of social psychology*. New York: Random House.

Rothstein, M., & Jackson, D. N. (1980). Decision making in the employment interview: An experimental approach. *Journal of Applied Psychology*, *63*, 271-283.

Rotter, J. (1966). Generalised expectancies for internal versus external control of reinforcement. *Psychological Monographs*, *80*, 609.

Rowe, P. M. (1963). Individual differences in selection decisions. *Journal of Applied Psychology*, *47*, 304-307.

Rowe, P. M. (1984). Decision processes in personnel selection. *Canadian Journal of Behavioural Science*, *16*, 326-337.

Rozelle, R. M., & Baxter, J. C. (1981). Influence of role pressures on the perceiver: Judgments of videotaped interviews varying judge accountability and responsibility. *Journal of Applied Psychology*, *66*, 437-441.

Russell, J. S., Persing, D. L., & Dunn, J. A. (1986). *A test of the self-fulfilling prophecy model of the interview process*. Unpublished manuscript.

Ryckman, W. G. (1982). *How to pass the employment interview (with flying colors)*. Homewood, IL: Dow Jones-Irwin.

Rynes, S. L. (in press). Recruitment, organizational entry and early work adjustment. In M. D. Dunnette (Ed.), *Handbook of industrial and organizational psychology* (2nd ed.). New York: John Wiley.

Rynes, S. L., & Boudreau, J. W. (1986). College recruiting in large organizations: Practice, evaluation, and research implications. *Personnel Psychology*, *39*, 729-758.

Rynes, S. L., Heneman, H. G., III, & Schwab, D. P. (1980). Individual reactions to organizational recruiting: A review. *Personnel Psychology*, *33*, 529-542.

Rynes, S. L., & Miller, H. E. (1983). Recruiter and job influences on candidates for employment. *Journal of Applied Psychology*, *68*, 147-154.

Sackett, G. P. (1978). *Observing behavior, Vol. II: Data collection and analysis methods*. Baltimore, MD: University Park Press.

Sackett, G. P. (1979). The lag sequential analysis of contingency and cyclicity in behavioral interaction research, In J. Orofsky (Ed.). *Handbook of infant development* (pp.504-572). New York: John Wiley.

Sackett, P. R. (1982). The interviewer as hypothesis tester: The effects of impressions of an applicant on interviewer questioning strategy. *Personnel Psychology*, *35*, 789-804.

Sackett, P. R., & Dreher, D. F. (1982a). *Face validity and empirical validity as determinants of selection decisions*. Paper presented at the annual meeting of the American Psychological Association, Washington, DC.

Sackett, P. R., & Dreher, G. F. (1982b). Constructs and assessment center dimensions: Some troubling empirical findings. *Journal of Applied Psychology*, *67*, 401-410.

Sackett, P. R., Zedeck, S., & Fogli, L. (1988). Relationships between measures of typical and maximum job performance. *Journal of Applied Psychology*, *73*, 482-486.

Schank, R. C., & Abelson, R. P. (1977). *Scripts, plans, goals, and understanding*. Hillsdale, NJ: Lawrence Erlbaum.

Schlenker, B. R. (1980). *Impression management: The self-concept, social identity, and interpersonal relations*. Monterey, CA: Brooks/Cole.

Schmidt, F. L., & Hunter, J. E. (1977). Development of a general solution to the problem of validity generalization. *Journal of Applied Psychology*, *62*, 529-540.

Schmidt, F. L., & Hunter, J. E. (1980). The future of criterion-related validity. *Personnel Psychology*, *33*, 41-60.

Schmidt, F. L., & Hunter, J. E. (1983). Individual differences in productivity: An empirical test of the estimates derived from studies of selection procedures utility. *Journal of Applied Psychology, 64*, 609-626.

Schmidt, F. L., Hunter, J. E., Outerbridge, A. N., & Trattner, M. H. (1986). The economic impact of job selection methods on size, productivity, and payroll costs of the federal work force: An empirically based demonstration. *Personnel Psychology, 39*, 1-29.

Schmidt, F. L., Hunter, J. E., & Pearlman, K. (1982). Assessing the economic impact of personnel programs on workforce productivity. *Personnel Psychology, 35*, 333-347.

Schmidt, F. L., Hunter, J. E. Pearlman, K., Hirsch, H. R., Sackett, P. R., Schmitt, N., Tenopyr, M. L., Kehoe, K., & Zedeck, S. (1985). Forty questions about validity generalization and meta-analysis. Commentary on forty questions about validity generalization and meta-analysis. *Personnel Psychology, 38*, 697-798.

Schmidt, F. L., Hunter, J. E., McKenzie, R., & Muldrow, T. W. (1979). Impact of valid selection procedures on workforce productivity. *Journal of Applied Psychology, 64*, 609-626.

Schmitt, N. (1976). Social and situational determinants of interview decisions: Implications for the employment interview. *Personnel Psychology, 29*, 79-101.

Schmitt, N., & Coyle, B. W. (1976). Applicant decisions in the employment interview. *Journal of Applied Psychology, 61*, 184-192.

Schmitt, N., Gooding, R. Z., Noe, R. A., & Kirsch, M. (1984). Meta-analyses of validity studies published between 1964 and 1982 and the investigation of study characteristics. *Personnel Psychology, 37*, 407-422.

Schmitt, N., & Ostroff, C. (1986). Operationalizing the "behavioral consistency" approach: Selection test development based on a content-oriented strategy. *Personnel Psychology, 39*, 91-108.

Schneider, B. (1976). *Staffing organizations*. Santa Monica, CA: Goodyear.

Schneider, B. (1978). Person-situation selection: A review of some ability-situation interaction research. *Personnel Psychology, 31*, 281-297.

Schneider, B. (1983). Interactionist psychology and organizational behavior. In L. L. Cummings & B. M. Staw (Eds.), *Research in organizational behavior* (Vol. 5, pp.1-31). Greenwich, CT: JAI.

Schneider, B., & Schmitt, N. (1986). *Staffing organizations*. Glenview, IL: Scott, Foresman.

Schneider, D. J. (1973). Implicit personality theory: A review. *Psychological Bulletin, 79*, 294-309.

Schneider, D. J., Hastorf, A. H., & Elsworth, P. C. (1979). *Person perception* (2nd ed.). Reading, MA: Addison-Wesley.

Schramm, W. (1953). How communication works. In W. Schramm (Ed.), *The process and effects of mass communication* (pp. 3-26). Urbana, IL: University of Illinois Press.

Schuh, A. J. (1978). Effects of an early interruption and note taking on listening accuracy and decision making in the interview. *Bulletin of the Psychonomic Society, 12*, 242-224.

Schuh, A. J. (1980). Verbal listening skill in the interview and personal characteristics of the listeners. *Bulletin of the Psychonomic Society, 15*, 125-127.

Schwab, D. P. (1980). Construct validity in organizational behavior. In B. M. Staw & L. L. Cummings (Eds.), *Research in organizational behavior* (Vol. 2, pp.3-43). Greenwich, CT: JAI.

Schwab, D. P. (1982). Recruiting and organizational participation. In K. M. Rowland & G. R. Ferris (Eds.), *Personnel management* (pp. 103-128). Boston: Allyn & Bacon.

Schwab, D. P., & Heneman, H. G. (1969). Relationship between structure and interviewer reliability in an employment situation. *Journal of Applied Psychology, 53*, 214-217.

Schwab, D. P., Heneman, H. H., & DeCotiis, T. A. (1975). Behaviorally anchored rating scales: A review of the literature. *Personnel Psychology, 28*, 549-562.

Schwab, D. P., Rynes, S. L., & Aldag, R. J. (1987). Theories and research on job search and choice. In K. M. Rowland & G. R. Ferris (Eds.), *Research in personnel and human resources management* (Vol. 5, pp. 129-166). Greenwich, CT.: JAI.

Schwartz, S., & Griffin, T. (1987). *Medical thinking: The psychology of medical judgment and decision making.* New York: Springer-Verlag.

Schwind, H. F. (1977). *New ways to evaluate teaching and training effectiveness.* Proceedings of the Adult Education Research Conference, Minneapolis.

Scott, W. D. (1915). Scientific selection of salesmen. *Advertising and Selling Magazine, 5*, 5-6.

Scott, W. D. (1916). Selection of employees by means of quantitative determinations. *Annuals of the American Political and Social Sciences, 65*, 182-193.

Scott, W. D., Bingham, W. V., & Whipple, G. M. (1916). Scientific selection of salesmen. *Salesmanship, 4*, 106-108.

Sechrest, L. (1963). Incremental validity: A recommendation. *Educational and Psychological Measurement, 23*, 153-158.

Sechrest, L. (1967). Incremental validity. In D. N. Jackson & S. Messick (Eds.), *Problems in human assessment*, New York; McGraw Hill.

Seigfried, W. E., & Pohlman, C. E. (1981). Order and task effects in the evaluation of female and male applicants. *Academic Psychology Bulletin, 3*, 89-96.

Shahani, C., & Dipboye, R. L. (1988). *Incremental contributions of the interview to college admissions decisions.* Unpublished manuscript.

Shannon, D., & Weaver, W. (1948). *The mathematical theory of communication.* Urbana: University of Illinois Press.

Siegel, J. M., & Steele, C. M. (1980). Environmental distraction and interpersonal judgments. *British Journal of Social and Clinical Psychology, 19*, 23-32.

Silverman, D., & Jones, J. (1975). *Organizational work.* London: Collin Macmillan.

Silverman, I. (1977). *The human subject in the psychological laboratory.* New York: Pergamon.

Simas, K., & McCarrey, M. (1979). Impact of recruiter authoritarianism and applicant sex on evaluation and selection decisions in a recruitment interview analogue study. *Journal of Applied Psychology, 64*, 483-491.

Simon, H. A. (1957). *Models of man.* New York: John Wiley.

Sims, H. P., & Gioia, D. A. (Eds.) (1986). *The thinking organization.* San Francisco: Jossey-Bass.

Skinner, B. F. (1956). A case history in scientific method. *American Psychologist, 11*, 221-233.

Slovic, P., & Lichtenstein, S. (1971). Comparison of Bayesian and regression approaches to the study of information processing in judgment. *Organizational Behavior and Human Performance, 6*, 649-744.

Smith v. American Service, 36 EPD 35,000 (1984).

Smith, P. C. (1976). Behaviors, results and organizational effectiveness: The problem of criteria. In M. D. Dunnette (Ed.), *Handbook of industrial organizational psychology.* Chicago: Rand McNally.

Snow, A. J. (1928). An experiment in the validity of judging human ability. *Journal of Applied Psychology, 8*, 339-346.

Snyder, M. (1974). The self-monitoring of expressive behavior. *Journal of Personality and Social Psychology, 30*, 526-537.

Snyder, M. (1981). Seek and ye shall find: Testing hypotheses about other people. In E. T. Higgins, C. P. Heiman, & M. P. Zanna (Eds.), *Social cognition: The Ontario symposium on personality and social psychology* (pp. 277-303). Hillsdale, NJ: Lawrence Erlbaum.

Snyder, M., & Swann, W. B., Jr. (1978). Hypothesis-testing in social interaction. *Journal of Personality and Social Psychology, 36,* 1202-1212.

Society for Industrial and Organizational Psychology, Inc. (1987). *Principles for the validation and use of personnel selection procedures.* (3rd ed.). College Park, MD: Author.

Soelberg, P. O. (1967). Unprogrammed decision making. *Industrial Management Review, 8,* 19-29.

Sparks, C. P., & Manese, W. R. (1970). Interview ratings with and without knowledge of pre-employment test scores. *The Experimental Publication System, 4,* 142.

Spriegel, W. R., & James, V. A. (1958). Trends in recruiting and selection practices. *Personnel, 35,* 42-48.

Springbett, B. M. (1958). Factors affecting the final decision in the employment interview. *Canadian Journal of Psychology, 12,* 13-22.

Staw, B. M. (1986). Organizational psychology and the pursuit of the happy/productive worker. *California Management Review, 28,* 40-53.

Staw, B. M., McKechnie, P. I., & Puffer, S. M. (1983). The justification of organizational performance. *Administrative Science Quarterly, 28,* 582-600.

Steel, R. P., & Ovalle, N. K. (1984). A review and meta-analysis of research on the relationship between behavioral intentions and employee turnover. *Journal of Applied Psychology, 69,* 673-686.

Stehle, W. (1983). *Zur Konzeption eines Personalauswahlverfahrens auf der Basis biographischer Daten [Conception of a personnel selection procedure based on biographical data].* Unpublished doctoral dissertation, University of Hohenheim, Stuttgart, West Germany.

Sterrett, J. H. (1978). The job interview: Body language and perceptions of potential effectiveness. *Journal of Applied Psychology, 63,* 388-390.

Stewart, C. J. & Cash, W. B. (1974). *Interviewing: Principles and practices.* Dubuque, IA: W. C. Brown.

Stoops, R. (1984). Reader survey supports market approach to recruitment. *Personnel Journal, 63,* 22-24.

Stoops, R. (1985). Nursing poor recruitment with a marketing approach. *Personnel Journal, 64,* 92-93.

Storms, M. D. (1973). Videotape and the attribution process: Reversing actors' and observers' points of view. *Journal of Personality and Social Psychology, 27,* 165-175.

Street, R. L. (1986). Interaction processes and outcomes in interviews. In M. L. McLaughlin (Ed.), *Communication Yearbook* (Vol. 9, pp. 215-251). Beverly Hills, CA: Sage.

Street, R. L., & Brady, R. M. (1982). Speech rate acceptance ranges as a function of evaluative domain, listener speech rate and communication context. *Communication Monographs, 49,* 290-308.

Street, R. L., & Murphy, T. L. (1987). Interpersonal orientation and speech behavior. *Communications Monographs, 54,* 42-62.

Struit, D. (Ed.) (1947) *Personnel research and test development in the bureau of naval personnel.* Princeton, NJ: Princeton University Press.

Swann, W. B., Pelham, B. W., & Roberts, D. C. (1987). Causal chunking: Memory and inference in ongoing interaction. *Journal of Personality and Social Psychology, 53,* 858-865.

Swets, J. A., Tanner, W. P., Jr., & Birdsall, T. G. (1961). Decision processes in perception. *Psychological Review, 68,* 301-340

Sydiaha, D. (1959). On the equivalence of clinical and statistical methods. *Journal of Applied Psychology, 43,* 395-401.

Sydiaha, D. (1961). Bales' interaction process analysis of personnel selection interviews. *Journal of Applied Psychology*, *45*, 393-401.

Taylor, M. S., & Sniezek, J. A. (1984). The college recruitment interview: Topical content and applicant reactions. *Journal of Occupational Psychology*, *57*, 157-168.

Taylor, M. S., & Bergmann, T. J. (1987). Organizational recruitment activities and applicants' reactions at different stages of the recruitment process. *Personnel Psychology*, *40*, 261-286.

Taylor, S. E., & Crocker, J. (1981). Schematic bases of social information processing. In E. T. Higgins, C. P. Herman, & M. P. Zanna, (Eds.), *Social Cognitions: The Ontario symposium on personality and social psychology* (pp. 459-524). Hillsdale, NJ: Lawrence Erlbaum.

Tedeschi, J. T. (Ed.) (1981). *Impression management theory and social psychological research*. New York: Academic Press.

Tedeschi, J. T., & Melburg, V. (1984). Impression management and influence in the organization. In S. Bacharach & E. J. Lawler (Eds.), *Research in the sociology of organizations*, (Vol. 3, pp. 31-58). Greenwich, CT: JAI.

Tengler, C. D., & Jablin, F. M. (1983). Effects of question type, orientation, and sequencing in the employment screening interview. *Communication Monographs*, *50*, 245-263.

Tenopyr, M. L. (1977). Content-construct confusion. *Personnel Psychology*, *30*, 47-54.

Tenopyr, M. L. (1987). *Policies and strategies underlying a personnel research operation*. Paper presented at the annual meeting for the Society of Industrial and Organizational Psychology, Atlanta, GA.

Tenopyr, M. L., & Oeltjen, P. D. (1982). Personnel selection and classification. *Annual Review of Psychology*, *33*, 581-618.

Terborg, J. R. (1977). Validation and extension of an individual differences model of work performance. *Organizational Behavior and Human Performance*, *18*, 188-216.

Terborg, J. R. (1981). Interactional psychology and research on human behavior in organizations. *Academy of Management Review*, *6*, 569-576.

Tessler, R., & Sushelsky, L. (1978). Effects of eye contact and social status on the perception of a job applicant in an employment interviewing situation. *Journal of Vocational Behavior*, *13*, 338-347.

Tetlock, P. E. (1983a). Accountability and the complexity of thought. *Journal of Personality and Social Psychology*, *45*, 74-83.

Tetlock, P. E. (1983b). Accountability and the perseverance of first impressions. *Social Psychology Quarterly*, *46*, 285-292.

Tetlock, P. E., (1985). Accountability: The neglected social context of judgment and choice. In L. L. Cummings & B. M. Staw (Eds.), *Research in organizational behavior* (Vol. 7, pp. 297-332). Greenwich, CT: JAI.

The Bureau of National Affairs (1983, May). *Employee selection procedures*. (ASPA-BNS Survey No. 45). Washington, DC: Author.

Thompson, D. E., & Thompson, T. A. (1982). Court standards for job analysis in test validation. *Personnel Psychology*, *35*, 865-874.

Thorndike, R. L. (1949). *Personnel selection: Test and measurement techniques*. New York: John Wiley.

Thorne v. City of El Segundo, 32 EPD 33,936 (1983).

Thornton, G. C., & Byham, W. C. (1982). *Assessment centers and managerial performance*. New York: Academic Press.

Thumin, F. J., & Barclay, A. G. (1980). Sequential validity: A new model for evaluating judgmental prediction in personnel selection. *Professional Psychology*, (February), 48-54.

Thurow, L. (1975). *Generating inequality*. New York: Basic Books.

Tiao, G. C., & Box, G. E. P. (1981). Modeling multiple time series with applications. *Journal of American Statistical Association, 76*, 802-816.

Tiao, G. C., & Tsay, R. S. (1983). Multiple time series modeling and extended sample cross-correlations. *Journal of Business and Economic Statistics, 1*, 43-56.

Tosi, H. L., & Einbender, S. W. (1985). The effects of the type and amount of information in sex discrimination research: A meta-analysis. *Academy of Management Review, 28*, 712-723.

Travers, L. B. (1941). Improving practical tests. *Personnel Journal, 20*, 129-133.

Tubiana, J. H., & Ben-Shakhar, G. (1982). An objective group questionnaire as a substitute for a personnel interview in the prediction of success in military training in Israel. *Personnel Psychology, 85*, 349-357.

Tucker, D. H. (1976). *Consulting the application form prior to the interview.* Unpublished master's thesis, University of Waterloo, Waterloo, Canada.

Tucker, D. H., & Rowe, P. M. (1979). Relationship between expectancy, causal attribution and final hiring decisions in the employment interview. *Journal of Applied Psychology, 64*, 27-34.

Tullar, W. L. (1986). *Relational control in the employment interview.* Paper presented at the 46th Annual Meeting National Academy of Management, Chicago, IL.

Tullar, W. L., Mullins, T. W., & Caldwell, S. A. (1979). Effects of interview length and applicant quality on interview decision time. *Journal of Applied Psychology, 64*, 669-674.

Tversky, A., & Kahneman, D. (1974). Judgment under uncertainty: Heuristics and biases. *Science, 185*, 1124-1131.

Tversky, A., & Kahneman, D. (1981). The framing of decisions and the psychology of choice. *Science, 211*, 453-458.

Ullman, J. C., & Gutteridge, T. G. (1973). The job search. *Journal of College Placement, 33*, 76-72.

Ulrich, L. & Trumbo, D. (1965). The selection interview since 1949. *Psychological Bulletin, 63*, 100-116.

Uniform Guidelines on Employee Selection Procedures. (1978). *Federal Register, 43*, 38290-38315.

Valenzi, E., & Andrews, I. R. (1973). Individual differences in the decision processes of employment interviewers. *Journal of Applied Psychology, 58*, 49-53.

Vance, R. J., Kuhnert, K. W., & Farr, J. L. (1978). Interview judgments: Using external criteria to compare behavioral and graphic scale ratings. *Organizational Behavior and Human Performance, 22*, 279-294.

Vitelles, M. S. (1932). *Industrial psychology.* New York: Norton.

Vogler, M. (1984). *The negativity bias in personnel selection: An attempt to modify decision-making processes.* Unpublished master's thesis, University of Waterloo, Waterloo, Canada.

von Baeyer, C., Shark, D., & Zanna, M. (1981). Impression management in the job interview. *Personality and Social Psychology Bulletin, 7*, 45-51.

Vroom, V. H. (1964). *Work and motivation.* New York: John Wiley.

Vroom, V. H. (1966). Organizational choice: A study of pre and post decision processes. *Organizational Behavior and Human Performance, 1*, 212-225.

Wagner, R. (1949). The employment interview: A critical review. *Personnel Psychology, 2*, 17-46.

Waldron, L. A. (1974). The validity of an employment interview independent of psychometric variables. *Australian Psychologist, 9*, 68-77.

Walton, R., & McKersie, R. (1965). *A behavioral theory of labor negotiations.* New York: McGraw-Hill.

Wanous, J. P. (1973). Effects of a realistic job preview on job acceptance, job attitudes, and job survival. *Journal of Applied Psychology, 51,* 327-332.

Wanous, J. P. (1977). Organizational entry: Newcomers moving from outside to inside. *Psychological Bulletin, 84,* 601-618.

Wanous, J. P. (1978). Realistic job previews: Can a procedure to reduce turnover also influence the relationship between abilities and performance? *Personnel Psychology, 31,* 249-258.

Wanous, J. P. (1980). *Organizational entry.* Reading: Addison-Wesley.

Washburn, P. V., & Hakel, M. D. (1973). Visual cue and verbal content as influences on impressions after simulated employment interviews. *Journal of Applied Psychology, 58,* 137-140.

Watson, K. M. (1982). An analysis of communication patterns: A method for discriminating leader and subordinate roles. *Academy of Management Journal, 25,* 107-120.

Watson, K. W., & Barker, L. L. (1984). Listening behavior: Definition and measurement. In R. N. Bostrom & B. H. Westley (Eds.), *Communication Yearbook* (Vol. 8, pp. 178-197). Beverly Hills: Sage.

Watson v. Fort Worth Bank and Trust, 487 U.S. 108 (1988).

Webster, E. C. (1964). *Decision making in the employment interview.* Montreal: Industrial Realtions Centre, McGill University.

Webster, E. C. (1982). *The employment interview: A social judgment process.* Schomberg, Ontario, Canada: S.I.P.

Weekley, J. A., & Gier, J. A. (1987). Reliability and validity of the situational interview for a sales position. *Journal of Applied Psychology, 72,* 484-487.

Weick, K. E. (1964). Organizations and unnoticed causes. *Administrative Science Quarterly, 14,* 294-303.

Weick, K. E. (1968). Systematic observational methods. In G. Lindzey & E. Aronson (Eds.), *Handbook of social psychology, II* (pp. 357-451). Reading, MA: Addison-Wesley.

Weick K. E., & Bougnon, M. G. (1986). Organizations as cognitive maps. In H. Sims & D. Gioia (Eds.), *The thinking organization* (pp. 102-135). San Francisco: Jossey-Bass.

Weiner, B. (1979). A theory of motivation for some classroom experiences. *Journal of Educational Psychology, 71,* 3-25.

Weiner, B. (1985). "Spontaneous" causal thinking. *Psychological Bulletin, 97,* 74-84.

Weiner, B., Amirkhan, J., Folkes, V. S., & Verette, J. A. (1987). An attributional analysis of excuse giving: Studies of a naive theory of emotion. *Journal of Personality and Social Psychology, 52,* 316-324.

Weiner, B., Frieze, I. H., Kukla, A., Reed, L., Rest, S., & Rosenbaum, R. M. (1971). *Perceiving the causes of success and failure.* Morristown, NJ: General Learning Press.

Weiner, B., & Kukla, A. (1970). An attributional analysis of achievement motivation. *Journal of Personality and Social Psychology, 15,* 1-20.

Weldon, E., & Gargano, G. M. (1985). Cognitive effort in additive task groups: The effects of shared responsibility on the quality of multiattribute judgments. *Organizational Behavior and Human Decision Processes, 36,* 348-361.

Wernimont, P. F. & Campbell, J. P. (1968). Signs, samples, and criteria. *Journal of Applied Psychology, 52,* 372-376.

Westlaw. (1987). West Publishing.

Wexley, K. N., & Nemeroff, W. F. (1974). The effects of racial prejudice, race of applicant, and biographical similarity on interviewer evaluations of job applicants. *Journal of Social and Behavioral Psychology, 14,* 66-78.

Wexley, K. N., Yukl, G. A., Kovacs, S. Z., & Sanders, R. E. (1972). Importance of contrast effects in employment interviews. *Journal of Applied Psychology, 56,* 45-48.

Wexley, K. N., Sanders, R. E. & Yukl, G. A. (1973). Training interviewers to eliminate contrast effects in employment interviews. *Journal of Applied Psychology, 57*, 233-236.

Whyte, W. F. (1955). *Men, money and motivation.* New York: Harper.

Wickelgren, W. A. (1981). Human learning and memory. *Annual Review of Psychology, 32*, 21-52.

Wiener, Y. & Schneiderman, M. L. (1974). Use of job information as a criterion in employment decisions of interviewers. *Journal of Applied Psychology, 59*, 699-704.

Wiesner, W. H., & Cronshaw, S. F. (1988). The moderating impact of interview format and degree of structure on interview validity. *The Journal of Occupational Psychology, 61*, 275-290.

Wiesner, W. H., & Cronshaw, S. F. (in press). A meta-analytic investigation of the impact of interview format and degree of structure on the validity of the employment interview. *Journal of Applied Psychology.*

Williams, K. J., DeNisi, A. S., Blenco, A. G., & Cafferty, T. P. (1985). The role of appraisal purpose: Effects of purpose on information acquisition and utilization. *Organizational Behavior and Human Decision Processes, 35*, 314-339.

Wood, R., & Mitchell, T. R. (1981). Manager behavior in a social context: The impact of impression management on attributions and disciplinary actions. *Organizational Behavior and Human Performance, 28*, 356-378.

Woodall, W. G., & Folger, J. P. (1985). Nonverbal cue context and episodic memory: On the availability and endurance of nonverbal behaviors as retrieval cues. *Communication Monographs, 52*, 319-333.

Word, C. O., Zanna, M. P., & Cooper, J. (1974). The nonverbal mediation of self-fulfilling prophecies in interracial interaction. *Journal of Experimental Social Psychology, 10*, 109-120.

Wortman, C. B. (1976). Causal attributions and personal control. In J. H. Harvey, W. J. Ickes, & R. F. Kidd (Eds.), *New directions in attribution research* (Vol. 1). Hillsdale, NJ: Lawrence Erlbaum.

Wright, O. R. (1969). Summary of research on the selection interview since 1964. *Personnel Psychology, 22*, 391-413.

Wright, P. M., Pursell, E. D., Lichtenfels, P. A., & Kennedy, R. (1986). *The structured interview: Additional studies and a meta-analysis.* Paper presented at the annual meeting Academy of Management, Chicago.

Wyer, R. S., & Srull, T. K. (1981). Category accessibility: Some theoretical and empircal issues concerning the processing of social information. In E. T. Higgins, C. P. Herman, & M. P. Zanna (Eds.), *Social Cognitions: The Ontario symposium on personality and social psychology* Hillsdale, NJ: Lawrence Erlbaum.

Wyer, R. S., & Srull, T. K. (1986). Human cognition in its social context. *Psychological Review, 93*, 322-339.

Yate, M. J. (1987a). *Hiring the best: A manager's guide to effective interviewing.* Boston: Bob Adams.

Yate, M. J. (1987b). *Knock 'em dead with great answers to tough questions.* Boston: Bob Adams.

Yate, M. J. (1988). How to knock 'em dead: Great answers to tough interview questions. In *Career opportunity update* (pp. 3-7). Fountain Valley, CA: Career Research Systems.

Yonge, K. A. (1956). The value of the interview: An orientation and a pilot study. *Journal of Applied Psychology, 40*, 25-31.

Young, D. M., & Beier, E. G. (1977). The role of applicant nonverbal communication in the employment interview. *Journal of Employment Counseling, 14*, 154-165.

Young, I. P., & Allison, B. (1982). Effects of candidate age and teaching experience on school superintendents and principals in selecting teachers. *Planning and Changing, 13*, 245-256.

Young, I. P., & Ponder, D. G. (1985). Salient factors affecting decision making in simulated teacher selection interviews. *Journal of Educational Equity and Leadership, 5*, 216-233.

Young, I. P., & Voss, G. (1986). Effects of chronological age, amount of information, and type of teaching position on administrators' perceptions of teacher candidates. *Journal of Educational Equity and Leadership, 6*, 27-44.

Zajonc, R. B. (1980). Feeling and thinking: Preferences need no inferences. *American Psychologist, 35*, 151-175.

Zedeck, S. (1977). An information processing model and approach to the study of motivation. *Organizational Behavior and Human Performance, 18*, 47-77.

Zedeck, S., & Cascio, W. F. (1982). Performance appraisal decisions as a function of rater training and purpose of the appraisal. *Journal of Applied Psychology, 67*, 752-758.

Zedeck, S., & Cascio, W. F. (1984). Psychological issues in personnel decisions. *Annual Review of Psychology, 35*, 461-518.

Zedeck, S., Tziner, A., & Middlestadt, S. E. (1983). Interviewer validity and reliability: An individual analysis approach. *Personnel Psychology, 36*, 355-370.

Zima, J. P. (1983). *Interviewing*. Chicago, IL: Science Research Associates.

About the Editors

Robert W. Eder is Associate Professor of Human Resources in the School of Hotel Administration at Cornell University. He received a Doctorate in Business Administration (D.B.A.) in Organizational Behavior from the University of Colorado at Boulder. Professor Eder was a recipient of the 1985 GTE award for faculty excellence in teaching and research, and has held managerial and professional positions in both the private and public sector with an emphasis on human service organizations. He has research interests in the areas of employee responses to supervisor feedback, performance appraisal systems, the employment interview, employee relations in advanced technology firms, and managerial effectiveness in the hospitality industry. Professor Eder has authored more than 30 articles which have appeared in publications such as *Organizational Behavior and Human Decision Processes*, *Journal of Management*, *Research in Personnel and Human Resources Management*, *Academy of Management Review*, and *The Cornell HRA Quarterly*.

Gerald R. Ferris is Professor of Labor and Industrial Relations and of Business Administration at the University of Illinois at Urbana-Champaign. He received a Ph.D. in Business Administration from the University of Illinois at Urbana-Champaign. Professor Ferris has research interests in the areas of social influence and organizational politics, performance evaluation, and the employment interview. He is the author of more than 40 articles which have appeared in such journals as the *Journal of Applied Psychology*, *Organizational Behavior and Human Performance*, *Personnel Psychology*, *Academy of Management Journal*, and *Academy of Management Review*. Professor Ferris is coeditor of the books, *Method & Analysis in Organizational Research*, *Personnel Management*, *Current Issues in Personnel Management*, and *Human Resources Management: Perspectives and Issues*, and serves as coeditor of the annual series *Research in Personnel and Human Resources Management*.

About the Contributors

Richard D. Arvey is Professor of Industrial Relations at the University of Minnesota. Professor Arvey's research interests and publications are in the areas of employee selection, the employment interview, discrimination and bias in employment decisions, job analysis, and job evaluation.

Robert A. Baron is Professor and Chair of the Department of Psychology, and Professor of Organizational Behavior, School of Management at Rensselaer Polytechnic Institute. Professor Baron's research interests and publications are in the areas of the interview process, and organizational conflict.

M. Ronald Buckley is Assistant Professor of Management in the College of Business Administration at the University of Oklahoma. Professor Buckley's research interests and publications focus on the employment interview, performance appraisal and feedback, construct validation, and methodologies designed to accurately assess the effectiveness of change interventions in organizations.

James E. Campion heads the Industrial-Organizational Psychology Program at the University of Houston and directs their Interviewing Institute. Professor Campion's research interests and publications are in the areas of assessment, training, and the employment interview.

Steven F. Cronshaw is Associate Professor of Psychology at the University of Guelph, Guelph, Ontario, Canada. Professor Cronshaw's research interests and publications are in the areas of human rights legislation and employment testing, selection utility, job evaluation, and leadership.

Robert L. Dipboye is Professor of Psychology at Rice University where he directs the Ph.D. program in I/O Psychology and the Center for Applied Psychological Systems. Professor Dipboye's current research interests and publications center on selection, especially the employment interview.

George F. Dreher is Associate Professor of Management at Indiana University, Bloomington. Professor Dreher's research interests and publications are in the areas of staffing and compensation systems.

Hubert S. Feild is the Edward L. Lowder Professor of Management at Auburn University. Professor Feild's research interests and publications are in the fields of human resource selection, personnel research methods, and legal issues in human resource management.

Uwe Funke is Assistant Lecturer of Organizational Psychology at the University of Stuttgart-Hohenheim, Stuttgart, West Germany. Professor Funke's research interests are in the areas of personnel selection, and training.

Robert D. Gatewood is Associate Professor of Management at the University of Georgia. Professor Gatewood's research interests and publications are in the fields of human resource selection, and psychometric measurement.

David C. Gilmore is Associate Professor of Psychology at the University of North Carolina at Charlotte. Professor Gilmore's research interests and publications focus on employee selection, especially the employment interview.

James G. Goodale is Senior Partner of Philbrook, Goodale Associates, a management consulting firm in Houston, Texas. Dr. Goodale has conducted numerous workshops on effective employment interviewing, and has published several books on interviewing.

Milton D. Hakel is Professor and Chair of the Department of Psychology at the University of Houston. Professor Hakel's research interests and publications center on the process dynamics in selection decisions, particularly with regard to the employment interview.

Peter Herriot is Professor of Occupational Psychology and Chairman of the Department of Occupational Psychology, Birkbeck College, University of London. Professor Herriot's research interests and publications focus on the social psychological approach to recruitment and selection.

Tom Janz is Professor of Management at the University of Calgary, Calgary, Alberta, Canada. Professor Janz's research interests and publications are in the areas of organizational performance development, motivation, and the employment interview, especially the use of behavior description interviewing techniques.

K. Michele Kacmar is a doctoral student in Management at Texas A & M University. Her current research interests include employee selection and recruitment processes.

Gary P. Latham is Professor and Chair of the Department of Management and Organization, and Ford Motor Research Affiliate Program Professor, at the University of Washington. Professor Latham's research interests and publications are in the areas of goal setting, performance appraisal, employee training, and the situational interview.

Robert C. Liden is Associate Professor of Organizational Behavior, Georgia Institute of Technology. Professor Liden's research interests and publications are in the areas of leadership, feedback, performance appraisal, and impression management in organizational settings.

Steven D. Maurer is Associate Professor of Management and Systems at Washington State University, Vancouver. Professor Maurer's research interests and publications are in the areas of recruitment and selection, with special applications to professional/technical employees.

Charles K. Parsons is Associate Professor of Organizational Behavior, Georgia Institute of Technology. Professor Parson's research interests and publications are in the areas of human resource methodology and behavioral aspects of information technology, including how organizations adapt to changing technologies and organizational environments.

Shannon L. Ratcliff is a doctoral student in Management at Texas A & M University. Her current research interests include justice and conciliation issues in unjust dismissal disputes.

Patricia M. Rowe is Professor and director of the graduate program in Industrial/Organizational Psychology at the University of Waterloo. Professor Rowe's research interests and publications continue to build upon her earlier work as a participant in the McGill studies, under the direction of Edward Webster.

Sara L. Rynes is Associate Professor of Personnel and Human Resource Studies at Cornell University. Professor Rynes's research interests and publications are in the areas of employee recruitment and selection, compensation, and career management.

Allen J. Schuh is Professor of Management and Finance in the School of Business and Economics at California State University, Hayward. Professor Schuh's research interests and publications include the employment interview, effectiveness evaluation, and employee training.

Heinz Schuler is Professor of Psychology at the University of Stuttgart-Hohenheim, Stuttgart, West Germany. Professor Schuler's research interests and publications focus on the improvement of employee selection instruments, and applicant views of the selection process.

William L. Tullar is Associate Professor of Management in the Bryan School of Business and Economics, University of North Carolina at Greensboro. Professor Tullar's research interests and publications are in the areas of organizational behavior and communications, with an emphasis on script theory and applications of expert systems to the interviewing process.

William Weitzel is Professor of Business Administration and Coordinator of the Human Resources faculty at the University of Oklahoma. Professor Weitzel's research interests and publications are in the areas of the employment interview, organizational decline, and employee feedback reactions.

Willi H. Wiesner is Assistant Professor in the Department of Management, Concordia University, Montreal, Quebec, Canada. Professor Wiesner's research interests and publications focus on the employment interview's validity and utility.